Heroes of the Age

Comparative Studies on Muslim Societies

General Editor: Barbara D. Metcalf

Heroes of the Age

Moral Fault Lines on the Afghan Frontier

DAVID B. EDWARDS

University of California Press

BERKELEY   LOS ANGELES   LONDON

University of California Press
Berkeley and Los Angeles, California

University of California Press, Ltd.
London, England

© 1996 by the Regents of the University of California

Library of Congress Cataloging-in-Publication Data

Edwards, David B.
    Heroes of the age : moral fault lines on the Afghan frontier / David
B. Edwards.
        p.   cm.—(Comparative studies on Muslim societies ; 21)
    Includes bibliographic references and index.
    ISBN 978-0-520-20064-7 (pbk. : alk. paper)
    1. Afghanistan—History. I. Title. II. Series.
  DS358.E38   1996
  958.1—dc20   95-31423
                                                      CIP

Printed in the United States of America

10   09

10   9   8   7   6   5

Contents

Maps

Acknowledgments

This project has evolved over a long time, and consequently there are many people and institutions to thank. The first is my grandmother, Florence Kruidenier, who became the first member of our family to visit Afghanistan in the late 1950s. A widow and world traveler, Grandma Flo captured the imagination of a small boy back in Iowa with her postcards and traveler's tales. There is one story in particular on which I hang much significance, a story about my grandmother staying up until dawn watching from the balcony of her hotel room as the camel caravans unloaded their wares. By the time I made it to Afghanistan, much that she had led me to expect was no longer the way it had been. Trucks had replaced most of the camel caravans, and those that remained never went into the city. But for all that, I've never regretted the journey nor doubted that it was my grandmother's caravan that carried me to Kabul. I remain grateful to her for that inspiration to travel and for the first-time feeling of the tidal power of stories to move and shape the imagination.

Two men exerted a different sort of influence that must also be acknowledged. Both are now gone, and both are missed. Louis Dupree, along with his wife, Nancy, treated my wife and me with kindness during our first stay in Kabul, and their unselfconscious joy in being there inspired me to more fully enjoy the opportunities of the moment. Sayyid Bahauddin Majrooh was a mentor during my time in Peshawar. For nearly two years we were neighbors, and I had the chance to spend many hours with him. A philosopher, a poet, a Sufi, a reporter, and sometimes a clown, he was also a devoted Afghan *mujahed*, and his brutal murder left a void that will not soon be filled.

In Pakistan a number of individuals helped me in a variety of ways. The most important of these individuals are Shahmahmood Miakhel, whose contribution to my work is discussed in the introduction, and Muhammad Nasim Stanazai, a good friend since 1983 who has helped immensely with translations and interpretations. Other friends, colleagues, and associates from Pakistan whom I would like to thank include Bruce Lohoff, formerly the head of the U.S. Education Foundation in Pakistan; Akbar S. Ahmed, who helped facilitate my research clearance; John Dixon, head of U.S.I.S. in Peshawar; Anwar Khan, the former head of the Area Studies Centre at Peshawar University, and Azmat Hayat Khan, the present head; Abdul Jabar Sabet, Abdullah Tora, and Wasil Nur, all formerly employed at the Centre; Rasul Amin and Hakim Taniwal, first of the Afghan Information Center and later of the Writers' Union for Free Afghanistan; the late Khalilullah Khalili, who spent generous amounts of his time educating me on things Afghan; and Dr. Zahir Ghazi Alam and his son, Zalmai, who lived with us for more than a year and became our extended family.

Among mentors, colleagues, and friends in the academy, I would like to acknowledge the support and inspiration of Jon Anderson, Lois Beck, John Bowen, Michael Brown, Bob Canfield, Steve Caton, Paul Dresch, Nancy Dupree, Dale Eickelman, Ken George, Susan Harding, Peter Just, Bob Jackall, Barbara Metcalf, Sherry Ortner, Bill Schorger, and Aram Yengoyan. Special thanks are also due to Bill Darrow, who provided crucial editorial suggestions on the first draft of the manuscript, and Margaret Mills, whose critical reading of this and other work has been invaluable to me. Jane Kepp and Anne Just also supplied helpful editorial assistance, and Mary Kennedy helped draft some of the maps that appear here.

My research in Peshawar was made possible by a Fulbright-Hays dissertation fellowship and a grant from the National Science Foundation. In the intervening years I have also received a Mellon Fellowship from Washington University and, most recently, a National Humanities Fellowship. I thank all of these institutions for their assistance as well as the University of Michigan, which provided financial support during my graduate career, and Williams College, which has generously supported my research since I arrived in 1989. During the writing of this book, I had the good fortune to be a fellow for a year and a half at the Center for Humanities and Social Sciences at Williams, and I want to thank Jean-Bernard Bucky for his support, along with that of the other faculty fellows who shared and enriched my time there.

I also want to acknowledge the debt I owe family members. My parents, Charles and Sue Edwards, have offered sometimes bemused but always unflagging support over the years in which this project has developed. So, for a far shorter period of time, have my children, Nick and Melody, who

I hope will someday experience Afghanistan under something like the conditions that I first came to know it. My wife, Holly, to whom this book is fondly dedicated, has been enmeshed in this project from its beginning. My experiences are hers, and whatever value might reside in these pages is her doing as much as it is my own.

Finally, I want to express my gratitude for the cooperation and kindness of the many Afghans who took the time to talk to me and, in many cases, agreed to tell their stories for the benefit of my tape recorder. There was nothing of compelling interest to be gained by speaking with me, and in some instances there was potentially some danger. Nevertheless, close to one hundred people chose to do so and, in the process, made my study possible. I can't say what motivated most people to talk with me, but I know that in at least some instances my informants believed that there was value in keeping oral histories alive. As a non-Muslim and an American, I might not have been their first choice for undertaking this assignment, but they still recognized the importance of someone doing it. This study uses only a fraction of the histories I collected, and it subjects those I did use to a form of interpretation that not all my informants might agree with or appreciate. Nevertheless, I hope that all Afghans who come into contact with this study will recognize the good faith with which it was undertaken and the sincere concern its author feels for Afghanistan, its people, and its future.

Significant Persons

Chapter 2

Samiullah Safi	Son of Sultan Muhammad Khan and narrator of the story recounted at the beginning of chapter 2
Sultan Muhammad Khan	Son of Talabuddin Akhundzada, the hakim of Pech Valley
Talabuddin Akhundzada	The hakim of Pech Valley who is killed in the story recounted at the beginning of chapter 2
'Ali Dost	Talabuddin Akhundzada's brother
Paindo	Talabuddin Akhundzada's cousin and rival who (along with his seven sons) is blamed for killing Talabuddin
Faizullah	Paindo's brother (unnamed in story)

Chapter 3

Abdur Rahman Khan	King of Afghanistan from 1880 to 1901
Dost Muhammad	Grandfather of Abdur Rahman Khan and king of Afghanistan (1819–39; 1842–63)

Muhammad Afzal Khan

Son of Dost Muhammad Khan, father to Abdur Rahman, and king of Afghanistan (1866–67)

Muhammad Azam Khan

Eldest son of Dost Muhammad, full brother of Muhammad Afzal, and king of Afghanistan (1867–69)

Sher 'Ali Khan

Son of Dost Muhammad, half brother of Muhammad Afzal and Muhammad Azam, father of Muhammad Isaq Khan, and king of Afghanistan (1863–66; 1869–79)

Muhammad Isaq Khan

Son of Muhammad Azam and rival to Abdur Rahman Khan

Chapter 4

Mulla of Hadda

Major religious figure in Afghanistan in the late nineteenth century. Born Najmuddin Akhundzada, he is also referred to in various stories and accounts as Hadda Sahib, the Hadda Mulla, and Mulla Najmuddin.

Akhund of Swat (Abdul Ghafur)

Teacher of the Mulla of Hadda and the progenitor of the *mianguls* of Swat, one line of which became the ruler (*wali*) of Swat

Abdul Baqi

Attendant of the Mulla of Hadda

Hazrat Sahib of Butkhak

Disciple of the Mulla of Hadda

Sufi Sahib of Batikot (and Faqirabad)

Disciple of the Mulla of Hadda

Mulla Sahib of Kajuri

Disciple of the Mulla of Hadda

Sayyid Ismail Pacha of Islampur

Disciple of the Mulla of Hadda

Haji Sahib of Turangzai

Disciple of the Mulla of Hadda

Ustad Sahib of Hadda

Disciple of the Mulla of Hadda and heir to the center at Hadda

Shaykh Sahib of Sangar	Disciple of the Mulla of Hadda
Mia Sahib of Baro	Disciple of the Mulla of Hadda
Mulla Sahib of Tagao	Disciple of the Mulla of Hadda
Manki Mulla	Religious scholar who was the Mulla of Hadda's principal rival on the frontier

Map 1. Afghanistan

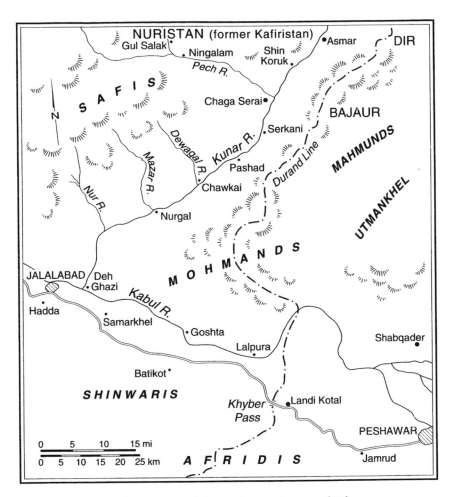

Map 2.   Eastern Afghanistan and the north-west frontier of Pakistan

1 Introduction

This book is about the lives of three great men from Afghanistan's past. It is also about the stories Afghan people tell one another about the past—stories in which men of quality are tested and, by dint of their single-mindedness, their courage, and their capacity, demonstrate the qualities of person and action by which greatness is achieved. The three men are a tribal khan, a Muslim saint, and a royal prince who became Afghanistan's king. Their stories come from a variety of sources. The khan's tale was recounted to me by his son and involves a feud in which the khan, while still a young boy, was required to avenge his father's murder. The Muslim saint is represented by a series of miracle stories told to me by offspring of his disciples; the stories center on how the saint came to wield spiritual and political authority along the Afghan frontier. The king, in princely fashion, is present through his own words—an autobiographical account of how he came to sit upon the Afghan throne and a proclamation in which he announces to his people the nature of his responsibility as their king and theirs as his subjects.

After surveying and comparing the moral meanings associated with these three lives in the first four chapters, I turn in the last chapter to a specific event: a widespread tribal uprising against the British Raj that broke out in the summer of 1897. This uprising was the severest attack on British colonial rule in India since the so-called Mutiny of 1857, and its principal leader was the Muslim saint whose life is examined in the third chapter. Through an analysis of both colonial and native accounts, I investigate the saint's role in this conflict, his relationship to the tribal groups that followed him, and the larger issue of how Islam traditionally functions as an encompassing framework of political association in frontier society. In addition, I also examine some of the structural reasons for the failure of this uprising, as well as the larger implications of these events for Afghanistan's future.

Throughout the book my concern is with the articulation of moral authority in Afghan society and the contradictions which different moral systems pose to one another and to themselves. The three great men whose lives I consider are icons of resoluteness. Each exemplifies a pure determinacy that stands outside the baser exchanges of average men, a determinacy that beckons even as it casts warnings of the perils that ensnarl those who would follow too closely an ideal. The final chapter on the events of 1897 records some of the dangers that arise when the determinant encounters the contingent and also draws attention to the moral threat posed by colonialism. Using the writings of another would-be hero, Winston Churchill, as a lens, I outline the moral significance attached to Islam by colonial authorities and indicate the larger, moral threat that the West was beginning to pose not only to Islamic religious leaders but also to tribesmen and kings as well.

Because my focus in this book is on the past, it might be said that this is a work of history, but my approach differs from traditional history in being centered on a few texts that are highlighted as cultural artifacts of a particular time and place. The search for logical coherence and chronological continuity in past lives and events is set aside here in favor of a different approach emphasizing the particular cultural coherences that can be found in and through stories. This approach has been pursued by a number of anthropologists interested in history, including Marshall Sahlins, whose rereading of Hawaiian historical texts has had an important influence on this work.[1]

My concern for the cultural meanings associated with particular texts was also influenced by Hayden White's oft-cited essay, "The Value of Narrativity in the Representation of Reality," in which he develops the point that "every historical narrative has as its latent or manifest purpose the desire to *moralize* the events of which it treats."[2] However, whereas White was interested in his essay in the development of historical consciousness in the West over a broad sweep of time and in the relationship of state authority to changing modes of narrative construction, I focus in this book on a single time and place and the way in which competing forms of moral authority find expression in different kinds of narrative texts.

The ultimate objective of this book is to shed light on the sources of contemporary civil strife in Afghanistan. While I am not the first to address this subject, I believe that most of those who have tried to make sense of the situation so far have been distracted by the action on the ground and have missed what might be called the *deep structure* of the conflict. One reflection of this problem is the emphasis that different studies have given to the various ideological dimensions of the war. For most of the decade following the Marxist revolution in 1978, analysts assumed that the centerpiece of Afghanistan's troubles was the dispute between Soviet-aligned Marxists and Islamic fundamentalists. But gradually, observers started to consider the role of ethnic and sectarian divisions in the conflict, and then finally, in the past few years, journalists and scholars of various orientations and persuasions began to wonder aloud if, after all, the British hadn't gotten it right in the first place. Afghanistan was once and would remain a singularly wild and anarchic place that could only be managed (if at all) by men of ruthless violence and ambition. So it has seemed to conventional wisdom, and so it is that attention has drifted away from the Afghan morass to other more significant and potentially pacifiable geopolitical hot spots.

All of the factors—Marxism, Islamic fundamentalism, ethnic and sectarian loyalties, and personal ambition—that commentators have marshaled to explain Afghanistan's problems have undoubtedly played a role in the conflict, but something else is at work here as well that has to do less with ideology, identity, and anarchy than with certain deep-seated moral contradictions that press against each other like tectonic plates at geological fault lines below the surface of events. In other words, Afghanistan's troubles derive less from divisions between groups or from the ambitious strivings of particular individuals than they do from the moral incoherence of Afghanistan itself.

This incoherence goes back to the rise of Islam, but it has been greatly exacerbated since the end of the nineteenth century, when the expansion of colonial empires into South and Central Asia led to the fabrication of a nation-state framework on the unstable foundation of Afghan society. The artificiality of the nation-state in this setting and its incommensurability with Afghan social and political realities have deepened inherent contradictions within Afghan culture, contradictions that have increased under the pressure of trying to construct and maintain a framework of unity in defiance of underlying discords. While various social, economic, and political factors have kept the Afghan polity together since its establishment one hundred years ago, the moral fault lines below the Afghan nation-state have not disappeared just because the surface configuration has changed. The underlying situation remains the same, and obscure tectonic shifts of which one is hardly aware are always capable of producing violent surges at unexpected moments.

One reflection of the fundamental artificiality of the Afghan nation-state is the absence of a moral discourse of statehood shared by a majority of its citizens. Afghanistan has great heroes that are recognized by all and a common set of events that are generally glorified (especially the nineteenth-century insurrections against British occupation). Together these heroes and events do constitute what might be called a myth of nationhood, but there is no corresponding myth of the state to go along with it. The result is that although most Afghans hold to some notion of shared identity with one another, that identity is articulated horizontally between individuals, tribes, and regions rather than vertically between the state and its citizens.

Drawing again on White's article on narrativity, I argue that if one of the requirements of state authority is to impose its vision of significance and necessity on events and to infuse this vision with "the odor of the *ideal*," then it can be said that one of the failures of the Afghan state and one of the causes of its present inchoate condition has been its own persistent inability to make itself a necessary element of the Afghan moral narrative.[3] In Afghanistan, other notions of community have persisted on an equal level with that of the state. Similarly, other moral orders have endured despite the development of an increasingly powerful central government, and they have continued to challenge the state in its assertions of legitimacy and its role in plotting the meaning and direction of ongoing events.

Traditionally, these contests of legitimacy have been discussed in terms of tribes and states, with Islamic leaders and institutions sometimes introduced as mediating elements in the relationship. In this study, however, I am less concerned with the social and institutional structure of this relationship than I am with the cultural principles that animated it, specifically, the principles of *honor, Islam,* and what I will call *rule* (i.e., state governance). My thesis is that honor, Islam, and rule represent distinct moral orders that are in many respects incompatible with one another. While this incompatibility has been mediated at various times by the delineation of distinct realms of activity within which tribes, states, and religious institutions have exerted their separate authority, the underlying incommensurability of honor, Islam, and rule persisted and became increasingly irreconcilable with the emergence of the nation-state.

In amplifying this thesis, I have located my study in a particular place—the eastern Afghan frontier—and a particular historical era—the late nineteenth century. The frontier is a critically important area because it was there that the pressure of British colonial rule was most dramatically felt and where the contradictions in Afghanistan's political status were most clearly illustrated.[4] The late nineteenth century was a crucial period in Afghan history for similar reasons. In 1879–80 Kabul was occupied by the British for the second time in forty years. Because of the disastrous nature of the earlier occupation, the British decided on this occasion to get out as fast as they could. To rule in their stead, they chose a young prince, Abdur Rahman, who was relatively unknown to them and who had spent most of his adult life in exile in Russian Central Asia.

When Abdur Rahman took command, the country he was given to rule was up in arms. Few of his nominal subjects were ready to accede to his authority, and other royal princes were prepared to vie for the favor of tribes and ethnic groups that were themselves eager to assert autonomy from Kabul. Over a period of twenty years, Amir Abdur Rahman succeeded in eliminating his dynastic competition, destroying regional warlords who sought to govern independently of Kabul, and suppressing local revolts. In doing so, he also managed to quiet the threat of outside colonial intervention. So long as he could control his own people and protect against Russian encroachment toward their borders, the British largely abstained from intervening in Afghanistan's internal affairs, although they did continue to exert control over the country's foreign affairs.[5]

But as the threat of direct colonial domination waned during Abdur Rahman's rule, a more insidious force began to be exerted on Afghan society in the form of the nation-state itself, the framework and mechanisms for which were initiated and implemented during Abdur Rahman's reign. As a number of recent scholars have demonstrated, the nation-state is not the natural and inevitable polity that we sometimes imagine it to be.[6] Nor is it just an administrative arrangement that can be applied anywhere, anytime, like an architectural blueprint. The nation-state is, rather, the product of particular historical events that occurred in a particular place on the globe. As a consequence of European colonial expansion to other regions of the world, the nation-state was imposed elsewhere, but as recent history has tragically shown, it has remained in many regions an unnatural transplant maintained solely through terror and repression.

In the case of Afghanistan, the imposition of this new framework of political relationship conflicted with the existing arrangement in which kings, seated at various times in Qandahar and Kabul, extended their authority into the precincts of autonomous local principalities and tribes, while the local principalities and tribes did their best to offset (or at least gain advantage from) these extensions of state control through assertions of their own power. The advent of the nation-state presented a new challenge to this arrangement, a challenge that was as much moral as it was practical, and it is the objective of this book to convey a sense both of the underlying principles of honor, Islam, and rule as they traditionally coexisted in Afghan society and of the way in which this coexistence was undermined by the appearance of the nation-state under and after Amir Abdur Rahman.

BEGINNINGS

In 1982, when I arrived in Peshawar to begin research for my Ph. D. dissertation in anthropology, the war in Afghanistan had already been under way for four years. During the next two years (and again for six months in 1986), I had the opportunity to watch its conduct from close at hand. In military terms, the mid-eighties was a period of protracted stalemate in which little was accomplished by either side. In ideological and political terms, however, this period was significant for being the time when what had seemed a fairly straightforward conflict between Marxism and Islam was clearly revealed to be something a great deal more complicated and contradictory. This was the time when the self-interested and parochial character of the Afghan resistance parties became unmistakably apparent, and large numbers of Afghan refugees began to lose their certainty as to war's meaning and value. It was also the period when the Afghan people as a whole began to confront the possibility that the conflict might go on for a very long time, that the millions who had gone into exile might be permanently dispossessed, and that the country they had left might come unglued for good.

The chaos I confronted in Peshawar was all the more remarkable to me because this was not my first trip to the region. Between 1975 and 1977, I had spent almost two years teaching English at a language center in Kabul. The mid-seventies were the golden age of economic development programs in Afghanistan, when teams from a half dozen nations vied with each other to bring the country "into the twentieth century"—or so they and most of the world imagined, for in those days the rightness and logic of development assistance seemed straightforward, and there were few outward signs of the trouble that lay ahead.

The late sixties and early seventies had witnessed a great deal of political turbulence, with violent student demonstrations a frequent occurrence, but the coup d'etat of President Muhammad Daud in July 1973 had brought some of the agitators into the government and pushed the remainder underground. The sole hint of any political unhappiness of which I was aware was a minor uprising that broke out in the Panjshir Valley north of Kabul on a holiday weekend during my first summer in Afghanistan. I became aware of this event only because it caused the cancellation of a bus trip that I had planned to the northern city of Mazar-i Sharif. The press made little mention of the problems in Panjshir, and I only discovered much later that there had been attacks that day against government installations throughout the country and that they all had been organized by student leaders of the Muslim Youth Organization (*sazman-i jawanan-i musulman*).[7]

When I left Afghanistan to attend graduate school, the idea I had in mind was to live in a mountain village somewhere in the Hindu Kush. The plan I had was a traditional one, long honored in anthropology, but it began to fall apart in the spring of 1978 when I saw headlines announcing the overthrow of President Daud and the establishment of a new revolutionary government in Kabul. Since I was in the early stages of my training, I had plenty of time to reorient the subject of my research plans and grant proposals from villages, kinship, and ritual toward other matters. What I didn't realize, however, was how little the existing anthropological works offered for understanding the kinds of dislocations and disturbances that I was to confront in my fieldwork.

The greatest dissonance I experienced between literature and reality came in my efforts to apply the various studies of tribe-state relations that I had read in graduate school to the actual situation I encountered in Peshawar. The problem was that the majority of these studies viewed tribes and states as discrete sociopolitical formations bound together in long-term dialectical arrangements. Tribes existed on the rural periphery, states were at the urban center, and each served to define the other in their opposition to one another. The classic expression of this opposition came from Morocco, where various scholars had encountered the local distinction between *bled l-makhzen* and *bled s-siba:* the land of governance versus the land of dissidence. Accompanying this general spatial opposition, anthropologists had discerned a set of schematic associations: the order of the state was thus opposed by the anarchy of the tribe; the commerce and cosmopolitanism of the city was set off against the barren wastes of the desert and mountain homeland; the artifice of the royal court contrasted with the rough-edged simplicity of the tribal guest house.

While the nature of the relationship between tribes and states has been amplified and refined by later scholars, the basic formula goes back to Ibn Khaldun, the great medieval historian whose analysis of North African dynastic politics established the framework for subsequent anthropological and historical studies of Middle Eastern politics. In Ibn Khaldun's view, tribes and states were linked in an enduring and oft-repeated cycle that begins when a desert tribe, fused by kinship and "group feeling" ('asabiyah), rises up to overthrow the existing dynasty. As the desert tribe accommodates itself to the decadent life of court and city, it loses the martial qualities and the sense of closeness that had made it powerful in the first place. Over three or four generations, the pace of decline quickens. Kings grow lazy and lose touch with the qualities of greatness that had originally brought their ancestors to the throne. Individuals pursue their own interests at the expense of their kinsmen, while the tribe abandons the group feeling that once made it a formidable fighting force. As the ruling group sinks into decline, other tribes consolidate their strength on the desert fringe and eventually push into the area of government control, doing to the ruling dynasty what its own ancestors had done earlier to their predecessors on the throne.

As I prepared to begin my fieldwork, I naturally assumed that Ibn Khaldun's model would help provide a theoretical understanding to the situation I would confront. After all, in its previous two hundred years, Afghanistan had witnessed a number of great clashes between the central government and various popular coalitions, almost all of which featured some combination of tribal groups from the eastern border area of the country taking up arms to overthrow the government. Sometimes the tribes succeeded, sometimes they did not. Regardless of the outcome, these conflicts did seem to occur at fairly regular intervals, and they appeared to follow what could be construed as a variant of the kind of cyclical pattern that Ibn Khaldun had discerned in the rise and fall of North African dynasties six centuries earlier.[8]

The most recent instance of this pattern asserting itself is, of course, the popular uprising that began in 1978. As in the past, coalitions of tribes and ethnic groups all over the country rose up to defend themselves against government intrusion in their lives. This time, the government proclaimed a Marxist line, which made it unique in Afghan history, but like other hated regimes before it, this one too allowed itself to serve as the puppet of foreign interests and promoted policies and engaged in practices that were viewed as offensive to popular morality. These characteristics made the Marxist regime seem quite like others that had come before it. Indeed, history appeared to be repeating itself: tribes and states once more were squaring off in one of those periodic clashes by which each side comes to define itself and the other by the difference between them.

Nevertheless, one of the first revelations I had on arriving in Peshawar was that it was extremely difficult to discern who the tribes were in this scenario. Peshawar was overrun with Afghan refugees in 1982, and although many of them identified themselves as members of particular tribes, those tribes had little if any concrete, corporate existence. Small, patrilineally related kin groups often lived together in the refugee camps I surveyed, but these groups seldom consisted of more than twenty or thirty families and only rarely had any connection to larger tribal structures. More important than tribal identity in the choice of residence was the time of arrival and the availability of sites on which to set up a tent. Likewise, it was as common to meet people who had chosen to live near in-laws, business partners, or former neighbors as it was to meet kinsmen living together.[9]

As difficult as it was to discern discrete tribes, it was equally hard to detect a government. This was Pakistan, after all, and although the Pakistani government was very much in evidence, the Afghan resistance movement with which I was concerned had spawned not a government but a shifting assortment of interest groups that passed themselves off as political parties. Shortly after the Soviet invasion, a Pakistani scholar counted over a hundred separate Afghan refugee political parties in Peshawar, each with its own office, manifesto, and, if it was lucky, letterhead.[10] The Pakistan government had forced all but ten of those parties to disband by the time I arrived in 1982; but while now better funded, the leadership and composition of the ten surviving parties remained unstable and subject to continual rearrangement.

There was another government, of course, in Kabul, but my position disallowed me from seeing it up close. Even if I had been able to observe the situation on the other side, I don't think I would have found it very different. All through the 1980s, the same sort of ethnic and personal factionalism that I observed in Peshawar was eating away at the Kabul regime as well, so that nowhere was one likely to find anything resembling the kind of developed, sophisticated court culture and government administration that one reads about in the traditional literature on Middle Eastern tribes and states.

Another problem with applying the classic tribe-state model to the Afghan situation was the overwhelming significance of Islam. In most studies of tribe-state relations that I had encountered as a graduate student, Islam was of secondary importance and tended to enter the political equation solely as an interstitial force: a politician wearing the guise of preacher, hereditary saint, or charismatic mystic arrives on the scene at a time of crisis and interposes himself between tribe and state as a mediator, power broker, or rabble-rouser. As usually described, the Islamic figure's turn on the stage is brief and his significance transitory. In almost all cases, he is viewed with suspicion—as an opportunist who dons a disguise to mislead the people and stir up trouble.

This depiction of Islam's role in political affairs makes some sense perhaps at certain points in Afghan and frontier history, but the persistent tendency to interpret the role of religious leaders in cynical terms struck me as biased, while the more general tendency to see their importance as medial and temporary also seemed inappropriate, particularly in the context I was witnessing. The war in Afghanistan had already been going on for four years when I began my research and is in its eighteenth year as I complete this book. Clearly, the notion of Islam as politically short-lived and interstitial was not working as it was supposed to, even if one assumed that this was simply a very long intermission between acts in the national drama. An even greater problem with seeing Islam simply as an intermediary force is that it fails to account for the moral and political authority wielded by Islamic leaders, an authority that, in my experience, was not reducible to their presumed position in the interstices of tribes and states.

While I was engaged in research, these incongruities led me to the conclusion that Ibn Khaldun's model had little to offer. Over time, however, I have come to change my mind and to see the problem as lying more in the direction in which Ibn Khaldun's successors have gone than in his original formulation itself. Specifically, I believe that modern scholars have tended to focus on (and in the process overreify) tribes and states as concrete social formations while underrepresenting the emphasis that Ibn Khaldun himself gave to the moral dimension of political relations. As concerned as he was with tribes, states, and Islam, Ibn Khaldun paid at least as much attention to the moral sentiments that made each of them unique: the "group feeling" that existed among tribesmen, the "royal authority" upon which kingship was based, and the "prophetic law" that sanctioned the pronouncements of Muslim divines.[11]

For me, perceiving the significance of the moral bases of political authority came not through any great, solitary insight, but as a result of the particular exigencies of my fieldwork situation. Historians working with archival sources tend to absorb the assumptions, rationales, and expectations of the state employees whose documents they are reading. Similarly, anthropologists who have lived and worked for a long time with a particular tribe tend to adopt that tribe's perspective and to see the world from its vantage. My situation, however, was different because it had no natural center of social gravity.

Peshawar was a chaotic and somewhat estranging place in which to conduct fieldwork. People were far from their homes, their native kin groups were generally scattered, and the formal political groupings that claimed to represent them attracted only transient respect and rarely generated much sense of shared identity. The only common cement was Islam, but there was a pervasive feeling of disillusionment here as well—not with Islam itself, but with the self-interested promotions that various leaders undertook in the name of Islam. Practically every day I would hear stories of minor corruption on the part of religious leaders alongside reports of street abductions and summary executions. And when leaders were not filling their pockets or spreading terror, they were making themselves objects of derision, as when a party leader in his sixties married a teenage girl.

The absence of stability was disorienting to me at first. Most anthropological accounts at that time tended to emphasize the endurance of the social order, not its destruction. In Peshawar, however, I could see or infer very little in the way of stability and therefore had to accustom myself to believe my own eyes, to locate my study in the reality around me, and finally to come to terms with what it means for a society to collapse upon itself. Although it seems a rather straightforward matter now, it was not a simple conclusion at the time. Repeatedly, I tried to write about things of which I had no direct experience, for instance, the social organization of tribes or the economic situation in Afghanistan prior to the war.

The reason I did so was simply the force of tradition. The models I had in my head for doing anthropology centered on the material, economic, and ritual substructures of everyday life around which villages and nomadic camping groups arranged themselves over time. Peshawar disallowed this sort of approach. Refugees also had to meet basic subsistence needs, of course, and many of the rituals of everyday life, from Friday prayers to female seclusion, were being maintained in Peshawar, just as they had been in Afghanistan. Yet, while the persistence of certain key cultural traits was an interesting subject in itself, it also seemed to mask an underlying process of dissolution that needed to be understood on its own terms.[12]

Although I didn't completely recognize it at the time, the turning point for my research came one day about a month after I had arrived in Peshawar. I was still staying at a hotel at the time and had gotten to know a fellow transient, an American from Los Angeles, who was in Peshawar to record sounds (background noises, music, local color) that might be used for a proposed docudrama on the war in Afghanistan. (The plot, as I recall, had to do with American mountaineers who set out to climb one of the peaks close to the Afghan-Pakistan border and get lost in a snowstorm, only to find themselves in an Afghan village in the middle of the war.) We became friendly, and when he proposed that I accompany him one day to record some Afghan musicians, I readily agreed.

Our destination was a small room above a cloth shop in the part of old Peshawar known as Qissa Khani: the Street of the Storytellers. As picturesque as the name sounds, I had always found it incongruous because one was more likely to hear the drone of a motor rickshaw or the pounding of a tinsmith there than the tale of a bard. On this occasion, however, the name proved appropriate, for in the bare room upstairs we found three musicians and a singer who proceeded to sing song after song of the war over the mountains. Some of the songs were exhortations to the tribes to rally against the infidels in Kabul; others were tragic laments for fallen martyrs. The author of most of the songs was a man named Rafiq Jan, whom I was not to meet until several years later; his songs, however, were to become important to me not only for their content and the connection they provided to the ethos of the war but also for the way they made me reconsider the direction of my own research.[13]

That afternoon in Qissa Khani began to reorient my attention from larger, more abstract matters, like "tribes" and "states," toward the opportunities that were immediately available and what the people right around me were actually doing, which, of course, was mostly getting by—preserving and supplementing their ration allotments, establishing and keeping up contacts with the various refugee political organizations, and obtaining various forms of assistance and sinecure from them. These activities could consume considerable amounts of time, but they still left a large part of the day free for the other principal occupation of refugees—talking and telling stories.

While I was ill-disposed to take this sort of activity very seriously at first, I eventually came to see it as the centerpiece of my ethnographic research. My initial reluctance to pay much attention to this activity stemmed from the fact that most of what I was hearing was a litany of gripes and complaints—all very predictable and pathetic for being so. Gradually, however, it dawned on me that this was actually a more serious and revealing discourse than I had imagined. Much of the conversation did consist of laments about inadequate ration allotments and reproachful comments regarding this or that party or leader, but I could also make out other persistent elements in the talk, the most notable of which was nostalgia for the past and for what might have been.

One focus of this nostalgia was the early part of the popular rebellion, which was seen as a time when people acted out of moral principle unsullied by self-interest. A second focus, at least among some of the refugees, was the absent king, Zahir Shah, who had been deposed in 1973 and was therefore relatively uncorrupted by more recent political events that had tarnished other leaders. Viewed in hindsight, Zahir Shah's reign (1933–73) seemed to many to be a long springtime of peace and gentility, and it was the unrealistic sense that such a time could come again that fueled the cult of his return.

Because Zahir Shah was still alive, many refugees pictured him as a "man on horseback" who might reappear to lead the nation to peace and reconciliation. The ex-king was not the only person put forward as the national savior, but in my experience he was the most commonly proposed candidate, probably because he was the best known and his reputation the least damaged. Many also romanticized the idea of kingship itself, which, for all its faults, had the virtue of fixing authority (and dynastic dissension) within a single family. Another name that was frequently mentioned was that of Ahmad Shah Massoud, the commander of Panjshir Valley (whose attack on President Daud's government in 1975 had disturbed my holiday bus trip). Massoud's reputation has since declined owing to his involvement in the long and destructive siege of Kabul that began in 1993, but in the mid-1980s many who would later denounce and belittle him entertained the notion that he might potentially rescue Afghanistan from the abyss.[14]

Regardless of their specific content, such discussions made clear to me that many Afghans felt a need to express their disillusionment by focusing on times and leaders other than those they currently faced. Zahir Shah, because of his association with a favorably remembered past, and Massoud, because of his dissociation from the immediate and despised situation in Peshawar, were both cast as potential champions—men who could, as champions have always done, destroy evil and reestablish order. No heroes emerged, of course, but the recurrent longing for the appearance of a champion encouraged me to begin to think about heroes, what they mean, and how they help to encode cultural and moral truths that are at the center of what is and is not present in Afghanistan today.

RECOLLECTING THE PAST

I should mention before proceeding further that I had originally received permission from the Pakistani government to conduct an ethnographic study of a refugee camp. My topic was to show how Afghans preserved their cultural identity in the camp context. Eventually, I was allowed four months to investigate this subject, but shortly after my arrival in the capital, Islamabad, I was told that the one research permit I had already received from the Ministry of Education was inadequate and I would need a second one from the Ministry of States and Frontier Regions. That would take months, I was warned (in fact, the permit wasn't issued until more than a year later), but in the meantime I could move to Peshawar, cash my fellowship checks, and make myself at home.

Like the Afghans I had come to study, I had plenty of time on my hands during this year of waiting, and I wasn't at all sure what to do with it. In their initial trepidation and uncertainty, anthropologists newly arrived in a village have long relied on a variety of mundane tasks to get them over the hurdle of the first few months. These tasks, which typically include such activities as measuring rice paddies and conducting household censuses, do not usually figure in the final ethnography (at least not these days), but they do serve to cushion the ethnographer from the more difficult enterprise of actually relating to people and making sense of what they are saying and doing. It was partially out of a similar desire to cushion myself from the strangeness of my surroundings that I turned to history and stories.

Although I was first encouraged in this direction by my experience listening to the musicians sing songs of war, one of the things that most appealed to me about the afternoon I spent in that room overlooking the Street of the Storytellers was that I could turn on my tape recorder, lie back, and let those on the other end of the microphone do the work. The tape recorder was a buffer that diffused interaction while also allowing me the comfort of knowing that I was collecting information that might somehow, someday prove useful. Eventually, as my language skills improved, I started taking a more aggressive role in my interviews; however, initially I took as my role not that of the investigative interviewer but that of the chronicler, and my rationale for doing so was that Peshawar was chock full of people whose life histories constituted a significant portion of Afghanistan's recent national history.

One of the ironies of the situation I encountered was that in displacing hundreds of thousands of people from their native villages, the war had laid bare a treasure trove of oral history. In the past, no one could ever have tapped more than a small part of this resource if only because the people one might have wanted to interview were too widely dispersed and often lived in remote villages that were difficult to reach. If a researcher could even discover the names of appropriate people to interview on a particular subject, he or she would then have had to find out where they lived and try to make arrangements to travel there. With luck, the potential interviewee would be home and willing to talk. If not, too bad.[15] The war significantly altered this situation, for one of the unintended consequences of the Marxist government's efforts to suppress the traditional rural elites was that many of those who had played a prominent role in earlier events (along with the sons and grandsons of those who had been important in earlier eras) were among the first to flee the country. Many of these elite families crossed the border into Pakistan, and a large percentage of them ended up in Peshawar.[16]

Not surprisingly, the greatest number of refugees came from the eastern provinces of Afghanistan, a fact that disposed me to focus on this region even though I would have preferred to concentrate on a Persian-speaking area. I had begun studying the Afghan dialect of Persian during my stay in Kabul in the mid-seventies, had continued it in graduate school, and by the time I arrived in Peshawar, was reasonably fluent. But the overwhelming preponderance of Pakhtu-speaking refugees from the east and the relative paucity of native Persian speakers obliged me to fix my attention on the eastern areas and start learning a second language. Fortunately, because I was interested in people who had been significant political actors or who were the offspring of such people, I found that I could usually conduct my interviews in Persian since this had been the principal language of commerce and the state and almost all of my subjects had sufficient mastery of the language to converse easily. This being the case (and given the fact that I never knew when the Pakistani government might take notice of my anomalous presence and decide to expel me as a security risk), my decision was the expedient one of falling back on Persian whenever possible, even if it meant that I was communicating with many informants in their second language.

Since I had not anticipated the possibility of conducting an oral-history project, the research plan I adopted during my first year in Peshawar was vaguely defined at best. There were people who had stories to tell. I was determined to capture these stories on tape, and later I would figure out what to do with them. All told, I conducted more than one hundred formal interviews with a wide variety of people. These included five of the seven principal party leaders, scores of mid-level officials, tribal elders from most of the major tribes in the border area, well-known and obscure Sufi religious leaders, ordinary Sufi disciples, former directors of the departments of tribal affairs and religious endowments, one former Justice Minister, a close confidant of King Zahir Shah, primary school teachers and university professors, poets, various nomads-cum-refugees (including both the camel-herding and truck-driving varieties), drug smugglers, former army officers, present *jihad* commanders, ex-communists, judges, religious teachers, mullas, Turkmen carpet dealers, an old Uzbek chief who'd fled from Central Asia as a young boy when the Bolsheviks took over, a variety of businessmen, newspaper editors, pamphleteers, and the grandson of the bandit Ajab Khan Afridi, who had gained renown in the 1920s for kidnapping the British girl Molly Ellis.

The list goes on, continuing in the same eclectic fashion. The only real criterion I imposed in deciding whom to interview was my sense of who had an interesting story to tell. Since I didn't have a clear idea of how I might finally focus the project, I also intentionally sought breadth, on the assumption that it was better to have too much than too little.[17] On one level, this mix of interview topics was exhilarating, but it was also disorienting. Despite my change of direction toward oral history, I still had some notion of following anthropological tradition and focusing on a single tribe or even some quarter of the city.

I abandoned this inclination only gradually and, in the meantime, felt quite perplexed by the indefiniteness of the interviews and the absence of any clear organizing principle that might help me decide what to do with all of the material I was collecting. Presaging the fate of the Hubble satellite with its flawed telescope lens, I found myself a long way from home trying to focus on a lot of distant objects that remained blurry no matter how I adjusted my instruments. Unlike the Hubble satellite, however, I did not ultimately need a rescue crew from home to salvage my mission (although my wife's arrival six months into my fieldwork certainly helped). Rather, I had simply to remind myself to attend to the opportunities that my research situation presented and not try to impose my preconceived ideas onto the material.

As I began to realize the value of responding to (as opposed to forcing myself upon) the situation, it became clear that Peshawar offered a scope that most anthropologists living within the precincts of a single group are not afforded. The disadvantage I suffered under, given my interest in what was going on across the border, was that I was not immersed in the social milieu of the people about whom I wanted to write, and consequently I could not produce the sort of traditional ethnographic study of a particular place at a particular time that has long been the stock-in-trade of anthropologists. At the same time, however, because of the number, diversity, and uniqueness of the informants upon whom I could draw, I had a wider field available to me than most anthropologists have. With the disparate ethnographic and historical sources at my disposal, I could hold within my lens a wider than usual terrain that still possessed considerable detail— something midway between the highly nuanced but closely cropped portraits generally produced by ethnographers and the long-range but fuzzy panoramas that historians usually provide from their documentary sources.

Samiullah Safi and Sultan Muhammad Khan

If my experience in Qissa Khani began to awaken me to what was going on around me, my encounter with Samiullah Safi, the narrator of the story of Sultan Muhammad Khan that will be told in chapter 2, opened me up to the historical possibilities of the moment. I met Safi (as he is called) at the office of the Afghan Information Center, a now defunct organization whose principal task at that time was to provide assistance for foreign journalists who wanted to report on the war inside Afghanistan. When I first arrived in Peshawar, I used to go over to the Afghan Information Center several times a week to chat with whoever happened to be there. Because the center catered to reporters from abroad, I fit in and was always made to feel welcome, something I especially appreciated during the first few months of my stay in Peshawar.

As I spent more time at the center, it quickly became clear that despite its nominal status as a cooperative, most of its work was performed by one man—Sayyid Bahauddin Majrooh, a former professor and dean at Kabul University, who long ago, in another life really, had attended university in France and written his Ph. D. dissertation on Hegel. Majrooh spoke French and English fluently, along with many other languages, and was possessed of rare intelligence and energy. Because the center generated a limited amount of day-to-day work, it had become a one-man operation—Majrooh being that man—and the other members usually spent their time sitting around a table in the living room gossiping with one another. That suited most just fine, but others were unhappy in their inactivity—among them Safi.

During the first few months, Safi was almost always at the information center. Sometimes there would be three or four others with him, sometimes eight or ten. Usually Majrooh would be sitting at a table in the next room, punching keys on his typewriter or talking in one of his various languages to some foreigner newly arrived and eager to head over the border. Most of the members of the center could speak at least a smattering of English, and the one job that many of them did do was to accompany and translate for this or that foreigner as they conducted their business in Peshawar. The only one who did not perform this job was Safi, and the reason seemed to me both his pride and the fact that, alone among the center members, he could speak none of the European languages that the visiting journalists knew. I don't remember exactly how I got to know Safi, but it probably had something to do with my being one of the few foreigners who could speak with him and appreciate his story and situation.

When Safi was a boy of five or six, his family had been exiled from Pech Valley because of his father's involvement in the *jang-i safi*, the War of the Safis. The Safis had long been one of the most dissident tribes in the country, and the jang-i safi, which broke out in the late 1940s and lasted for more than a year, had severely tested the authority of the Afghan government. Prior to the present civil war, this conflict was generally recognized as the last great tribal rebellion in Afghanistan—the final act in the ancient drama of tribe-state conflict in this traditionally anarchic region. Safi's father had been a leader of that failed uprising and suffered nearly two decades of imprisonment and exile as the price of his leadership.

His family had also paid the price, being transported across the country and forced to live, first, in the western city of Herat and, later, in several isolated cities in the far north. Eventually, in the mid-1960s, the government allowed the family to move to Kabul, where Safi attended the university. This was during the so-called Democratic Era, when independent newspapers and political parties were permitted to operate openly for the first time. Safi's family benefited from the climate of liberalization as well, being given the opportunity to return to their native Pech Valley for the first time since the uprising twenty years earlier.

Shortly after their return, Safi announced his own decision to run in the parliamentary election as the deputy from Pech. Despite his having been away for most of his life, Safi won that election, a testament to the deep and abiding respect that the people of Pech had for his father. Safi stayed in the parliament until it was disbanded by Muhammad Daud following his bloodless coup d'etat of July 1973. Thereafter, Safi held various government jobs, including the editorship of a folklore journal. When the Marxist Khalqi party took power in April 1978, Safi began making preparations to return to Pech, which was among the first regions to experience anti-government agitation following the coup. Safi managed to leave Kabul with his family in December, and on his arrival in Pech, he immediately assumed a leadership role in the burgeoning rebellion against the Marxist regime.

Safi stayed in Pech for more than a year, planning strategy and rallying support for the rebels from neighboring tribes. Late in 1980, however, ten months after the Soviet invasion, Safi had been forced to leave Pech for Pakistan and had not returned. The initial impetus for his departure was a major Soviet operation targeted on Pech, but the reason he had not gone back was his ongoing dispute with local mullas. Independent tribal leaders like himself had come under pressure from religious leaders aligned with the Peshawar parties. Gradually, after much bickering and maneuvering on both sides, the mullas had won out, and the only tribal leaders who could maintain their position were those who accepted the mullas' terms and their ultimate control of the military situation and the society.

My encounter with Safi came about a year after his departure from Pech. I knew nothing of this history before the interview, and it is my recollection that the reason I suggested an interview in the first place had as much to do with his availability as with any perception on my part that his story might be a particularly significant one. I don't recall exactly how I phrased it, but (in keeping with my graduate school lessons) I let him know that I wanted to find out about "tribes and honor and Islam." Whatever I said, it was enough to get him to tell me his story and the story of his family, particularly that of his father, Sultan Muhammad Khan.

To this day I don't really know why Safi talked with me, but over a period of several weeks we spent nearly fifteen hours together taping an extensive inventory of stories about his father's life and his own. During these tapings, Safi was very much in charge. I would occasionally ask a question, but the basic agenda was his, as he told me (and the tape recorder) what he thought I (and it) should know. After we had finished, however, Safi said nothing more about the interview and never asked me what I was going to do with all the material we had recorded. He did tell me that I was free to use it any way I saw fit, but he never inquired as to what way that might be. Then, a few months after we finished the interviews, he drifted away from the information center, and I stopped seeing him with any frequency. Occasionally I would run into him on the street or at someone's house, but we pretty much forgot about each other.

Despite losing track of Safi, I grew increasingly fascinated by the stories he had given me as I listened to them again and again during the process of translating and transcribing the tapes. In attending to Safi's stories, I decided that somehow I would keep these artifacts in the final text that I produced. Stories were important in and of themselves, I concluded, and I did not want simply to extract from them some pulpy mash of facts that could be reconstituted within my own narrative history. My interaction with Safi also led me to abandon the traditional questions I had brought with me from graduate school and focus instead on the particular lives that were being revealed to me in my various interviews.[18]

Although I had not anticipated this emphasis when I set out to do my research, it was not altogether surprising that I should move in this direction, for the book that had first made me consider going into anthropology had been Clifford Geertz's *Islam Observed.* In this work Geertz contrasted Islamic cultural styles in Morocco and Java, and he did so by considering the very different personae of legendary saints: a rough-and-ready firebrand from the tribal hinterland of Morocco and a quietist yogi-like divine from the peasant heartland of Java. Geertz's portrayal of these two saints as "axial figures," each of whom exemplified a particular cultural "style," undoubtedly influenced my decision to view Safi's father as an axial figure—not of Afghan Islam but of Afghan honor. Sultan Muhammad Khan's fame in the tribal areas was well attested, and he was repeatedly mentioned by others from the frontier region as a man of great deeds who defended his personal and family honor with notorious zeal. This reputation and the wonderfully evocative quality of the stories themselves encouraged me to portray Sultan Muhammad in a way comparable to Geertz's handling of the Moroccan (Sidi Lahsen Lyusi) and the Javanese (Sunan Kalidjaga).

As I was beginning to see Safi's father as exemplary, however, the stories I was hearing also encouraged me to question the very notion of the axial figure, because many of the narratives seemed too extreme to be in any sense representative of a lifestyle or normative of the way honor should be followed. As often as Sultan Muhammad appears to exemplify the tenets of honor, he also appears to breach them, and the violence inherent in his stories also made me wonder about the viability of society itself when such passions were loosed. But for all the confusion they engendered in me, the stories still existed, and the detail and conviction with which they were told convinced me that they were grounded in empirical reality, just as the testimony of others besides Safi convinced me of the heroic stature of the man.

My sense of uncertainty as to how to interpret Safi's stories of his father's life began to develop while I was still in Peshawar, but the feeling didn't solidify until much later, when I was writing this book and casting about for a title. I had stewed over this issue for a long time, assuming that there must be something wrong with a book that couldn't find a title for itself. Finally, a Persian phrase came to my mind, a phrase I had heard many times in relation to great men of the past: *qahraman-i zaman*, hero of the age. The term was normally reserved for mythic figures from the distant past such as the warrior-poet Khushhal Khan Khattak or the great champion Rustam, from Firdausi's *Shahnama*. The phrase was rarely applied to a living person and never, in my hearing, to a Muslim saint. Still, it had a nice ring and might even convey a hint of irony, given the morass in which Afghan politics and political leaders were currently trapped. More importantly, it was appropriate to the subject of the great lives that define particular times, which is what the book was going to be about. What I didn't recognize right away was the aptness of the title in relation to the equivocal legacy of heroes. The word *qahraman* derives from the Arabic root *qahr*, meaning to subdue or gain mastery over something or someone. As it is used in the two relevant languages to this study—Persian and Pakhtu—other meanings have also accrued to the root form: rage, fury, wrath, calamity—all of which convey a sense of violence and disequilibrium.

What this etymology signifies to me is something that scholars of Greek myths have long realized: as praiseworthy as heroes might be, they are also dangerous. Noble and memorable, indeed, they also stand outside the normal orbit of human interaction and are never entirely fit for ordinary society.[19] In Afghanistan, no less than in other cultures at other times, heroes are an ambivalent blessing. On the one hand, they embody through their deeds the axiomatic truths by which societies define themselves. On the other, they strain the limits of what societies can tolerate if they are to survive. The hero rarely knows his place; he creates his own space at the expense of others and in doing so almost invariably transgresses the limits and agreements around which the normal commerce of daily life takes shape.

Shahmahmood and the Mulla of Hadda

Although Safi's stories were to occupy a considerable portion of my thoughts over the next few years, the interviews themselves were over quickly, and Safi was soon gone as well. The next part of my research would not go so easily, for it involved untangling the complex histories of the Islamic parties that then dominated the refugee political scene.

When I arrived in Peshawar in 1982, there were ten recognized resis-
tance parties aligned in two coalitions: the Seven Party Unity (*ettehad-i
haft gana*) and the Three Party Unity (*ettehad-i se guna*). The Seven
Party Unity was the more radical and included among its members the
Islamic Party (*hizb-i islami*), headed by Gulbuddin Hekmatyar, and the
Islamic Society (*jam'iyyat-i islami*), directed by Professor Burhanuddin
Rabbani. The Three Party Unity, the more traditional alliance, counted
among its members a party directed by an old-style religious scholar—the
Movement for Islamic Revolution (*harakat-i inqilab-i islami*) of Maulavi
Muhammad Nabi Muhammadi—and two parties affiliated with the heads
of prominent spiritual families: the National Liberation Front (*jabha-yi
nejat-i milli*), run by Hazrat Sibghatullah Mujadidi, and the National Islamic Front (*mahaz-i milli islami*), whose leader was Sayyid Ahmad Gailani.

Although I had been keeping abreast of events before my arrival in
Peshawar and was aware of the ascendance of these parties, the reality of
the world that they had created was something I was not prepared for,
even after two years in Kabul. If anything, my time there was to blame
for my confusion because the situation in Peshawar was so radically different from what I had known in Kabul. Where once I had seen bureau-
crats in karakul hats and Western suits whizzing past in their chauffeur-
driven Volga sedans, I now found myself staring at turban-draped mullas
squeezed between kalashnikov-toting bodyguards in bright, new Toyota
Land Cruisers. Where before there had been the one smirking photograph
of President Daud surveying every tea shop and staring down from every
eminence, Peshawar claimed a hive of would-be Dauds, all buzzing madly
about but none managing to dominate the rest.

As an anthropologist with spare time, I immediately wanted to investigate how this situation had come to be but also knew from my reading of
the literature on Afghanistan that very little had been written on Afghan
Islam—a subject that had appeared just a few years earlier to have only
an antiquarian significance in the modern world.[20] The world that the
refugees created in Peshawar was a world full-blown, a world that seemed
to have sprung up as if by some mysterious process of spontaneous generation. This could not be the case, of course, but I also recognized that it
would require a considerable amount of digging to discover where these
multiple Islams had come from and how they had claimed center stage.

Addressing this issue required that I start to unravel the web of person-
alities, parties, and alliances that was all around me. In turn, doing so
required that I spend a large percentage of my time at the various party

headquarters, interviewing officials high and low and gradually constructing from their testimony a chronological history and an ideological map that would help me first keep the different factions straight in my mind and then explain where they had come from and what they represented for the future. While I was occupied fixing the coordinates of the present confusion, I was also interested in uncovering some sense of the moral force of Islam—the ideational center around which these party satellites were spinning in their various irregular orbits. The creation of new parties was not all there was to Islam; fragmentation and discord might be what one saw on the surface, but there had to be something else going on as well—some profound pull that kept Islam at the center of people's thoughts and affections despite the abuses to which it was subjected by the parties.

Perhaps because I had already "found" Sultan Muhammad Khan, I began to focus my efforts on discovering some comparable figure who could exemplify and encapsulate the moral imperatives of Islam as Sultan Muhammad Khan seemed to exemplify and encapsulate those of honor. Ironically, the soundman from Los Angeles who had led me to the poems of Rafiq Jan also had an indirect hand in my finding the exemplary figure I was seeking, for he introduced me to a young Afghan named Shahmahmood Miakhel, who would lead me in turn to a historic figure as representative of Afghanistan's Islamic past as Sultan Muhammad Khan was of the traditional culture of tribal honor.

When I met him, Shahmahmood was working as the soundman's paid assistant. He was, in fact, my acquaintance's contact with the musicians on Qissa Khani. After the soundman returned to the United States, I saw Shahmahmood from time to time, but not that often because in the early months of my stay I was still hoping to work with Persian-speaking refugees from the north rather than with Pakhtu-speakers from the frontier, where Shahmahmood's home was. We stayed in touch, however, and eventually started working together, at first occasionally, and later daily. By the time I left Peshawar, we were together most of the time, and even now, more than a decade later, we remain close friends and sometime collaborators.

Shahmahmood's family was not exceedingly wealthy but was prominent in its area because its members were recognized as *sayyids*, or descendants of the Prophet Muhammad. The family also traced descent from an important saint—Mia 'Ali Sahib—whose shrine outside of Jalalabad was one of the best known and most frequented in eastern Afghanistan. Mia 'Ali Sahib had lived many centuries before, but Shahmahmood's grandfather had gained his own small following as a Sufi *pir*, or master, in the area of Kunar Province where he settled his family. The grandfather had been a government official but abandoned his career to devote himself full-time to religion as a disciple of his own Sufi master, Serkano Mia Sahib. Serkano Mia Sahib was also from Kunar, and he was one of the principal deputies of an even more famous master, the Mulla of Hadda.

As my interest in matters of religion became more apparent, Shahmahmood started talking more and more about this Mulla of Hadda, and he mentioned that there were a number of families then living in Peshawar who had a connection to the Mulla. As I contacted members of these families and interviewed them, I began to realize that the Mulla might provide a useful focus for my research into the role of Islam in tribal society. He had operated along the frontier in the later part of the nineteenth century, and it was clear from the way people spoke of him that his life held a special resonance for them. His Islam was the real Islam, many would tell me. The way he did things was the right way.

In a strange way that I only gradually appreciated, the Mulla seemed somewhat like Samiullah Safi's father. Both men were larger-than-life figures, and both were associated with a period in the past that was only dimly recollected but was nevertheless thought of as purer than the present. The era of men like Sultan Muhammad and the Mulla of Hadda was a mythic one, when people acted not for themselves but for higher principles. In the minds of many Afghans, men nowadays are corrupt and let all sorts of mitigating factors intrude upon their response to events. But the Mulla of Hadda and Sultan Muhammad Khan were different. They did not vacillate and collude as men do today. They were exemplars who adhered to a moral code to the end.

As the history of the Mulla of Hadda became clearer to me, I began to consider using the story of his life as a counterpoint to that of Sultan Muhammad Khan; however, several problems arose that made the two life histories incommensurable. First, whereas Sultan Muhammad's story had come from one source, his son, I was hearing the Mulla's story from a dozen different people, all of whom revealed significant pieces of the puzzle. Second, the various stories I was hearing did not arrange themselves into a coherent life history as Safi's stories did. To the contrary, the layering of story upon story by different informants seemed to deepen the mystery of the life I was investigating rather than to clarify it, and the main reason for this increasing obscurity was that almost all of the stories I collected were centered on *miracles* that the Mulla of Hadda had performed.

The question I had to answer was how I could fabricate a life history out of a series of disconnected stories, all of which focused on some action that, the rational part of my brain told me, had never happened in the first place. It appeared to me that the answer was embodied in the basic assumption that was coming to guide the study—namely, that all stories moralize the history with which they are concerned. The notion of *moralizing history* implied a process of perception and interpretation by which meaning was attached to events.[21] This was essentially a cultural process, and its result would necessarily vary depending on the background of those who would mold (largely unconsciously, but never nonculturally) the raw data of events according to the metaphysical principles and narrative conventions that were available to them.

Someone who imagines history as the sum of great and ignominious deeds performed by the ancestors of the living will tell one kind of story; someone who envisions the events of the world as unfolding according to a divine plan will tell another. The task for an anthropologist delving into the realm of the historian was less to assemble the "facts" of a particular historical situation than to preserve the texture of the original stories in which historical facts were embedded and to use those stories to illuminate the cultural imagination of those who took part in the events that those stories recalled. What mattered then was not merely that the life history of an Islamic saint and a tribal khan be told, but that the narrative genres themselves within which their stories were encoded be highlighted and treated as centrally important evidence in the search for historical meaning.[22]

I increasingly understood that the story *as a story* was itself a mirror for viewing society, and it was therefore critical that the integrity of different narrative genres be respected and understood in and of themselves. This was especially true with regard to the stories that were told of the Mulla of Hadda. The fact that the majority of these stories recounted miraculous transformations and voyages undertaken by the Mulla had to be recognized as significant in itself and not treated as a cultural idiosyncrasy to be overcome and seen through. His was the life of a saint—a man endowed with supernatural powers beyond the ken of ordinary men—and the analytical challenge in making sense of that life was how to respect the integrity of miracles in the cultural construction of his narrative identity.

The Missing Life

Having decided to focus on the lives of a tribal khan and a Muslim saint as a means of gaining access to the moral bases of honor and Islam, I began to realize the need for a life history of an individual from the same historical period that could illuminate the moral order represented by the state. On what basis did Afghan rulers command allegiance, and how did they legitimate their authority? In trying to answer these questions, I quickly confronted a fundamental problem: there was no one to ask—no one with a narrative connection to the royal family comparable to Safi's with Sultan Muhammad Khan or to the descendants of the Mulla of Hadda's disciples' with the great saint. The strangeness of this fact should not be overlooked. Members of the Durrani tribe that had ruled Afghanistan almost uninterruptedly from 1747 to 1978 simply were not in evidence in this, the capital of the resistance movement that was trying to unseat those who had swept the Durranis from power.

As unexpected as the hegemony of Islamic political parties seemed to me on my arrival, this absence of Durranis was odder still, for when I had lived in Kabul in the 1970s, members of the ruling Muhammadzai lineage of the Durrani tribe were everywhere to be seen and very much the first among the Kabul elite. In many of the most important offices, in the largest homes, in the fashionable restaurants and discotheques then sprouting up in Kabul, they were ones you saw, and theirs were the names you most often heard. Now they were gone—the former kings and king-pins of Afghan society—all dead or vanished to one or another Western capital where many of them had long-standing connections and probably bank accounts as well. In their absence, I had to find another informant, equal to those I had already discovered, who could provide access to the ethos of rulership in Afghan culture.

Because I had chosen to focus on the Mulla of Hadda, I was particularly eager to establish some link to the king of his day: Amir Abdur Rahman Khan. In almost every account I heard of the Mulla's life, Abdur Rahman's name also came up, and the references were usually negative because the Amir had tried to capture the Mulla on several occasions and had actually imprisoned several of his disciples, including the grandfathers of two of my informants. Nevertheless, I did not get a uniformly disapproving sense of the Amir from the stories in which he figured, and rarely did I hear outright condemnations of his actions. I sensed instead, even from these informants, that kings operated according to a different morality and a different set of cultural expectations. Abdur Rahman may have been cruel to his subjects. He may have been inadequately respectful of the saints and scholars of his realm, and he probably earned the divine retribution that was his in the end. But then again, he was the king. His lot was not the same as other men's, and it was understood that he would adhere to norms other than their own. Ultimately, everyone seemed to admit, a king had to be judged on a different scale. If many believed that Abdur Rahman exceeded what a king should do, then they also acknowledged their own inadequacy to evaluate his excesses with any certainty.

As I began to recognize the distinctiveness of Abdur Rahman's moral station, I also became aware of the way in which his reign appeared to function as something of a divide in people's minds, and one of the main reasons for this appears to have been his association with the founding of the nation-state. I don't recall anyone making this connection between the Amir and the nation-state explicitly, for the nation-state as a concept was not something that most people talked about. Instead, what was fixed on were those concrete manifestations of the nation-state's appearance for which Abdur Rahman was largely responsible and in relationship to which many of my informants made their judgments of him.

The most prominent of these manifestations was the Durand Line, which was established in 1893 at British insistence and delineated the frontier between the areas of British and Afghan control. While no British subject was ever allowed to enter tribal territory to survey the actual line and no cairns were ever set in place to show where Afghan sovereignty ended and British sovereignty began, the Durand Line nevertheless became, in different ways for different constituencies, an important symbol both of British domination in the area and of the changing role and character of the Afghan state. For tribal informants, the Durand Line had the particular significance of differentiating and dividing what previously had been singular and whole. The land of the tribes was free territory unencumbered by government control. *Yaghistan*, it was sometimes called— the land of the *yaghi*, the rebel, the unruly, the one who obeyed his own law. The tribes fought among themselves. They nursed bitter enmities and rarely, if ever, made common cause. But this they could agree upon: in comparison to the fragmented, hierarchical, and regulated world of the state (*hukumat*), theirs was an undivided world, a world of sure ethical standards and fierce loyalties.[23] And this too they knew: the recognition and universal acceptance of this social and political order began to fall apart when the Durand Line intruded and forced upon them a different sort of moral order than the one they knew and understood.

From a Muslim point of view, the Durand Line was equally problematic, not only because it reflected the growing control of an infidel regime, but also because it divided the land in terms alien to their own. Great Britain, India, Afghanistan—these were categories that confounded the fundamental division of the world between the *dar al-islam*, the land of

Islam, and the *dar al-harb*, the land of war. The dar al-Islam is the territory of those who have submitted to God's dominion. The dar al-harb is land controlled by non-Muslims, and it is subject to contestation because those who live there have not yet accepted God's dominion. Muslims also accept as legitimate the existence of separate polities within the dar al-Islam because God has decreed that individual tribes and races must come together in communities and obey kings drawn from among themselves. But there is no precedent in Islam for the nation-state, and as we shall see, one focus of particular antipathy was the creation of the Durand Line, which many Muslims viewed as an act of capitulation to an infidel power for which Abdur Rahman bore most of the responsibility.

As my fieldwork came to a close, the evidence I was accumulating pointed ever more insistently to the importance of Abdur Rahman for my study, but I was getting no closer to finding the informant or informants who could provide the kinds of personal stories I needed to complete my study. No one had the kind of personal stories I needed. No one produced testimony comparable to what I had been given by Samiullah Safi and the descendants of the Mulla of Hadda's disciples. I left Peshawar loaded down with tapes and transcripts but missing one critical piece of the puzzle that I had determined to solve. I didn't realize it until much later, but the informant I needed had been available to me all along. That informant was Abdur Rahman, who made himself accessible to inspection through several invaluable documents: an autobiographical account depicting the trials and adventures of his early years and a royal proclamation enunciating the Amir's understanding of the moral ties of kingly authority.[24]

CONTESTED DOMAINS

In the last chapter of this book, I will keep the focus on narrative that holds sway elsewhere, but I will shift attention from persons to events: specifically, a conflict (referred to by the British as an "uprising" and by the people of the frontier as a "jihad") that broke out in the summer of 1897 along the border between British India and Afghanistan. This uprising/jihad was led by religious leaders, the most important of whom was the Mulla of Hadda, and most of its participants were Pakhtun tribesmen from eastern Afghanistan and the autonomous districts of the frontier. Standing on the sidelines—perhaps complicit in the attack, perhaps not—was the Afghan amir, Abdur Rahman Khan.

The initial reason for my focusing on the frontier war of 1897 as the subject for the last chapter was the serendipity of discovering accounts of those events from three distinctly different points of view. The first of these accounts came via several descendants of the Mulla's disciples. The story that they told involved the Mulla's miraculous escape from imminent capture by British troops near the village of Jarobi, high in the mountains of the Mohmand territory. Initially I didn't know what to do with this story because it had no dates attached to it, and it was unclear what battle was being discussed. But the story possessed a singular dramatic quality, and it was still very much in my mind when I later read accounts of the events of 1897 written by the British war correspondent H. Woosnam Mills, who accompanied the expeditionary force that was sent into Mohmand territory to punish the tribe for its participation in the attacks.

One of the stated goals of the expeditionary force was to capture the Mulla of Hadda, and Mills spun a vivid tale of the British troops braving enemy fire and a thunderous monsoon storm as they entered Jarobi in pursuit of the elusive Mulla. As I read the account, I noticed that a number of elements in Mills's story corresponded with elements in the miracle story I had heard in Peshawar, and it became clear to me that the two stories concerned the same set of events. What was less clear was how to reconcile the two accounts—how to make them speak to one another. The two stories reflected such different notions of agency, of meaning, and of reality itself that a simple, straightforward account of "what happened" seemed not only impossible but also somewhat beside the point.

The problem got even more complex in 1986 when I went back to Peshawar for six months of additional fieldwork. During that trip I met and interviewed Shahmund, a man about seventy years old who was an elder of the Mohmand tribe. His branch of the tribe was the one that the Mulla of Hadda had lived with when he was with the Mohmands, and according to Shahmund's version of history, it was his own grandfather who carried the Mulla away from the field of battle and saved him from capture. Shahmund's story was short and didn't provide many details from the battle, but it did suggest that there was a third way to view events, a way that reflected a tribal understanding of the world that was distinctly different from the understandings which informed the other two accounts.

The congruent but contradictory stories of the Mulla's escape from Jarobi is what first drew my attention to the uprising of 1897, but the more I investigated these events and thought about them, the more I realized that their significance transcended the events themselves and the issues of narrative representation that their historical recounting raised. Viewed against the backdrop of the anti-Soviet resistance that was raging when I first heard and read these accounts, the earlier conflict could be seen as connected in some way to the later, if only because both were led by Islamic leaders and viewed as Islamic holy wars against foreign, infidel invasions.

However, the differences between the two were at least as striking as the similarities. Gone, for the most part, from the recent conflict were miracles and the fantastic claims of divine complicity in the outcome of events. Gone too was the overwhelming sense of conviction and certainty that, all accounts agree, the people of the frontier felt when the rising first began. In the place of miracles and emotions, what one saw were political parties and more or less shrewd politicians spouting ideological formulas and cadging money and arms from foreign governments. Examples of heartfelt Islamic devotion were much in evidence—from the innumerable daily sacrifices and deprivations that refugees and civilians uncomplainingly accepted for the greater good of the struggle to the corporal immolation of tens of thousands of mujahidin martyrs—but so too was the sense of abiding suspicion conveyed in so many ways by so many Afghans: suspicion that ambitious leaders were systematically corrupting the faith, that the Islam they represented was not the Islam the people as a whole believed in and practiced, that the struggles of the present were more about baser matters and concerns than the idealized struggles of the past.

The forms of Islamic ideology and political practice that one observed in the 1980s had many points in common with those one heard and read about from the turn of the century, but there seemed to be as many differences, and it became clear to me that to understand the present I had first to understand the past and the transformations that had been wrought between past and present. Beyond this, however, it also began to become apparent that the uprising/jihad of 1897 could serve not simply as a baseline for measuring change: its significance was not just as an illustration of traditional Islam that could be erected and set next to the contemporary variant. Rather, it seemed that past and present were intertwined and that one could make out in the events of that distant summer not just arrayed armies of men but also opposed moral visions that, combined and reconfigured, would transform the political landscape of Afghan society.

The role of the Durand Line as symbol and substance of changing political relations has already been alluded to, but what I began to see more directly as I considered the long-forgotten colonial conflict was the deeper, cultural threat that the colonial vision of progress and civilization represented to the Mulla and the Islam he embodied. At the time of the uprising/jihad of 1897, this threat was still a distant one that had not yet been articulated in a language or form that made it directly accessible to the tribal people of the frontier; however, one could also see the challenge that the colonial vision posed, particularly if one paid attention to the contrary ways in which the colonial conflict was portrayed and meaning assigned by different sides.

Of special significance in this regard is the interpretation of the "irrational" features of the uprising: an erratic holy man promising miracles and the end of British rule in India, farmers abandoning their fields and flocks in the middle of the growing season, otherwise normal villagers assaulting fortified forts with little more than pitchforks in their hands. Various political and economic factors could be marshaled as contributory to the climate of discontent; but, as the following statement suggests, British authorities and commentators of the time recognized that the ultimate cause was not something accessible to rational analysis: "after having studied the attitude of the tribes from the first burst of their energy through the varied phases of their resistance, and the final collapse of the majority of sections, one is inclined to sum the causes of the outbreak up under three heads: the first of which is fanaticism; the second, fanaticism; and the third, *fanaticism.*" [25]

Fanaticism (along with related terms like *barbarism* and *mad mullahs*) constitutes a key trope in British accounts of native unruliness, and one which is as significant for understanding the moral threat presented by British imperialism as the Durand Line is for understanding the practical political and economic challenge of colonial authority. Thus, if the Durand Line can be said to represent the spatial imposition of an exogenous order over an existing social organization, the terminology of fanaticism represented a similar sort of superimposition of an all-encompassing binary conceptual grid on the existing cultural topology.

To uncover the structural implications of this conjunction, I begin chapter 5 by focusing on the writings of a different sort of hero: young Winston Churchill, who, in his first foray into the political arena, was an eyewitness to the frontier war and its aftermath. Because of his involvement in the conflict, his passionate commitment to imperial rule, and his expressive power as a writer, Churchill makes an appropriate and articulate spokesman for the British point of view on the tribal rising. Churchill's dispatches and correspondence from the frontier provide both a dramatic chronicle of the events themselves and a passionate polemic on the significance of the conflict for British interests and ideals.

At the same time, Churchill also supplied us with another document that, I will argue, effectively negates—or at least relativizes—the terms of moral absolutism that infuse his dispatches. This document, an unpublished treatise on political oratory that Churchill happened to be working on during the same summer of 1897, discusses the requirements and techniques that enable a political speaker to win an audience to his side. In providing us these insights into the practical nature of political authority, Churchill also, quite unintentionally, provided a ground for dissolving the rational grid that dictated the interpretation of the combined tribal/Islamic assault on colonial control.

Using Churchill's treatise as a starting point, I continue on to a consideration of the cultural and organizational bases of the uprising and then conclude with a comparison of the three stories of the Mulla of Hadda's escape from Jarobi glen. Throughout the several stages of this analysis, my aim is to try to reconstitute the cultural logic of the "fanaticism" that inspired the frontier people to mount a movement of resistance against British power. At the same time, I also try to lay the groundwork for considering the manner in which the rationalist paradigm introduced to the region by the British would later integrate itself within the hitherto self-contained moral matrix of Afghan politics: the matrix of honor, Islam, and rule to which I will now turn.

2   The Making of Sultan Muhammad Khan

My name is Samiullah. I am known as Safi. My father is Sultan Muhammad Khan from the area of Morchil in Pech Valley of Kunar. My grandfather's name was Talabuddin, but he was famous by the name *Akhundzada* [son of a religious scholar]. I don't know his background, but this much I do know. My father at that time was about thirteen or fourteen years old. He was the eldest child of my grandfather—my father was. He had two other sons who were small. One of them could eat solids. The other was still nursing. My grandfather had three wives, and these three boys were from each of the mothers—each one separate.

At that time, the government had the regulation that whoever was the elder of the tribe—if he was pious and if he had a reputation among the people (from both the religious and tribal point of view) of being firm—the government would recognize this sort of person and give them the authority over the region. In this way, my grandfather became the administrator [*hakim*] of the area. His name was Talabuddin Khan but he was known as Akhundzada since his father was also a man of religion. He had studied in a religious school [*madrasa*], although he didn't do the work of a mulla. But he was an individual who was knowledgeable about religious matters and other things, and for this reason they would refer to him as an *akhund* [religious scholar].

In addition to this, he was a landowner. The original place of my grandfather was Gul Salak, not Morchil. He had land in Morchil, but at that time this area of Morchil was the border line between the regions of the Nuristanis and Safis. One of our places is named Samtal, which is about twenty minutes by foot from Nuristan.

Samtal also belonged to my father. It was originally a Nuristani area, but they had sold it to my grandfather. It happened this way that as long as my grandfather was alive, some of the people who had land there in Morchil sold their land to my grandfather and left. At that time, my grandfather was living in Morchil, which is to say it belonged to us. But the original place of his tribe, the place of the sword, of coming and going, living and dying, among the tribe, that place was called Gul Salak which includes three side valleys, within Pech Valley, which is itself associated with one district administration ['alaqadari] of Chapa Dara. They also call this valley Mahsud Dara.

There were originally two tribes living in Pech: Nuristanis and Safis. The Nuristanis were, well, Nuristanis, but the Safis are three brothers: one of them is remembered as Mahsud, one by the name of Gurbuz, and the other by the name of Wadir. We are from the line of Mahsud. My tribe is Mahsud, in the line of Safi. This valley is known as Mahsud Dara.

This that I'm telling you, I don't know if it's important, but I think its interesting. However important it might be, it is interesting.

My grandfather—his oldest son became my father—Sultan Muhammad Khan. Some man from that same village of Gul Salak, whose name I have forgotten, said to my grandfather, "I will give my daughter to your son. I will give her to you, you give her to whichever son you want." He agreed. They were twenty-two people. They were twenty-two *malatar*—close cousins. This man who gave his daughter to my father (my father at that time was small and didn't have any wife), he had seven young sons. But he didn't have much inherited land. He didn't have land. But my grandfather had the power of the government and the power of the tribe and of the land in his hands.

This plot was arranged between them. The man who wanted to give his daughter to my father and who had talked with my grandfather, he invited my grandfather to his house. I'm not sure if that same girl later married or not; I believe that she didn't get married.

My father, who was small, said to his father, "You yourself have a rifle. You also have servants, and you have soldiers that you are not going to take with you? For security, you should always take your own servants with you with their rifles." My grandfather said to his son, "Here, I am with people who are of my own tribe. I haven't done any treachery to these people. Why should the government soldiers or my own servants come and go with me?" He would get on his horse and go alone.

Although he was still little, my father didn't accept this reasoning from him. "You must always take an armed person with you when you come and go. You can't say that something bad won't happen, that someone won't attempt to kill you." But, my grandfather said, "I am an akhundzada, and I have never harmed anyone. Why should I take someone with me?"

He didn't accept my father's advice and went off and came to a bridge which is between Gul Salak and Morchil. [Gul Salak] is about a half-hour away by foot, but my grandfather had fixed the road so you could go by horse. He went back and forth on horseback. He came to the bridge. He was on the bridge, he was crossing over the river. The man who had offered his daughter to my grandfather, he was crouching with his seven sons. They had taken cover. Their rifles were in their hands. He was on his horse and had arrived at the bridge. They shot him, and he fell from his horse.

When my father heard the sound of gunfire, he becomes worried that something had happened. He leaves there, running, and when he arrives, his father is still alive. He had fallen onto the bridge, on the wooden bridge. He places his head on his chest, and his father says to him, "My son, God has given me paradise because I am a pure martyr [shahid]. I have never deprived anyone of their rights, so be careful that you don't ruin the Day of Judgment [akherat] for me."

Then, my father says to him, "Matters of death are the work of the dead. The dead have no rights over the work of the living. I am alive. If I do not have the force and power in me to take revenge on one person for every bullet that has struck your body, then I would not be your son. Swallow your grief. You should take care of your final moments. You know, and your God knows. I know, and the living know."

They bring him back and bury him. After that, my father goes to some other place outside of Pech Valley where some friends of my grandfather lived. He went there, and there he immediately begins to learn the study of writing and reading. They call it *mursalat* [the skills of a scribe]. He learns these. My father would say that, "I learned forty *mursalat*. Forty *mursalat*. In the space of two months, I learned forty *mursalat*." What these forty *mursalat* really amounted to were the kind of letters that the scribes of old would write. Petitions and invitations and that sort of thing. *Gulistan* and *Bustan*—this kind of book—and religious knowledge.[1] Of course, at that time, all of these things were quite common. He learned them.

Then my father comes, and the first wife my father takes, through her, God gives him his first son. The name of that first son is Jandad Khan. Last year he died of natural causes in Pech Valley. At the time that his son Jandad Khan is born in his house, my father's *mama* [mother's brother] goes to see my father.

At the time that his son is born, he isn't there. The reason is that he is afraid. He is afraid because he has two little brothers, one of whom is an infant and the other has just taken his first steps. Except for them, he is alone, and because of this he is afraid that they [his father's enemies] might try to kill him now while he is here. So he would go to the homes of his friends and his father's friends. There he was studying, and then one day he comes to Dir. Dir—the one they call "the Nawab of Dir"—he was there. The Dir Nawab was acquainted and had had a relationship with my grandfather. For example, one would send some people to the other, if something happened and the situation required. They had a friendship. I think that this was during the time of Abdur Rahman Khan [1880 to 1901]. I don't know whether or not the Durand Line had been established yet, but the friendship with my grandfather was from that time.

Anyway, he was studying there when my father's *mama* comes and says to his nephew, "Let's go to the homeland. God has delivered a child in your home." He goes there with him and passes some time there with his child. Sometimes he would giggle with my father, and my father would be gentle with him. Then this *mama* of his sensed the love that was growing between father and child and says to him, "I believe that you have become a cuckold [*daus*]. You have become a cuckold and a pimp [*dala*]."

My father doesn't understand what he's saying and says, "Why?"

He replies, "As long as you enjoy this love of your child, you will remain dala."

Then my father understood what he meant by these words. The

meaning of his words was this: "If you are preoccupied with your child and the love of children and family and woman and this sort of thing, with this sort of love, then you will forget about your father. You will forget about the murderers of your father, and after that, maybe you will compromise with them. Maybe you will go on with your life." His real meaning was this.

After that, my father leaves. He leaves again. I'm not sure if he was in Asmar or where. He was with one of his father's friends since he was a boy and had no friends of his own. All of his friends were the friends of his father's. He studied there.

Then news came to him. Someone informed him that, "Your mother congratulates you that she has gained revenge for your father. She has taken his revenge."

He comes home, and all of the people, all of his friends and relations think that he must be happy since his mother, with the help of his mama, had killed the murderer of her husband—that is to say, the big man. His seven sons were still alive. The people thought he would be happy, and they congratulate him. But the color had gone from him. He doesn't say a thing, and when he reaches the house, he severely punishes his mother. My father would never talk about it since he understood the rights of a mother from the point of view of Islam. My father never said, "I did this act." But others say that he sat his mother down some place and put out her eyes. He blinded the eyes of his own mother.

He blinded her because, "You have subjected me to the taunts and ridicule [*tana* and *paighur*] of the tribe. [People will say that] 'the son of Talabuddin Akhundzada was never born. His wife gained his revenge. His wife took his vengeance. He didn't have a son.' You have ruined my name and reputation in the tribe. When you committed this act, you thought that you were taking revenge for my father or for your husband, but instead you have lost my position in the tribe. You have placed me under the paighur of the people who say that, 'Talab Akhundzada died without issue. He is childless. He didn't have a son. He didn't have a man. He didn't have a youth who would take revenge for his own father. His wife took his revenge.'" For this reason it is said he blinded his own mother, but I was never able to question him about this matter because he was a very severe man. And he never said, "I did this thing."

Whenever he would come, he would only pay his respects to his mother. A man was appointed for her. Until her death, he gave her food. He would put food in her mouth. But he didn't do anything. He wouldn't sit with her to talk or to get her advice on some matters—never. [From that time] my father developed a reaction against women in general that, whatever had to be done, a man had to do it, and he shouldn't take the advice of a woman since the mentality of a woman is of a certain kind. They don't understand.

He had another experience which caused him to have this reaction against women. While he was alive, I often argued with him that this wasn't good. The rights of women and men are the same. They must be equal. But he would reply, "Take good care of your wife and love her. Be kind to her. Don't beat her. Treat her gently. But on important matters a man must never take the advice of a woman, even if she is his mother. Whatever he does, he must not tell her." This was his attitude.

After that, my father is at home. We had some land some place that shared a boundary with those same men who had killed my grandfather, that is to say, the enemies of my father. They were coming, and they had this plot where they would tell my father, Sultan Muhammad Khan, to come and correctly mark the boundary line of this land. They wanted to take him there. "He is just a boy. If he has a servant or someone else with him, we will kill him too. What do other people care about him? And anyway we are one body, and we are many in number."

Then they were leaving to come here. But, before this, what does my father do but plant a woman in the house of these enemies of his. He gives her a salary. He gives her clothes—secretly— so that he would be informed of every plan that they might come up with. One day before, she tells my father. At that time, he must have been seventeen or eighteen years old, anyway less than twenty, and maybe only sixteen. She informs him of the decision they had come to, and the decision was such that [their] mother had brought a Qur'an to her seven boys and [said to them], "You should not go. This poor boy. You have killed his father and now you will kill him. This isn't a good thing to do. You have made a marriage bond with him. You gave my daughter to him, and even now this girl is in our house. This is not good. What wrong has he done?"

She beseeches them with the Qur'an, but they don't accept that Qur'an. Well, that woman who was in their house, whoever she was, she comes and tells my father the following: "In the morning they will come. They have this plan to take you some place to divide the land. But you must know." My father understands.

The seven young men—all wearing the same clothes, all of them [carrying] rifles—they come, and when they reach the fort they call to my father, "Come, let's go!"

My father is inside the house. He wouldn't go outside. He sends a person to tell them, "You should go. However much land you need, and wherever you want to place the boundary—that is up to you. You decide yourselves, and take one or two white beards with you. I am sick. I have some difficulties, but when you come back from there, eat some food with me. Have lunch with me."

They replied, "Fine. Not today, tomorrow." And one of them took some dirt like this in his hand. The dirt was in his hand, and he buried a stick into [the dirt] and struck it like this, flicking it away, and said [to his brothers], "This is little Sultan, you know? We can kill him tomorrow. Today, we'll go and set the boundary ourselves, to our own liking, and come back later." So when they came back from that place, they would return here, to the house of my father.

[At my father's house] there are some people who are with my father: his servants and in-laws, his mother's kinsmen and others. He says to all of them, "As long as you have been here and lived with me, whether or not we have given you a salary, whether we have given a lot or a little, this life has been in this measure that you have always had our guns on your shoulders. Today, however, I have no need of those of you who work for a wage. I am alone, and my two brothers are small. Those of you who are with me for the sake of my friendship and who are not afraid of losing their heads stay. The rest of you go."

All of them came to his side and [said], "We don't serve you for the sake of your barley, or because of your crops or for your money. All of us have our own difficulties. We have our own problems—many of them. But, since each of us calls himself a man, we are here, and we have brought our rifles. From long ago, your father has saved us from many sorrows. He has defended our rights. Therefore, if you are to die, we should die first—whatever you order us to do."

Except for my father, no one has any idea what the plan is. After this, he tells them that this is the situation, that these same ones are coming back and this is the plan we have. He tells them, "We are going to kill them right here. We will kill all of them."

Then they are there. They have sat down for the meal. Each of the servants chooses one person: "I have this one and I have that one." Some of them are sitting amongst them. My father's mama is seated with them, and my father is standing, and right then and there they shoot them. They shoot, and one young boy who is the same age as my father escapes. He escapes, wounded, falls by a tree, and grabs the roots of the tree like this. Then my father shoots him with a pistol. He shoots him with the pistol, but then he takes his head in his arms. And my father cries because he had been his friend. He had been his friend and playmate, and for this reason he cries. He cries a lot, so much so that people say he didn't eat any food for a week. He was simply crying, not thinking of anything else except this friend of his. But, since he had become his enemy, he was obliged to kill him.

And then they are on seven bedstands with red mattresses and, in those days, they had a kind of silk shawl. Over each of them they drape a fine silk shawl. And then they send word to their paternal cousins and others to "come and take away your dead." They come and take them. Then they bury them. Some among those paternal cousins of theirs then begin to get revenge for them, and a feud began. My father—all of them by himself—since his two brothers were small, but he acts in such a way that in total about twenty-two of these enemies are killed. He kills twenty-two of them.

Their women remain. My father says to all of these women, "You are like my own sisters or my own daughters. I will give you to whomever you desire." Since by the law of inheritance, it was up to my father. No one else had any rights over them. No one was left from their family, other than youngsters. Naturally, some of them had wives, some didn't. Some of them who had wives didn't have young children. With those to whom he gives [women], my father establishes relationships, just as though he had given them his own daughter. It was that sort of relationship.

From then on, whenever my father went out on horseback, he took other men and horses with him. Every time he approached a house where one of these women was living, he would get off his horse one kilometer away and lead it until he was one kilometer past the house. Then he would get back on the horse. He would never ride by. He did this because he did not want to humiliate them by showing haughtiness [*kibr*] toward them. This is kibr.

"They, what did they want to do? They wanted to kill me; they killed my father, and for this they were killed. The marital tie was also a kind of plot, a conspiracy. They wanted to establish a marital alliance, and then kill my father, and me. I was small. They would have killed me. And then my inheritance, the authority. They would have [taken] it for themselves because there would be no heir. This was their original intention, there was nothing else. Then, what did God do? God did the work that they wanted to do to us—God did this to them. In return, we could not be proud [*gharur*]. We could not do kibr. [That was] first, and second was this, that since they are *namus*,[2] one must show respect to them. Since they are not men—they are namus—and one should not pass by their houses on horseback. These things he didn't do—ever."

The people saw this. The people saw the kind of thing my father was doing, and at the same time, the people saw what modesty he had with regard to namus and other things that concerned the tribe. The tribe said good things about this. This is how he defends these things.

In this manner, it reached such a point that my older brother, Jandad—one day, my older brother Jandad came upon one of our enemies who was a distant cousin of those others (who had been killed in the feud). Jandad thought to himself, "Ah, they are from that family, from our enemies." This man's wife was with him, and he said to him, "Drop your rifle!" He put down his rifle, and his rifle was taken away from him.

Since the wife of this enemy was with him and this older brother of mine, Jandad, took away his rifle, this—in *afghaniyat* [the customs of Afghans], in our tribe, in *pakhtunwali* [the code of Pakhtuns]—this is a very great dishonor, a very great paighur. That an armed man should put his gun down: a gun is not dropped as long as you are alive, and his wife was also with him.

When this all happened, what did my father do? What did he do about this situation? My father sent for my brother. [Jandad's] own mother locked him in a room. It was winter, and she put him in this room without any clothes except a pair of shorts. And women brought water. My father was seated in a chair to watch him, a long horse whip in his hand, and he told the mother—the mother of this brother of mine—"Pour water on him." They poured cold water on him, and my father beat him. The whole tribe heard of this.

He said, "I will kill him in this manner since he has done something very dishonorable [*be ghairati*]. He was your enemy, and so many of them were killed. He is from that same lineage, and we must show respect for them. He told him to drop his rifle and then took it from him. He did this in front of his wife, and he didn't have this right." He himself was the husband of a woman. My brother had a wife, and his wife and all the others were standing and watching.

For three days and nights he wasn't given any food, and he was beaten. They gave him just enough food that he wouldn't die of starvation and a little bit of water, and then they beat him.

Finally, my father's brothers, especially that brother of his who lives in Samtal, he came to see him. His name was Abdul Qudus Khan. Abdul Qudus Khan had two wives. He comes to his brother—my father—and says, "If you kill this boy, I will divorce these two wives of mine. Then you marry them, or anyone else can marry them, and I will go, in whatever direction I end up going."

My father is afraid that if he releases his wives and divorces them that it will be very bad, one more disgrace. He wouldn't have cared if Abdul Qudus had died or killed himself, but if he had divorced his wives, that would have been something else. And Abdul Qudus had said, "If you kill him, I will divorce these two wives of mine, and when they are divorced I will go away." So he was obliged to release him, but he gathered the whole tribe together, and he disowned his own son. This disowning continued until 1346 or 47 [1967 or 68]. My father was in his final moments. He was dying, and the whole tribe came together and said to him, "Forgive your son whom you have disowned."

He replied, "If I forgive him, may God not forgive me." This is the kind of single-mindedness and determination he had. You see? Later, he was about to die. There was hardly anyone around. I was also away in the army, and one of my brothers named Shah Khusrau said to him, "Father, pray for us."

My father accepted his request but said, "I disown Torab and you should not speak with him." He also disowned him, this other son, Torab, who is older and is now in our homeland [because] he was with his brother, Jandad. These two fingers, he cut off like that, and forgave all of his children but these two sons. All of the men and women of our family were there and saw that even in his last moments his resolve had not left him. They thought that even if we ask him to forgive everyone, these two others will not be included. He cut off these two fingers and except for them forgave everyone else.

MYTH AND HISTORY

The story you have just read is the first story that Samiullah Safi told me. It is the story he chose to begin with, the story he felt compelled to tell first of all. Hours of stories followed this one, some having to do with his father, most with himself and the various stages that his life had passed through including a childhood spent in exile in distant parts of the country, student days at Kabul University during the era of protests and demonstrations in the mid-1960s, his tenure as a parliamentary deputy in the late 1960s and early 1970s, his career as a leader of the anti-government resistance in the Pech Valley after the Marxist Revolution in 1978, and finally his exile to Peshawar following the takeover of the resistance by Islamic parties after the Soviet invasion in 1979. All told, Safi talked for more than twelve hours, and the transcripts of the many stories he told me go on for several hundred pages of single-spaced text. Of all the stories, however, this first one, the one of Sultan Muhammad's revenge, is the one I have always come back to, the one that, to my mind at least, reveals more about the irreducible values of tribal culture than any other story that Safi ever told me or that I have encountered elsewhere.

Before Safi and I began our interviews, I told him that I wanted to find out about tribes and honor in Pakhtun society. I don't remember exactly how I expressed my interests, but given that Safi was one of the first people I interviewed during my two years in Peshawar, I'm quite sure that the questions I had for him were basic ones of the "What is honor and what does it mean to you?" variety. As it turned out, it didn't really matter what I asked him. He had his own agenda, and during our time together I asked him very few questions. Every morning for a period of several weeks, we would meet at my home in Peshawar over a pot of black tea, a pack of cigarettes, and a Sony tape recorder. Sometimes other Afghan friends would sit in, but usually it was just Safi and me: Safi doing most of the talking and I almost all of the listening, trying to keep up with the rapid flow of the Dari Persian that Safi had learned fluently during his years in exile away from Pech Valley.

However I might have framed my questions about tribal honor, Safi complied in a way that made sense to him, even if it was not immediately evident to me what he was up to or how I might make use of what he had given me. His manner of responding to my crude questions was not with analysis, but rather with a story, a story that he prefaced by saying, "This that I'm telling you—I don't know if it's important, but I think it's interesting [*delchasp*]. However important it might be, it is interesting." That's not an especially grandiose claim. It is, in fact, a lot less grand a claim than some of those that I make for the story myself. But as straightforward as Safi's description of the story appears to be, I find it revealing because it indicates that the narrator realized this story would seem notable to me in some way. It also suggests that, perhaps more than most people, Safi was able to objectify his family lore and to see it as illustrative of some larger process or pattern of social life extending beyond itself. Perhaps this is because Safi himself was educated and had worked as a writer and editor in Kabul. Perhaps it is because he spent much of his life among strangers. Whatever the reason, in seeing the story as potentially useful to me, Safi also seems to have been signaling his own estrangement from it. At the very least, he demonstrated that he was sufficiently outside the orbit of his own society and sufficiently aware of the orbit that I was operating in to have a fairly clear idea of the difference that lay between us. Be that as it may, the question that must be of concern at present is how to analyze a narrative like this one. I have been mulling this story over for a long time, but I have never been able to completely convince myself that I understand it or that I know what depths to sound. One reason for this uncertainty is that the story of Sultan Muhammad's revenge seems so radically to blur the traditional boundary between myth and history.

Distinctions between myth and history are artificial, of course, but they still have a hold over us. They still must be negotiated, and in terms of such negotiation this story is strangely anomalous, in part because it seems too close in time for the kind of story it purports to be. Many of the characters in Safi's tale are only recently deceased, and the events themselves occurred within—or just over the horizon—of living memory. If there is no one around who specifically remembers all of these events, there are those who remember some of them; and those from whom Safi heard the story are in all probability those who also witnessed it and perhaps even joined with his father in the climactic slaughter in the guest house. For these reasons, the story has a grain and texture that we usually associate with history, with chronicle, with the narrative recounting of events as people actually remember them in that near temporal space in which specific accounts can still be checked against personal memory.

Despite the historical proximity of the recounted events, however, the story also has a mythic quality to it—like the *Oresteia* or a medieval fairy tale that seems, at once, too hideous in its excesses and too elegant in its symmetries to be of real lives and actual happenings. The reader almost senses that he or she is a spectator at an ancient drama—the sort in which a mother's appearance in the first act foreshadows another in the last, vengeance always redresses deceit, and dramatic oaths of honor are intoned at climactic junctures and in a voice loud enough that even those in the back rows might hear them. There are also moments in this story that seem too perfect to be believed as real-life experience, such as the scene in which Talabuddin tells his son not to "ruin his Paradise" while lying prostrate on a bridge, not unlike the bridge called *sirat* that all Muslims must cross to enter the gates of Heaven.

And there is the sheer economy of the story, with every moment carefully plotted, every extraneous event removed (including the narratively anticlimactic deaths of twenty-two of the enemy), every detail somehow contributing to the coherence of the whole. Let one example suffice—the moment early on when Safi introduces the antagonist of the story: "A man from Gul Salak—I have forgotten his name—said to my grandfather ... " Here we are embarking on a story about how one man overcomes tremendous obstacles to gain his identity, and the first person we encounter is a man who has lost his name. A lapse on the part of the narrator perhaps, but we are shortly to discover that such lapses have tremendous resonance in a culture where one's name is literally worth dying, or killing, for. However, there is an irony in this lapse, as well, that again blurs the distinction between myth and history, for no matter how much Safi might wish that the enemy's name be forgotten, the story of Sultan Muhammad's revenge is sufficiently within the range of remembering that some details, including this one, can be checked out. The edited portions of the narrative—the parts that were dissonant in tone or out of keeping with the moral tenor of the whole—remain accessible. They have not yet been swept away with the decomposition of memory, and consequently we can still ascertain that the name of Sultan Muhammad's enemy has not been forgotten, even if—in a culturally more meaningful sense—it has been lost because the dead man has no heirs, no one to claim him as his father, his grandfather, his ancestor.

In the process of my research, I have been able to discover other pertinent facts that likewise confound the mythic consolidation of the tale. The
most important of these concerns the background of the story: how it
all began. The beginning is clear-cut in Safi's rendition. A man from a
neighboring village—a man who had many adult children but little land—
offered his daughter in marriage to one of Talabuddin's sons. Talabuddin,
who had a lot of land but only three small sons, went to fetch the girl but
was ambushed and killed on his way. Safi's description of events makes it
quite clear why the killing occurred and leaves little room for alternative
interpretations.

However, another informant from the area has offered additional information that complicates the meaning of the story by making it less certain
when and why the feud between the two families first got under way.
According to this alternate version, Talabuddin's murder was not the
opening scene in this drama. Rather, it was one of a series of acts in a
long-standing enmity that involved many other people not mentioned in
Safi's narrative. The man with seven sons whom Safi does not name was
known as Paindo, and he was a *tarbur,* or close paternal cousin, of Talabuddin's. Paternal cousins are natural rivals in Pakhtun society. The term
tarbur, in fact, connotes "enemy," which Pakhtuns themselves explain by
referring to the common interest that cousins have in the inheritable lands
of their paternal grandfather and to the tendency of cousins to vie with
one another for primacy and prestige within the family.

That these two tarburs—Talabuddin and Paindo—should be at odds
with one another was very much according to form, but it is still uncertain
whether or not they were engaged in enmity with one another prior to
the events recounted in Safi's story. The other informant was unclear on
this. What was more certain in his mind was that Paindo was feuding with
another family closely allied with Talabuddin's brother, 'Ali Dost. One
day, 'Ali Dost, who is not mentioned at all in Safi's story, was accompanying his allies to Gul Salak when Paindo and his sons ambushed them
along the path. During the attack, 'Ali Dost killed Paindo's brother, Faizul-
lah, and thereby initiated (or extended) the feud that would later lead to
Talabuddin's death.

According to my other Safi informant, tribal elders from the area con-
vened an assembly (*jirga*) to resolve the dispute and came to the decision
that Paindo should give a daughter to the family of Talabuddin. The reasoning behind this decision was apparently that 'Ali Dost's honor had
been injured when Paindo's side attacked his guests. (As will be discussed
further on, the obligation of a host to his guest is fundamental in Pakhtun

culture.) ʿAli Dost was consequently duty-bound to protect his guests and could not be held personally liable for the death of Paindo's brother because ʿAli Dost was only doing what honor required. At the same time, the jirga recognized that it was in everyone's interest for violence between the families to cease, and the chances of reconciliation were much greater if the two families were joined by marriage. To bring about this end, the jirga decreed that Paindo should give his daughter to one of Talabuddin's sons, and it was for this purpose that Talabuddin set off from his village on the day of his death.

This additional information complicates the story but does not fundamentally contradict it. Instead of recounting a complex and morally ambiguous history, Safi has simplified events, reducing them to their bare narrative essentials and introducing a more straightforward plot and a clearer sense of a beginning and end (which reality had refused to provide). Safi's version also imparts a clear sense of moral responsibility, at least as regards the relations between the two families: Talabuddin innocently, if naively, set off to get a bride for his son and was treacherously murdered for reasons of greed. Blame here can be readily affixed, which helps to explain, if not entirely excuse, the excesses that Sultan Muhammad later commits in pursuit of his revenge.

The new information confounds the simple moral equation by introducing at least the possibility that events were more ethically ambiguous than Safi made them out to be, particularly if the tribal assembly reached the decision reported to me. According to other Pakhtuns I have talked to (including some experienced tribal negotiators), most jirgas dealing with conflicts such as this one would require that the family of the murderer give a woman to the family of the victim, regardless of which side was ultimately liable for the violence. If Paindo had been judged accountable for the ambush of ʿAli Dost's allies, he or one of his sons might have been exiled from the community, his house might have been burnt, or the family might have been forced to pay a hefty compensation. But because his family had suffered a death, it would have been unusual for the jirga to compound their loss—and humiliation—by making them give up a daughter to their enemies in addition to the brother they had already lost.

Why would the jirga have decided that Talabuddin should receive the woman? Was it because this incident was preceded by others in which Paindo's family was held accountable? Was it because the honor of Talabuddin's family had been mortally impugned by the attack on their guests? Or was it because Talabuddin, as the governor of the area, had sufficient power to turn the results to his own favor, thereby contravening the sanctity of the jirga as the arbiter of honor in tribal life? If one of the former possibilities is correct, then the basic moral equation Safi set up still holds, but if the latter possibility is closer to the truth, then perhaps Talabuddin's killers had a more compelling motive than mere greed. Perhaps because of his position as a powerful landowner and government official, Talabuddin felt he could gain an advantage over his cousin. Perhaps he felt invulnerable in his own home territory, and it was arrogance (kibr) rather than piety that made him leave home without a bodyguard. Perhaps, as well, Paindo's attack on Talabuddin was not launched by greed but as an honorable defiance to a rival cousin who was unbalancing the rough equality of tribal cousins and fast turning himself into an overlord.

These speculations rest on uncertain ground, of course, but the fact that they can be entertained at all reminds us that we can never know for sure how historically accurate Safi's tale really is. It also indicates that we should set aside any aspirations we might harbor for discovering the "plain facts" of history. We are in a world of stories, and the absolutes we encounter here are made-up ones while the rendition of history meets other requirements than mere truth. The ultimately uncertain truth value of the story does not lessen its interest, however. In some ways, it makes it more interesting, for we can see in the interstices between myth and history the shaping influence of the moral imagination as it has passed over this particular outcropping of events in the course of myriad retellings.

In the tale of Sultan Muhammad's revenge, we confront a rendering of a historical event that is the product not of Safi alone or of any other single author but of many. We know this to be the case because no single voice could possibly have known all the parts of the story and because its main protagonist was himself silent on critical matters that only he could have known about but that have nevertheless found expression within the narrative frame. This being the case, we can see in this account not merely the working of one man's imagination but the operation of a cultural logic fashioning meaning from experience and fixing value to memory.

At the same time, while it is clear that the account has a strong moral dimension, it is also equally the case that aspects of the story do not readily lend themselves to what might be called common-sense interpretation, even when those doing the common-sense interpreting are other Afghans. Although most of the actions recounted in the narrative are perfectly comprehensible to a native audience, there are some that blur cultural distinctions between right and wrong and violate one set of customary expectations in the process of fulfilling another. Three scenes in particular stand out as extreme, even to Afghans brought up on stories of feud and retribution. They are Sultan Muhammad's denial of his father's dying request, the blinding of his mother, and the slaughter of the seven sons in the guest house.

The actions recounted in these scenes touch raw nerves and occasion awkward silences when recounted in company, and I have found that Afghans to whom I have told the story find these parts as troubling as I do, despite their bringing different cultural resources to the story. This being the case, I had to confront the fact that a straightforward exegesis (along the lines of "he does this because in Afghan culture they believe that . . . ") was insufficient to the contradictions embodied in the story and that it was necessary to search out deeper meanings than those immediately evident even to Afghan listeners. The idea of stretching my analysis beyond the boundaries of the native point of view bothered me at first: if this story was strange and distasteful to Afghans, what use could I make of it in my exposition on the moral logic of honor? And besides, what right did I have to impose an interpretation on their stories that went beyond what Afghans themselves would recognize as legitimate and apparent?

Increasingly, however, I have come to accept the necessity of this sort of interpretation and to feel that the only stories worth writing about, in one's own or another culture, are the troubling ones that are full of contradictions and that defy easy exegesis. This point became especially clear to me when I started reading bedtime books to my son. Like most children, he has an insatiable appetite for stories and often wants to hear the same ones over and over. Like most adults, I enjoy reading aloud but found the experience of repeating the same story night after night to be trying at first. Gradually, however, I have gotten used to repetition and in the process have gained a much clearer sense of what makes a story affecting than I ever got from reading books one time through to the end.

The sum of my experience is this: simplistic stories devoid of morally ambiguous characters and narrative complexity quickly wear thin, both for the child and the parent. The worst of all stories are those that seek to be charming, but a close second are those stories that rework classic fairy tales, gutting them of their contradictions, their violence, their perverse strangeness. Such reworkings are usually undertaken to make the classic tales less offensive to modern ears, but they achieve this objective at the expense of the stories' integrity and leave little behind that might catch (or fester) in the imagination of a child or an adult.

Applying this experience to my reading of Safi's tale, I have been emboldened to think that what matters most in this story are precisely its moments of excess and transgression, for it is in these moments that we come to see the story's horrible fascination and glimpse the troubling contradictions that rest at the core of Sultan Muhammad's world and that Pakhtuns themselves are aware of, at least subliminally. The strategy for the remainder of this chapter, then, will be to focus on what I have marked off as the three pivotal transgressions in the story, both as a way of illuminating the meaning of the story as a whole and as a means of comprehending the cultural logic of honor.

FATHERS AND SONS

One of the underpinnings of the story of Sultan Muhammad's revenge is the principle of patrilineal descent and the relationship between fathers and sons. Like people in other parts of the Middle East, Pakhtuns accord special significance to kinship through the paternal line, and many, if not most, refer to themselves as members of a larger grouping (*qaum*) that includes all those who claim descent from a common patrilineal ancestor. Thus, for example, members of the royal family that ruled Afghanistan prior to the 1978 revolution belonged to the "Muhammadzai" lineage: those who claim to be "sons of" (*zai*) an earlier Muhammad, though not the Prophet Muhammad.

In the course of my investigations, I have frequently encountered individuals who, when asked to substantiate their claim to being "from the so-and-so-zai tribe," can provide from memory a genealogy that is ten or eleven generations deep and more or less inclusive of all parallel lines that have branched off from their own within the last four or five generations. This depth of genealogical knowledge is far from general (many Pakhtuns can tell you their grandfather's name and little else), and the practical implications of claiming common patrilineal descent varies widely. But it is doubtless the case that patrilineal descent is of tremendous moral import even for those without extensive patrilineal connections.

One expression of this significance is the respect paid to paternal ancestors who are accorded unquestioned respect by the very fact of their being in the category of *nikagan*, or "grandfathers." Being a grandfather (singular, *nika*) means first of all that a man lived long enough and productively enough to propagate the line. This in turn implies that the ancestor's name, at least for a time, will be preserved in genealogies and will be remembered by those who come after him and who owe him their respect by the mere fact that he made them possible. In a profound way, attacks against one's ancestor(s) are defamations of oneself, while conversely the honor (*nang*) of an ancestor is honor reflected through oneself. The logic of this can be seen in the following statement of Shahmund, a venerable elder of the Isakhel branch of the Mohmand tribe. The Isakhel are among the branches of the tribe known as *sarhad* (frontier) Mohmands because their territory straddles the Afghanistan-Pakistan border. Other Pakhtuns generally acknowledge the sarhad Mohmands as exemplars of Pakhtun culture in its uncorrupted state, and Shahmund demonstrates the merit of this assessment by the manner in which he describes a man who had recently been selected to a position of power within the tribe:

> I'm sure that this family will not be destroyed by the will of God because if there is goodness among them God will not destroy them. If someone is a gambler or a vagabond, God will destroy his family. . . . What finally happens is God's doing. They are better than other people. "The sword of real iron cuts" [*tura pa asil ghutsa kawi*]. For example, Faiz Gul is the brother of Haji Reza Khan. Since Faiz Gul is a good-for-nothing, his son is just like him. His grandson is also nothing. Since Haji Reza Khan is a good man, his sons are also like him. His grandsons are also like him, and maybe his grandsons' sons will be even better than him.

In the world view of the speaker (as of Sultan Muhammad), a man carries the honor of his father as his primary legacy, and, before he has done anything in the world, he will be judged by the actions of his forebears. A man of good stock—like the clean-cutting sword—is said to be *asil:* pure, uncorrupted, authentic. This quality can be diluted in a number of ways—for example, by having a mother who is from another tribe or, worse yet, another ethnic group—but so long as a man is known to have a Pakhtun father and paternal grandfathers, then it is understood that he is at least capable of honor.[3]

In both the action inscribed in the narrative (as well as in the act of narration itself), the relation of father and son provides the central axis of Sultan Muhammad's story, but the first instance in which the father-son relationship presents itself as a relevant factor is not in fact within the story itself. Rather, it is embedded in Talabuddin's honorific surname, Akhundzada (son of an akhund). While not developed explicitly by the narrator, the fact that Talabuddin was known by this name is important, for it tells us a great deal about who he was and how he came to hold the position of power that he did.

In Kunar Province, there are four renowned families known by the name Akhundzada. Three of these families are located in villages along the main branch of the Kunar River (in Kus Kunar, Khas Kunar, and Narang), and the fourth is Safi's family in Gul Salak of Pech Valley. While the exact histories of these families is unclear, it is known that the apical ancestor of each of these families was a religious figure and that all four of these ancestors lived within the last hundred years. In two cases (the families in Kus Kunar and Khas Kunar), it appears that the paterfamilias was an outsider brought to the village to serve as prayer leader and religious teacher, whereas the families of the other two akhunds were both indigenous to the villages in which they lived. Regardless of their original situations, the sons of all four of these pious fathers succeeded in parlaying the initial spiritual influence of their forebears into political power in their areas.

The specifics of how this came about are obscure, but it appears that the principal factor in all four cases was the role that the succeeding generation played as mediators with the central government, probably during the late nineteenth and early twentieth centuries when Amir Abdur Rahman (1880–1901) and his son Amir Habibullah (1901–1919) were consolidating power in the Kunar Valley.[4] Religious families could play this role effectively for a variety of reasons. In relation to the needs of the government, religious families tended to be literate and more conversant in the ethos and practical requirements of government service than the average person brought up in the tribe. This was especially true of families that had been brought into the tribe from elsewhere and therefore had kinship ties and other connections that most native tribesmen lacked. In addition, religious families enjoyed the privilege of being simultaneously inside and outside the tribes with which they lived. This status meant that while they were knowledgeable of tribal ways and tended to be trusted because of their local residence in tribal areas, they also could withdraw themselves from tribal feuds without loss of prestige to themselves.

Since religious figures were frequently placed in inter- and intra-tribal mediatory roles during times of conflict or dispute, it was not difficult for them to take the further step of mediating between tribe and government. In taking on this role, religious figures also had certain perquisites that they could draw upon to advance their position. The most important of these was authority over the Holy Book itself, which tribesmen revered but which most were unable to read. Because of the sacred but generally inaccessible status of the Qur'an, those who could quote from its pages had a tremendous advantage that could be used, for example, to excoriate those who exhibited inadequate religiosity in their everyday lives or who participated in unsanctioned political activities. This kind of tactic did not always work, of course, and tribesmen no less than peasant farmers and city dwellers were ready to condemn those who used Islam for personal advantage. However, under certain circumstances, such as those that existed in Kunar in the early part of the century, religious status could be used to advantage, and for the four akhundzada families of Kunar, the combination of religious prestige, a tribal base, and government backing proved decisive in acquiring power, land, and privilege.

From the story of Sultan Muhammad's revenge, we also know that religious status, particularly when combined with "the power of the government and the power of the tribe and of land" could also prove troublesome and contradictory. In fact, we must conclude that it is precisely this unwholesome combination of personal statuses that brought about the first confrontation in the story: that between Talabuddin Akhundzada and his son, Sultan Muhammad, when the latter decided to travel unescorted outside of his village. This is a strange and barely credible scene. After all, Sultan Muhammad is said to be only a twelve- or thirteen-year-old boy at the time, and it is hard to imagine a child of this age lecturing his father in so open and worldly a manner, particularly in a social context that values paternal authority as highly as this one. It is also, of course, difficult to imagine that the father would be so naive as to travel alone in the area given the position he occupied and the existence of ongoing rivalries.

What then motivates the father? From what the story tells us, we are meant to believe that the father acts out of trust. He has faith in his fellow men. Because he has acted fairly with others in his community, he trusts that they will act fairly with him. His logic is simple. It is the logic of a man of religion, a pious Muslim. Perhaps like many old men in Pakhtun society, he wants to retreat from life, to finally immerse himself in religion and piety before death arrives to close the book of his deeds. This is a legitimate sort of progression in the life of any man, but Talabuddin is not any man: he is hakim, he is a landowner, he is a man who lived life fully enough to acquire the rivals and enemies that are the sign of one's status and worth in this world.

Talabuddin, in other words, is still too fully invested in the world to legitimately seek divestment. As such, his action can only be judged as intentionally self-destructive and morally indefensible since his destruction in all likelihood will also mean the destruction of his family. In the moral universe of the tribe, the father's incaution must be viewed as profoundly criminal, for by refusing to acknowledge the reality of violence, Talabuddin visits upon his son the curse of that violence. In contradiction to the statement of principle attributed to Talabuddin in his dying moments, the most basic fact of life in the tribal universe is that all men are not "brothers," at least not in any simplistic sense. They are, rather, "tarburs" and, one must also assume, enemies, now or in the future.[5]

Talabuddin, of course, knows the continual threat which exists even (or especially) from one's own kinsmen, and his failure to acknowledge it occasions his death and the transgression of his son's disobedience to his dying request. Thus, while it would appear on one level that it is the treachery of the enemy that sets the action of the story into motion, on another level, it is Talabuddin's recklessness that matters more. This incaution is, in a certain sense, the original sin of the story, and its import is signaled by the incongruity in the opening scene of the son giving advice and thereby reversing roles with his father.

Similarly, when Sultan Muhammad reaches his dying father, he gives the boy an order which he cannot obey and which is based on a moral presupposition that does not apply in this world. The order may not seem remarkable to us, but it is in fact a mark of supreme arrogance: the arrogance of a man who, in his concern for his own status, ignores the social community that is the legitimate arbiter of status; the arrogance of one who worries more about his own situation than that of his dependents; the arrogance of a believer who abrogates to himself what is rightfully God's alone, namely the determination of who is and is not "a pure martyr." Preternaturally wise in the ways of the world, Sultan Muhammad refuses his father's command and in doing so breaches one code of tribal life (obedience to one's father) in order to satisfy another (the necessity of taking revenge for an act of violence committed against a close kinsman).

The binding nature of Sultan Muhammad's obligation to avenge his father's death is spelled out in dramatic fashion when he says to his father, "I am alive. If I do not have the force and power in me to take revenge on one person for every bullet that has struck your body, then I would not be your son." This statement makes clear that Sultan Muhammad's status as his father's son has been placed in jeopardy. In Pakhtun culture, the symbolic status of being a son is the fundamental precondition of male identity. Detachment from one's father means that one is alienated from the honor which the father represents and from the community of individuals bound by their shared concern for honor. Thus, in a very real sense, a man without a father is a man without identity; but at the same time, having a father, we come to understand, is not presupposed by being alive. A man may, in the course of events, lose his father (or his claim to identity through the father) and be forced to prove that he is in fact the son of a man. Such is the case with Sultan Muhammad, but the tragic irony here is that regaining the identity of being his father's son requires

Sultan Muhammad to refuse his father's dying command. The son's disobedience condemns the father to damnation (in the religious terms invoked by the father), just as the father's allowing himself to be killed has condemned the son to a sort of living damnation (in society's terms): the damnation of being exiled from one's group and of losing the most basic claim to identity, the claim of having a father.

A final issue must concern us before moving on to the second transgression in this story. That issue concerns the significance of Sultan Muhammad's disobedience outside the confines of the story itself. In addressing this matter, we must first recall that the action inscribed in this story is not real, even if it may be true. We don't know what motivated the father to do what he did, and we must suspect even the basic "facts" of the story, especially those facts that would tell us what transpired between father and son at the father's death. Whose words are these that Safi recounts and who preserved them for posterity? Only Sultan Muhammad was there after all. Is this dialogue based on his own testimony (a somewhat unlikely possibility given his general reticence to discuss his own life), or do these words rather represent what might have or should have been said?

Are they, in other words, a response developed later by untold other voices to explain and resolve both Sultan Muhammad's relation to his particular father and—more generally—the ambiguous ties that join all fathers and sons in Pakhtun culture? There being no other eyewitnesses to provide even the barest Rashomon-like balance to the available narrative, we will never know what portion of this story corresponds to real events and what portion is made-up. However, on the assumption that all historical narratives reflect to some degree a sense of what ought to have happened rather than what did, my tendency in this case is to believe that here, too, what *should have been* said came over time to be what *was* said, and it did so in a fashion that corresponded with the ambivalent feelings men generally have about their fathers.

In Pakhtun society, so long as the father is alive, the son will always be subordinate. He will always be forced to serve his father and will be, to one degree or another, a dependent in terms of his material stake in the world and the voice that he is able to exert in familial and societal affairs.[6] The first symbolic severing of this dependence comes with the boy's marriage and, even more important, the birth of his first male child. At this moment, the boy truly joins the tribe, both in the literal sense that his name will be included as a significant link in the chain of genealogical memory that constitutes the tribe and in the more personal and emotionally charged sense that he now stands as an independent actor who radiates his own honor as well as the reflected glory of his antecedent fathers. The birth of a son is thus integral to the construction of a man's identity, but this construction is based on the perpetuation of the same kind of psychic subjection of the son's identity to that of his father that the father himself experienced in his early life. For his son, as for himself, this subjection will continue at full strength until the birth of his own male offspring and will only cease altogether when his father departs the world.

Given the centrality of the father-son relationship within Pakhtun society (and the status of the father as the one who makes the son what he is while also denying him the chance to become what he wants to be), it is clear that the account of Sultan Muhammad's disobedience to his father's last command taps into a powerful current, a current that has a strong resonance with Pakhtun men who know all too well the contrary pulls of paternal obedience and personal affirmation. In a way that is eerily reminiscent of other myths (including the psychoanalytic ur-tale contained in *Totem and Taboo*), the story can be seen as a kind of patricide by which obedience to paternal authority is violently rejected. This act of resistance is only a story, of course, but it nevertheless reflects the psychic turbulence which patriarchal authority creates in a society that measures the merits of men both by the status of their paternal ancestors and the degree of independence they manage to muster in worldly affairs. The story of Sultan Muhammad's denial of his father's command gives dramatic form to this ambivalence, and does so in a way that allows the son to affirm both his paternity (what his father stands for as opposed to who he actually is) and at least the potentiality of his selfhood in the face of the father's willful suppression.

MEN AND WOMEN

After Talabuddin's death and burial, the second part of Sultan Muhammad's story begins. So long as his father's murder remains unavenged, the boy will remain in an existential limbo, a fact dramatically demonstrated by his leaving the insular world of his tribe and taking up residence with allies of his father's. The narrator does not know exactly when all of these events took place, but his surmise that it was "during the time of Abdur Rahman Khan" provides one of our few hints as to what was going on in the larger world outside Pech Valley. This was before the establishment of national borders, when local potentates like the Nawab of Dir wielded nearly as much influence in the area as the government in Kabul itself, and Sultan Muhammad avails himself of the Nawab's offer of asylum to provide for his needs and protect himself from the further violence of his enemies.

Sultan Muhammad settles into the life of the Nawab of Dir's court, learning to read and write (one assumes he did not acquire these skills in Pech) and eventually mastering the calligraphic and rhetorical techniques associated with the scribal class. These were accomplishments in which Sultan Muhammad clearly took pride, but even as he marveled in his mastering of the forty "mursalat" of the scribe, he also must have felt the sting of his diminished status as an employee of a man who had once been his father's friend. The reprieve offered by the Nawab is a costly one for Sultan Muhammad that requires his physical and moral estrangement from his native land. Exile, he must come to realize, will end only when he rejects his dependence on others and takes the necessary steps to avenge the murder of his father. Before fully absorbing this lesson, however, Sultan Muhammad must endure humiliations that elucidate (for him and for the story's listeners) the full extent of his alienation and liminality.

The first humiliation arises from the birth of his son during his absence from Pech. We don't know exactly when this event takes place; Sultan Muhammad's age is omitted, as is the identity of his wife and when they got married. In my later research, however, I did manage to discover that this wife was Sultan Muhammad's stepsister: the daughter of Talabuddin's third wife by an earlier, deceased husband (himself a cousin of Talabuddin).[7] Since this information is not relevant to the narrative, Samiullah has not included it; but what he has provided—and what is underscored in the story—is the contradiction to Sultan Muhammad's own status that the birth of a son brings into being.

In Pakhtun society, the birth of a son is normally the occasion for general celebration and personal recognition for the father. This is one of the highlights of any man's life—a moment for ceremonially firing rifles into the sky and feasting family and friends. However, in this instance, the news that a son has been born is delivered in a somber, almost funereal manner: "Let us go to the homeland. God has delivered a child in your home." As the scene develops, it becomes clear that the brusque tone of the original message was not accidental, and we see that the maternal uncle (mama) does not intend to let happiness be a part of his nephew's response to his good fortune. So long as his debt to his father remains unpaid, Sultan Muhammad will not be allowed to enjoy the fruits of his newly gained status in society.

The nature of this debt is made clear to Sultan Muhammad by his mama, who forces the young man to recognize the shame and incongruity of lavishing affection on his infant son while his own relationship with his father remains unresolved. The uncle's message is that if Sultan Muhammad is to return to Pech and live a normal life with normal affections, he must do so on the tribe's terms. It is worth noting here that the mama has a special place in Pakhtun culture. He is one of the few senior males with whom a boy can talk and enjoy an informal and uninhibited relationship, and this closeness helps to offset the formality that usually characterizes the relationship between a boy and his senior agnatic relatives, especially his father and his paternal uncles.

In this instance, the mama uses his trusting relationship with his nephew to say directly to his face what others would say behind his back. The terms that the mama throws at Sultan Muhammad—*daus* and *dala*—don't translate well into contemporary English with its impoverished vocabulary of honor, but they are especially offensive and insulting to Pakhtun ears. To call a man "daus" is to accuse him of being unable to preserve the sexual honor of his wife, even potentially of offering his wife to other men. It is to say that the normally sacrosanct domestic quarter of his home is violable and that he himself has not the power to defend his home, his lands, or his women (wives, mother, sisters, daughters)—all of which, individually and collectively, constitute a man's namus.

It could be said that a man's namus are all those things he has that other men might desire and whose inviolability to those desires constitutes the primary criterion of his worth in the tribe.[8] A man who is incapable of defending his namus is referred to as daus. "Cuckold" is probably the closest approximation to the word and captures some aspects of it, but it completely loses the affective power of the word *daus*, along with its many possible applications—for example, to men who spend all of their time in the company of women, who are continually nagged and scolded by their wives, or who choose to live with their fathers-in-law.

Dala is frequently used as a synonym for *daus* but also carries the meaning of someone who is weightless and without substance—a man who, out of ignorance or moral perversity, debases honor by inaction or by action undertaken solely for personal advantage. Like *daus*, *dala* is a term that is invoked rarely and then only with due caution. If the mama did not enjoy a trusting relationship with his nephew, his use of these words would be understood as the kind of mortal insult that could only be redressed by deadly violence. Because they are uttered by the mama, however, the words stand as a warning of the fate that befalls a man who is unmindful of the implications of his actions.

If his mama's words are a warning of the ridicule that will follow if he does not achieve vengeance for his father, the actions of his mother are the realization of this possibility. The responsibility for taking revenge should fall to the wife of a slain man only if there is no male heir to take up the challenge. The precipitous action of Sultan Muhammad's mother denies the son the opportunity to fulfill his obligation and obtain social recognition as the son who has avenged his father. In a fundamental way, the mother has condemned the son not so much to disgrace as to a perpetual state of liminality. As the uncle has warned, Sultan Muhammad cannot reside within the tribe as a full equal of other men so long as he has not avenged his father's death. Once the mother has taken matters into her own hands, the opportunity no longer exists for Sultan Muhammad to effect his own revenge. From the tribe's point of view, a life has been squared with a life. The debt (*por*) is paid, and if further violence were to be initiated, the perpetrator would himself come to be thought of as the responsible party. Sultan Muhammad presumably knows this and knows as well that his opportunity for redemption has slipped beyond his reach.[9]

Sultan Muhammad's response involves two actions: first, the blinding of his mother and, second, the elaboration and execution of his own plan to bring about vengeance for his father's murder without bringing down upon his head the indignation of the tribe. The first of these two acts is the more difficult to comprehend and brings to mind what would seem to be a discrepancy between how the mother and the majority of others have interpreted her actions and how Sultan Muhammad himself has conceived of them. Thus, the narrator tells us that "all of the people, all of his friends and relations think that he must be happy" with the news that revenge has been achieved and the debt of honor erased. I have also asked other Pakhtuns what their reaction would be, and while they understand logically the reasons for Sultan Muhammad's displeasure, they also express surprise and outright abhorrence at the brutality of his actions.

Such responses make one wonder just what is going on, and so too does the fact that Safi interjects his own explanation into the narrative, an explanation that is couched in the direct speech of the father, even though he also states that the father never talked about the incident. Safi's interpretation is, in fact, a tangle of made-up quotes belonging not only to his father but also to "the tribe": "You have subjected me to the tana and paighur of the tribe: 'The son of Talabuddin Akhundzada was never born.

His wife gained his revenge. His wife took his vengeance. He didn't have a son.' You have ruined my name and reputation in the tribe." What Safi's explanation seems to indicate, first of all, is his own understanding of the problematic, and perhaps transgressive, nature of his father's action and, second, his attempt to make sense of that action in a language that will make sense to me, an outsider, and that will also accurately reflect the cultural realities.

Despite the confusing syntax of Safi's explanation, it accomplishes both purposes in an admirably succinct manner, for he shows how his father has internalized and amplified the external judgments of the people as the basis of his own self-judgment. The anthropologist Julian Pitt-Rivers has noted that "Honour is the value of a person in his own eyes, but also in the eyes of his society. It is his estimation of his own worth, his *claim* to pride, but it is also the acknowledgement of that claim, his excellence recognized by society, his *right* to pride."[10] In the case of Sultan Muhammad, we see this relationship played out to its logical conclusion, a conclusion that results in a man renouncing all other claims on his person but that of honor. For Sultan Muhammad, honor is not to be gauged in any componental sense by what he does (e.g., by feeding guests, by carrying a gun, or even by gaining revenge). It is rather to be gauged by who he is. In this sense, Sultan Muhammad is attuned to the inexorable logic of honor to a degree that others, who are bound and determined by other sorts of loyalties and affections, are not. Hearing this tale unfold, the listener understands that while Sultan Muhammad may be a man obsessed, he is also a man who knows more fully than other men what honor means.

Perhaps the listener also understands that honor unmediated by countervailing attachments is finally corrosive of social life—perhaps, but perhaps not. At any rate, we must conclude that when Sultan Muhammad punishes his mother, it is not in a fit of rage or pique. To the contrary, it is, like all of his actions, a "rational" and coherent response to a situation that threatens not only his own existence but the ethical presuppositions of honor that underpin the society. The response is certainly heartless, but those who expect something less extreme do so out of concern for something other than honor.

Even if we grant the rationality of punishment given Sultan Muhammad's ethic of honor, we are still left to wonder why the punishment chosen was blinding. In considering this question, it is helpful to know something about the circumstances under which the mother carried out the revenge for her husband's murder. The story itself does not provide this information, but additional research has helped fill this gap. One important piece of information that has been retrieved is that after Talabuddin's death, it was arranged for his widow, Sultan Muhammad's mother, to marry Paindo. This may seem an odd choice, but it makes sense if several factors are taken into consideration. The first of these is that in Pakhtun society widows are almost always remarried to a close agnatic relative of the husband. Talabuddin's brother, 'Ali Dost, would normally have been the logical choice for her to remarry, but for reasons that remain obscure it was decided that she would marry Talabuddin's more distant cousin, Paindo, instead.[11]

A second relevant factor in the decision was that Paindo's responsibility for the murder had not been proven. Since Talabuddin was alone at the time of this murder and the murderers themselves had acted covertly, no one knew for certain who was guilty of the crime. Consequently, while most people assumed that Paindo and his sons were guilty of the deed, responsibility could be denied by Paindo himself, even as he stepped forward to marry the dead man's widow and, presumably, seize hold of at least part of his estate. According to tribal informants, this plot was foiled when Sultan Muhammad's mother and her brother—the same mama who retrieved Sultan Muhammad from Dir—murdered Paindo when he appeared to claim his bride.

In acting as she did, the mother may have balanced a debt of honor according to an objective calculus, but from Sultan Muhammad's personal vantage, she did so in a way that compromised the integrity of his namus (by allowing Paindo even to think that he could claim Sultan Muhammad's home as his own) and that abrogated a right and duty (that of revenge) that was primarily his to uphold. While the mother's actions achieved the desired end, the means by which this end was brought about were potentially open to public censure and, of greater importance ultimately, they entailed the usurpation of a role properly belonging to him. That the arrogation of Sultan Muhammad's rightful role is the ultimate meaning of this scene is indicated by the nature of the punishment that Sultan Muhammad inflicts, for in blinding his mother, he engages in a form of punishment that appears to be uncommon in the tribal world but is more familiar in the context of the state. While I have never come across any reports of blinding as a punishment in tribal society, I have encountered accounts of blinding as a punishment for crimes of state, the most important being the usurpation of royal power by a functionary of the court. One example is a famous case from the early nineteenth century involving the chief minister to the royal court, Wazir Fateh Shah, who had his eyes torn out by the dissolute ruler, Shah Mahmud. The purported reason was that Shah Mahmud, briefly emerging from his perpetual stupor, was upset when he realized how much power and influence his minister had come to wield in his court. A second example is more recent and comes from the late nineteenth century during the reign of Amir Abdur Rahman, who is also the subject of the next chapter. According to Frank Martin, a British engineer who worked in the Amir's court, blinding was a punishment sometimes inflicted on prisoners "who try to escape from prison or from the country—synonymous terms almost."[12] An additional purpose underlying blinding in this instance is that the punishment makes the criminal dependent, whereas before he had acted in a manner that was excessively independent and evasive of royal authority.

The congruent logic of the punishment in this historical instance and in Sultan Muhammad's story is apparent. A minister (*wazir*) is not the equal of kings. He is properly a functionary, dependent upon the patronage of the king. Nevertheless, wazirs could gain considerable power in their management of the court and its affairs. When this power spilled out from the interior of the court to the exterior realm of politics, then the wazir was seen as overstepping his role. In a similar fashion, Pakhtun women can also exercise considerable power in the internal administration of their families. They often manage finances and ensure the proper feeding of guests, and they also quite frequently consult with their husbands (or nag them if necessary) in matters of familial concern. However, women, like wazirs, have a dependent status and are rarely expected to act independently in the political realm. In the case of Sultan Muhammad's mother, the nature of her "crime" was precisely that of acting beyond the limits of her culturally prescribed role. If she had committed adultery, then the penalty of death (for her and her partner) would have been expected, but her mistake was that of overreaching her authority as a mother, a wife, and a woman. Blinding was a coherent response in this circumstance because it made the wrongdoer passive and dependent where before she had been excessively active and independent.

Beyond this culturally grounded interpretation of blinding, Sultan Muhammad's act has an additional value within the confines of the story. Because of women's ability to move in and out of interior spaces that are restricted to men, they see more than men do. Although veiled from the sight of others as they move about in the public realm, women's own sight is unhampered, and they can observe the actions of men there just as they can also pass into their own world and see what is going on behind closed doors. The freedom to look into the inner worlds that men seal off from other men and to let others know what they see gives women considerable power over men. In this light, the act of blinding can be thought of as a practical, although inevitably futile, response to limit the power of surveillance with which women are culturally endowed.

After blinding his mother, Sultan Muhammad did not ignore her needs. A man was assigned to care for her, and Sultan Muhammad continued to pay her nominal respect, which was her due. Thereafter, however, he never indulged in the normal intimacies that are expected between mothers and sons, and—the narrator emphasizes—he never asked advice of his mother again and later warned his son of the dangers of female involvement in male affairs. Love is fine in its place, we are to conclude, and brutality toward women is to be censured, but the man of honor must be cautious that his judgment is not clouded by their advice. To allow this to happen is to make oneself vulnerable to the dangers which women embody: the danger of becoming the object of public ridicule, the danger of having extraneous considerations interjected in the course of pursuing honorable objectives, and the danger of having events slip out of one's control.

FRIENDS AND ENEMIES

There is much more that could be said about the role of women in this story, as well as about male-female relations in Pakhtun society generally, but I want to turn now to the third of the story's transgressions: the slaughter of the seven brothers in Sultan Muhammad's guest house. In order to make sense of this knot in the narrative, it is first necessary to consider the cultural logic and social structure of revenge in Pakhtun society.

Among Pakhtuns, all men of common descent are viewed as *sials* of one another. The term *sial* has the explicit meaning of "equal," but it also has the more commonly understood connotation of "rival." In theory, all members of a tribe are equal (and rival) to one another, and the killing of a poor tribesman in a feud is viewed as nominally equivalent to that of a wealthy man in tribal legal precedents. The only male residents in the tribal community who are not considered equal to other men are servants (*nokaran*), tenant farmers (*dehqan*), and client groups such as barbers and blacksmiths, collectively referred to as *hamsaya* ("same shade," i.e., those living in the shade of a patron or of the tribe), who do not possess their own honor but rather share in the reflected honor of those under whose protection they live.

Rivalries in Pakhtun society generally coalesce along lines of age, wealth, and kinship relation—which delineation means that men of the same generation are more likely to become rivals than are men of different generations. Similarly, men of traditionally influential households will also tend to view each other (and be viewed by their fellows) as competitors for status and prestige if not also for land and women. Beyond such situational rivalries, every man also has a natural rival in his patrilateral first cousin, the aforementioned tarbur. When the word *tarbur* is joined with the suffix *wali*, it connotes something along the lines of "cousin competition" and is used to describe the endemic gamesmanship, rivalry, and sometimes open hostility that is thought to exist inevitably between the sons of brothers.

Most situations in which *tarburwali* comes into play are of an innocent sort. First cousins, for example, are expected to try to show each other up whether the opportunity arises in a sporting competition or in battle with some other group. The reward for proving oneself the better of one's cousin is the intangible advantage of being referred to as a "good youth" (*kha tzwan*). Whereas the term *tarburwali* is most often used in reference to first cousin rivalry, that all males in a tribe are categorically referred to as tarburs of one another means that the competition known as tarburwali can and frequently does extend beyond the range of first cousins to include all males of the same generation belonging to a tribe or tribal lineage. When good-natured rivalry escalates to deadly violence, the dynamic of reciprocal exchange that governs that violence is known as *badal*.

In its most general sense, badal signifies simply "exchange" and thus can be used to describe such phenomena as linked marriages in which two men marry each others' sisters. But badal is most commonly used to refer to exchanges of violence, most importantly, revenge killings, which, like marriage, are structured and regulated by custom. Revenge killings represent an extreme situation, but the very possibility of their occurrence sets the terms by which relationships in Pakhtun society are conceived, and they engender the common understanding that all alliances are necessarily formed because of the present existence or future likelihood of violent feud: which is to say, the existence of opposition creates the need for community. This conceptual complementarity is transformed into a practical unity of those allies who defend one another (*malatar*: those who bind their waists together) over and against the group of enemies (*dushmanan*) who, in different contexts, can be composed of one's cousins, a collateral tribal lineage, another tribe, or a temporary alliance of various kinsmen and allies not strictly related by ties of patrilineal descent.[13]

A basic comprehension of the logic and structure of badal is a necessary prelude to uncovering the meaning of the story of Sultan Muhammad's revenge, for in certain respects this whole tale can be read as an extended meditation on the fragile nature of social community in the tribal world. Any act of friendship (*dosti*) can quickly turn into an act of enmity (*dushmani*). Every alliance can become a feud, and all that prevents this from happening is the individual's vigilant concern for defending his honor, which, in the final analysis, is all that he has. The narrative progression of Sultan Muhammad's story clearly reflects the structural logic of badal—from the initial act of violence by the enemy to the final destruction of the twenty-two members of the opposing faction. Like other feud stories that one hears in Afghanistan (and the Middle East in general), this story replays a number of familiar refrains: for example, the tendency to attribute base intentions, treacherous practices, and breaches of taboo to your enemy; and the tendency for violence to escalate with every stage in the progression of the feud.

Despite these common threads, Sultan Muhammad's story stands out as different from most other feud stories in several respects. First, few feud stories end in the total annihilation of one's enemies. As Emrys Peters and other anthropologists have noted, feuds tend to have no set beginning, just as they have no determinate end. In many cases, the origins of a feud are lost in a mythic past, and even as the tenor of a feud will change—occasionally rising to snarling ferocity in response to a killing or other offense, more often keeping to a low growl of mutual intimidation— it is generally presumed that a feud will have no resolution, if only because no outcome could ever be equally satisfactory to both sides and, in a more general sense, the feud is too important for it to be allowed to end.[14]

Without an ongoing arena of competition, young men have no avenue by which to prove their mettle. Feuds provide this arena, and even when older men want to see a feud resolved, young men usually want to see it prolonged.[15] Likewise, for the group as a whole, feuds provide individuals with their most vivid stirrings of identity and the principal context within which they can feel themselves to be part of a unified community. The feud story in this narrative therefore stands apart because it does have both a beginning and an end, the beginning being possible to inscribe as a beginning because the ending has happened, which is to say, it is because the enemy is annihilated that Safi can begin the narrative part of his tale with the declaration "Some man from Gul Salak, whose name I have forgotten, said to my grandfather. . . . "

The second feature of this story that sets it apart from other feud stories is the constructed character of Sultan Muhammad's "vengeance group." Feuds almost always develop between related branches of a single tribe and are more often than not the product of cousin rivalries. As has been noted, the only rivalry worth pursuing is with an equal: to become entangled with someone who is not one's equal raises that individual in the eyes of others and lowers oneself. In this case, however, Sultan Muhammad allies himself with an assortment of relatives (mostly affinal and maternal) and lower-caste tenant farmers (most of whom we assume either do not belong to the Safi tribe or are Safis who have had to accept the demeaning status of working for others).[16] Although the members of Sultan Muhammad's vengeance group are not agnatically related and many appear to be his servants and tenant farmers, the request that he makes of them and their ceremonial response to it explicitly erase the contradiction of their alliance with the principle that patrilineal descent should be the basis of partnership in defense of honor. The ethical significance of this exchange of oaths is initially signaled by its being presented in dialogue rather than simply being reported by the narrator. Quoting this exchange allows the narrator to show the ethical status of the pact and the voluntary compliance of those who are party to it.[17]

In his address, Sultan Muhammad indicates that the cement binding him to all those who would choose to join with him is their common readiness to die for the sake of higher ideals. Sultan Muhammad does allude rather conspicuously to the fact that he is the salary-giver and provider of arms for the group, but he then denies the importance of these factors in comparison to the friendship and mutual regard that bring them together. The implicit message here is that while Sultan Muhammad may be their superior they will show themselves to be his equal in honor by their willingness to sacrifice their heads in the cause of honor. In their response, Sultan Muhammad's allies likewise hint at the economic nature of their relationship, but they then set this matter aside as an irrelevant consideration. Instead, they praise the murdered father for his loyalty in the past and commit themselves to Sultan Muhammad's cause, not because of anything he has done, but because he is his father's son and therefore worthy of respect. The mutual obliviousness to the exact nature of the undertaking and to the risks it entails demonstrates the disinterestedness of the parties to this negotiation and the moral righteousness of their bond (a righteousness that offsets and obscures the variegated nature of their social structural ties).[18]

The third and final way in which this story is different from most feud stories is in its apparent attribution of treachery to family members. Feud stories are often full of incidents in which people are killed while praying or guns are fired in a saintly shrine or a mosque, but these actions are always carried out by enemies, not by allies. Here, however, we are confronted with what is a clear transgression of cultural norms when Sultan Muhammad lures his enemies into the sacred precincts of his guest house (*hujra*) in order to murder them. Just as there are examples of political blindings in Afghan history, so there are examples of kings laying out lavish banquets for their guests and then slaughtering them. However, I am unfamiliar with any instances—other than this one—of a tribal host violating the sanctity of his hujra in this way.

In Pakhtun culture, hospitality (*melmastia*) is a central principle and a core feature of identity. All Pakhtuns, rich and poor alike, pride themselves on their readiness to feed and care for their guests, even if it means denying themselves and their families. For the khan in particular, feeding many guests is one of the primary ways to convert wealth into power and respect, not simply because it ties people to him in a dependent relationship, but also because it allows the khan to demonstrate his personal humility and his corresponding commitment to the ideals of his culture. This attitude is demonstrated in a myriad of ways seen daily in Pakhtun communities, for example, when a host personally presents each of his guests with a pitcher of water and bowl to wash their hands before a meal is served or when a host carries in the platter of food for his guests and then sits off to the side until they have finished their meal. As the primary site where the rituals of hospitality are played out, the hujra takes on a special significance as the symbol of the khan's identity and the way in which he wants to be viewed by his fellow tribesmen.

Like hospitality, offering shelter and protection to all who request it is another sacred value of Pakhtun culture. Known as *nanawatai*, this principle requires that an individual safeguards those who place themselves under his control, even it means sacrificing his own life to do it.[19] A common narrative motif in Pakhtun culture is thus of the tribesman fleeing from one set of enemies who is forced to seek refuge from a third party with whom he has also been feuding. The person from whom refuge is sought invariably accepts the request, refusing to surrender the enemy now under his protection, even if it means having to fight the enemies of his sworn enemy. Nanawatai is a principle that Pakhtuns not only talk about but also put into practice and that they invoke in discussing the virtues and merits of individuals. A man cannot expect to be accorded respect if he refuses to shelter those who (to use the Pakhtun phrase) "seize his skirt" (*laman niwul*) any more than he can if he is stingy with his resources or lax in monitoring the behavior of female family members. In the story of Sultan Muhammad, however, we see both the principles of protection and hospitality violated. What are we to make of this? Is it not the case then that in gaining his revenge Sultan Muhammad has sacrificed any claim he might have had to the honorable regard and respect of others?

The contradiction is not an easy one to resolve, but there are several steps that might be taken to help explain this part of the story. The first is to relate Sultan Muhammad's actions to those of his enemy and thereby evaluate the degree to which the prior offenses of the enemy made Sultan Muhammad's response qualitatively reciprocal and therefore justified. One incident from the story that is relevant here is the denial by the seven sons of their mother's plea that they desist from their plan of violence against Sultan Muhammad. The description of the mother, Qur'an in hand, begging her sons to spare Sultan Muhammad's life presents a profound and disturbing image to Pakhtuns, for it is recognized that the violation of such a sacred request is likely to bring ill tidings to those responsible.

In a more general sense as well, the sons' refusal to heed their mother's appeal can be seen as qualitatively similar to a violation of the principle of nanawatai. When one side to a conflict wishes to sue for peace, they will frequently signal their intention by sending a delegation of women carrying Qur'ans and accompanied by one or more mullas to the compound of their enemy. The women will go into the domestic quarters and lower their shawls so that their hair and faces are revealed. This gesture, which replicates what women normally do when visiting relatives, signals the readiness of the women's male kinsmen to negotiate and enter into friendly relations with their enemies. Likewise, when someone has accidentally injured or killed another person, the family of the responsible party will signal its responsibility and desire for peace by sending women with Qur'ans to the victim's home. When women have crossed the lines of conflict in this way, all fighting must cease, and those who refuse to acquiesce are recognized to have violated the law of nanawatai. The action of the sons is not precisely the same, but it is similar. In both situations, the relevant fact is that women holding holy Qur'ans have placed themselves in harm's way in order to secure a truce. Those who are implicated by this act are obliged to comply, at least temporarily, and the failure of the seven sons to honor their obligation places them in a position of moral culpability for what follows.

A similar logic can be applied to the scene in which the seven sons first confront Sultan Muhammad and ask him to accompany them to mark the boundary between their properties. Sultan Muhammad refuses, feigning illness, but sends a messenger to tell them to take "however much land you need, and wherever you want to place the boundary—that is up to you. You decide yourself, and take two white beards with you." On one level, Sultan Muhammad's words can be interpreted as an elaborate deception: pretending to be sick, he makes his enemies think he is afraid and furthers this impression by sending them a message that seems to indicate his abject willingness to capitulate to their demands. That this act is part of a plan to trap his enemies demonstrates Sultan Muhammad's cunning and perhaps helps to justify his violation of the norms of hospitality. Cleverness, particularly when placed in the service of honor, is a laudable virtue in Pakhtun society, and to some extent at least, the end (reclaiming honor) can be said to legitimate the means (violation of the rule of hospitality).[20]

This much is going on, I think, but there is an additional message embedded in Sultan Muhammad's words as well—a message that the seven sons rashly overlook in their rush to seize their rival's land and destroy his name. As all Pakhtuns know, someone who willingly relinquishes his ancestral land is the most ignoble of creatures, for he has not only sacrificed his claim to social identity and membership in councils of the tribe, he has also "sold the bones of his fathers." A man without land may be pitied for his poverty, but if he is otherwise brave and steadfast he will still have the respect of those around him. A man who sells his land or who abandons it to his enemies is in another category, however. Such a man is seen as cowardly (be ghairati) and unworthy of the respect of others in his society. Attacks against land are attacks against honor, and they cannot go unrequited if the victim of the attack has any intention of retaining his name and place in society.[21]

Given the symbolic significance of defending one's land, it can be argued that when Sultan Muhammad expressed his willingness to have Paindo's sons move his boundary markers, he was actually up to something more complicated and devious than it appeared on the surface. Feigning timid concurrence to his enemies' demands, Sultan Muhammad succeeded in duping Paindo's sons into believing that he was not man enough to defend his land. This was the impression that his message conveyed, and it was under its spell that they set off to disenfranchise Sultan Muhammad of his inherited estate. At his suggestion, they also presumably brought along a number of old "white beards" to witness the act, but what they seem not to have recognized is that these same old men could also serve Sultan Muhammad's interests. Specifically, they could act as witnesses to an act of unlawful and immoral trespass egregiously perpetrated in broad daylight for all to see.

In this sense, it can be argued that Sultan Muhammad's appearance of acquiescence was actually intended to provide a pretext for attacking his enemies, a pretext that he hitherto lacked. From the tribe's point of view, Paindo's murder would have wiped the slate clean between the two families. Each side had lost a man of comparable rank, and no one had any right to pursue the feud any farther. However, once Paindo's seven sons violated "the bones of Sultan Muhammad's father," he had all the pretext he needed to escalate the feud to the next level. The sons, of course, didn't recognize this possibility, but in the context of the story that ignorance is a mark of their greed and stupidity, just as it is also a sign of Sultan Muhammad's singular cleverness.

The endpoint of the present argument is that the seven sons of Paindo have sealed their own fate. By ignoring their mother's plea for mercy and ignobly stealing Sultan Muhammad's land, they have given Sultan Muhammad adequate cause for seeking their deaths. From a cultural and a narrative point of view, there seems to be considerable justification for viewing the logic of the slaughter in this way. However, I am not ultimately convinced by this argument. In the final analysis, I cannot fully believe that these rationales are sufficient to solve the problem that this scene raises in regard to understanding Sultan Muhammad's position in Pakhtun society or honor as a cultural system and moral logic. In a sense, the variables that I have provided are rationalizations, present in the text no doubt, but still inadequate to explain, much less erase, the transgressive quality of Sultan Muhammad's actions.

This being the case, I would take the analysis of the story one step further by admitting the morally contradictory features of the tale while also trying to place them in a more inclusive, less strictly componential framework. In my view, the story of Sultan Muhammad's revenge is about all I have claimed it to be, but it is also finally about something else as well—the impossibility of honor unmitigated by other principles as a basis of social action. In following Sultan Muhammad's actions and the events that he brings about, the listener (reader) cannot help but notice the cost to the individual and to the society of an unswerving adherence to honor. No man, we are led to understand, could possibly care more for honor than Sultan Muhammad, and no man understands its terrible logic better than he or realizes it more completely in his life. At the same time, no man pays a greater price, and the price he pays is one to which society at large must also contribute. The first installment on that price comes when Sultan Muhammad must disobey his dying father. The second and third are met when Sultan Muhammad is compelled to withhold his love from his infant son and then when he blinds his mother, thereby forever estranging her from himself. After this, Sultan Muhammad's path leads to two final sacrifices, one of which, ironically, is the sacrifice of his own status as a host, a man who offers hospitality and protection, a man of honor. This dimension of Sultan Muhammad's sacrifice derives from the perception, logically arrived at given the presuppositions of honor, that it is only when he has gained his own revenge that it can be said of him that he even exists (that when his father died he left behind a child who could become a man of honor).

In this sense, to kill his enemies in the guest house can be understood as an act of renunciation by which Sultan Muhammad signals his willingness to give up what he values most—his own status—so that he can exist at all within the threshold of honor. The existence he seeks is of necessity a cursed state of incompleteness: a state in which antagonism is the existential condition for one's identity as an individual and as a member of a group; a state in which an individual is forever in the thrall of those whom he respects and those whom he despises; a state in which the man of power and authority is finally as dependent on others as the man of basest means and aspirations.

The last and in some ways most poignant of all the sacrifices that Sultan Muhammad must make in regaining his claim to honor is the killing of his friend, which appears in the story as the denouement of the climactic slaughter in the guest house. Interestingly, this is the only one of Sultan Muhammad's actions that elicits an emotional response, and it is an effusive one at that: "And my father cries because he had been his friend. He had been his friend and playmate, and for this reason he cries. He cries a lot, so much so that people say he didn't eat food for a week. He was simply crying, not thinking of anything else except this friend of his. But, since he had become his enemy, he was obliged to kill him."

Given its placement in the story and the emphasis that it is given, one is led to see this murder of the friend as especially significant, and this view is strengthened when one takes into consideration the value that Pakhtuns attach to friendship as an ideal. The most common word that

Pakhtuns use for friend is *andiwal.* The prefix of this word, *andi,* literally means the bundle that makes up half the load carried on the back of a camel, horse, or other pack animal. Combined with the suffix *wal,* the word refers to the second bundle carried on the other side of the animal's back to balance the load. The sense of the term is thus that friends are comparable to a pair of fully loaded saddlebags that balance and support one another on the journey of life. When one has a friend with whom to share life's burdens, the journey proceeds smoothly; but for those who do not, the journey is likely to be torturous and slow.

That this linguistic metaphor of friendship correlates with Pakhtun cultural realities is substantiated by research that Charles Lindholm has conducted among Pakhtuns in the Swat valley of Pakistan. As Lindholm has noted (and my own experience confirms), the Pakhtun ideal of friendship is much more intense than the casual concept of friendship that generally prevails in the West:

> [Pakhtun] Friends should be together constantly; they should completely trust one another and reveal all their secrets to one another. . . . The friend should be willing to sacrifice himself in total devotion to the will of the other. His affection must be spontaneous, without reservation, and all-consuming. The true friend is called 'naked chest' because the hearts of both parties are bared to one another, thus sweeping away the pervasive secrecy and mistrust of . . . society.[22]

The extent of Sultan Muhammad's emotional response to the death of his friend indicates the applicability of Lindholm's assertion to the Afghan context, just as Lindholm's analysis helps us to realize the toll which obedience to honor has exacted on Sultan Muhammad's soul. For Pakhtuns, the friend represents the possibility of an uncomplicated, unmediated relationship contracted outside the bounds of kinship and honor. The friend is a refuge from the distrust and suspicion that are ubiquitous everywhere else in tribal society.[23] In destroying this refuge of trust then, Sultan Muhammad has destroyed the last part of his self that is responsive to something other than honor. All other attachments have gone before. At each stage of the story, Sultan Muhammad has been forced to renounce some part of his identity, some affection that contradicts the inexorable demands of honor, and the last and perhaps greatest of these sacrifices is that of his childhood friend whose life is dearer than his own.

The triumph of honor is thus complete: parental love, the bond between men and women, social respect as a host and protector of other men, and finally friendship—all have been sacrificed on the altar of honor. And if we still question the genesis of Sultan Muhammad's actions, the narrative provides some further suggestions in the care that he subsequently takes to uphold the sanctity of honor: care, for example, in attending to the bodies of his enemies and, later, care in demonstrating the proper respect to the wives of his fallen victims. To show disrespect for one's enemies would be to show disrespect for honor itself and would throw into doubt the very foundation upon which this act of extreme vengeance has been undertaken. Sultan Muhammad, we are to suppose, has not acted for himself or for his own advancement. Rather, he has been motivated solely by his absolute and unwavering concern for honor. That alone could justify the magnitude of his revenge, and that alone, we are asked to believe, is what Sultan Muhammad strove to uphold.

CODA: JANDAD'S PUNISHMENT

The story of Sultan Muhammad's revenge has introduced us to a man who fully understands the logic of honor and carries that logic to its ultimate conclusion. But what are we finally to conclude from his story? If, as Hayden White has argued, "narrativity . . . is intimately related to, if not a function of, the impulse to moralize reality," what is the ultimate moral message of this tale of vengeance and resolve?[24] One answer perhaps is provided by Safi when he declares (again speaking his father's lines) his father's rationale for treating the female kin of his enemies with circumspection and respect: "we could not be proud [*gharur*]. We could not do kibr. [That was] first, and second was this, that since they are namus, one must show respect to this namus."

Act, in other words, not in pursuit of self-interest but for honor. So long as one's motivations are pure, one can be assured that God's sanction and society's approval will follow. And indeed, this was the case, as "God did the work that they wanted to do to us" while "the people saw the kind of thing my father was doing, and at the same time the people saw what modesty he had with regard to namus and other things that concerned the tribe. The tribe said good things about this. This is how he defends these things."

Thus, the tale would appear to conclude logically. This, in fact, is its natural terminus, but when Safi recounted the story of his father's revenge he did not stop here. Instead, he glided past the conclusion of the first story of his father's revenge to tell of another incident many years later that involved his eldest brother, Jandad. Jandad, it will be recalled, was introduced in the story as the infant whose affections Sultan Muhammad denied. Here, we see him as a young man seeking to demonstrate, as all young men should do, his courage and prowess. However, in disarming this rival, Jandad also shows a heedlessness to the dictates of honor, a heedlessness that his father has good reason to fear and condemn. In the Pakhtun world, the rifle is the symbolic marker of a man's identity as a man. To take away someone's rifle is therefore extremely provocative; to do so in front of his wife is far worse, virtually a form of sexual assault which conveys the message that the wife is the assailant's to possess. Whatever Jandad may have had in mind when he took his rival's weapon, his action represented a serious breach of Pakhtun norms; and given the care with which Sultan Muhammad has treated his enemies and the female relatives of his fallen foe, it can also be said that Jandad's impulsiveness has threatened his father's efforts to live a life utterly ruled by honor's dictates.

While one can understand the logic of Sultan Muhammad's response, one is still left gaping at its severity and also wonders at the narrator's motivation in appending this additional episode to the earlier story. What could have motivated Safi to continue on past the natural ending of the first story to tell the second? Both episodes involve relations with Paindo's family and are linked in that way. Both also involve the concept of namus, but the placement of the two episodes back-to-back does not have the effect of clarifying the meaning of namus or of explicating the meaning of the story more generally. Rather, its central effect is to place in doubt, if not actually undermine, the sense of the narrative and with it, the ethical foundations of Sultan Muhammad's actions. More specifically, Safi's inclusion of this story of Jandad's punishment raises some basic questions that might otherwise have remained unasked: When does the pursuit of personal honor go beyond the bounds of what is just and commendable? At what point does the *kha tzwan*—the good youth—become the *badmash*—the reprobate or outlaw? The answer Safi explicitly provides is that it happens when an individual acts in an arrogant fashion to advance himself and his own interests to the detriment of society's norms and expectations. At critical junctures, however, Safi's father has contravened this principle by disregarding the views of the community, for example, when he blinds his mother or, in this case, when he punishes and disowns Jandad. Reading these episodes, one must wonder whether an individual is, in fact, acting in an honorable manner if he insists on upholding a standard of morality that exceeds that of his neighbors. Is not such a man guilty of the sin of arrogance, or kibr, that the story so vehemently decries?

Safi does not tell us his opinion on this question, but his inclusion of these alternative endings has forced us to confront it directly. If we are to make sense of the story, we must make sense of these contradictory clos-ings, for they highlight the ultimate ambiguity of Sultan Muhammad's actions and the ambivalent nature of honor itself. Let me then conclude this examination of honor as a moral system by considering in somewhat greater depth the significance of Jandad's actions and Sultan Muhammad's response to them.

From Sultan Muhammad's perspective, Jandad's sin is to violate an-other man's namus, a term that comprises all those things with which a Pakhtun man surrounds himself—rifles, land, women—and that collec-tively constitute his claim to honor. Without women in his home, without land to his name, without a rifle to shoulder, a man is weightless and naked (*luchak*). But, namus can also be defined as all those things—rifles, land, women—that are inherently desirable, that other men will in the normal course of events seek to possess, and that must at all costs be defended. Those things that give substance to a man's claim to honor thus also make him vulnerable. The more namus, the greater the honor that accrues, but along with this greater honor comes greater susceptibility to assault. In this way, the attainment of honor—that most cherished of possessions—requires exposure to dishonor. The individual who would be respected must make himself vulnerable: the more so the better. In this system, there is no stopping point, no resting place, only greater risks, as long as a man lives or chooses to play the game.[25]

That Sultan Muhammad took a total of nine wives indicates the extent to which he understood this logic. The ability to secure more wives dem-onstrated his power and his prowess, but at a considerable cost. For in taking these wives, Sultan Muhammad increased his vulnerability both to other men in his society and to the women themselves since women gain power in and to the degree that men require them in order to become and remain competitive in the arena of honor. Here then is one of the central dilemmas of honor as a cultural system. The ultimate objective of the man of honor is to exhibit independence in his actions and to sustain the appearance that he is not dependent upon or determined by any other individual. In seeking that independence of action, however, the man of honor must become dependent on women who, although categorically in-ferior to him, are yet capable of denying him the social respect that is his most cherished desire.

The most poignant manifestation of this predicament is found in the pervasive fear of paighur, or public ridicule. It will be recalled that the motivation Safi cites as the reason Sultan Muhammad blinded his mother was that she had brought ridicule upon him. Such reasoning is not at all unusual, nor is the association of paighur with women. Thus, while insults can emanate from any quarter, the worst are those voiced by women, for they can be neither rejoined nor rebutted. The ability women have to comment on their husband's sexual prowess, to observe the private behavior of their male in-laws, and to move as visitors between households puts them in the privileged position of witnessing and potentially reporting on all aspects of male activity.[26] And because men are always under the gaze of women and because women are capable of shaming men through their verbal and physical indiscretions, male power, which seeks to be absolute, is finite at its core.

These indications of female power lend to Sultan Muhammad's tale, and to all like it, a curious sense of pathos. The man of honor, we see, is no übermensch living by his own dictates and in satisfaction of his own desires. He is rather a desperate sort of fixer, fearless in his way no doubt, but destined to engage in the futile activity of making solid and whole what is by its nature hollow and incomplete. No matter how great the individual, there is no escape from this trap, for as Alasdair MacIntyre has noted about such cultures, the hero lacks "the capacity to detach [him]self from any particular standpoint or point of view, to step backwards, as it were, and view and judge that standpoint or point of view from outside. In heroic society there is no 'outside' except that of the stranger. A man who tried to withdraw himself from his given position in heroic society would be engaged in the enterprise of trying to make himself disappear."[27]

No "heroic" society, including this one, is oblivious to the existence of other moral codes. No society lacks an outside to the degree that MacIntyre claims, but the point is still an important one. In Sultan Muhammad's case, several alternative moralities were available for the choosing. His grandfather, after all, was an akhund (a man of religion), the father had become a hakim (a man of the government), and the boy himself had the option of following either of these paths if he had so desired, particularly after he was forced into exile from his home community. However, once Sultan Muhammad decided to return to Pech, all of his options disappeared. From this point on, there was, as MacIntyre states, no "outside" from which to ponder his situation, no half-measure or negotiated settlement that would allow him to fully reclaim and keep his former status.

Sultan Muhammad certainly knew all of this. He understood that his father's status and position made his own challenge greater. His father, after all, had been a man of renown before his turn to religion, and the son, once he chose to meet the challenge, would necessarily attract rivals and enmities of his own. Since his father was now dead and the family had proven vulnerable to assault from its enemies, the certainty of further attacks had increased, even after his mother succeeded in avenging his father's killing. If he was to be known as the son of a Pakhtun father and stand on the same footing as his father, he would have to gain his own vengeance.

And once vengeance was achieved, vigilance could not end. The commitment had to be lifelong, first, because anything less would cast suspicion upon his original motives in killing Paindo's sons and, second, because he, better than anyone else, knew the misfortune that could befall one who wavers. He, better than anyone, understood the suffering that comes to the family of a man who deludes himself into believing that he could suddenly change loyalties and become someone different than the man he was known to be. Other moralities and devotions will intrude from time to time to challenge the primacy of honor in the tribal homeland, but for the man who enters honor's realm, there is no way to avoid its dictates or its contradictions. Sultan Muhammad knew this better than most men, and his story is an enduring testament to the price and peril such knowledge entails.

3   The Reign of the Iron Amir

I am Amir Abdur Rahman Khan, the king [*padshah*] of Afghanistan. During the time of my reign, I have always been sympathetic
and benevolent to you people of Afghanistan, and I have not overlooked my responsibility to you for a single moment. I have told
you people a lot through books of advice, publications of preachings, and in many other ways. I have now prepared a map [*naqsha*]
of your own country and also a map of those countries which are
located on the four sides of your country [see map 3]. If you people consider well the map which is drawn for you, it will allow you
to see with your eyes how blessings may accrue to you in your religion [*din*] and also in this world [*dunya*].

There are enough details of the affairs of your religion and your
life in this world on this map for you to understand that everyone's share [*nasib*] is determined by God on the basis of his merit,
circumstances, and capabilities. Your king also pays attention to
these ranks among the people. He has appointed each one of you in
one of these ranks from the commander-in-chief to the common
soldier. Each one stands in his own place and position, and hence
you people should be grateful to God and to the king. In whatever
rank and position you are and wherever you stand look downward
to know how many people are lower than you. When you look
downward and see your high rank and position you will receive
three blessings [*ni'mat*]. First is the consent and contentment of
God, for it is written, "If you express your gratitude to God for the
blessings He has given you, He will increase them for you." Second is the approbation and good will of your ruler for you. The
third is that you can keep that rank or position that you have, and

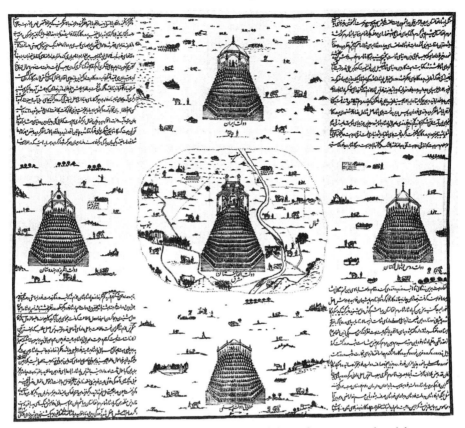

Map 3. Proclamation and map issued by Amir Abdur Rahman. Reproduced from Curzon, *Tales of Travel.*

you can be hopeful for more progress and promotion in the future. God has said that "if you are grateful for His blessings, He will increase them for you." The increase of blessings, in fact, is progress in rank [*daraja*]. All other blessings of the world are apparently related to the rise in grade and gaining advancement. When one makes progress and [earns] promotion, he can easily obtain other blessings and privileges.

But if you people are not contented with your present state and neglect to offer your thanks to God, and do not look to those who are inferior to you in position, but rather envy those who are above you, and ask in your hearts why such persons are superior to yourselves, you lay the foundation of envy and hatred, and cause many calamities to fall upon you. First, you bring down God's anger on you because it means that you criticize God. People can get something only if God wants to give it to them. No doubt if God likes someone, He leads him to the right path and makes him do good things and makes him honest in his life and job to achieve good services. On the basis of these qualities which God has given to a person, He will undoubtedly make the king benevolent towards him and give him promotions. In addition to this, [recitation of the phrase] "I take refuge in God" is, first of all, infidelity. Second, the person will face the calamity and misfortune of not being grateful to God. Being ungrateful for God's blessing can decrease God's blessings and the honor that God bestows upon the human being. Third, one will definitely fall down from the position he has, and when one falls down from a high position, two things happen to him. First, he will break his neck. When one breaks one's neck, it means he has lost everything in this world and in the other world [akhira]. If you break your neck, you will remain in a state of unconsciousness for so many years. When you become conscious you will see that someone else has occupied your position because the work of the world cannot be stopped for a person. When one leaves someone else occupies his position. When you lose your position, you will be walking down a street in a state of disgrace [be abru] and dishonor [be ghairat]. No one will even mention your name. You will be forgotten. If they mention your name, they will curse you. You will become famous for being foolish and ignorant. You will not be able to obtain the position that you lost to the very end of your life. These kinds of behavior also have another bitter fruit which is the destruction of the base of your religion and your life in this world. That is to say, if you do not look downward but rather look only upward, and if you are led by spite [bughz], contumacy ['anad], and envy [hasad], and if you make envy and spite the watchwords of your life, and if you feel happiness over the disgrace of others, and if you accept corruption as a way of life, the neighbors around you will laugh at your way of life night and day. All the countries will criticize your way of life. At that time you will not be able to do anything useful. You will be regretful and remorseful.

Please be cautious! Think wisely and listen carefully to my words and sayings, I who am the king of you people of Afghanistan. Listen, obey, and weigh well what I am saying to you, for no use can come from lamenting later if you do something wrong now. This advice is for all of you, from the commander-in-chief down to the common soldier and also for the subjects who are inferior to all. It has been said that a common soldier who stands with a gun on his shoulder to fulfill his duty has the lowest rank in all the military, but he shall look downward to the common subjects [ra'iyat] who are even lower in rank than him. He shall think to himself that once he was one of them, but now because of the grace of God and due to the kindness of the king he has obtained this rank. You should sympathize with the subjects, who are your own tribesmen and who are continually employed in cultivating their lands, in cutting their crops, in thrashing their corn, in gathering in the harvests, and in winnowing the wheat from the chaff. They are also occupied in commerce and undergo hardships and troubles by night and by day and only enjoy a portion of the produce themselves after they have paid the taxes which are necessary for the expenses of the state. Whatever money and goods I, the king of Afghanistan, take from the people is spent every month for you the people of the army. It therefore behooves you all, whether you are high ranking commanders, soldiers, or subjects, to be grateful, because all that you pay to your government is given back to your brothers, sons, and tribesmen. It is as if their own money is spent by their own government for their own brothers and their own sons. By doing so, God is pleased, religion prospers, and our dignity and honor are preserved. In a like manner, the subjects should also be grateful, so that God's blessings may increase day by day, for it is written that, "Those of you who are grateful for My blessings shall have them increased." It is therefore incumbent on you to be grateful both to God and to your king. You people have to gird your loins and honestly serve your religion and state. In doing so, you have to have only one objective and that should be the welfare and prosperity of your religion and state and obedience to your king. Obeying the order of the king with complete devotion and loyalty is just like obeying the commands of God. It is based on this verse of the Qur'an: "Obey Allah, his Prophet, and the king who is from among you." Thus it is incumbent on all of you, on account of the ranks and responsibilities that you have, to be thankful for this blessing which is the obedience of God.

The most important thing for you to know is that the kindness and mercy of the king for his subjects is like the kindness and mercy of a father for his son. In the same way that the kindness and mercy of a father is natural towards his son, the kindness and mercy of the king to his subjects is also natural. This is also the command of God to the king that he should be kind to his subjects. But when a father notices that his son is involved in illegal activities, then he will try to admonish or reprimand him. The reprimand of a son by his father to prevent him from committing a crime is not a sign of unkindness to the son, but rather should be considered as a kind of favor to him since a father does not want his son to have a bad name and habits. In the same way, the king has the same feelings towards his subjects as a father has towards his son. The king only wishes to spread the blessings of peace and order among his subjects if they do anything wrong. The king wants his subjects to be happy, prosperous, and have a good reputation and name. As long as the son is young and ignorant, he will hate his father's words, actions, and exhortations. But when he gets older and becomes endowed with wisdom and intelligence, then he will never consider anyone kinder and dearer than his father. By that time, he may have no other desire than obeying his father's wishes. As the ruler of you people of Afghanistan, my objective and desire towards you is the same as the desire that a father has for his son. I want a good name for you. I want to be kind to you. This is my desire. If you are wise enough to understand and benefit from my advice, you will see that your religion will flourish and that your country will be prosperous. May it so please God.

This was written on the day of Sunday, the thirteenth day of the month of *Jamadi al-Sani,* 1316.

MAPPING THE STATE

Amir Abdur Rahman, who ruled Afghanistan from 1880 until his death in 1901, was never content to command his subjects. He also wanted to school them, to teach them how to better perform their divinely appointed duties as workers in the field, as subjects, as human beings. Throughout his reign, he published numerous pamphlets and broadsides instructing his people on a variety of topics. The document translated above, which could probably be categorized as a *firman,* or proclamation, was one expression of this tendency. According to Lord Curzon, who visited Abdur

Rahman in Kabul and who later reproduced the firman in a book of travel memoirs, the original document was huge—five feet by four and a half feet—and printed on canvas. As both a map and a public lecture, its size and durability were required by the fact that the proclamation was designed to be "read out in the bazaars and mosques of all the principal towns and posted in every village" as a way "to stimulate the patriotism and ensure the due subordination of his people and incidentally to render them more amenable to military conscription."[1]

The date appended to the end of the document translates to 1898 in the Christian calendar, eighteen years after Abdur Rahman ascended the throne and just three years before his death. That year was a time of relative peace in the kingdom. The last of the many rebellions that had punctuated Abdur Rahman's reign ended two years before, and no ambitious kinsman loomed on the horizon to challenge the Amir's right to dynastic supremacy; however, from the evidence of this document, it does not appear that Abdur Rahman relaxed his guard even at this moment, when other rulers might have retired into the confines of their harems. To the contrary, the old warrior remained wary to the end, for he knew how tenuously held were the reins of power and believed as well that he would have been long since dead if any of his retainers had had the resolve or resourcefulness to do him in.[2] That he proved to be one of the few Afghan monarchs who died in bed and in power can be explained not only by his vigilance, but also by the fact that he availed himself of every opportunity to demonstrate the force of his will and the moral imperative of his rule to those around him and to the nation at large.

I have reproduced the firman in its entirety because it provides a succinct précis of the moral principles of kingship that Abdur Rahman hoped to instill in his subjects. While the language of the proclamation might lead one to suspect that these are venerated principles of rule, there is no indication that this is the case. Indeed, that Abdur Rahman felt the need to produce this proclamation in outsized form and to have it carried around the country lends the impression that these principles were neither time-honored nor widely accepted; so too does the fact that, since its founding in 1747, the central state had been subject to repeated upheavals and therefore Abdur Rahman had been required to expend the majority of his labors for most of two decades to protect his throne and gradually consolidate the authority of his state.

The proclamation, however, makes one think otherwise. It conveys an impression of confidence. Its attitude is both lofty and paternalistic, pietistic and exhortatory. In one sense, a primer on the obligations of rulers and those they ruled, in another, it is a warning to those who would defy the king and incur his wrath. While we cannot take its message at face value and assume that Abdur Rahman's subjects held these principles to be self-evident, we can nevertheless use this document as a source for understanding the moral foundation of kingship as envisioned by the ruler who essentially founded the modern Afghan state. More than anyone since the Ahmad Shah Durrani, the founder of the kingdom of Kabul, Abdur Rahman made Afghanistan a reality. He is the Iron Amir, who brought the disparate and antagonistic tribes and petty chiefdoms to heel; he is the ruler who transformed a small cohort of scribes into an administrative bureaucracy; he is the general who molded a motley collection of mercenaries and militias into a standing army; he, more than anyone else, is the visionary who established the boundaries, the offices, the apparatus of the modern nation-state.

These developments have been well analyzed by other scholars and need not be reanalyzed here, but what has been less well attended to and does need to be considered are the moral imperatives that animated, provoked, and legitimated the practical measures that were transforming the kingdom into a new species of state.[3] The time when these changes were occurring represents a crucial moment in Afghan history. It was a time not just of internal change but also of external peril, with the Russian and British empires at the peak of their power and advancing from the north and east. Given the state of imperial competition, consolidation was not just a matter of private ambition; it was also a practical necessity, and the proclamation gives us an idea of the grounds on which Abdur Rahman imagined such consolidation might be justified and sold to his people.

Besides containing text, the proclamation also has on it an image, an image that is part map and part icon and that tells us a great deal about kingship and the kind of community that Abdur Rahman imagined Afghanistan to be. Given that over ninety percent of the population at the time was illiterate and given the size of the original artifact, we must conclude that, even more than the words, it was the image on the document that mattered. This is what people saw first even as they listened to someone else—a government official or a mulla perhaps—read the words. In addition to the text then, it is also important that we consider what the people might have seen when they stared up at this *mappa mundi* of the Afghan universe.

The image that Abdur Rahman asks his subjects to survey shows five multitiered structures, each surmounted by a canopied pavilion. The five structures are arrayed in a cruciform grid, the centermost one being labeled in small letters at its base "The Government of Afghanistan." The pavilion at the top of this innermost edifice is of a traditional design often seen in Afghan architecture—two short minarets rising above three columned arches. Several other unidentified (though probably recognizable) buildings can be seen in the center section of the picture, each connected to the others by little roads. Snaking vertically through the terrain is a large river, apparently the Oxus, since it is on the side of the image labeled "North." On the "East" side of the map (which is on the lower half of the map), one notices rocky crags that apparently indicate the rugged Pamir Mountains on Afghanistan's northeastern border. Other than these few features, no other geographical details are provided except the boundary itself—a dotted line that frames the central oval representing Afghanistan (map 3).

Beyond the borders, there are four other structures, all more or less identical in size. The topmost structure on the map, which is on the side labeled "West," is identified as "the Government of Iran" and surmounted by a canopy design that is at least vaguely reminiscent of Iranian shrine architecture. The building on the right side of the image (to the "North") is referred to as "Government of Russia and Northern Turkistan" and bears a spire with a Christian cross at its top. The structure on the bottom, or "East" side, is the "Government of China," and its pagoda-like form appears Chinese in inspiration. The last edifice, on the "South" side of Afghanistan, is marked as the "English Government in Hindustan" and is crowned with a cross and pediment that seem to represent an Anglican church.

In the opening sentences of his proclamation, Abdur Rahman tells his subjects that they should "look at this map carefully and think about it deeply, so that you will see with your eyes the ways of life from which you can get benefit in your religion and also in this world." Perhaps, but for us, deciphering the image is difficult without the aid of the surrounding text because we are not subjects of the Amir and our eyes are blurred by many more media images than the few that came before the Afghan people in 1898. However, even without the text, certain lessons are still available to us. One such lesson is that Afghanistan exists as a state among other states, and from the visual geometry of the interlocking images, we might also conclude that each of these states has its own allotted portion of the earth. (The text immediately informs us of the correctness of this deduction when it notes, "You can understand that everyone's share is determined by God on the basis of his merit, circumstances, and capabilities." Divine apportionment as the basis of all social and political relationships is a central tenet at work here, and the text and image reinforce this basic principle.)

We can also conclude from an inspection of the map that the world is divided into domains and that each of these domains is ruled by a government. In visual terms, rulership is represented by the towers, the height and solidity of which reflect the power and stability of the separate regimes. That all five of these towers are more or less equally stable at their base and tall at their summit tells us perhaps that all are equal in their sovereign authority. This is not an unexpected assertion from our point of view, but it is surprising when we consider it in historical and political context. When the Amir published this proclamation, 'Afghanistan' was a relatively novel idea (not long before it had been referred to as the kingdom of Kabul), and it was an idea that had only really come into being because policy makers in London had come to the conclusion that a buffer state on their northwestern flank would be more useful to British interests than the perennially mutating satrapy that had existed up until that point. Here, shortly after that decision, we see the Afghan amir claiming a status for his state equal to that of apparently more stable states on his borders and, in the process, abandoning any grander aspirations for expansion into the Indian subcontinent or central Asia.

That is one of the surprising notions intimated by the map. Another comes when one considers its religious iconography and the clear association of states with religious symbols. That association is an established one from an Islamic point of view, but what is more interesting is the Amir's apparent acceptance of Afghanistan's status as an Islamic nation bordered on two sides by non-Muslim states. If we take into account the fact that Abdur Rahman was given protection in Russian-held Tashkent for the ten years prior to his ascension to the throne, his position makes sense, but we must assume that his apparent avowal of the notion that God has apportioned the share of each state, including that of non-Muslim ones ruling over Muslim populations, would have been a difficult idea for many of his more religious subjects to accept.

One more point about the towers concerns their relation to the people represented on the map. Close inspection of the towers indicates that each tier is articulated by the black silhouettes of people lined up shoulder to shoulder. Given the evidence in the text, it is clear that we are supposed to see these silhouettes as people who occupy appointed positions in the government. These are the ones whom the Amir addresses when he declares, "He has appointed each one of you in one of these ranks from the commander-in-chief to a common soldier. Each one stands in his own place and position, and hence you people should be grateful to God and to the king."

Below the tower, in the expanse of landscape that represents the Amir's domain, we are confronted with a more pastoral and spacious scene in which we can make out scattered dark figures engaged in a variety of domestic pursuits such as tilling the soil, driving bullocks, and carrying bundles of straw on their backs. In the text, these figures are referred to as "common subjects . . . working night and day on the farm, shoveling, reaping, and cultivating to get the produce [of the land], they separate wheat from straw." The Amir wants his soldiers and officials to look on these common folk and be grateful that their lot in life is better than that of their peasant kinsmen, but he has another objective as well and that is for his people to set aside the traditional understanding of themselves as members of separate communities accepting the suzerain authority of a king conceived of as the first among equals.

In place of this conception of kingship, the Amir propagates—in the visual language of the map—the novel idea of Afghanistan as a single, undivided community unified by common obedience to a sovereign authority. While the people are to go about their business in the fields below, the ruler must go about his, high astride the tower of state. From this lofty vantage, he can supervise the peaceful pursuits of his peasant subjects and survey as well (at eye-level and with unblinking vigilance) his fellow rulers, who stand in their towers beyond the borders of the kingdom. What divisions there are in this imagined community of Abdur Rahman's are those of apportioned rank; otherwise, no divisions, whether of tribe, ethnicity, religion, or language, are recognized. To the contrary, all subjects are defined by either the position they hold (a position bestowed by the king) or the tasks they perform (tasks determined ultimately by God and carried out in the shadow of the state).[4]

The map also indicates something else about the state—that it is bounded. Boundaries, it would seem, are important, and it is somewhat surprising that they appear this way, given that Abdur Rahman had grudgingly accepted the British demand for a demarcated border between Afghanistan and India only five years earlier. At the time, he had suspected that British cartographers would use the opportunity to remove parts of his dominion, and he also worried that his own ability to control his subjects, particularly the recalcitrant border tribes, would somehow be diminished and constrained by the presence of fixed boundary lines. But just a few short years later, he is displaying to his people a visual representation of that very border he had been so loath to accept. The question which this image raises is not so much why he accepted the boundary line—that question can be answered if one considers the state of relations with Great Britain and the power it wielded in the region—but, rather, why he seems to have embraced the idea of the border to such an extent that he would proudly advertise its existence.[5] How is it that an act of capitulation had become a point of pride with his people?

On the most mundane level, of course, recognized boundaries offered some protection against external encroachment; because the border was sparsely guarded, this protection was more diplomatic than military, but it was still something that could be counted on. To my mind, however, a more important factor in explaining Abdur Rahman's acceptance of the boundary is the help it provided in legitimating his regime and his sometimes draconian policies to his subjects. This reason can be seen in the following analogy taken from the Amir's autobiography:

> It is easy to understand that before furnishing a house one must think of making or finding a house to furnish; and in case of building a house it must be surrounded by walls to keep the goods safe which are put in it; and if the house is full of holes, ditches, snakes, scorpions, etc., it is necessary to get rid of these before anyone can live in it. In the same way, it was of the first and greatest importance to mark out a boundary line all around Afghanistan.

A prosaic image no doubt, but one that the humblest Afghan could readily identify with and abstract from. Who could object, after all, to the importance of "a strong wall around the country, shaping it, as it were, into a house"? And who could argue against the need "to clear that house of all the injurious scorpions existing in it, scorpions that formed a great obstacle in the way of peace and progress"? As Abdur Rahman goes on to explain, the scorpions he is referring to are "those hundreds of petty chiefs, plunderers, robbers, and cutthroats, who were the cause of everlasting trouble in Afghanistan." To end their depredations, the Amir had to resort to desperate measures that included "breaking down the feudal and tribal system," but the result, he was quick to note, was the creation of "one grand community under one law and under one rule."[6]

THE ONCE AND FUTURE KING

The visual images adorning the proclamation created an idealized picture of the Afghan nation as Abdur Rahman wished his subjects to see it. I now want to examine in greater depth the principles of monarchical authority by which he thought that nation should be ruled. Monarchical authority, of course, is illuminated on the map we have been analyzing (can a more striking depiction of the king's stature and power be imagined than this image of the great tower looming over the agrarian landscape?), but it is more systematically revealed in the accompanying text, which neatly articulates the principles of kingship on which Abdur Rahman based his rule. In explicating these principles, I will make reference both to the proclamation itself, which supplies the essential outline of those principles, and to the previously cited autobiography, which demonstrates in dramatic fashion the way in which Abdur Rahman saw these principles guiding and defining his own life experience.

Originally published in Kabul in 1886 as *Pandnama-i dunya wa din* (*Book of Advice on the World and Religion*), the autobiography details the trials and tribulations of the Amir's early years up to his ascension of the Afghan throne in 1880. The work was translated from Persian into English by a Punjabi official named Sultan Mahomed Khan (who had served for many years as a secretary [*munshi*] to the Amir) and was then published in London as the first volume of *The Life of Abdur Rahman Khan: Amir of Afghanistan* (1900). While Afghan historians have questioned the extent of Abdur Rahman's input on the second volume (which provides an account of the Amir's daily life and the government he established), they have confirmed that the first volume is a more or less faithful rendition of the Persian pandnama previously published under the Amir's direction in Kabul.[7]

Periodically tapped for information on Abdur Rahman's early life and the historical events of that time, the narrative contained in volume one of *The Life* has been otherwise overlooked by scholars, and its virtues, both as a story and as a treatise on kingship, have been largely ignored. This is a strange oversight, if only because Abdur Rahman's life history is a fascinating tale of adventure and intrigue. As the translator of the autobiography notes in his preface, Abdur Rahman's early life is "like a chapter of the 'Arabian Nights,' [and] the reader cannot help being interested to notice that a monarch like the Amir, setting aside the idea of boasting, should condescend to make a clear statement of how he was a prisoner in fetters at one time, and a cook at another; a Viceroy at one time, and a subject of the Viceroy at another; a general at one time, and under the command of the general at another; an engineer and a blacksmith at one time, and a ruler at another."[8]

Beyond its sheer drama, however, the story of Abdur Rahman's early life deserves attention for what it tells us about the Amir's vision of kingship and his understanding of the reciprocal obligations of ruler and ruled. Written originally as a book of advice, *The Life* retains its sense of moral instruction even in its English incarnation. The Amir wanted the readers of the original work to learn from his life and to follow his example, and this sense of direction, injunction, and exhortation is visible in the account of his life experiences, just as it is in his official proclamation. In the case of the life history, however, the idiom of instruction is more often stories than outright admonition, and we are thus afforded the opportunity, as we watch Abdur Rahman's odyssey from displaced heir to rightful king, to see enacted the principles of royal authority that are abstractly delineated in the royal firman.

A second merit of *The Life* is its coherence as a narrative. While it is replete with interesting characters and strange encounters, the story of Abdur Rahman's early life is not a pointless picaresque. Rather, it is a clearly moralized account of a king's coming of age and bears a striking similarity to the saga of Sultan Muhammad's youthful ordeal that was presented in the last chapter. The story of Abdur Rahman's youth is far more detailed, of course, and the canvas is broader, but the essential outline of both stories is much the same, and the moral pivot around which each revolves is the relationship between father and son.

Like Sultan Muhammad's father, Abdur Rahman's father, Muhammad Afzal, was a man of influence and authority, but in his case the authority was on a grand scale. Muhammad Afzal was, in fact, the eldest son of the Afghan amir, Dost Muhammad, who twice ruled the kingdom of Kabul (1826–38, 1842–63). As the narrative begins in 1853, Abdur Rahman is called away from his mother's home in Kabul to join his father, who is serving as governor of Afghan Turkistan. Though only nine years old, Abdur Rahman was Muhammad Afzal's eldest son, and it was time for him to sit by his father's side and imbibe the lessons of rulership. Much of the first part of the story is taken up with a depiction of the joys and vicissitudes of this apprenticeship. But we also encounter our first indications of the misunderstandings that are to plague Abdur Rahman's relationship with his father; they are, in fact, the same sort of tensions that we have already seen in the story of Sultan Muhammad and his father.

The first sign of trouble occurs when Abdur Rahman is about fourteen years old. He has been assigned by his father to serve as the governor of Tashkurgan district, but shortly after beginning his appointment, he is rebuked by his father for reducing the taxes of his impoverished subjects and giving presents to some of his loyal attendants. Abdur Rahman resigns over this infringement on his authority, but he gets into even more trouble with his father shortly thereafter when a treacherous advisor persuades his father that his son has taken up wine and hashish. Trusting the word of his advisors over that of his son, Muhammad Afzal has Abdur Rahman thrown in prison, where he languishes in chains for a year.

Abdur Rahman eventually regains his father's favor and the command of his father's armies, but after serving faithfully and well in this capacity, Abdur Rahman's position in society is again endangered by another error of judgment on the part of his father. These events transpire following the death of Amir Dost Muhammad in 1863. The great amir had ruled for more than thirty years, and his demise created a power vacuum in which his two eldest sons, Muhammad Afzal and Muhammad Azam, were pitted against their younger half-brother, Sher 'Ali Khan, who had succeeded in gaining the favor of the late amir prior to his death. Through the first of many acts of treachery, Sher 'Ali managed to defeat Muhammad Azam, and he then turned his attention to Muhammad Afzal who, as Dost Muhammad's oldest son, had the strongest claim to the throne.

Although he enjoyed a stronger position than Sher 'Ali, Muhammad Afzal once again committed a fatal error. This was the error of trust—the same offense that precipitated Sultan Muhammad's travails when his father set off alone and unprotected to claim a bride. In that case, the incautious father had rejected the warning of his worldly wise son, and here too we find Abdur Rahman cautioning his father when a messenger from Sher 'Ali arrives in their camp carrying a Qur'an and professing good faith: "My father being deceived by these assurances, took the Koran on his eyes, and kissed it, starting out for the camp of Shere Ali, leaving his army to return, although they all begged him to fight it out."[9]

Against his son's advice, Muhammad Afzal sets off for Sher 'Ali's camp and is soon taken prisoner. As one would expect, Abdur Rahman prepares to retaliate for this treachery, but before he can do so, he receives a letter from his father threatening to "disown" him if he took to the field.[10] At this juncture, there is a slight deviation in the two stories, for unlike Sultan Muhammad, Abdur Rahman decides to obey his father's wishes. This choice proves significant for the meaning of the story, but on a narrative level Abdur Rahman's obedience has the same effect as Sultan Muhammad's disobedience, as Abdur Rahman is abandoned by his troops and—like Sultan Muhammad—forced to take refuge with one of his father's old allies, in this case, the king of Bokhara.

Residence in the Bokharan court places Abdur Rahman in the same ambiguous situation that Sultan Muhammad faced in exile when he had

to choose between returning to Pech and accepting the secure but demeaning status of a court scribe. In Abdur Rahman's case, the dilemma is
presented to him shortly after his arrival in court when a message arrives
indicating that the king "wishes to make you one of his Court officials, so
that you should attend on him every day." Like Sultan Muhammad, Abdur Rahman declines the offer and adds the comment, "I had never been
a servant, and did not know how to behave as one."[11]

Abdur Rahman's father was taken prisoner in the summer of 1864.
Two years later, in May 1866, Abdur Rahman returns to Afghanistan to
release his father and gain for him the throne from which he had been
deprived. To do so, he has to raise an army, a task that requires the same
sort of diplomacy employed by Sultan Muhammad when he gathered together his grim band of avengers. This skill is evident in the following
letter which Abdur Rahman wrote to his former troops, then under the
command of a treacherous relative: "You are my army, therefore I will
not fight against you. If you wish to kill me, I will come to the fort tomorrow, and you shall shoot me, and obtain rewards for killing your old
employer."[12]

This appeal to honor and old loyalties (like that of Sultan Muhammad)
"melted their hearts," and he is soon able to engage and defeat Sher 'Ali
in battle. Following the release of his father from Sher 'Ali's clutches,
Abdur Rahman enters Kabul at the head of his victorious army and immediately avails himself of the opportunity to read "the Khutba [Friday ser-
mon] in the name of my father as king." Responding to Abdur Rahman's
lead, "the chiefs gathered together to congratulate [Muhammad Afzal] on
becoming amir, saying that he being the rightful heir, they were pleased
to acknowledge him as their ruler."[13]

Thus Abdur Rahman achieves redress for the wrongs he has suffered,
and we see enacted once again what would appear to be a paradigmatic
narrative of fathers and sons, dispossession and vindication. The difference
here, of course, is that father and son are reconciled. In this case, obedience
to the father has allowed both father and son to reclaim their rightful
place in society, or so it would appear, but the story does not end here.
Within a year of mounting the throne, Abdur Rahman's father is dead,
and Abdur Rahman has ceded his own right to the throne in favor of his
uncle, Muhammad Azam. Like his older brother, Muhammad Azam is
prone to misjudgment and heeds the advice of courtiers who convince him
of Abdur Rahman's bad intentions. He therefore dispatches Abdur Rahman to the north and loses his assistance when the army of the resilient

Sher 'Ali threatens from the south. Because of Muhammad Azam's cruelty, once-loyal troops desert to Sher 'Ali's side, and Abdur Rahman, with his uncle in tow, must flee to Turkistan. There he remains until 1880, when he finally succeeds in claiming the throne for himself.

Regardless of these later complications in the story (which repeat rather than alter its principal themes), a remarkable series of parallels can be noted between the "coming of age" narratives of Sultan Muhammad Khan and Abdur Rahman. In both cases, certain basic cultural preoccupations are illustrated, among them the ambivalent relations that the two protagonists enjoy with their fathers (an ambivalence that is as much structurally given as individually arrived at), the persistent threat posed by paternal cousins (Paindo and his brood in the first story, Sher 'Ali and his in the other), the danger of trusting those inferior in rank to oneself (be they women or courtiers), and perhaps most important of all, the overriding importance of continually remembering who you are and adhering to the responsibilities entailed for you by your situation and station (as seen in the exemplary actions of Sultan Muhammad and Abdur Rahman themselves). In both stories, the failure of senior kinsmen to abide by this last precept creates the obstacles that each protagonist encounters in the course of the narrative, and it is finally only the steadfastness and resolve of the hero that allows these obstacles to be conquered and the moral order to right itself.

The similarity in these two otherwise disparate stories indicates that we are in the presence of something like a "cultural script," but at the same time it is important to note that there are significant differences in the stories as well. Thus, despite the commonalities outlined above, these two stories are ultimately *about* very different things, and they illustrate dissimilar principles of social action and political relationship. Quite simply, Sultan Muhammad's story is about the individual requirements of honor and the moral authority that joins together the coequals who claim common descent in the universe of tribal relations. Abdur Rahman's story, on the other hand, is about the personal requirements of kingship and the hierarchical moral authority binding the monarch to his dependent and subservient subjects. Both honor and kingship as moral systems draw elements from each other; both, in fact, have the intrinsic capacity of being transformed into the other. But, in their basic constitutions, the two systems are opposed, and it is therefore necessary to focus on the nature of the differences that lie between them in order to understand how they can also be, in certain respects, alike.

THE ARMATURE OF ROYAL RULE

Having provided some background on Abdur Rahman's life, I now want to relate principles of kingly authority contained in the proclamation that was reproduced and translated at the beginning of this chapter to specific episodes in Abdur Rahman's life story. The organization of this section will be thematic rather than chronological, as I will outline three aspects of kingship revealed in the proclamation and correlate them with scenes and situations found in the autobiography. The three aspects to be explored are those of king as instrument of God's sovereignty, king as patriarch and kinsman, and king as grantor of benefits and rewards.

God and King

The first and most important principle of Islamic kingship, be it an Afghan version or any other, is the paramountcy of God as creator of the universe and the ultimate judge of human affairs. All power in nature and society emanates from God. It is God who "determines the share" that everyone receives, which is to say, the station that they are born into and the capability which they have to improve their situation. As creatures of God, people can achieve something only if God allows them to do so. If He does not, then no amount of effort can alter their destiny. The proclamation builds on this principle of divine control by closely aligning the interests of the monarch with those of God. The king, like other human beings, is subject to God's ultimate authority, and he too will be judged for his actions and his obedience to divine commandments. But in distinction from other people, the king has been allotted an added burden—that of ensuring the general order that will enable those subject to his authority to fulfill their assigned duties as Muslim believers.[14]

In the autobiography the most dramatic means by which Abdur Rahman conveys his belief in the obligation of the ruler to provide the conditions within which his subjects can fulfill their religious obligations is through his portraits of unjust rulers who fail to live up to their divinely appointed responsibilities. The most egregious of these rulers was the king of Bokhara, whom Abdur Rahman encountered several times on his travels in central Asia. During one journey to the Bokharan court, there occurred an episode that is emblematic of this ruler's sins.

Abdur Rahman was passing a village when he spies "a high piece of ground, which had been prepared to receive the tents of the king." The ground was covered with blood, which Abdur Rahman assumes was "due to the amount of cows killed for charity to celebrate the king's victory" in a recent campaign. On inquiring of the local residents why the sacrifice had not been performed further from the tents, however, he is informed that this was not the blood of cows but of men. Fifteen days earlier the king's tents had been pitched in this spot, and one thousand prisoners had been brought before the king, who had ordered their throats cut in front of him. Abdur Rahman's response to this news is "shock" that prisoners should be treated in this way, and he goes on to ruminate that the then ongoing conquest of Turkistan by the Russians was caused by "the neglect of the Muslim rulers of God and His religion. They make the true believers slaves, and kill human beings, who are God's creation, without fault." Ordering his soldiers "to cover over the blood with earth, in the shape of graves," Abdur Rahman laments, "Bokhara, which had the reputation of being a very religious country, acted so contrarily to the teachings of Mahomet. I regretted the carelessness of the Muslims who are mad in their own conceit, so that the unbelievers, finding them ignorant and hostile to each other, take advantage of this." [15]

If Abdur Rahman portrays the king of Bokhara as a ruler who ignores his responsibility to uphold God's law, he paints himself as a ruler who succeeds in this responsibility and is favored by God for doing so. One way God expresses His favor is through a series of miracles that aid Abdur Rahman before he assumes the reins of royal power. The first of these interventions occurs while Abdur Rahman is still a young man and serving as governor of Kataghan in northern Afghanistan. He receives a letter from his fiancée and first cousin, the daughter of his uncle Muhammad Azam, who wrote that the letter was to be delivered into his hands, that it was to be shown to no one else, and that he himself was to write and seal the reply. Never having paid attention to his studies and consequently unable to read or write, Abdur Rahman "wept bitterly" out of frustration and shame, for "while I boasted of being such a fine man, I was really most unmanly, being so ignorant."

On retiring that evening, Abdur Rahman prays to God "with all humility, beseeching the souls of the Saints to intercede" for him and asking that his heart and mind be enlightened so that he would not be "ashamed in the eyes of Thy creation." After Abdur Rahman falls asleep, a holy man appears to him and twice tells him to rise and write. Both times, the younger man raises his head from his bed only to fall back asleep, but the third utterance of the command is punctuated with the threat: "If you sleep again, I shall pierce your chest with my staff." At this, Abdur Rahman rises and begins to search his memory for the letters he had learned as a child. One by one they come back, and before dawn he is writing words in an awkward scrawl. By late afternoon, he is responding to his fiancée's letter and perusing official correspondence. The holy man's intervention thus enables him both to maintain privacy in his domestic relations and to overcome that great obstacle to proper rule—overreliance on court advisors.[16]

In the course of his autobiography Abdur Rahman recounts several other divinely inspired dreams "from which I drew much comfort, as they gave me hope that I should not fail in my mission as a king, and that I should be successful in the end."[17] Perhaps the most dramatic occurs just before he leaves Turkestan to make his drive on Kabul. In this dream, two angels take him by the arms and bring him into the presence of a man he does not recognize: "He had a very mild, gentle face, of oval shape, a round beard, and beautiful long eyebrows and eyelashes. He was wearing a large loose garment of a blue color, and a white turban. His whole appearance was the perfection of beauty and gentle nature." Seated beside the man, whom he perceives to be a ruler of some sort, are four other men—two on each side and all dressed in Arab robes. Into this august assembly is brought a man who, when asked a silent question "in the unspoken language of the eyes," replies that he "will destroy the churches of other religions and build them into mosques, if I am made king." The sovereign is displeased with this answer and orders that the man be taken away. Then the same question is asked of Abdur Rahman who responds that he "will do justice and break the idols and [uphold the Islamic declaration of faith] instead." Hearing these words, the sovereign's four companions look at him with kindly expressions on their faces:

> It was an expression of consent to appoint me king. I was inspired at the same moment with the knowledge that the king was the Blessed Prophet Mahomed, the two men at his right hand were his companions Abu-Bekr and Osman; the two at his left hand were his companions Omar and Ali. Upon this I awoke, and was so happy to believe that the Prophet and his Four Companions, whose authority it is to appoint the sovereigns of Islam, had chosen me as the future amir.[18]

Like many Islamic rulers before him, Abdur Rahman uses dreams not only to legitimate his efforts but also to lend them a sense of inevitability. This practice can be seen in a series of episodes that occurs just as Abdur Rahman, accompanied by a tiny contingent of cavalry, is setting off on his final, desperate bid for power in 1880. On the eve of his departure from central Asia, he has a dream in which a saint tells him to take one of the flags flying over his nearby tomb and "erect that flag in front of thine army, and thou shalt always be victorious." Abdur Rahman does as he is told but, shortly after setting out for Kabul, is confronted by an opposing army that he guesses to be 10,000 men strong. Despite the numerical superiority of the force arrayed against him, Abdur Rahman never loses heart or wavers from his goal: "I knew that no courage, however great, could succeed against such a number, but as I had given my life for the service of God, and knew all the verses of the Koran which promise rewards to those who sacrifice themselves for the suffering, to me 10,000 were the same as 1,000,000.[19]

The next day, as he marches to face the enemy contingent, an astonishing sight greets his eyes. "The enemy began to disperse gradually in different directions, as if under the influence of an evil spirit. I could not understand what had happened. In the meantime, a body of sowars [cavalry] belonging to the Mir of Badakhshan . . . was approaching from another direction praising God." Soon thousands of chiefs and common people from the surrounding areas are flocking to his camp and swearing fealty to his cause, an outcome that he explains thus: "A wise man will understand how I conquered the hearts of these 20,000 men in one day, because the hearts of men are in the hands of God, who turned them that day towards me."[20]

Such are the claims of kings, of course, but it is still important to recognize the significance to a ruler of his being able not only to convince the people that God supported his cause but also to believe it himself. If a ruler can convince the people that God is behind him, and if he can support that conviction through successful action, then popular support will mushroom. Likewise, if a leader can convince himself of his own divinely favored status, he can act in a fearless manner that befits his station. While it is undoubtedly true that many of those rendered fearless in this way wind up dead, those who survive are fortified by their survival and become formidable indeed. Abdur Rahman is one such survivor who was favored by circumstances and possessed of the requisite credentials to achieve what he took to be his destiny.

Kingship and Kinship

Patriarchal authority is the binding cement of Afghan society, and it is therefore not surprising that Abdur Rahman exploits that tie in the proclamation when he notes "the kindness and mercy of the king for his subjects" is as natural as "the kindness and mercy of a father" for his son. Like a father, the king's desire for his subjects is that they should earn a good name for themselves and accomplish in their lives what God has given them the capability to achieve.[21] If instead they act in illicit ways and disobey lawful commands, their ruler, acting again like a dutiful father, is required to reprimand and punish his subjects in order lead them back to the right path and preserve the general prosperity of the community at large.

According to Bernard Lewis, the use of patriarchal symbols of authority is unusual in Islamic political writings, and one rarely finds instances in which a king is referred to as the "father" of his country.[22] The language of the proclamation suggests, however, that patriarchal images are vitally important in Afghan political culture, and that conclusion is buttressed if we consider the evidence of the autobiography, in which virtually every important political relationship is negotiated in and evaluated through the terminology and ideology of kinship relations. One area in which this can be seen is in the relationship between dynastic rivals. The first such example in the book occurs between Abdur Rahman's father, Muhammad Afzal, and his younger half-brother, Sher ʿAli Khan. The meeting between them that is described below was initiated by Sher ʿAli after he has learned from his spies that Muhammad Afzal's army is "too strong for him to stand against, and that he must resort to intrigues, or he would meet with defeat."

> Shere Ali, listening to this, sent Sultan Ali, son of Sirdar Kuhandil of Kandahar, with an oath on the Koran, in which he undertook to look upon [Muhammad Afzal] as his father, and saying he was determined not to disgrace the name of their father Dost Mahomed by fighting against his son. My father being deceived by these assurances, took the Koran on his eyes, and kissed it, starting out for the camp of Shere Ali. . . . On his arrival at his brother's camp [Sher ʿAli] walked out to welcome him, and kissed his stirrups, thus treacherously flattering him, and expressing his sorrow for thinking of going to war with his elder brother.[23]

Not long after this scene, Sher ʿAli breaks his oath to Abdur Rahman's father and throws him in prison. As mentioned earlier, Sher ʿAli's power was short-lived—within two years, he was overthrown and Muhammad Afzal was installed on the throne. The issue of succession again arose when Muhammad Afzal died a short time later, but the bloody battle that most observers expected between the dead Amir's brother, Muhammad Azam, and his eldest son, Abdur Rahman, never transpired. The following description of the meeting between Abdur Rahman and his uncle purports to tell why:

> Three days after [the funeral], I said to my uncle (Mahomed Azim) that as long as my father was alive, he was his younger brother, and I was as a

younger brother to him (my uncle); now my father was dead, I would look upon him as occupying his place, and I would take his myself, leaving my place to his eldest son. My uncle replied that I was the rightful heir, being the late amir's son, and he would be my servant. But I replied: "Your white beard, uncle of mine, makes it unfitting for you to be a servant of any one. I am young, and therefore will serve as I served my father."[24]

In the first of these two scenes, the illegitimacy and infidelity of the pretender, Sher 'Ali, is illustrated in multiple ways: by his breaking of a sacred oath, by his treacherous invocation of his grandfather's name to a kinsman he was conspiring to destroy, and finally by his use of kinship etiquette to lull his rival into a false sense of security. In the second vignette, the respect properly shown by a son to his father is invoked as a model for the decorum that a subject should exhibit to his king. Use of this kinship model in the latter instance allows a potential political crisis (in which the principle of seniority conflicts with that of lineal succession) to be peacefully resolved.

Another arena in which kinship terminology is used as a basis for negotiating uncertain political relationships is in meetings between unrelated rulers. An example of this sort of negotiation can be seen in Abdur Rahman's description of his arrival at the court of the Khan of Khiva:

> They fired fifty guns as a salute to me, and the Khan walked out to receive me. I dismounted, and we shook hands, and hand-in-hand we walked into the Durbar hall. . . . We spoke together for two hours, during which time he told me that he regarded me as his elder brother, as his father Mahomed Amin was most friendly to my father at the time of his residence at Balkh, and he thanked God that we had met. He offered me two of the seven cities now under his rule, and at any time I chose to go to Balkh, he would lend me 100,000 sowars and footmen, who would conquer the city for me, so that we might remain friends and neighbors.[25]

In analyzing this scene, it is useful to point out that in traditional Afghan society there are a limited number of relational frames which can be used to structure encounters between unfamiliar people, and of those frames that are available the one most frequently called upon is that of kinship. Time and again I have observed that when first introduced, Afghans will question one another in order to find a prior connection between them. The questioning continues as long as it takes to discover a point of reference: an uncle of one of the two men whose cousin had married a relative of the other man's, an elder brother of one of the men who had been a classmate of the other's, and so on. Once a connection has been uncovered, the two men greet each other all over again, familiarly hugging each other and reciting the litany of salutations appropriate to their newly discovered relationship. From that moment on, they will address each other with such terms as are appropriate to that relationship.

Although the meeting between the Khan of Khiva and Abdur Rahman occurred more than a century ago and in a different world, it appears that a similar dynamic is going on as the Khan declares Abdur Rahman to be his "elder brother" because Abdur Rahman's father had long ago played host to his father. In modeling their own relationship on the earlier one of their fathers, the Khan of Khiva not only provides a set of protocols for their interaction but also imparts dignity to his guest, who is, as they both recognize, in a dependent and highly vulnerable situation.

If the khan of Khiva is the epitome of the noble and generous king, the antithesis of this ideal can be seen in his neighbor, the king of Bokhara, who was renowned not only for his cruelty (evidence of which was shown in the last section) but also for his decadence and incivility. In keeping with this reputation, the first meeting between Abdur Rahman and the Bokharan ruler is notable for its cynical manipulation of ritual to gain advantage. Thus, before he has even greeted Abdur Rahman (whose father, as governor of Afghan Turkistan, was well known to him), the king feasts Abdur Rahman and his retainers for nine days and sends them expensive gifts. The generosity of their host is much admired until, at the conclusion of the feast, a messenger arrives to inform Abdur Rahman that he is expected to reciprocate in kind. Never one to be caught unawares, Abdur Rahman has brought sufficient valuables with him to meet the king's demand for tribute, but Abdur Rahman is less forthcoming when he is told by the king's doorkeeper that before entering the royal sanctum, he should stoop over so that the coins which he intends to present the king can be placed on his back. Abdur Rahman's curt response to this demand ("I am created by God, and shall kneel to no one but Him") annoys the doorkeeper, "who had never heard such a reply from any one before" and is disinclined to allow him entrance. However, another courtier intervenes, and Abdur Rahman is at last allowed to meet his royal host.

Instead of bowing to his host, Abdur Rahman says, "in the ordinary way, 'Salam Aleikum' ('Peace be on you')." Not appearing to mind the informality of the greeting, the king chats amicably for some minutes but after that single meeting ignores his guest until some two months have passed. Finally, the king dispatches one of his servants to inform Abdur Rahman that he is kindly disposed toward him and "therefore it was advisable that I should give him 1000 sovereigns and three handsome page-boys" as a sign of good faith. Abdur Rahman refuses this extortion, replying, "These boys are to me as sons. To give gold away is the part of sovereigns. I gave to the king presents, according to the custom, and now I expect gifts and grants from him in return." Ten days after this exchange, the same servant returns, this time to offer Abdur Rahman a position as a court official. Abdur Rahman is once again outraged by his host's behavior, and he signals his displeasure with a declaration of his independence and equal standing: " 'Neither is a camel's load on my back, or am I on a camel's back,' i.e., 'Neither the king of subjects, [n]or a subject of the king.' "[26]

For the king of Bokhara, there is apparently no basis for relationship except the hierarchical one of master and servant, and in his hands this relationship is an exploitative and estranging one. Abdur Rahman, however, expresses a contrary notion of the master-servant relationship that highlights the naturalness and mutual benefit animating this bond. This ideal is evident throughout the proclamation that begins this chapter, one of the main themes of which is that God has determined that mankind should be divided into ranks, that certain men should occupy superior positions, and that others should serve and obey them. While this relationship undoubtedly has the potential for exploitation, the proclamation translated at the beginning of the chapter indicates that the wise ruler will prevent this from happening by treating his subjects with paternal concern and benevolence: "Whatever money and goods I, the king of Afghanistan, take from the people is spent every month for you the people of the army. . . . It is as if [the people's] own money is spent by their own government for their own brothers and sons."

In a world of contending dynastic rivals with no strong central government, troops were quick to change sides if they felt it was in their interest to do so, and kinship was one of the few idioms a leader had at his disposal to bind men to his cause. This is readily apparent in the proclamation and throughout the life history as well. One typical example from the latter work is provided below. The scene takes place in northern Afghanistan where Abdur Rahman's father is governor. Although still a young man, Abdur Rahman has just been appointed commander-in-chief of his father's army, and he is meeting his troops for the first time: "I found the army of Kataghan very pleased to see me, and I conveyed to the soldiers a message from my father, that he looked upon them all as sons, and felt the same fatherly affection for them as he felt for me, Abdur Rahman. At this they cried out with joy, saying, 'Every one of us will sacrifice his life for our father, Sirdar Mahomed Afzul Khan.' "[27]

Kinship is the bedrock of traditional Afghan social relations, of course, but it is important to realize that its appropriation in a context like this one can also alter its meaning in fundamental ways. For an officer in command of an army—or a ruler governing a nation—the expression of a kinship relationship between himself and those under him is an explicitly metaphoric act, which says, in effect, "I am like unto you as a father to his children." Such a statement is expansive and potentially far-reaching in its consequences, for the man who utters these words is not simply trying to ingratiate himself with those beneath him. He is also attempting to transform their relationship in such a way that he can expect the same devotion from men who are in effect strangers that a father can expect from his sons.

For the tribe, on the other hand, kinship is a more rigidly applied idiom of relationship that has the effect of dividing groups from one another and making them more self-reliant. Tribesmen are also capable of using kinship metaphorically and of referring to non-kin acquaintances by kin terms, but the application of kinship categories to non-kin is generally interjected as a temporary measure to solidify a relationship until such time as actual marital ties can be established to make it substantial. Thus, kinship in tribal culture tends always toward the real. Fictive uses blur discrepancies and gaps, but only so as to preserve the integrity of the original frame, which remains inviolate and unbreachable. Kinship, in this sense, serves as a barrier to the world beyond the tribe, for so long as individuals remember who their kin are and honor their obligations to them, the distinction between insider and outsider can be upheld, and the world beyond the tribal homeland can be better kept at bay.

Gratitude and Ingratitude

In Islam, the relationship between ruler and ruled is premised on the belief that mankind stands in a covenantal relationship with God and that all worldly pacts partake of the moral force of the divine covenant binding mankind to God. As Roy Mottahedeh points out in his study of kingship in eleventh-century Buyid Iran, "In the Koran, benefits that God has granted to men, for which men are repeatedly urged to be 'grateful,' extend from the very substances of life and the beauty of creation to the blessing of revelation and the Koran itself. . . . The Koran repeatedly emphasizes that the Believer is 'thankful' (*shâkir*) for these countless benefits; and that gratitude is one of the basic spiritual qualities that accompanies true belief."[28]

The proclamation that introduces this chapter extends the Qur'anic principle of gratitude binding believer to God to include the relationship between subject and king. Thus, the proclamation informs us that positions and salaries received from the state cannot be looked upon merely as compensation for work performed; rather, they are the divinely sanctioned gifts of God, and those persons who have the temerity to bemoan their rank or to complain about the size of their portion demonstrate ingratitude not just to their king but also to God. Calculations of a material nature are clearly inappropriate within the domain of the state, and those who view the king simply as their employer debase the spiritual foundation of kingship and undermine their own position in this world and in the hereafter.

Given the importance of the military to the stability of the throne and given the fact that the army was originally composed to a large degree of tribal levies and recruits whose loyalty to the king was often questionable, it is not surprising that Abdur Rahman refers specifically to his army in the proclamation and that he cautions them in several places against invidious comparisons with those who have a higher position or larger salary than themselves. As I discussed in the last chapter, the ethos of tribal culture is one that accentuates rivalry by encouraging individuals to uphold their own rights to preeminence in the face of self-assertions by others. The functional result of this imperative in the tribal context is to limit the development of social stratification as successful individuals attract an ever-increasing number of rivals and are ultimately forced to rely on the assistance of a corresponding number of allies to protect themselves from assault and offense.

Abdur Rahman seems to have recognized the fundamental tension that existed between the egalitarian ethos animating tribal contests of valor and supremacy and the hierarchical ethos on which a successful army depended. If the proclamation is any indication, it would also appear that the Amir realized that, when transplanted to the ranks of the army, the tribal ethos of rivalrous comparison and continual self-assertion represented a serious challenge to the government's authority and his own particular efforts to institutionalize an army based on ordered ranks in which those lower in the hierarchy obeyed those higher up.[29]

Past rulers had been content to rely on the fealty of retainers and soldiers whose personal loyalty was ensured through their receipt of favors, positions, and booty. But Abdur Rahman's own experience indicated the fickleness of such loyalty, and he sought to break with this tradition in his plan to create a more rationalized army and impersonal government bureaucracy. This ambition to alter the way in which people viewed their personal circumstances is seen in the proclamation in which he informs those who serve him to evaluate their worldly fortunes not—as in the case of Sultan Muhammad—by "what people say," but by the objective measure of their "progress in rank." The status of the individual should not be judged in relation to the position (or wealth or success) of a rival individual, but rather by the rank which the individual has achieved. Accordingly, if one wants to best a rival, the proper strategy is not to attack him directly but rather to be a better soldier than he and thereby gain advancement above him in the ranks.

The fact that a soldier (or other employee of the state) focuses his ambition on promotion reflects his obedience to the king and his gratitude for the position he enjoys in the world. Contrarily, disobedience to those above one in rank and an unwillingness to fully accept one's position in the hierarchy reflect the fundamental ingratitude of an individual. Frequently in Afghan history, disobedience to the king has been justified as obedience to God, but Abdur Rahman speaks out in the proclamation against those who preface their own acts of disobedience to the state by "taking refuge in God." Recitation of the phrase "I take refuge in God" is a means by which an individual indicates his indifference to state sanctions and his obedience to God as the final arbiter of human actions. Those who "take refuge in God" indicate their readiness to defy the ruler's anger and risk punishment in order to carry out what they take to be a proper and justified action. Abdur Rahman, however, cautions those who might contemplate disobedience to his orders that such disobedience will be harshly judged not only by the state but also by God who has designated the Amir as his sovereign authority in temporal affairs.

Disobedience to the state and coveting the position of superiors in the administrative and military hierarchy are both examples of ingratitude, and Abdur Rahman demonstrates the seriousness with which he views these sins by the amount of space that he devotes to cautioning those who might contemplate either path of action. The ultimate sanction, of course, is that God will judge the individual harshly and send him to Hell. Abdur Rahman invokes this penalty in the proclamation, but he pays far more attention to those penalties that he himself is in a position to administer and that he knows have a particular resonance in Afghan culture. Thus, the Amir promises those who are ungrateful that not only will they lose their position and the privileges associated with their positions, but also they will suffer shame and humiliation: "When you lose your position, you will be walking down a street in a state of disgrace (*be abru*) and dishonor (*be ghairat*). No one will even mention your name. You will be forgotten. If they mention your name, they will curse you. You will become famous for being foolish and ignorant."

This, of course, is language we have encountered before. Abdur Rahman's threats are ones that derive ultimately from the tribal lexicon of honor and that presumably would work especially well among the deracinated tribesmen who serve in his army. At any rate, the fact that he feels the need to invoke such threats here indicates that, however much progress he may have made in transforming and modernizing the apparatus of rule, he recognizes both the danger which the ethos of honor still represents to the state and its potential utility if its injunctions can be harnessed to the interests of state rule.

Turning to the autobiographical narrative, we see that if there is a single thread running throughout this work, it is this same theme of gratitude and obedience that is so evident in the proclamation. Whenever Abdur Rahman introduces an individual into his narrative, the reader quickly discovers whether that individual was loyal or disloyal to the author. Likewise, virtually all of the misfortunes that befall Abdur Rahman in the course of his journey to the throne of Kabul come about because of the treachery of one or another individual who chooses to act out of self-interest rather than gratitude for his benefactor and rightful ruler.

Given the many misfortunes detailed in the autobiography, it is not surprising that in this document we find many more examples of ingratitude than of fidelity, but the latter do exist and are instructive. One such example is in the actions of a servant named Parawana Khan, who accompanied Abdur Rahman through both of his periods of exile and remained "the most beloved" of the Amir's subjects "up to the last moment of his life."[30] The extent of this man's loyalty can be gauged by the fact that he allowed himself to be sold into slavery on at least three occasions when Abdur Rahman needed money. Each time, he remained in bondage until his patron could secure the funds to redeem him. A second case of abiding loyalty is provided by the story of an unnamed servant of Abdur Rahim, one of Abdur Rahman's close companions, who accompanied the Amir during his several exiles:

> Imagine our gratitude when a servant of Abdur Rahim came from Kabul on foot to bring us 2000 sovereigns. The man had formerly been Abdur Rahim's treasurer, and having no shoes, had bound up his feet (which were torn and bleeding) with bits of carpet. He asked leave to return to Kabul to look after the family of Abdur Rahim, and also to execute further commissions for us. I gave him permission to return, also offering him a horse,

which he refused, preferring to go on foot in case we might need the horse for our own use.[31]

As exemplary as these stories are, the most telling case is that of Abdur Rahman himself who encounters tremendous hardships in his early life due to the loyalty that he displays to those in power over him. The most dramatic demonstration of Abdur Rahman's constancy comes in his relationship with his uncle, Muhammad Azam, who repeatedly ignores the sage advice of his nephew in favor of the self-interested counsel of his courtiers. One instance of this occurs shortly after his uncle's assumption of power following the death of Abdur Rahman's father. At the time, Muhammad Azam's younger brother and perennial rival, Sher 'Ali, remained in the field, and Abdur Rahman wanted to stay in Kabul to help defend the capital in case of attack. Not trusting his nephew, however, Muhammad Azam sends Abdur Rahman to conduct operations in the north where he could be of no assistance if an attack on Kabul were undertaken: "My uncle would not heed any of my advice, writing that if I was his friend I would go; if I was not, I could do as I chose. I was much disappointed, and felt inclined to write: 'If I am not afraid of Shere Ali's enmity, I am not afraid of yours.' But, on second thoughts, I desisted, considering that as I had put him on the throne, I ought to uphold him in everything."[32] One mistake follows another until Sher 'Ali takes control of Kabul. When Abdur Rahman sends a letter to military officers who had defected to Sher 'Ali's side, he receives the reply that "they hated my uncle, and being tired of his cruelties, had joined Shere Ali; also adding that, if my uncle were not with me, they would submit to me."[33] Not heeding these requests, Abdur Rahman remains loyal to his uncle, the result of which is continued defeat and the liquidation of his once considerable treasuries.

Thus commences Abdur Rahman's second and longest exile from Afghanistan, and it is clear from his repeated descriptions of his uncle's mistakes in judgment, of his intransigence when confronted with his errors, and of his cruelty to his subjects that Abdur Rahman felt that the fate of defeat and exile would have been avoided if he had been ruler instead of his uncle. Nevertheless, the lesson we are to learn from this episode in his life is that once he made the decision to support his uncle's claim to the kingship and took the oath of allegiance, he never wavered in his loyalty, continuing to accompany him as they searched for a place of refuge and even to minister to him when he was stricken with illness. As he self-righteously notes at one point in the narrative of their exile in central Asia, "I was more fond of him than his own son was, for during his illness, which lasted forty days, Sarwar had only called twice to inquire after his father's health, occupying himself instead with private business."[34]

Far more plentiful than depictions of loyalty are illustrations of disloyalty, particularly of servants who fail to reciprocate the trust and care of their patron. One example occurs during Abdur Rahman's first exile in Bokhara when a number of his servants abandon him to work in the service of the king of Bokhara. Given what we come to know of this particular king, we are perhaps intended to draw the conclusion that a king such as this deserves servants such as these, but Abdur Rahman is nevertheless greatly offended when, on encountering these same servants in the court of the Bokharan king, they "ignored me, not even salaaming."[35] Even greater outrage is expressed when disloyalty comes from men of noble birth and station who have benefited from the kindness and friendship of Abdur Rahman and his family in the past but then betray their benefactors. Such is the case with one Sultan Ahmad Khan, an officer in the army of Abdur Rahman's father, who was captured by Sher 'Ali Khan at the battle of Herat. Muhammad Afzal had secured his release and appointed him as the governor of the central Hazarajat province, but he responded to this act of generosity on the part of Abdur Rahman's father by abandoning his post to join the ranks of his former tormentor, Sher 'Ali Khan, who then made him the head of his cavalry. In this position, he later took up arms against the man who had once rescued him, an act that leads Abdur Rahman to the following rumination: "What can be thought of the character of one who fights against the man to whom he owes his freedom, and joins him who took him prisoner? An evil-minded man cannot be made good by culture. In gardens grow flowers, and in jungles grow thorns."[36]

While Abdur Rahman peppers his narrative with comments on this or that ingrate he has had the misfortune to encounter, he reserves some of his harshest denunciations for the ministers and officials who haunt the court. More consistently than any other class of people, it is these courtiers who bring grief to Abdur Rahman and his family. As we have seen, it was a court official who first caused the young Abdur Rahman to become estranged from his father when he convinced his father that he had begun drinking wine and smoking hashish, and it was in large part on the advice of his court officials that his father was led into the trap that resulted in his imprisonment. Abdur Rahman's uncle was equally prone to weakness in the face of his advisors' admonitions, and the Amir blamed courtly "mischief-makers" for bringing about his uncle's overthrow since it was they who "turned my uncle against me, persuading him that while I was in Kabul his influence was limited." [37]

Reading Abdur Rahman's fulminations against ministers of court, one is reminded of Sultan Muhammad's words concerning the danger of listening to the advice of women. Sultan Muhammad, it will be recalled, believed that female involvement in male affairs was necessarily deleterious to the interests of the male. A woman's perspective was simply not the same as a man's, and the interjection of women's concerns tended to confuse issues and weaken the ability and willingness of men to act in a manner appropriate to their station.

Advisors, it would appear, have a similar effect on kings; their perspective is also different and their interests do not always coincide with those of the ruler. Advisors, like women, have their place and their utility, but when the ruler allows them to get too close, he blurs the necessary distinction between ruler and ruled and encourages his subordinates to imagine that they are entitled to power and privileges to which they are by nature unsuited and undeserving. One imagines that Sultan Muhammad and Abdur Rahman would both have shared the opinion that any individual who allowed the difference between male and female, king and courtier to be transgressed deserved the fate he received, for it is in the nature of women and courtiers alike to act out of self-interest, and it is consequently the responsibility of the dominant party to control that self-interest and to keep their subordinates in their proper place.[38]

While Abdur Rahman is consistently scathing in his comments on court officials, the tone of most of his statements tends to the sardonic and rueful rather than censorious and damning. Since they are not his equals, court officials are not as much to blame for their actions as those who empower, and thereby ruin, them. The same cannot be said of members of his own family who follow the path of self-interested treachery. Among this number the one who stands out is Abdur Rahman's paternal cousin—his tarbur—Ishaq Khan, whose rebellion in 1888 was the most serious challenge Abdur Rahman faced during his reign. As the story of Sultan Muhammad illustrated, paternal cousins are perennial rivals and, under the right circumstances, can become the most vicious of enemies. But because they are the closest of kin, they also share in one another's honor, a fact that undoubtedly contributed to Abdur Rahman's belittlement of his "disloyal and traitorous cousin" as "an illegitimate child of Mir Azim, my uncle, and his mother was an Armenian Christian girl, who was one of the women in the harem, and not one of my uncle's wives."[39] Following the traditional pattern of attributing the bad character of a rival to the defects of his parent, Abdur Rahman reminds his reader of the many services he had rendered for both his uncle and his cousin and then notes: "These kindnesses were all forgotten, and my readers can form their opinion of the ingratitude of Ishak. It must also be remembered that all the mischief caused in our family was from the hands of Mir Azim, who made my father and Shere Ali enemies to each other. The same love of mischief-making was in the nature of Azim's son, Ishak, and was sure to show itself sooner or later." [40]

The first of the cousin's sins is the betrayal of an oath ("signed and sealed by Mahomed Ishak" in a Qur'an) according to which he offered his cousin "loyalty, sincerity, and allegiance." [41] Trusting the veracity of this oath, the Amir placed complete trust in the younger cousin and, upon appointing him as his viceroy and governor in Turkistan, instructed his other governors and officers to "look upon Mahomed Ishak Khan at all times as my brother and son." For his part, Ishaq Khan sent frequent missives to Kabul assuring the Amir of "his obedience and faithfulness" and always addressed his cousin "as a most sincere son and obedient servant would address his father and master. He signed his letters, 'Your slave and humble servant, Mahomed Ishak.' " [42]

Abdur Rahman claims that throughout the period preceding Muhammad Ishaq's rebellion, he continued to supply his cousin with the best armaments available to help him defend the northern border and repeatedly dispatched additional funds to augment the revenues he obtained locally so that he would always be able to pay his troops and meet his other expenses. The son proved "as false as his father," however, for all the while that he was receiving aid from Kabul, he was "collecting gold and guns, making secret preparations, and intriguing against me." [43] The ultimate sign of Ishaq's falsehood was his adoption of the guise of "a holy saint and a very virtuous strict Muslim" in order to lure the people of Turkistan to his cause:

> He would get up early in the small hours of the morning to attend prayers in the mosque, a procedure which misled one portion of the Mahomedans, namely, the mullahs, who only care for those people who say long prayers and keep fasts without taking their actions into account. . . . The second deceit that Ishak practiced upon the uneducated Mahomedans was that in addition to being an ecclesiastical leader and mullah, he entered into the group of the disciples of one of the Dervishes of the Nakhshbandis. [44]

According to Abdur Rahman, all of these exertions were no more than a ruse to entrap the gullible Turkman people into supporting Ishaq Khan's cause, but he went even further than this into the realm of blasphemy when, after the commencement of his revolt, he undertook to strike his own coins and placed upon them an invocation that placed himself in the syntactical position reserved for the Prophet Mohammad himself: " 'Lâ illah Amir Mahomed Ishak Khan' (There is no God but one, and Mahomed Ishak Khan is His Amir)."[45] Through these various deceits, Ishaq Khan is able to field an army even greater than Abdur Rahman's own, but in the end, he is undone by his own cowardice and the will of God: "Though the enemy's forces were at first victorious, and my army was defeated, yet still, as it was the wish of God that I should continue to be the ruler of the flock of His creation—His people of Afghanistan—the enemy fled, and the victory was in my hands."[46] Thus ingratitude receives its just reward, thus the man of impure ancestry and improper ambition meets his preordained end.

While all ingratitude is bound to receive the punishment it deserves, Abdur Rahman is quick to assume responsibility for expediting this process whenever possible—and in ways that ensure that others will take note. One such instance crops up early in the narrative and involves a group of bandits that had been posing as merchants so as to prey on traders traveling the road between Badakhshan and Kataghan:

> On questioning these men, they owned they had acted as highwaymen for the past two years, owing to the contempt in which they held the Afghans, and although they offered 2000 rupees per head to purchase their lives, I ordered them all to be blown from the guns, as they had committed many crimes on my unoffending people. This punishment was carried out on market day, so that their flesh should be eaten by the dogs of the camp, and their bones remain lying about till the festival was over.[47]

Blowing criminals from the mouths of cannons was a common form of execution under the Iron Amir. So too was the expedient of hanging highwaymen in cages by the side of the road so that their bleached bones would serve as a deterrent to all those who might consider banditry a desirable career path.[48] On several occasions, the Amir also chose the less thunderous, but no less effective route of public humiliation, particularly with local potentates or religious leaders who chose to defy his authority. Such was the case of a Badakhshani chief who demanded that Abdur Rahman release the merchant/highwaymen who had been causing him so much trouble. Unbeknownst to the local chief, the bandits were already dead, but Abdur Rahman nevertheless decided to teach the chief a lesson through the instrument of his messenger: "Without further conversation I ordered my servants to pull out his beard and moustache, and to dye his eyebrows like a woman's. I then took him to the place where the remains of the merchants lay, and put his beard and moustache in a gold cloth, advising him to take it to his Mir, both as a caution, and as a reply to the letter he had written me."[49]

One of the more grandiloquent of the Amir's various punishments was the construction of towers made from the skulls of rebels who rose up against the government. On at least three such occasions, the Amir had towers built "to strike fear into the hearts of those still alive."[50] As dramatic as this gesture was, however, it was by no means extraordinary, for the Amir confessed without apparent compunction or compassion to having executed 120,000 people during his life. Those who were most likely to incur the Amir's wrath were, of course, those who rebelled against his authority, but even the most ordinary of criminal acts was viewed as treasonous and liable to exemplary, if not summary, justice. This can be seen in the following description penned by Lord Curzon after his visit to Kabul:

> Crimes such as robbery or rape were punished with fiendish severity. Men were blown from guns, or thrown down a dark well, or beaten to death, or flayed alive, or tortured in the offending member. For instance, one of the favourite penalties for petty larceny was to amputate the hand at the wrist, the raw stump being then plunged into boiling oil. One official who had outraged a woman was stripped naked and placed in a hole dug for the purpose on the top of a high hill outside Kabul. It was in mid-winter; and water was then poured upon him until he was converted into an icicle and frozen alive. As the Amir sardonically remarked, "He would never be too hot again."[51]

British writers of the time (perhaps no more than those who quote them) were fond of citing examples of Oriental violence and cruelty, but Curzon at least was equally quick to rationalize this behavior in relation to the difficulty of exercising rule in this corner of the globe.[52] The Afghan, Curzon wrote, is "one of the most turbulent people in the world by force alike of his character and of arms." Whereas "no previous sovereign had ever ridden the wild Afghan steed with so cruel a bit, none had given so large a measure of unity to the kingdom" as had Abdur Rahman.[53] In like manner, Abdur Rahman asked those who condemned the harshness of his rule to compare the state of the kingdom at the close of the nineteenth century with the situation that existed twenty years earlier when he took power or even with the situation that existed across the border in the British-controlled tribal districts, where "nobody can move a step without being protected by a strong body-guard."[54]

In Afghanistan, according to the Amir, "persons possessing great riches and wealth can travel safely throughout my dominions, by night as well as by day." The hired robbers and thieves that had preyed on travelers in the past were gone. Merchants could pass unmolested on the roads, and in towns and villages throughout the country people could count on a degree of security and courts of redress to prevent the tyrannical excesses and lawlessness that had kept the country in a state of continuous alarm. Perhaps his was a reign of terror, but from Abdur Rahman's point of view the terror he directed was aimed solely at the ungrateful few—be they bandits, rebels, or local despots—who threatened the order and stability of the nation. Whatever their identity and whatever their crime, it was these criminals who disturbed the security of the realm and they alone who broke the covenant ordained by God and upheld by His Amir.

KINGSHIP AND HONOR

Having outlined some of the principles of monarchical rule set forth by Amir Abdur Rahman and the ideal of kingship and state rule that they embody, I now want to compare in a more general way the moral imperatives of kingship indicated in this chapter with those of honor that were developed in the examination of Sultan Muhammad's story. A number of similarities between the two life histories were noted earlier in this chapter, but it was also pointed out that while these two narratives shared a number of common features, they were finally about different things and illustrated opposing notions of individual action and the nature of moral authority. In concluding this chapter, I want to consider these differences more systematically, first by making some general comments concerning the kinds of texts we have been examining and then by comparing the organizing principles that can be discerned in each.

Person

With regard to the story of Sultan Muhammad's coming of age, the most important fact to note is that it was *about* rather than *by* him. Thus, the version of the story that we read was one told by his son. Compressed within the rendering of the events of Sultan Muhammad's early life that I have recorded here are, of course, many earlier tellings that the son has absorbed and made his own, but what must be noted is that it is not finally Sultan Muhammad's story or his version of events that is inscribed, but someone else's. In the course of the telling, the son "quotes" his father several times, giving him a place within the text in which his own interpretation can be set forth, but regardless of such concessions, it is clear that the text belongs to the son (and to those others who tell it) and not to the man whose actions it purports to record. The father's quotes are patently fictitious, and his presence and position in the text are wholly dependent upon the narrator, who is free to tell the story according to his own recollection and those of others who remember the life and times of Sultan Muhammad Khan.

This situation is obvious, but it is important to stress because it shows the dependent status of Sultan Muhammad in relation to his own history. The way he is remembered is not within his control, and given the ethos of tribal culture, this is exactly as it should be; which is to say, the fact that the memory of this man of action is held hostage by those who come after him is entirely in keeping with the cultural concern for reputation, for "what people say." Securing the respect of those around him was, after all, what motivated Sultan Muhammad. More than anything else, he sought through his actions to secure the encomium "the tribe said good things" about what he had done. For him, this approval was what was at stake. So it is just and fitting, first, that we discover this man not in his own words, but in those of someone from his own tribe; second, that it be someone who has come after him (we see thereby that his actions have outlived his presence on the earth—the mark of greatness in this cultural system); and, finally, that it be his own son (whose honor is most directly implicated and who has most to gain by the endurance of the father's life in the collective memory of his people).

The situation with Abdur Rahman is very different, for whereas the tribesman was ultimately dependent on what others would say about him, the king asserted his right to have his own say and to shape what people thought of him and how they interpreted his actions. Thus, when we look at the proclamation and autobiography, what is most striking (particularly next to the story of Sultan Muhammad) is the overpowering voice of the protagonist himself. The proclamation illustrates this quality most succinctly, for here we encounter the Amir looming in front of us from the very first statement: "I am Amir Abdur Rahman, King of Afghanistan." Just imagine the scene of government agents throughout the country intoning those words, raising their voices to be heard, declaring that they are "Amir Abdur Rahman, King of Afghanistan!" Each individual spokesman, in making this declaration, became an extension of the king. Each magnified the royal presence and made the Amir's subjects aware that in a tangible sense he was there, that it was his voice they were hearing, and that in ways they could barely fathom he was able to be among them and to hear what they were saying in the privacy of their own homes, perhaps even in their own thoughts. "Please be cautious!" he warns. "Think wisely and listen carefully to my words and sayings, I who am the king of you people of Afghanistan. Listen, obey, and weigh well what I am saying to you, for no use can come from lamenting later if you do something wrong now."

If we recall that the original text was printed on a canvas five feet wide by four and a half feet tall and that it was designed to be carried from town to town and read aloud in public, then it becomes clear that its intent was not just to school the king's subjects; it was also meant to produce a kind of awe and trepidation in the audience as each person listened to the Amir's message with its mixture of paternalistic compassion and dire threat, its references to everyday pursuits side-by-side with lofty quotations from the Qur'an, and its juxtaposition of simple homilies familiar to peasants and tribesmen with elevated rhetorical idioms common to courtiers and kings.

Although we don't know how listeners would have reacted to the public reading of this text, it is quite obvious that they would not have comprehended all of it in a single hearing. Much of its language is more formal than ordinary people would have been accustomed to, and that being the case, one wonders what effect might have been intended by the use of obscure language. One can only speculate on this question, but it does seem quite probable that obscurity would have been used to overawe the populace by conveying the sense of a ruler "out there" who knows more about the world-at-large and local activities than the person listening to his words. The intimidating effect of formal Persian idioms intoned before an audience of common people would have been reinforced by the admixture of Qur'anic quotation which lent the imprimatur of scriptural sanction to the Amir's declarations.

The different modes of "self" presentation in the story of Sultan Muhammad and the proclamation of Abdur Rahman are significant, for whereas the man of honor is ultimately powerless to shape what matters to him most, the king asserts a more active control over his subjects: to school them, to cajole them, to threaten, and finally, to punish them. For Abdur Rahman, "what people say" was not significant, at least not in the same way that it was for Sultan Muhammad, because the Amir had no equals in honor. The fact of sovereignty put Abdur Rahman above the concerns of reputation and appearance, above even honor itself, for the dynamics of honor entail the existence of others who can claim a more or less equal standing. Having no equals other than his fellow rulers, Abdur

Rahman was able to posit his honor beyond the reach of challenge and his actions and person as answerable only to God.

The most telling difference between the textual persona of Sultan Muhammad in his social context and that of Abdur Rahman in his is expressed in the lines that summarize the two texts. In Sultan Muhammad's case, it would be the statement "People said good things about this," which indicates that it is the tribe that stands as the final arbiter of his virtue. In contrast, Abdur Rahman's proclamation ends with the Amir himself in charge, as shown by his final statement: "I want a good name for you. I want to be kind to you. This is my desire. If you are wise enough to understand and benefit from my advice, you will see that your religion will flourish and that your country will be prosperous. May it so please God."

The irony here, however, is that while Abdur Rahman did not need to worry about "what people said" in relation to his own honor, he did worry about their utterances in relation to his own power. The Iron Amir, in fact, was as deathly afraid of his subjects' words as Sultan Muhammad was of his neighbors', and he went to extreme lengths to find out who was saying what to whom and when. According to one observer, the Amir was so obsessed by the possibility that his subjects might be conspiring against him that he set up an elaborate network of spies and informers modeled on the Czarist intelligence system that he had seen in operation during his exile in Tashkent:

> Consequently, every fourth man was a "reportchee" (spy), who sent in his private reports to the Amir. These spies were of all classes and ranks, and every large house had one or two spies among the servants who reported all they saw and heard, and as it is a custom of the country for servants to sit in the same room as their master . . . they of course hear all that is said at any time. . . . The Amir had spies in the houses of his sons, and among the women of their harems, and spies in his own harem too, while his wives and his sons in their turn, had their spies among his servants, who informed them of all that concerned themselves.[55]

Probably more than any Afghan ruler before or since, Abdur Rahman depended on spies and informers to uncover conspiracies and confound his enemies, both within the confines of the court and in the distant corners of his kingdom. Even up to his death, when he was confined by illness to his bed, it is said that the Iron Amir continued to send out his spies, receive his reports, and prepare for the secret betrayers who would seek his undoing. Thus, even the mighty Amir, who never hesitated to speak for himself and announce his virtues to the world, found himself as entrapped by others' words as did the honor-bound tribal khan.

Devotion

Another comparison between the two sets of texts centers on the role of Islam. In Sultan Muhammad's narrative, Islamic principles (or the local interpretation thereof) are seen sometimes to contradict those of honor, for example, when Sultan Muhammad contravenes his father's desire for a martyr's death. However, when Sultan Muhammad has finally triumphed over his rivals and all is well and done, he is quick to depict God not merely as compliant with his actions, but also as complicit: "Then what did God do? God did the work that they wanted to do to us."

God (through His Prophet and saints) plays a similar interventionist role in Abdur Rahman's life history through the miraculous visions that lead the once and future king toward his rightful place as head of the Afghan state. Likewise, in the proclamation, we see the manner in which Abdur Rahman invoked appropriate Qur'anic sources to bolster his authority and warn those who contemplated disobedience to his rule. Like Sultan Muhammad, Abdur Rahman not only used Islam to justify his own actions but also condemned those of his enemies who used religion to legitimate their purposes; and he too takes his ultimate victory over those enemies as divine providence: "This is the experience of my life, that if they have true hearts in the service of God, He will ensure their success. The result of my belief is, that I am a king to-day." [56]

Despite the apparent conviction with which he expresses his claims to divine support, Abdur Rahman feared the power of religious leaders who, after all, made claims similar to his own and had the credentials and insignias of religious standing to back up those claims. In response to their challenge, Abdur Rahman expressed his own contemptuous view that many religious figures "taught as Islamic religion strange doctrines which were never in the teaching of Mahomed, yet which have been the cause of the downfall of all Islamic nations in every country. They taught that people were never to do any work, but only to live on the property of others, and to fight against each other." [57]

Of this noxious breed, none was more objectionable to Abdur Rahman than Najmuddin Akhundzada, also known as the Mulla of Hadda (whose life will be discussed in the next chapter). In the Amir's view, the Mulla of Hadda was the epitome of the "priestly" breed who would gladly "extort money from the people" while leading them down the path of sedition. The Amir was convinced that the vast majority of his subjects would be content with their lot were it not for these troublemakers who were all too eager to kindle insurrection and thereby violate God's intention for mankind: "Allah says in the Holy Koran, by His Blessed Prophet, Mahomed, 'Live ye on God's earth with justice and peace, and do not be the cause of quarrels and bloodshed, as the Almighty Allah loveth not those who break the peace on His earth.' Alas! the actions of the priests are quite contrary to the teachings of the religion to which they belong."[58]

The bitterness that Abdur Rahman evinces in this passage does not simply derive from anger over the role of religious leaders in leading people astray; it was also their success at calling into question the ideological foundations of his rule that enraged him. Thus, while unruly tribes represented a practical danger to his control of the throne, the challenge posed by the mullas was more pernicious, for theirs, finally, was a moral threat. And as we shall see in the following chapter, it was one that plagued the Amir up to (and even after) the end of his days.

Obedience

While the principle of obedience plays a role in the cultures of honor and kingship, the nature of that role is very different in each. This difference is evident if we consider, first, Sultan Muhammad's decision to disobey his father and, second, Abdur Rahman's consistent determination to follow the commands of his father (and, later, those of his uncle). In the story of Sultan Muhammad, regaining the status of being "the son of Talabuddin Akhundzada" is represented as more important than obedience to the father. Obeying the father would entail that he lose his identity as his father's offspring in the eyes of his peers. This being the case, he casts off the obligation to obey so that he may exist.

This sort of disobedience to a senior kinsman never occurs with Abdur Rahman and (his autobiography would have us believe) is never contemplated. To the contrary, he complies with the orders of his father and uncle even when that compliance makes him vulnerable to his enemies and causes him to act in a manner that is contrary to the way he believes a king should act. Obedience, it is clear, is more important than being right and must be accepted even when it puts in doubt the personal honor of the one who obeys. This being the case, we must conclude that just as he was when he was the son of a king, so he expected his subjects to be now that he was "as a father" to them. Just as he risked death and dishonor to obey his leader, so he assumed the same unquestioning loyalty on the part of those who now followed him.

Here then is a crucial difference in the application of kinship in the tribal and kingly molds, for while obedience to one's father (and other senior agnates) is an important and respected tradition in the tribal world, it is one that is in continual conflict with the expectation that sons will also seek their own self-determination. The same is not true with kings, for they are inclined to judge individuals principally by the obedience that they display to sovereign commands. In the universe of ruler and ruled, obedience holds sway over all other obligations that an individual might have, including the obligation to uphold one's own honor. Those who insist on prosecuting their own vendettas rather than seeking redress through the offices of the state are committing violence not only against their enemy but also against the king, to whom is restricted the rightful use of force.[59]

Obligation

The next principle to be considered is that of obligation. In developing the comparison in this case, I want to focus on a single scene from the earlier story—that in which Sultan Muhammad brings his in-laws, servants, and tenant farmers together and seeks their assistance in carrying out his plan of revenge. This encounter comes at a crucial juncture in the story, and it provides us with our most concrete sense of how community is negotiated and maintained in the tribe. As noted in the earlier discussion of this meeting, cooperation is brought about through the mutual acceptance of the honor and right to self-determination on the part of each individual. Unlike similar scenes of negotiation in the story of Abdur Rahman, there is no claim of benefit on the part of the dominant individual, nor is there any obligation imposed or gratitude expected. To the contrary, the servants and tenant farmers of Sultan Muhammad make reference to gratitude only to deny its significance ("We don't serve you for the sake of your barley, or because of your crops or for your money").

The loyalty called forth and sworn to in the meeting of Sultan Muhammad and his followers is a situationally circumscribed one calibrated to ongoing actions and outcomes rather than fixed statuses, obligations, and privileges. The oath that the tenants undertake is a pledge of assistance toward the accomplishment of a specific task, and even if they do not know what that task is when they make their pledge, they do know that theirs is not an obligation in perpetuity and that the task expected of them is restricted in nature—even though the labor asked of them may involve their death, it will not entail their subordination, and when it is completed, so too will their obligation cease. There is, of course, an awareness on the part of leader and follower alike of an ongoing liability that attends the followers' assistance, and this liability is no doubt recognized as a reason why continued association and assistance will be called for, but the oath itself, as it is expressed in the story, in no way impinges upon the sovereignty of those individuals who freely undertake it. This is the critical difference between the oath sworn between tribesmen and that which subjects swear to their ruler, for the subject does relinquish his independence when he accepts the benefit of the king. Benefit betokens gratitude, which in turn calls forth an obligation to obey.

Like Sultan Muhammad's tenants, the subjects of the king are bound by economic ties of exchange, but in contrast to the situation of the tenants, it is neither legitimate nor meritorious for subjects to deny the permanent nature of these ties or the dependency they imply. The oaths that subjects take to their king are binding and sanctify the covenantal relationship of king and subject, much as the act of prayer sanctifies and binds the believer in submission to God. That being the case, it is not surprising that those who break oaths are portrayed in Abdur Rahman's story as particularly pernicious. As much apostates as traitors, those who are ungrateful to their benefactors are unfaithful as well to God, and Abdur Rahman assures us that they will feel God's wrath, either directly or secondhand through the agency of God's representative, the king.

Punishment

Discussion of ingratitude brings us naturally to the subject of violence that seems so conspicuously a part of both Sultan Muhammad's and Abdur Rahman's lives. Like Sultan Muhammad, Abdur Rahman uses violence as an instrument of moral suasion, albeit one that is obsessively and self-righteously wielded. At the same time, the moral valence of violence in each case is starkly different, a fact that is succinctly demonstrated if one considers a point of correspondence in each man's history: specifically, their punishment by freezing of men who have compromised the honor of women. The first story, it will be recalled, ended with an account of how Jandad took away a rival's rifle in front of the man's wife and how Sultan Muhammad punished his son for this act by strapping him in a chair and having freezing water poured over his head. In Lord Curzon's account of his visit to Abdur Rahman's court, we find an analogous story in which a man is thrown in a hole in the middle of the winter and covered with water until he turns into an icicle. The nature of the man's crime is not detailed, but Curzon does inform us that he has "outraged a woman." Despite the appearance of similarity between the two accounts, their chief effect is to highlight the difference between Sultan Muhammad and the Amir, for however severe the punishment may have been that he ordered, Abdur Rahman was still exercising a prerogative of his position. As king of Afghanistan, he had the right to retaliate to the extent of his power against an offender because it was his honor (as well as the woman's) that was violated in the commission of this crime. To paraphrase Michel Foucault (in his discussion of crime and punishment in eighteenth-century France), any crime committed within the realm of a king was recognized as a crime against the ruler himself, for "the crime attacks the sovereign: it attacks him personally, since the law represents the will of the sovereign; it attacks him physically, since the force of the law is the force of the prince." [60]

Although it would be simplistic and misleading to draw too many parallels between eighteenth-century France and late-nineteenth-century Afghanistan, Foucault's explanation for why French kings sanctioned severe forms of torture does help to make sense of Abdur Rahman's employment of equally brutal punishments. In both contexts, public executions were less about law and legality than they were about reactivating the diminished power of the state by reconstituting the injured presence of the sovereign. This was especially true of executions that posited a metonymic relationship between offense and penalty—such as when a "hot-blooded" rapist is turned into an icicle. In these cases, the penalty quite literally fits the crime and in the process, reinstates that part of the sovereign's authority compromised by the original infraction.

The same logic does not apply to Sultan Muhammad's violence because in tribal society each individual retains for himself the right of redress. When Jandad Khan disarmed his rival in front of his rival's wife, the insult was absorbed by the rival, who must seek his own revenge. As Sultan Muhammad came to realize in his own moment of crisis, no one else can gain vengeance for a man, least of all a relative of the attacker. But whereas Sultan Muhammad has applied this rule in his own life, he has not extended the same courtesy to his enemies. Rather, he has arrogated to himself the exercise of vengeance, and in doing so has transgressed not only against the rights of his enemies but also against the tribe as a whole which alone has the power to punish criminal acts (as opposed to acts of violence between rivals). [61]

That is to say, the tribe ascribes to itself the right of collectively punishing individuals who offend public morality. Whatever the crime, it is the tribe as a whole, acting through the tribal assembly (*jirga*) and in accordance with tribal precedents (*nerkh*), that traditionally decides on the form of punishment befitting any given crime and carries that punishment out. To this degree then, the tribe claims sovereignty for itself just as surely as the king, and generally the only occasion when an individual will act unilaterally against another member of the tribe is in retaliation for a personal assault that has offended his honor; however, in such cases it is not punishment that is being exacted but revenge, and the range of violence that can be inflicted is limited to a reciprocal exchange of deadly force and excludes further acts of humiliation and compensatory violence which remain the sole prerogative of the tribe.

Of the several transgressions committed by Sultan Muhammad, the punishment of Jandad is perhaps his worst since it involves an arrogation of an act of collective violence by an individual. In assuming the right to punish his son in the way that he did, Sultan Muhammad not only violated a fundamental rule of tribal culture, he also exposed the most serious contradiction afflicting the society bound by honor. That contradiction is the mutually irreconcilable desire of each individual to demonstrate his precedence over all other individuals and the opposite need of society for all individuals to submit equally to its customary codes and moral strictures. When individuals like Sultan Muhammad can exercise summary justice, they destroy the balance of power between individual desire and social restraint that must prevail if the society is to survive.

The same logic does not apply in the case of Abdur Rahman, for he is allowed, even expected, to operate by a set of ethical principles that demarcate a fundamentally different set of responsibilities and privileges for the ruler than for those he rules. At the same time, whereas Abdur Rahman has the right to monopolize the use of force and is obliged to administer justice to those who infringe upon this right, the creative forms of the violence that he employs and the incommensurate relation between crime and punishment that characterize his administration of justice place him outside the bounds of what is assumed just and appropriate, especially for a Muslim ruler. Turning rapists into icicles, blinding escaped prisoners, leaving highwayman to die in cages—none of these are condoned under Islamic law, and their employment by Abdur Rahman made him subject to criticism from tribal and Muslim opponents alike.

In both tribal and Islamic law, a clear relationship is maintained between the seriousness of the crime and the severity of the punishment, but one of the hallmarks of Abdur Rahman's justice was a disregard for proportion—a disregard evinced in ways both grandiose (the construction of his skull towers) and arbitrary (the summary execution of a tannery worker for the theft of a piece of leather, the beating of the pregnant wife of a sweeper who was absent from his job, the dismemberment of men who had spread rumors of the Amir's death). These examples are by no means isolated, and they leave one with the question of why Abdur Rahman resorted to such cruel punishment for even the most insignificant of crimes.

I am not sure of the answer, but it appears that Abdur Rahman's extreme actions in defense of his throne are similar to those of Sultan Muhammad in defense of his honor, at least in part because both cases are so problematic. As in Sultan Muhammad's story, where the inherent contradictions of honor are made accessible to view by being played out to an extreme degree, Abdur Rahman's history reveals the inherent contradictions of kingship, one element of which is reflected in the Qur'anic injunction (cited by the Amir in his proclamation) to "obey Allah, His Prophet, and the King who is from among you." In the king's eyes, his mandate is from God and Muhammad, to whom he is joined in the hierarchy of authority. From the point of view of those who are ruled, however, the king is "from among" them and therefore more like them than not. Because of his position, the king is entitled to certain perquisites and privileges, but he is never more than the first among equals, and any king who forgets that he is "from among" the people is guilty of arrogance and potentially liable to forfeiture of his claim to rule.

The dialectics of governance and dissent in Afghanistan have long centered on whether the king is primarily the representative of God to the people or of the people to God. The king's subjects, particularly those from the tribal areas, viewed the king as a khan writ large. As with a khan, they were obliged to pay respect to the king and obey his orders, but they were partially aloof; and to the extent that they demonstrated obedience in their actions, they did so in a way that made it clear that loyalty was freely offered—for now—but could as easily be withheld if circumstances warranted. Kings themselves, on the other hand, tended to adhere to the notion that their power was divinely ordained and that they were entitled by their position to demand absolute compliance on the part of their subjects.

In the case of Abdur Rahman, in particular, compliance alone appears to have been insufficient. His desire, it appears, was to see gratitude reflected in the eyes of his subjects, and if it was not forthcoming, then he would at least see fear. The desire to have his authority confirmed in the expression and posture of those he ruled led him to exercise ever greater increments of force. While that force helped secure the reins of power for the Amir, it did not endear him to his subjects. To the contrary, it seems to have hardened the resolve of many of his people to demonstrate their own status as men of honor and independence.[62] To this extent then, the predicament of Abdur Rahman was like that of Sultan Muhammad who, as he enlarged his status as a man of namus, also made himself ever more vulnerable to the assaults of his rivals. As Abdur Rahman increased his power (to preserve and protect his status as king), he also exposed himself to the assaults of his subjects who viewed his expanded power as a diminution of their own.

CODA: THE DEATH OF THE KING

As we saw at the end of the last chapter, Sultan Muhammad's obsession with honor led to the alienation of many members of his family: honor pursued ultimately meant a family estranged. But what of Abdur Rahman? What was the ultimate result of his obsessive pursuit of power and the prerogatives of kingly authority? Abdur Rahman was one of the few Afghan rulers who died in bed while still in power, and this knowledge might lead us to the conclusion that all finally was well in the kingdom of the Iron Amir. However, the peacefulness of Abdur Rahman's death masks several important facts, the first of which is that his ability to retain power was largely a result of his having so thoroughly terrorized the population that no one dared challenge his rule, even during his last years, when he was bedridden and intermittently deranged from his various illnesses.

The relative tranquillity of his passing also obscures the popular response to the Amir's death, which was anything but calm. According to the testimony of Frank Martin, an English engineer resident at the Afghan court at the time of Abdur Rahman's death, it was "confidently expected by the people of all classes in Kabul that the death of the amir would be the signal for a general insurrection, in which the army would lead."[63] Throughout the capital, the population prepared for calamity, the wealthy burying their treasure, the Europeans barring their doors and loading whatever weapons they had at hand, and everyone hoarding flour, water, and other basic provisions in preparation for the expected tumult. The city's residents were not the only ones mindful of trouble, however, for news of the Amir's impending death quickly spread to the outlying areas, leading many to descend from the mountains so that they would be there when the king finally expired: "Wild-looking, scantily dressed men came down in numbers from the mountains, carrying battle-axes and old flintlocks, and overran Kabul and the roads round about, for the news of the Amir's death had acted on them like the sight of a dead carcass on vultures, and caused them to flock round from great distances in an incredibly short space of time to see what looting was going."[64]

As Martin records, the rural peoples who came to Kabul as word of the Amir's death spread had their eyes set on booty, but it wasn't just lucre that drew them from their villages and encampments. Something else also motivated them—a desire for vengeance against the ruler who had so long and successfully suppressed their revolts, forced their acquiescence to his rules, and exacted summary justice when they failed to comply with his commands. The people may not have been able to gain their revenge while the king was alive, but it appears that they hoped to make up for this deficiency by wreaking indignities on the king's body after his death.

Thus, on the day of the funeral, Martin was informed that there was a plot afoot "to get the amir's body on the way to the tomb . . . and cut it into pieces that dogs might eat it."[65] This ignoble and religiously improper end was, of course, little different from that suffered by many of the Amir's own victims, a fact certainly not lost on the throngs who crowded the route along which the Amir's body would have to pass: "The road from the hills along the route, were black with people about two o'clock that day, waiting for the funeral procession to pass, and there was a general air of suppressed excitement among all the people as the time fixed for the funeral drew near, which showed itself in a quickness of movement and alert look, foreign to their usual leisurely style, and betrayed the nervous excitement under which all labored."[66] Given that Islamic law enjoins that a corpse must be buried by sundown on the day of the death, the host of people that formed along the procession route had had less than twenty-four hours to hear the news, leave their homes, and make their way to the capital. Rumors of Abdur Rahman's imminent demise had long been circulating, so his death was certainly not unexpected, although this fact does not make less remarkable the speed with which the Amir's subjects responded to intimations of his passing.

But finally, the hopes that the crowd might have had to disrupt the procession never materialized. No one was to have the satisfaction of watching the great king's body rent to pieces and fed to the dogs, for reports of the intended disruption caused court officials to change their plans. Instead of the regal funeral that had been ordained—a funeral that was to have culminated with the king's burial in a specially-built shrine outside Kabul—the court officials (whose loyalty and trustworthiness Abdur Rahman had so often suspected) chose to follow the safest course of action, which was to inter the Amir's corpse on the grounds of his palace. Rather than risk a popular frenzy, the ministers of court opted for the ignoble measure of depositing the remains of the Iron Amir, the man who had almost single-handedly forged the Afghan nation, in a hastily dug trench as close to his deathbed as they could manage.

Thus the story of Abdur Rahman ends in a fashion not unlike that of Sultan Muhammad, for just as the status of the man of honor needed continual protection from the potential slights of those around him, so the authority of the great amir is seen finally to be founded not on lofty principles, but rather on fear and intimidation. Just as the tribal hero was condemned to a life of ceaseless vigilance that isolated him even from his own family, so this mightiest of rulers—the man who had "ridden the wild Afghan steed"—spent the last years of his life fretting in solitude over his enemies' plots and received a final burial whose dispatch would have shamed the memory of the poorest peasant. The power Abdur Rahman wielded—a power that he claimed emanated from God Himself and that he represented to his people as a mighty tower looming over the Afghan countryside—proved ultimately insufficient to guarantee him the most basic of dignities. For in the end, the subjects he addressed so grandly in his proclamation, the subjects he looked upon as his children and whose gratitude and obedience he so forthrightly expected, wanted nothing so much as to tear him limb from limb.

4 The Lives of an Afghan Saint

There are many miracles of Hadda Sahib. Maulana Abdul Baqi, who was Hadda Sahib's servant and lived his entire life in the same room with Hadda Sahib, told the following story:

After the evening prayers, Hadda Sahib would come back to his room, perform three hundred prayers, and recite fifteen verses [*aya*] of the Qur'an.

One night, Hadda Sahib was sitting on his prayer carpet with the door closed. I was wrapped in my blanket but still awake. All of a sudden, I heard someone say, "Salam aleikum," and Hadda Sahib replied, "Walekum asalam."

I looked out from under my blanket to see who it was. I hadn't seen the door open, and no one could fit through the small opening in the ceiling. How could anyone have entered? Then I saw that it was a snake, and his head was on Hadda Sahib's prayer carpet.

Hadda Sahib said, "What do you want?"

The snake said, "Dear Sir, I have come from *koh-i qaf* [the mystical mountain of Qaf]."

He said, "Why have you come?"

The snake said, "I have come from *peristan* [the land of the fairies]. I want to marry a man's daughter, but she is from a noble family. Her father will not allow me to marry her. I know that she is devoted to you and that she has received *tariqat* [mystical teaching] from you, so I am asking you to go with me to *bagh-i haram* [the Forbidden Garden]."

Hadda Sahib said, "Where is Hadda and where is the Forbidden Garden?

"The snake said, "Dear Sir, you ride on my shoulder, and in the blink of an eye I will deliver you there."

Hadda Sahib said, "I will give you a letter, and your problems will be over."

"But if you don't go yourself," the snake replied, "there will be no solution."

(For this reason, Hadda Sahib felt obliged to go with him. Abdul Baqi said that) at this moment, when I realized that Hadda Sahib was ready to go with him, I threw off my blanket and sat up in my bed. Hadda Sahib said to me in Afghani [*Pakhtu*], "There is much time left before morning prayers. Go back to sleep."

I said, "Dear Sir, I can't sleep anymore if you're going. I don't want to sleep, if you're going to leave me behind."

He said, "Where are you and where is the Forbidden Garden?"

"I don't want to stay if you're going," I replied, and then he told me, "Okay, if you accept my advice. Perform your ablutions and say two sets of prayers."

He permitted me to say my prayers on his prayer carpet, and when I had finished, the snake placed his head on the carpet. He turned himself into his original shape [as a dragon] and made himself ready for Hadda Sahib to sit on his wing. But Hadda Sahib said, "God has not made me so useless that I must go on your back. Put Abdul Baqi on your shoulder and come along."

(Abdul Baqi swore by God that when they reached the Forbidden Garden, all of the people—even the king of the place—were standing to receive Hadda Sahib even though it was the middle of the night. His spiritual quality [*ruhaniyat*] was so extraordinary that even the king of those people was present to welcome Hadda Sahib.)

When we reached there and had sat down, we saw that they had prepared all sorts of different fruits from the garden. I said to myself, "Who will believe me when I go back to Hadda." Then I took a sample of every unfamiliar fruit I could find, and I tied them up in my handkerchief so that I could bring some memento back with us.

In one night, Hadda Sahib performed seventy wedding ceremonies. When all those people who were engaged to the daughters of rich men heard the news that Hadda Sahib was there, they came to him, and he performed seventy marriages. When these weddings were finished, Hadda Sahib said that he would go back.

They strongly insisted that he stay with them, but Hadda Sahib said that he wouldn't be delayed any further.

In short, I took my handkerchief. The dragon put me back on his shoulder. The dragon was the prince of Peristan. Soon we were back in Hadda, and the roof and ceiling of our room rose up so that no one would know [that we had been gone]. When Hadda Sahib and I were sitting back in the room, the roof and ceiling returned to their place. The mulla was reciting the morning call to prayer.

I was in a hurry to tell the others that we had gone to the Forbidden Garden, but as we left for the mosque, Hadda Sahib said, "Be careful not to tell anyone what we did."

My next thought was to open the handkerchief in front of the others so that they would ask about the fruit. When I opened the handkerchief, however, I was amazed that all of the fruit had turned into the same kind of fruit that we have in our own land. Even if I swore, no one would believe me. This was one of his extraordinary actions.

TWICE-TOLD TALES

I heard the story of the Mulla of Hadda's journey to the magical Mountain of Qaf one day in 1983 when I was in the home of an Afghan refugee in Peshawar. The narrator, Fazil Aziz, was the nephew of one of the Mulla of Hadda's principal deputies (a man known as the Hazrat Sahib of Butkhak), but I am unsure of how he came to hear this particular tale. He never told me, and I never thought to ask. He had so many stories like this one—stories of miraculous journeys, uncanny apparitions, and upwellings of power. If I had asked him the source of the story, I doubt he would have known for sure, any more than Samiullah Safi could have told me where or under what circumstances he had heard the story of his father's revenge for the first time. There is one difference, however, and that is the purported existence of a manuscript written early in the twentieth century by the Mulla of Hadda's companion, the Abdul Baqi of the story. As the narrative itself indicates, Abdul Baqi went everywhere with the Mulla (also known as Hadda Sahib) and became one of the primary guardians of the great man's legacy after his death in 1903. I don't know what ultimately became of Abdul Baqi. I don't know how long Abdul Baqi lived or what he did after Hadda Sahib died. Residents of Hadda identify the small grave next to the Mulla's tomb as that of Abdul Baqi, but no one who remembers these stories knows much about the man, and I suspect that, like his mentor, he never married and died childless.

Abdul Baqi's manuscript also proved to be elusive. The only copy that I ever heard of was kept in the library at the Mulla's old center (*khanaqa*) at Hadda. In the late 1940s, the government had taken over the center and converted the informal *madrasa* (religious school) that had continued operating there after Hadda Sahib's death into a formal government institution. Despite the change of management, the book of the Mulla's miracles remained on the shelf, but after the Soviet invasion, the entire library was reportedly evacuated to Pakistan by members of the Hizb-i Islami political party. Presumably, the book, along with the rest of the Mulla's library, is somewhere in Peshawar, but informal inquiries on my part failed to elicit any response.

Regardless of the absence of what might well be the *ur*-text, I found no lack of stories about the life of the Mulla. To the contrary, in the course of my interviews in Peshawar, Hadda Sahib's name came up repeatedly, and it quickly became apparent that he would be an appropriate focus for my examination of traditional religious authority in Afghanistan. Like Sultan Muhammad and Amir Abdur Rahman, the Mulla of Hadda was portrayed as an exemplary figure of a kind rarely encountered anymore. He was also someone whose course of action consistently embroiled him in controversy and contention, especially with the state but also with the tribes who supplied his principal base of support.

The Mulla of Hadda was also an appropriate focal point for my efforts because he passed most of his adult life in the eastern frontier region and because the period of his greatest activity and influence came during the last two decades of the nineteenth century—the same time that Abdur Rahman sat on the throne in Kabul and Sultan Muhammad came of age in Pech Valley. The Mulla also beckoned because of the sheer abundance of informants available for me to interview about his life and times. Since Najmuddin Akhundzada, the Mulla of Hadda, had died eighty years earlier, I was unable to find anyone who had actually seen him in person; however, I was able to find sixteen men in and around Peshawar who had some direct connection to him.

Of the sixteen persons I interviewed in depth, all but two were descendants of one of the Mulla's twelve principal deputies.[1] As noted, the Mulla never married and had no children. Since he was originally from the region of Ghazni (several hundred miles south of Kabul), he also does not appear to have had any other relatives living in the eastern part of the country. That being the case, the people with whom I talked were the best available sources for learning about the Mulla of Hadda, and their usefulness in this regard was not limited by the fact that they were not blood relatives.

To the contrary, since the renown of their own ancestor was a direct result of his having been a disciple of the Mulla, they retained a vital interest in keeping the Mulla's memory alive. The stories they told about the Mulla's life and activities were correspondingly detailed and lively. There was just one problem: almost all the stories I heard were fantastic accounts of the Mulla's miracles. These accounts would be interwoven with scattered bits of seemingly reliable biographical information, but the narrative heart of almost all the stories I heard was otherworldly. The question I faced then was what to do with them? What historical sense and cultural significance could be imparted to stories about magical journeys and occult occurrences?

The story that introduces this chapter is typical of the stories I heard and is representative of the analytical problem I faced. Here is a dramatic instance of the Mulla's power and influence, an influence that extends beyond this world to the magical realm of Koh-i Qaf itself. But what is the connection between this world and that, and between the miracle story as a narrative genre and the actual figures whose lives are remembered within them? Given the rational disbelief to which we are heir, the analytical challenge that is presented by such stories is how to salvage some remainder of the Mulla's life and meaning that time and cultural difference have largely destroyed. In attempting this act of reclamation, my strategy is to use the narratives of miraculous events that are available as a lens for perceiving, if not the actual landscape, then at least the moral one and how the Mulla was situated in that space a century ago.

Few of the stories I will refer to are so marvelous as the one that introduces this chapter, but most have some element of the fabulous in them and consequently represent the sort of "folk" history that traditional historians have tended to discount. Such stories are nevertheless a reservoir of information on religious belief and practice, not as abstract formulations but as lived realities. Thus, just as stories of family feuds crystallize the cultural logic of honor, and government firmans reveal the moral imperatives of kingship, so miracle tales provide an avenue for understanding the cultural significance of Islam in tribal society. The performance of miracles is only one element in the persona of a religious leader, of course, but it is in many ways the most visible and transcendent of saintly attributes, and it is also the primary means by which the religious leader demonstrates the source and nature of the power and authority that religion exerts in the world.

According to Islamic theological doctrines (to which all local cultural beliefs refer at least in part), there are two kinds of miracles: those associated with the prophets and those associated with the saints (*awliya*). Miracles of the saints are called *kiramat*, and while it is understood that saints are possessed of uncanny gifts and graces, it is also recognized (at least by the more orthodox and knowledgeable) that God alone is ultimately responsible for miracles and that saints themselves serve simply as channels for divine action.[2] At the same time, saints are privy to sights and sounds beyond those experienced by normal human beings. Because of their piety and persistence in the path in divine insight, God has rewarded a few good men (and fewer women) access to the extrasensory plane of experience known as the *batin*. Outside of God and his prophets, only the saints are vouchsafed personal knowledge of this hidden realm. They alone among the living have been endowed with the capacity to operate within and between the domains of both the apparent (*zahir*) and the hidden, and it is only through the occasional appearance of what the rest of us take as a miracle that we become even vaguely and momentarily aware of a more complex reality than that which daily meets our eye.

Despite the fact that belief in miracles is common to many Muslim cultures (indeed, to many cultures throughout the world), the subject has received a great deal less attention from anthropologists than it has from the people they study. One reason for this lacuna is certainly the difficulty of negotiating between the subjective experience of those who believe that miracles can and do take place in the world with some regularity and the skeptical attitude of most scholars that miracles are figments of particular minds and particular places. One way of overcoming this impasse is offered by Michael Gilsenan, who has focused not on what miracles are, but on the way in which they operate in and through popular discourse.

A central feature of his analysis is the insight that whatever miracles might be in reality, they are experienced first as stories. These stories, generally "endless versions and varieties of 'the same' miracle," constitute what is known of the hidden realm and reveal to the believer recurring instances of God's presence in human affairs.[3] The ubiquity of miracles in everyday discourse creates a predisposition to interpret events as reflections of an alternative causality so that everyday congruences of circumstances that might otherwise be dismissed as coincidence, luck, or happenstance are continually subjected to scrutiny for evidence of the involvement of some external agency. Simply stated, saints and the miracles they perform provide "a scheme of interpretation by means of which [people] explain and apprehend the multiple hazards and changes that play so great a part in their lives."[4]

Gilsenan's approach may not tell us what miracles are, but it does suggest that perhaps the best way to view them is as stories. Through stories, miracles first come into existence, a fact that became especially apparent to me when I realized that most of the miracle stories that were attributed to a particular saint were also attributed to others. In my interviews, I noticed that I was able to find variants of almost every miracle, although these different stories would often be told about different individuals. For example, I collected eight different versions of miracle stories having to do with the sudden appearance of many guests at the door of the saint's dining area (*langar*) and his miraculous generation of food to feed them. In each case, the details are different but the central miracle is the same. Of these eight stories, five are told about the Mulla of Hadda, and the other three are attributed to his disciples.

In a similar vein, I collected two stories whose central narrative element was a mistake made in the construction of the saint's shrine. In one case, a rug that had been especially woven for the tomb of one of the Mulla's deputies was found to be too large for the available space. In the second variation, a roof beam that had been cut was found to be too short. In both instances, the error was miraculously corrected during the night and discovered the next day: the rug being found to fit the floor of the tomb just perfectly and the beam to extend just far enough to support the roof. After leaving Pakistan, I was able to augment these two stories with a third that I found recounted in a letter to the editor published in a journal in 1882 and concerning the Akhund of Swat, who was the teacher of the Mulla of Hadda: this version of the story also had to do with a short roof beam—in this case, one intended for a new mosque—that was lengthened overnight through the miraculous intervention of the Akhund.[5]

My point in mentioning these similarities is not to cast doubt upon the originality of the stories or the veracity of the storytellers. To the contrary, what strikes me as interesting about these "twice-told tales" is precisely the way in which they substantiate Gilsenan's argument that miracles are above all else a discursive vehicle by means of which a certain kind of ethos and worldview are made real and apparent. This being the case, I want to proceed with my investigation into the life of the Mulla by means of the stories that are still remembered from his life. Whatever these stories lack in the way of precise facts and dates, they do allow us entry to an otherwise closed universe and provide us the opportunity to make sense of the moral logic that the Mulla invoked and embodied in his words and actions. These ultimately are what matter, and it is to these topics that most of the chapter will be devoted.

FATHERS AND SONS

One day when Mulla Najmuddin was in the Mahabat Khan Mosque in Peshawar, an old man came up and told him to stitch up his torn sandals. Najmuddin did so. Then the old man advised him to go see Akhund Sahib of Swat and become his disciple. So Najmuddin went to Swat and slept the night in the mosque of the Akhund.

Early the next morning the Akhund of Swat called out, "Pasanai Mulla, come here!"[6] Since he had only been there one night, he did not respond, but again the Akhund of Swat called out, "The last mulla come here!" Najmuddin thought that the Akhund Sahib was calling someone else and not him because the Akhund didn't know him. Then the Akhund called out his name, "Mulla Najmuddin, come here!"

Najmuddin went over to him and saw the old man he had met in the Mahabat Khan mosque. He performed the ceremony [of *zikr*—the spiritual exercises of the Sufi order] and became the Akhund of Swat's disciple. Other disciples were full of wonder why this person who had only spent a night there was called and received so much attention because others spend days and nights waiting to see him up close.

After some time, the Akhund of Swat told him to go and settle in Hadda, the place of the infidels, and to propagate Islam and *tariqat* [the Sufi path]. Hadda Sahib built a mosque and settled there. Gradually, he became famous.[7]

In beginning this excursion into a distant life, we should first start by considering what is known with certainty, even if it is minimal and ambiguous at best. While all of the informants with whom I talked agreed that the Mulla was a Pakhtun by birth and originally from the Ghazni area, there was some difference of opinion regarding the tribe into which he had been born and the place where he had grown up. One person claimed that Najmuddin was from the Suleiman Khel tribe and lived originally in

Shilgar near Ghazni. Several others indicated that he was from a branch of the Suleiman Khel known as the Musa Khel but believed that he was from the region of Katawaz. Still others said that he was from the Andar tribe and came from Ghazni proper. One thing that is agreed upon is that Najmuddin was the son of a religious teacher, an akhund, which is the reason why he (like Sultan Muhammad's father) bore the honorific title "akhundzada." Unlike Talabuddin Akhundzada, however, who parlayed his father's status as a religious teacher into a government position for himself, Najmuddin chose a different career, expanding on the minimal base of identity as the son of an akhund to pursue a religious education.

One possible reason for this career choice is indicated in the comment made by some of my informants that Najmuddin's mother was a widow and that he spent his childhood as a "poor shepherd." If, as is likely, Najmuddin's father was an "akhund" prior to his death, he probably served in the capacity of a village *imam*, leading communal prayers and teaching local children rudimentary phrases of the Qur'an and the basic customary practices expected of Muslims.[8] Those who serve as village imams are generally among the poorest members of a tribe, and their position is usually a salaried one, which means that whoever holds it is considered a dependent, or *hamsaya*, of others in the village.[9] Whatever the specific arrangement between Najmuddin's family and the community in which he lived, it is fair to assume that they probably occupied an inferior status and, consequently, that in leaving his natal village Najmuddin was also leaving a position of some socioeconomic disadvantage.

The second fact that we know about Najmuddin's early life is that he initially pursued the itinerant career of a religious student (*talab ul-'elm*). In choosing to become a religious student, Najmuddin was following a path trod by many poor young men before him who recognized the fact that religious education offered one of the few available avenues out of the fixed matrix of kinship and economic circumstances into which they had been born. Few individuals in nineteenth-century Afghanistan would have considered the possibility of moving outside their own village and region. Indeed, there were few incentives to do so and many not to. Most villages were self-contained units: marriages were contracted within the domain of co-resident kin, and there were itinerant merchants and moneylenders who could handle those economic transactions that village people required. Despite (or perhaps because of) the self-sufficiency of the village, however, not all people were happy to remain where they were born. Social inferiority, poverty, intellectual curiosity—many factors could propel a person outward, but there were only a limited number of avenues by which to withdraw from one's people.

On the most basic level, travel was uncertain and often dangerous, and the only people who took to the roads regularly were nomads and traders, both groups being hereditary castes skilled at negotiating the hazards and intricacies of moving from place to place. For the solitary individual, there were few available situations affording escape from the social and economic givens of birth, and the most readily accessible of these was that of the religious seeker, who was not only given a modicum of respect for his learning and commitment, but who also enjoyed a degree of immunity from harm on the highway that other travelers lacked. Generally recognizable by his scrawny beard and sack of books, the religious adept was hardly worth the attention of a self-respecting bandit who, in all probability, would also have thought twice before waylaying a seeker and thereby risking divine retribution.

In Afghanistan there was no paramount center of religious learning to which an aspiring scholar like Najmuddin would have gravitated. Shi'i students would have had Qom, Najaf, or Mashhad as their destinations; accomplished students in the subcontinent would have gone to Aligarh or Deoband, and in Egypt, there was the great university complex at al-Azhar. But in Afghanistan, the usual pattern was for students to study with whichever mullas were available in the immediate vicinity of their homes, and for most that degree of study was sufficient. More ambitious and talented students like Najmuddin quickly exhausted this source of knowledge, however, and had to go further afield to satisfy their thirst for education, usually following the leads of other students they met who would tell them about a particular scholar in such-and-such a village who had memorized so many traditions (*hadith*) of the Prophet or was known for some other scholastic accomplishment.

The religious seeker sought not only the scriptural learning to be found in books, but also the esoteric wisdom that one gained from a spiritual master: a *pir*. In some Islamic countries, there was a strict division between the scholarly tradition and the mystical practices associated with *tasawuf*, or Sufism, but in Afghanistan rigid distinctions were not made between the scriptural and spiritual paths or between acquired and inspired forms of knowledge.[10] Many, if not most, mullas were engaged in Sufi practices as well as in reading books, and it was not at all uncommon for a mulla to become the disciple (*murid*) of a pir. Likewise, the best-known religious leaders—men like Mulla Mushk-i Alam who led the Afghan resistance against the British during the second Anglo-Afghan war—were Sufi masters intimately familiar with the mystic realm and also respected scholars, deferred to in matters of scripture.

In pursuit of his education, Najmuddin first traveled to Kabul where he lived for some time in the Tandur Sazi quarter of the city prior to going to Peshawar where he met the Akhund of Swat, purportedly at the Mahabat Khan mosque. Little is known as to when Najmuddin might have been in Kabul, but a date around 1850 can be supposed, given the knowledge that the Mulla of Hadda was an old man at his death in 1903.[11] It also isn't known how long Najmuddin spent in Kabul, but after some time he did embark for India, which was the usual destination for the majority of serious religious students. Most of those who made the journey gravitated to religious schools in Peshawar or elsewhere in the Pakhtu-speaking frontier area. A few of the most ambitious went further to the great Deoband madrasa, and those that completed the course of study at this institution earned the title of *maulavi* or *moulana*. In the case of Najmuddin, I have been able to discover little concrete information about his education in India, but it is likely that he made it as far as Peshawar and was attending classes at one of that city's madrasas prior to his encounter with the Akhund of Swat.

The story of Najmuddin's life really begins at the moment of this meeting, for the Akhund was clearly the mentor that Najmuddin had set out from Afghanistan to meet. At the time, the Akhund was one of the most prominent and respected Islamic figures in India (indeed, he was sufficiently famous that when he died in 1877 he was given an obituary in *The Times* of London).[12] It is not known exactly when Najmuddin visited Swat nor where or how he might have fit in with the other deputies of the Akhund, but stories indicate that he possessed the sort of spiritual adeptness that waits less for instruction than for recognition. As the story that begins this section reveals, the match between the old pir and the young devotee was inspired, a fact that is made evident not only in the speed with which the young man learns each spiritual exercise, or *zikr*, but also in the miraculous manner in which he is guided to the Akhund.[13] The uncanny meeting of pir and disciple is a common narrative motif in the life histories of Afghan saints, and its significance is in removing the relationship between pir and disciple from the realm of contingent fortune and placing it solidly within the domain of the necessary and inevitable. The true disciple does not simply go out and find a pir to teach him lessons so that he in turn can set up his own spiritual shop; rather, the pir knows beforehand who his most important disciples will be and brings them to him. By taking this active role, the pir is not merely "recruiting" followers; he is also expediting a preordained end, and in the process making the relationship of pir and disciple as concrete and necessary in its own sphere as the blood tie of father and son is in the universe of tribes.

In Pakhtun culture, it is believed that the father is the true progenitor of his children. Mothers provide wombs within which the fetus grows, but the father's sperm provides both the spark and the material of creation. In the realm of religious relationships, the pir can likewise serve as the active agent in spiritual self-reproduction, first bringing the disciple into proximity to himself and then infusing him with the substance of spiritual life in the form of the divine words of the zikr.[14] In most instances, the pir will eventually send the disciple off to train students of his own, but from then on the name of the disciple will be connected to that of his pir (like that of a son to his father) in the chain of transmission (*silsila*) by which the authority and traditions of the Sufi order, or *tariqat*, are passed on from generation to generation.

In Najmuddin's case, he received permission from the Akhund to teach all four of the major Sufi orders represented on the eastern frontier. In providing this permission, the Akhund also ensured that Najmuddin's name would henceforth be enshrined in the spiritual genealogies of those four orders and that his and Najmuddin's names would continue to be linked like that of father and son in the genealogy of a tribe. For a would-be pir like Najmuddin, inclusion in such a chain of transmission was as significant for his future prospects as connection to a tribal lineage was to a khan like Sultan Muhammad or being the grandson of Amir Dost Muhammad was to an ambitious prince like Abdur Rahman. In all three cases, genealogical connection was the sine qua non of identity upon which all other claims to social respect and influence were inevitably based.[15]

This being the case, it can be said that when Najmuddin made the decision to leave his natal home in southern Ghazni, he was not simply going off in search of religious education and spiritual enlightenment; in a real sense, he was exchanging one father for another. Born the son of a nameless "akhund," Najmuddin was transformed by a miraculous act of appropriation into a spiritual son of the Akhund of Swat, who bequeathed to him what were to become the most important features of his identity: his status as a pir, his right to give instruction to disciples, and his prestige as the recognized spiritual heir of a great saint. Given the significance of this act of recognition between spiritual father and son, we can identify an important point of connection between the first two stories of Sultan Muhammad and Abdur Rahman and this one of Najmuddin Akhundzada, for in all three cases one of the constitutive narrative themes has been the substantiation of paternity as the basis of cultural identity.

In all of these stories, paternity has provided one of the constitutive problems which had to be overcome before identity itself could be attained. Sultan Muhammad's challenge was to substantiate his claim to relationship with his father by avenging his death. Abdur Rahman's was to exhibit unswerving loyalty to his father despite his father's repeated errors in judgment. For Najmuddin, the initial challenge was to go out and find the one true spiritual father who alone was destined to initiate him into the mysteries of the spiritual realm. In all three of these very different but also very similar stories, the solution to the problem of paternity is the foundation upon which the individual constructs his identity: as khan, as amir, and as pir. As we will see, the establishment of his spiritual paternity not only afforded Najmuddin Akhundzada the right to call himself a pir and to gather disciples of his own. It also led to the creation of a larger, more multiply inflected identity, one dimension of which was his association with his desert outpost at Hadda.

IDENTITY AND PLACE

Najmuddin became a follower of Swat Sahib [the Akhund of Swat] who told him to continue seeking knowledge. He prayed for him, and as a result he made great progress. The scriptural knowledge of Hadda Sahib was very advanced. When he had finished his studies, he went back to Swat Sahib who made him his deputy. Then he gave him permission to return to Afghanistan, but not to his own area. "You should choose a place that will become a fortress for Islam." When Swat Sahib told him this, he gave him a single rupee from his pocket. As he was leaving Swat, [Najmuddin] gave that rupee to a religious mendicant [*faqir*]. As he traveled, other people gave him money which he always distributed to the poor. Finally, he reached Hadda, which was close to the border with the English. Since he had been told by Swat Sahib to go to a place that would be a fortress for Islam, he chose Hadda which was near the English border. Another reason he chose Hadda was that religious devotees should live in a deserted place where they wouldn't bother anyone. Hadda was a dry, deserted, uncultivated place. There were a few nomads, but they didn't have land there. It was just a desert of God.

Hadda was also the name of an idol-worshipping king. His name was Hadda, and he had lived a long time ago, but idols are still found there.[16]

Individuals who are appointed as deputies to their pirs usually leave the presence of their pir, sometimes to return to their home areas or, as seems more often to be the case, to settle elsewhere. In some cases, villagers from a particular region will come to an established pir and request that he send some holy person to live in their village, usually because of an ongoing dispute that the religious person might help to dampen or because of the prestige and religious merit that might accrue by his presence. We don't know precisely why Najmuddin chose to go to Hadda. Some stories indicate that he was sent there by the Akhund. Others say that he had already established himself in Hadda prior to going to Swat. The former story is the one more often heard, but there is no definite evidence either way. Regardless of how he got there, there is no doubt that Hadda had certain physical and social characteristics that might recommend themselves to a pir far more than they would to a khan.

Although part of the area later came under irrigation from a government-built dam, one hundred years ago the area was apparently desert-like in its aridity and lack of vegetation. It was sparsely and sporadically populated by a mixture of local groups who would graze their animals and grow a few crops, as well as by pastoral nomads who would pass through the area on their way to India each winter. Located just a few kilometers outside the provincial capital of Jalalabad, Hadda was within the domain of the state, but also relatively near to the border with British India and the Mohmand and Shinwari tribal territories that straddled it. Being close to Jalalabad meant that Hadda was easily accessible and could be frequently visited; being close to the tribal territories along the frontier (but not within the territory of any one tribe) meant that the Mulla had ready means to evade encapsulation and control by the state.[17]

In addition to being marginal in a variety of economic, social, and political senses, Hadda was also marginal in a historic and religious sense as well since it was the former site of an extensive sixth-century Buddhist complex, ruins of which are still visible today. That this center of Buddhist worship became the site of a Sufi *khanaqa*, or center, was not coincidental. The site's "pagan" history was, in fact, one of its most attractive characteristics. As one informant expressed it, "Swat Sahib told him to make the house of idols (*butkhana*) into the place of *la illah il-lallah* (There is no god but Allah)." Constructing a mosque and religious center on "pagan" grounds was a common practice in South Asia: the Quwwat ul-Islam mosque in Delhi, which is made from the stones of a Hindu temple, is one example; so too is the mosque/temple at Ayodhya where fierce Hindu/Muslim fighting broke out in 1993. At least one of Hadda Sahib's disciples—the Hazrat Sahib of Butkhak (idol-dust)—repeated his master's example by locating his center on (or near) the site of a pre-Islamic ruin.

The symbolism of this practice is obvious, but Hadda had other symbolic attributes that the Mulla also appears to have recognized. Hadda, one person told me, was "a lonely place . . . like the cave on Mount Hira" which the Prophet Muhammad used to frequent for periods of private meditation. This attribution of separateness and the implicit linkage between Muhammad and Najmuddin are important for several reasons. First, Najmuddin, like Muhammad, was an ascetic who gained his connection to God through solitary meditation and prayer. Isolation from society was an important precondition for his acquisition of the spiritual insight and power that would later manifest themselves in a variety of ways, among them his performance of miracles. Second, separation from society and its entanglements and obligations was a necessary precondition for a figure like Najmuddin to establish himself as an independent political actor.

The extent to which a religious figure is bound by involuntary ties of obligation is the extent to which his status is compromised. This is true whether the ties are those of kinship or of clientage. In either case, the man of religion is constrained in the positions and actions he can take by the commitments that others can impose upon him. However, Najmuddin's choice of Hadda appears to have obviated this problem, for in removing himself from his natal kin group, he loosed himself from the pull of familial responsibility and public opinion that—as the case of Sultan Muhammad demonstrated—keep even the strongest individuals within the orbit of tribal morality.

The independence that Najmuddin achieved through social separation is seen in the names by which he came to be known. In addition to their given names, most Afghans in my experience also have at least one other identifying title, and it is usually this that others use to address them. Such titles generally refer to the individual's tribe, kin group, native area, or hereditary occupation.[18] In Najmuddin's case (and that of many religious figures like him), what stands out about his titles is that they are his own creation. Religious leaders are practically the only ones in their society having the power to name themselves rather than having a name imposed upon them. Thus, to his contemporaries, as well as to posterity, Najmuddin became what he himself chose to become—the *sahib*, or master, of Hadda.

Achieving recognition as the "master of Hadda" meant not only that Najmuddin had established an identity on his own terms, it also meant that he had evaded the limitations that other markers would have placed upon him. In writing of a parallel pattern of identification among Islamic saints in Morocco, Paul Rabinow has commented that the identification of a religious personage as "master" of a place "is not simply a case of association, or a territorial designation, but it is a claim, an assertion of a more profound connection . . an aggressive statement of a deep, emphatic, empathetic attachment of a mutual spiritual branding."[19] In contrast to this what is significant in Najmuddin's identification with Hadda was not so much the sense of attachment that it demonstrates as the sense of detachment. What was Hadda after all but a barren wasteland and a collection of ruins? Whatever significance the place had was not finally because of the place itself but because of the person, and what the person asserted in his association with this (non)place was essentially his own right to forge an identity outside the established matrices of kinship and co-residence. He would create himself anew, and Hadda provided the perfect place in which to effect this transformation. ,

If we compare the relationship of identity and place in the case of Hadda Sahib with that of Sultan Muhammad Khan, what stands out is the degree to which the tribal leader's identity involves a connection both to place and to group. Sultan Muhammad could only achieve his true identity by gaining the respect of the group to which he belonged in the place where he was born, and once he had done so, his identity was ever after linked with the Safi tribe and the Pech Valley. Abdur Rahman Khan, too, was a partial man so long as he lived in exile from Afghanistan. Although exile served to test his character and to school him in the verities of his station, the flowering of his own identity could only come about when he returned to Kabul to reclaim his birthright as the eldest son of the eldest son of the great amir, Dost Muhammad Khan.

Hadda Sahib's identity was very different from this. Abandoning both his birthplace and his birthright, his exile was in fact an escape, a process by which he acquired a new identity through the agency of a spiritual father and the adoption of a new homeland. The character of this new home is also significant, for in laying claim to a small expanse of desert ground, the Mulla of Hadda indicated the otherworldly source of his authority and implicitly rejected the criteria of wealth and power by which social status was elsewhere accrued and measured.

DISCIPLINE AND POWER

This story goes back to the time when Hadda Sahib was living in Hadda, and people were anxious to have him as their guest. But Hadda Sahib would not eat luxurious food. He wouldn't eat all the delicacies like pilau and chicken. I heard this [story] from the people who lived at that time that one of the rich people of the area insisted on inviting him [for a meal], so finally Hadda Sahib told him, "I will only accept your invitation on one condition." That person prepared many different dishes for him, but he told him that his condition was that he be alone in the room while he was eating.

Hadda Sahib had a horse and a cat. It was a very big cat. When they reached the house of the man who had invited them, he closed all the doors and windows after him. But the person was curious what Hadda Sahib would do with the food and how he would eat. So he made a small hole in the door beforehand to watch what was going on inside. He saw [Hadda Sahib] take a leg [of the chicken] and bring it close to his *nafs* [here meaning "senses," but more generally meaning "carnal self"] to smell it, and then he put it in front of the cat so that the cat could eat it.[20]

* * *

· Abdul Baqi Sahib has written the story that one day Hadda Sahib told him, "One of the distinguished friends of God has arrived. Let us go and welcome him."

All of us went out, and everyone wondered what had happened. They saw that a religious mendicant [*malang*] had come. The malang had two dogs with him. When Hadda Sahib went up to him, the person didn't pay any attention to him. He didn't shake hands with him. He didn't take into account that "this is Hadda Sahib, and I should pay attention to him." Nothing. He went toward the langar [dining area], and Sahib followed him.

When they reached the langar, Hadda Sahib went up to the malang, who said to him, "Mullah Najmuddin, feed my dogs!"

Then Hadda Sahib gave the order to slaughter a good sheep and give it to the dogs. The malang stayed for two or three nights without eating or talking to anyone. Then he finally left with his dogs, and Mia Abdul Baqi asked Hadda Sahib who the malang was. Hadda Sahib replied that he was an [Indian] religious mendicant [*qalandar*] who had come from India to inspect him. One of the dogs was a devil, and the other was the carnal desire [nafs] which he had expelled from his body. That is why he fed them and didn't eat himself.[21]

Many stories told of Hadda Sahib emphasize the single-mindedness of his piety and his disregard for the normal demands of the body. Thus, one of the things that is still remembered about Hadda Sahib is how he restricted his meals to a few pieces of plain barley bread and a semi-poisonous vegetable that no one else would eat but that he boiled and served unadulterated with any oil or spices to offset its bitter taste. It is also said that his piety led him to retreat frequently from society for extended periods of time. Known as *chilla* for the forty (*chil*) days which most individuals spend in isolation, such retreats were made in emulation of the periods which the Prophet Muhammad would spend by himself in meditation and prayer. During the period of chilla, the individual closets himself in a separate room (*chilla khana*) away from the comings and goings of the religious center. In his isolated chamber, the devotee eats only enough food to sustain himself and otherwise concentrates his thoughts on God.[22]

Periods of solitary meditation and fasting constitute one part of a larger set of disciplinary practices whose purpose was the purification of the individual's nafs. In Sufi cosmology, it is said that the individual's struggle to purify his soul is analogous to the holy wars initiated in defense of Islam. Both are forms of jihad, or struggle; and, in the view of Sufis, the jihad against unbelievers is of lesser importance than the jihad undertaken against the carnal nafs.[23] The basic instrument in this battle is the practice of zikr, for it is through the act of repeatedly reciting the phrases of the zikr that the individual comes both to cleanse his own soul of its desires and to know the oneness of God.

According to the precepts of the Qaderiya order, which is the most influential Sufi school on the eastern frontier, the adept must master eight zikrs, each of which consists of an Arabic phrase that is recited a set number of times in a given session. Each zikr centers on a different phrase, and each phrase employs different focal points and patterns of breathing that are designed to concentrate the disciple's mind on a particular aspect of the divine presence.[24] When the pir feels that his disciple has mastered each particular lesson, he will teach him the next until the sequence is complete. This may take anywhere from a few months to a lifetime. Most disciples, in fact, never complete the sequence, and it sometimes happens that a disciple who has completed all of his lessons is ordered by his pir to begin all over again.

Zikrs are obviously quite simple in themselves, and it would be no problem for a disciple to begin practicing them on his own without the permission of his pir. However, freelancing by disciples is strictly forbidden for several reasons. First, it is felt that such experimentation is unproductive and even dangerous without the guidance of the pir. The pir alone is capable of monitoring the disciple's progress and ensuring that he is reciting a particular phrase in the correct manner to produce the desired results. Those who experiment with zikr without proper preparation and guidance can be overcome by the experience, and it is generally believed that many of the wandering faqirs and dervishes one sees on the street are individuals who got too close to the divine source and forever lost touch with earthly reality as a result. Such individuals are thereafter irradiated by the experience, and while they may be unpredictable and dangerous as a result, it is also the case that they sometimes can become the channel for outbursts of divine energy.[25]

Like the faqirs one meets on the street, Hadda Sahib was thought to have experienced the divine, but unlike them he could control the power thus unleashed. Expressed in the formal terms of Sufi cosmology, Hadda Sahib (through the benevolent tutelage of his pir, the personal discipline of ascetic practice, and the spiritual exercise of zikr, prayer, and meditation) had learned to conquer his nafs and thereby escape the prison of bodily sensation and desire that obscure the universe of divine energies and potentialities from most of humanity.[26] Once he had achieved this degree of mastery, Hadda Sahib could unlock the treasure trove of hidden knowledge ('elm-i batini) and tap into the source of divine power, the power to manifest actions that other men wonder at and call "miraculous." Only the prophets and God's chosen saints have personal knowledge of God and with it the power to perform miracles. For them, the veil has been lifted, and the truth revealed. "A miracle cannot be manifested except in a state of unveiledness (kashf), which is the rank of proximity (qurb)" that is attained by only a select few.[27]

If we compare the power that emanates from the pir with that of the other great man of the tribal frontier—the khan—we notice the different ontological bases of their greatness. In the case of the khan, greatness derives in the first place from the quality of his ancestry, his *nasab*. Ancestry alone is not enough, however, for the man of greatness must demonstrate his qualities of person through a continual vigilance and readiness to take up challenges and redress any and all slights to his honor and reputation. In the process, the man of honor might very well be called upon to endure great hardships and perhaps even to sacrifice his life over objectively inconsequential matters, but it is in his willingness to do so and in his ability to recognize the implication of honor in the mundane that his own claim to greatness principally rests.

In the case of the saint, biology is important, but not in a definitive way. That is to say, a man who can claim descent from the Prophet Muhammad (sayyid) or from one of the recognized saints of the past is accorded respect for his ancestry and is thought to possess a natural propensity and talent for spiritual matters, but the realization of this potentiality is no more automatic in the realm of religion than in the domain of the tribe. Furthermore, it is also possible for greatness to manifest itself in someone of humble parentage like Hadda Sahib. As already noted, the "ancestry" that ultimately matters most is that provided by the pir whose advancement of favored disciples serves to incorporate them into the genealogy of the Sufi order(s) to which he himself has gained membership. While such incorporation into a spiritual genealogy is a sine qua non of true and lasting greatness, it is also insufficient, for the saint must also demonstrate his character and quality through his own acts.

In contrast to the khan, the most characteristic of a saint's acts are expected to be undertaken away from the glare of public inspection. Above all else, it is the self-mortification, the denial of bodily pleasures, and the continual prayer and worship that set the saint apart and mark him as extraordinary or, in local parlance, *buzurg:* large or great. While these acts of self-denial are not intended for public consumption, they come to be witnessed by others, shaped in the form of stories, and then marshaled as evidence of the saint's absolute devotion to God. These stories confirm the moral reputation of the pir, as well as his dangerousness, for just as a man like Sultan Muhammad excites the unease of those around him through the single-mindedness of his resolve, so stories of the saint's solitary exertions also generate as much concern as awe. Such men are unlike other men. They do not make the compromises other men accept. They attack life rather than negotiate it, and this approach gives them a sort of power: a power born as much in other men's uncertainty as in the saint's own capacities.

BENEFIT AND GRATITUDE

There was a Hindu in Peshawar who lived in extreme poverty and destitution. (Hadda Sahib was very famous as a person of jihad, piety and knowledge. He also had a langar even though he was poor and didn't own even a hand's breadth of land while he was alive. He didn't have any close relatives in Hadda—no cousins or uncles, nephews, or nieces. But he had a langar which is still operating by the blessing of God for hundreds of people who are the sons and grandsons of his deputies—like Sufi Sahib, Hazrat Sahib of Butkhak, Ustad Sahib of Hadda. On behalf of their descendants in Peshawar, his langar is still going on. This is because of his spiritual power [*baraka*]. This blessing is because of his tariqat.) This [Hindu] went to the langar thinking, "He has money, and maybe he will give me something if I beg for his mercy."

He left [Peshawar], and when he arrived at Hadda, Hadda Sahib saw him and told his servants, "A Hindu has come here. Dunk him in the pool."

The servants came and took the Hindu in his clothes and dunked him in the water. When he came up, they dunked him again, and then they did it again, and when he came up, there was a bag of coins in his hand.

When the Hindu came out of the water, he told Hadda Sahib, "Sir, it's enough. I can only carry this much money." The Hindu left happy, and *sahib-i mubarak* [blessed saint] just continued with his usual worship.

There is another story like this one that people tell. Another person went to [Hadda Sahib] and told him that, "I am very poor. I have a wife and children and don't have enough to feed them. I am handicapped. I don't have any job, and I can't work."

Hadda Sahib ordered his servants to fill his bag with corn. The servants took hold of the man's hand and led him to the langar where they filled his bag with corn. The man was amazed by this action and thought to himself, "This corn cannot feed us for even a day. I came with such great hope, but see what he has done."

He placed the bag on his shoulder and thought to himself, "As soon as I get away from this place I will throw away the corn." When he went away, he opened the bag to throw [the corn] out, but suddenly he saw that all of the corn had turned into jewels, money, and silver. So he closed the bag up and became happy. "He has actually given me money. This isn't corn. I had thought that it was corn, but it is not."[28]

* * *

Hadda Sahib had a great shaykh who wrote down all of the stories of his life in a book. Now this book is with Hizb-i Islami because Hizb-i Islami brought the library of Hadda Sahib to Peshawar. It's with Gulbuddin [Gulbuddin Hekmatyar, the leader of Hizb-i Islami]. This book was a manuscript. It wasn't printed. The name of the book is "Mia Abdul Baqi." The person who wrote the book was Mia Abdul Baqi. He named the book after himself.

Abdul Baqi wrote, "In the langar everything had been eaten up, and nobody had brought anything. I went to Hadda Sahib and told him, 'Dear Sir, there is nothing in the langar. People are hungry, but there's nothing.'

"Hadda Sahib told him, 'Come back in an hour.'

"When I returned after an hour, he said, 'Wash yourself and do ablution.'

"[When I finished], he said, 'Sit down and do zikr, and then come back to me in the last hour of the night.'

"When I went back, Hadda Sahib picked up his prayer carpet, and under it was a lot of money—gold coins. He filled his hand and gave it to me. My shawl became so heavy that I couldn't lift it, but the same amount of money was still lying there."

Abdul Baqi also wrote, "One day, everything in the langar had been eaten when Shaykh Pacha Sahib of Islampur arrived with 1,500 people. The food was completely gone. Finished. Someone told Hadda Sahib that Pacha Sahib had come and that he had many people with him. Here, he showed two miracles.

"One of the miracles was that Hadda Sahib told him that the number of people [with Pacha Sahib] was 1,497. Hadda Sahib said 'Three short of 1,500.' The next [miracle] was that he told him, 'Go and I think you will find two pots full of food.' The shaykhs hadn't seen any food before, but when we went there, we saw that they were full of food.

"There were only a few pieces of bread left over, but Hadda Sahib himself went [to the langar] and covered the leftover bread with his shawl. They were taking bread from under the shawl until they had fed all of the people, and after they had fed all of those people, the amount of bread that was left was the same as it had been in the beginning. They were taking food from those two pots and bread from under the shawl until all the people had eaten enough food.

"Hadda Sahib replied that, 'There are a total of 1,497 people with Pacha Sahib.'

"Someone else came up and said, 'Look! Two pots of food are full!' When we went [to the kitchen], we saw that two pots had suddenly filled up.

"All of the bread had been eaten, and only a few broken pieces remained. Hadda Sahib came and spread his shawl over them, and when he removed it, there were so many pieces that even after everyone had eaten some were still left over." [29]

The center of activity for all those who came to visit Hadda Sahib was the guest-house-cum-dining-hall known as the langar which was the principal institution through which the pir connected with both the immediate circle of his deputies and disciples and the community at large. In the present day, there are relatively few active langars compared to the number that existed in the late nineteenth century, and what few there were in Afghanistan prior to the 1978 revolution have, to the best of my knowledge, ceased (or severely cut back) operation.[30] Each of the langars served food to travelers, pilgrims, and local people on a daily basis. According to the son of one of Hadda Sahib's deputies, the Kajuri Mulla, there were "never less than thirty, forty, or fifty people in my father's langar." Many of these people were travelers "who were completely unknown. They would eat food and then go and didn't stay around. . . . In my memory, there were never fewer than twenty travelers in the langar."[31] While little information exists as to who the visitors to Hadda might have been, it is reasonable to assume that the majority were pilgrims who wanted to partake in the mysterious power (baraka) of the great man and perhaps as well to receive some relief from the vagaries and hardships of life. As a vehicle for divine intervention, the pir offered the hope of reprieve from bad harvests, infertility, sick children and other afflictions commonly experienced by rich and poor alike.

In addition to the ordinary people who were attracted to Hadda, there were undoubtedly some pilgrims, like the young Najmuddin himself, who would have journeyed to Hadda to imbibe the wisdom of the holy man. These scholars and seekers would have come to Hadda in search of spiritual insight, and they would have come with the hope that the great Mulla of Hadda was the longed-for master who would initiate them into the higher realms of scriptural and esoteric knowledge. Some who made the journey undoubtedly were disappointed and eventually moved on to study with other mullas and pirs. A few whom the Mulla encouraged remained for longer periods of time, and the best of these—those who succeeded in establishing a lasting bond with the pir—were anointed as his deputies. Almost all of these deputies either returned to their native villages or were sent out to new locations by Hadda Sahib, but they would have continued coming back to visit their pir once a year or so to receive new lessons or simply to pay their respects.[32]

According to the grandson of Ustad Sahib of Hadda, the langar at Hadda required many servants (shaykhs) and an elaborate organization to function properly: "In the langar, there were people who were in charge of bread making, meat slaughtering, distributing the food, tending to the guests, and cleaning the mosque. For every one of these responsibilities, there was a shaykh who was assigned to take care of the duty."[33] The number of Hadda Sahib's attendants probably says as much about the prevalence of the dispossessed on the frontier as it does about the size and scope of the langar itself. Without a large-scale government presence or any major urban areas in the immediate vicinity, there were few places where the outcast and the exiled could go, and one function the pir and his langar served was to provide an alternative community for those with nowhere to go. As the grandson of Sufi Sahib of Batikot explained, there were hundreds of these shaykhs at Sufi Sahib's langar, but no one was sure where they came from or to what tribe or group they originally belonged:

> Children would come from everywhere and grow up there, or a person would come, stay there, and eventually be given a wife. In Hisarak, Kot, Batikot, Dawarkhel-i Qabayel . . . there are compounds near to where Sufi Sahib had his langars. These are known as the compounds of the shaykhs, and there are also graveyards known as the graveyards of the shaykhs. Wherever they came from, they were serving in the langar, and people gave them wives, a place to live, and they would choose to stay there. They served the people and worked in the langar.

Even if these descriptions of the size and complexity of the langar are inflated, there is no doubt that they were important institutions that provided a social space unlike any other in the frontier region. This being the case, one question that arises is how exactly the Mulla and his deputies managed to keep their storehouses full enough to feed the multitude of pilgrims who came for short visits and the smaller but still significant number of scholars and shaykhs who came and stayed. According to all of the testimony that I heard, the most common arrangement for supplying the langar was for the local people to jointly agree to supply needed commodities to it on a regular basis. Such an arrangement is described as follows by Shams ul-Haq Pirzada, the son of the Kajuri Mulla:

> The organization [*silsila*] of the langar was like this. . . . Once a year, for instance after harvest, those who were able would provide as much as they could—so many kilos of wheat, so many of this or that . . . All of the disciples from different villages would do this. Some would bring money. Some firewood—we never paid for this. Since we lived near the mountains, the mountain people would bring it, dried cheese and oil and that sort of thing. It wasn't necessarily once a year. . . . If you were alive, and you went to see [the pir], you would bring something to him. If I went once, after a month, it would come back to my mind to go again. When he was coming, the next time he didn't want to come empty-handed.[34]

Whatever the actual arrangement might have been, the ethos at the center of the operation of the langar was one of boundless and uncalculated generosity on the part of the pir. All who came to the langar were to be served regardless of their wealth or position, and many stories illustrate this principle by showing a particular pir treating a poor beggar with the same or a greater level of attention and generosity as he did the visiting noble.[35] Some pirs also made it a habit not only to make food available to their guests, but also to personally lay before their guests the cloth on which food was eaten. Some also apparently insisted on giving their visitors a gift prior to their departure, as was the case with Kajuri Sahib: "When you left, he would put his hand in his pocket. If 1,000 rupees, or 2,000, or a ten rupee note, or one rupee came out, whatever it was, he would give it to you—definitely."

The most telling expression of the ethos of the langar is found in the stories about the miraculous generation of money or food for provisioning the langar. This is probably the most common theme of all the stories that I collected concerning Hadda Sahib and his deputies, and the frequency with which different versions of this theme appear makes me believe that it is one of the most important elements of the pir's persona. Specifically, what seems to be most important is the denial of normal patterns of economic production and exchange. Thus, on the one hand, the stories obscure the fact that the pir was involved in long-standing relationships with local people who supplied him with the resources for the langar, and on the other, the stories show the pir giving endlessly to others and thereby negating the usual patterns of reciprocity that structure exchange relations.

If the stories are to be believed, the pir receives all of the assistance he needs from God. People may bring their donations, but when the store-house of the langar threatens to dry up, the pir calls on God to restore its bounty. Furthermore, normal sorts of exchange don't matter. The pir gives food and gifts to those who need it without consideration of return. His gifts represent unselfish acts of generosity that are made possible not only by his own miraculous powers but also by the expectation that every ru-pee expended will be matched by ten or a hundred rupees returned later on. To some extent, it might appear that what is going on here is a kind of divine pyramid scheme, according to which the apparently boundless ability of the charismatic leader to give occasions more gifts which in turn lead to more bounty. The charismatic leader keeps the operation going by appearing to disavow any concern for the banal details of economic value or advantage. His attitude is one of total uninterest in the economic ex-change that underwrites the langar, and by maintaining this air of other-worldliness he increases the mystery surrounding the institution and mystifies the role which the people themselves play in keeping it viable.

While I think there is some truth to this sort of analysis—mystification is central to the operation of the langar and to the miracle stories that encode the langar's operation—viewing the langar solely in such instru-mental terms would be misguided. The langar cannot be reduced to a counterfeit confidence game. Its significance transcends this sort of reduc-tionism and must be analyzed not simply in terms of its own operation but rather in relation to the larger matrices of frontier society. Thus, while much of what a pir "does" for people (from "curing" them of diseases to teaching them zikrs) is relatively difficult to understand and even more difficult to assess, the langar is a public space and performs a public func-tion, and in so doing allows us to consider the nature of the pir's symbolic presence and moral authority.

In approaching this issue, it is perhaps most pertinent to begin by com-paring the langar as an institution and as a symbol of the pir's power to the other institution in tribal society that the langar most resembles: the guest house of the khan. As has been noted, the guest house, or hujra, is one of the prime elements in the tribal khan's social persona. As much as anything, it is the khan's ability to feed people that substantiates his own reputation as a man of substance: literally, a man who is "heavy" or *drund*. No individual who sought the title and position of khan could effect this claim without maintaining an active guest house where sup-porters, co-villagers, and strangers could gather and partake of the big man's hospitality.

In its heyday, the langar functioned in a similar fashion, providing the pir with an institutional base from which he could extend his influence into society and gather people to him. But while most tribal khans extended their hospitality to a narrow range of relatives, retainers, and guests, the langar served the needs of a wider public, functioning not only as a dining hall and dormitory for those close to the pir but also as a way station for travelers, as a place of congregation for neighboring tribes (and sometimes of mediation when those tribes were engaged in hostilities), and finally as a refuge for the many outcasts of society (not a few of whom assumed the status of shaykhs and stayed on as servants of the pir). In assuming these larger and more ecumenical functions, the langar provided a partial corrective to the insular propensities of the frontier tribes, bringing the tribes into contact with each other and with the world beyond their borders. The presence of langars meant that people could travel more easily. It meant that there existed a place where individuals from different, sometimes warring, groups could sit down together without anyone having the upper hand.[36] As visitors, no one assumed the identity of host or guest; all were equals and equally bound to respect the ethical precepts that governed the sacred precincts of the pir's center.

As an institution, the langar differs from the hujra in another way, and that is in how it formalizes relations of hierarchy and authority. We have noted previously that those who repeatedly attended the guest house of the khan would eventually be considered a companion or retainer (*malgarai*). Repeatedly accepting the hospitality of another individual without offering hospitality of one's own implies that one has accepted an inferior status relative to the other. Those who attend the khan can do so indefinitely, but it is understood that, when called upon, they will serve their benefactor and come to his aid. In the meantime, however, the khan's retainers preserve the facade of autonomy and even of equality in their relations with the khan, and only rarely, and in subtle ways, does one notice that there is a status difference between the khan and those around him.

The same is not the case with those who become disciples of a pir, for in accepting lessons from the pir and partaking of his food and his blessing, they implicitly accept a different status relative to the pir than to any other human being. This is the status of being "in the *band*" of the pir, which means in essence that they are to the pir as slaves are to their master. Compared with the relatively indistinct gestures of respect offered by a retainer or client to the khan he serves, the disciple is expected to act out more dramatic expressions of obeisance, as can be seen in the following "obligations and manners" (*shartuna au adabuna*) for disciples taken from a pamphlet prepared by Haji Muhammad Amin, a Pakistani Pakhtun whose pir was a disciple of a disciple of the Mulla of Hadda:

- the disciple should show politeness [*adab*] and modesty [*hiya*] in front of his pir
- the disciple should be "like a dead body in front of the pir" [which is to say, he should be quiet and non-assertive]
- the disciple should accept that the orders of the pir are obligatory [*wajeb*]
- the disciple should perform service [*khedmat*] for the pir with love [*mahabat*] and devotion [*ekhlas*]
- when going to visit the pir, the disciple should be sure to take some present—if he is poor, then he should take him a flower or even a clean stone
- when going to the pir's house, the disciple should consider himself a servant rather than expect to be treated with the respect due a guest[37]

We cannot say with certainty that these and other rules set forth in this pamphlet would have been applicable to Hadda Sahib's disciples, but given that they were written down by a disciple of Haji Sahib of Turangzai, one of the Mulla of Hadda's principal deputies, it seems fair to conclude that similar rules would have applied in the Mulla's time. If this assumption is accepted, then what stands out is the degree to which these rules of conduct contrast with the ethos of self-determination that otherwise held sway in the frontier region and that was so prominently displayed in the story of Sultan Muhammad Khan.

As discussed in the first chapter, the principal form of obedience that is expected of an individual in Pakhtun society is that which a son must show to his father and other senior patrilineal kin. In all other encounters, Pakhtun men try to meet one another on an equal footing, carefully reciprocating all signs of deference and respect so that the pretense of equality can be maintained even when the relationship is distinctly hierarchical (as in the case of a khan and his retainers). The author of the Sufi pamphlet, however, would seem to contravene the ethos of self-determination in his delineation of the protocols of discipleship, for not only is the pir to whom these signs of respect are shown not a senior kinsman, but the customary forms of regard due to him exceed those that a Pakhtun man would show even to his father.[38]

This being the case, what then is the explanation for this apparent difference between Sufi protocols and Pakhtun custom? What is the reason not only for self-effacement in the presence of the pir, but also for the larger set of disciplinary customs that encourage self-abnegation and mortification of the flesh? To some extent, the answer to these questions lies in the nature of mystical practice generally. The Sufi adept, like his counterpart in Christian, Buddhist, and Hindu mystical traditions, seeks to break away from the world of sensory gratification and ego-fulfillment, and the practices of self-denial help him to achieve that condition.

Beyond this general similarity with other mystical practices, the answer to these questions also lies in the particular character of Pakhtun culture, particularly its unusual severity—a severity that might lead an initiate to view Sufi discipline as a release from worldly stress rather than a trial to be endured. Leading the life of a Pakhtun requires relentless vigilance and restraint. A person is always under inspection and subject to censure or insult; consequently, he or she must always remain cognizant of the potential slights, insinuations, and assaults to which an individual is subject in the universe of honor-shame transactions. So long as a person remains in the village among his or her own people, the expectations of honor hold sway. There is no respite, even in the privacy of the domestic quarters, where competitive pressures are often as rife as they are in the public domain.

In the presence of the pir, however, a new sort of ethos takes hold: a non-economizing one of obedience and acceptance. No longer are there worries about reciprocal obligations. Whatever a person gives in the way of material goods for the operation of the langar is returned in the form of a sometimes tangible, sometimes intangible blessing. Likewise, even though the acts of deference paid to the pir are often returned with indifference or even abuse, it is not a matter of concern. The disciple does not feel slighted or aggrieved, for the ways of the saints are mysterious; therefore, the disciple must simply accept his treatment, for calculations of goods given and goods gained or of honors paid and received are not in accordance with the saintly ethos.

When the disciple is in the precincts of his pir, he conforms to the pir's rules, and he is grateful for the opportunity to do so, for the palpable recompense of his obedience is a unique sort of freedom that he can experience nowhere else. This freedom comes from letting go, from dropping the ever-present vigilance that an individual must maintain in the perilous world of tribal culture. Because the pir is situated outside the domain of day-to-day social and political relations, the disciple knows that his interactions with the pir are separate from the rest of his life and can be left behind when the everyday world is reentered.[39]

PURITY AND POLITICS

Once when Hadda Sahib was staying in Jalalabad, he said to Hazrat Sahib of Butkhak, "Go outside and listen, and tell me what you hear."

It was a peaceful night, and Hazrat Sahib soon came back inside. Hadda Sahib asked him, "What did you hear?"

Hazrat Sahib replied, "Dear Sir, I listened in every direction, and I heard nothing but the sound of people praising God and zikr."

Hadda Sahib said, "Once when I was a student, I was walking along in the heat of the summer and passed by Jalalabad. (Jalalabad is now very developed, but long ago it was a desert. Around the city there was only sand and no trees—only a kind of white plant that grew in the sand. It was just a small town. Nothing was there.) When I reached Reg-i Shahmard Khan, I put down my books. It was summer and hot. When I reached Reg-i Shahmard Khan, I just fell down. I spread my shawl out on the ground, but because of the heat and the mosquitoes, I couldn't sleep. I was also hearing the sound of singing and music rising up.

"I raised my head, turned my face to the sky, and said, 'Oh God, please send a person to change all these evil acts to positive ones. Change the people's corruption [*fasad-i'alam*] to the people's improvement [*aslah-i'alam*].'

"I prayed and prayed and prayed, and then I went to Swat Sahib and took his hand, and after he accepted me and made me his deputy, he gave me permission to come to Hadda (which is located about five or six miles south of Jalalabad). Swat Sahib told me, 'You shall stay there.'

"As I told you, when I was passing through there, I didn't hear any sound except that of music and nonsense, shouting, screaming, and carrying on. But tonight you are telling me that you hear the sound of [people] praising God and zikr. See how God has changed this place from that time until now. The changes will come through a person who himself has accepted the change. If he himself has not changed, then he cannot change others."[40]

There is an odd disparity between the respect that was shown to the pir and his lack of concrete authority. Scores of people came to pay their respects to the pir, and many of those who visited humbled themselves before the great man in token of their respect, but in practical terms the pir's authority did not extend much beyond the limits of his own center; for example, whereas the pir had a staff of attendant shaykhs to tend to his needs and handle the daily management of the langar, he did not have a force that could be called on to support him in the way that a khan's cohort of retainers could be called on to bully an adversary or appropriate a piece of land. Likewise, the nonresident disciples visited the center only intermittently and resumed their other commitments once they were out of the pir's presence, and only under certain rare circumstances would they enlist en masse to accomplish a political objective.

Although pirs could not extend their influence in the forceful ways available to a khan or a ruler, they did possess certain means by which to advance their authority. One was a practice known as *amir bil maruf* (commanding people to the proper practice and faith), according to which the pir would summon other scholars and Sufis to accompany him on a tour of local villages. In each village, the pir and other members of his entourage would preach in the mosque, encouraging the people to abandon those traditional customs that were not condoned in Islam and to embrace those that were. The customs most often enjoined included such time-honored practices as the collection of bride-price (*wulja*) and interest (*sud*), as well as singing and dancing at weddings and other celebrations.

While religious condemnations of customary practices were couched in the language of piety and proper worship, they also had clear political overtones, and there was at least one instance in which the Mulla's efforts to purify the faith brought him into competition with another religious leader who was also intent on extending his authority in the frontier. That other leader was the Mulla of Manki (Manki being a village on the British side of the border within the British zone of control), who was also a disciple of the Akhund of Swat, and, like Hadda Sahib, a figure of some renown among the frontier tribes. Though the details of their relationship are sketchy, it appears that the Mulla of Manki and Hadda Sahib had a long-standing rivalry that finally culminated in 1896 when the two religious leaders faced off over an issue of how properly to perform the act of prayer (*namaz* or *salat*).

Specifically, their dispute centered on the issue of whether it was appropriate for the worshipper to raise his finger at certain specific points in the sequence of recitations and prostrations that make up the prayer ritual. Hadda Sahib, citing one set of Traditions (hadith) of the Prophet Muhammad, claimed that it was. The Manki Mulla, marshaling his scriptural evidence, argued the opposite point of view—that the finger should not be raised. At stake in this confrontation was not only the proper conduct of ritual but also who was to be recognized as the paramount authority on religious matters in the frontier region. In April 1896 the two rivals met in the Mohmand village of Gandhab in front of an assembly of about eight thousand mullahs and spectators and, over several days, debated their respective positions.[41]

Such debates were nothing new to the frontier. In fact, they appear to have been treated as something of a sport and often attracted a large audience of spectators. Few of these spectators would have understood the theological nuances under debate, but that would not have prevented them from enjoying the sight of men squared off in contest, as illustrated in this description by Sayyid Bahauddin Majrooh:

> The best fight was disputation between two well-known maulavis. Each one would come with a large following of his students and donkey-loads of commentary books in Arabic. Arguments against arguments, objections against objections, books against books were produced. The disputation, interrupted by prayers, meals and sleep, was resumed the following morning and would continue for days. Strong emotion of anger, exchange of insults and occasionally physical fighting among the rival students were integral parts of the art of disputation.[42]

Sometimes debates would be sponsored by members of a particular tribe or village who would supply room and board for the disputants and their followers. In other cases, a debate might be paid for by a local chief, who would pit a religious scholar resident in his area against that of a rival leader, in order to gain merit and prestige for himself. In the case of the debate between Hadda Sahib and the Manki Mulla, however, it appears that the two principal protagonists were operating independently and on their own behalf.[43] Given this fact, the dispute is significant for showing the ways in which spiritual leaders could become embroiled in the same kind of political entanglements that engaged other political figures in the frontier region. As noted previously, a man of honor is judged by the rivals he keeps. The more famous an individual becomes, the more likely it is that he will attract the attention of others who want what he has. The most common form of rivalry is tarburwali, which pits patrilateral first cousins against one another. Variations of such rivalries are found in almost every frontier village, and, as the story of Sultan Muhammad illustrates, in their many permutations they constitute a fundamental element of Pakhtun social structure.[44]

While the Hadda and Manki Mullas were outside of the tribal system, they do not seem to have been exempt from the rivalries that the tribal system engendered. To the contrary, their own competition can be thought of as a variation on the tarburwali pattern since both Hadda Sahib and Manki Mulla were disciples of the Akhund of Swat and therefore something like "spiritual cousins." In the tribal universe, cousin rivalry is endemic at least in part because cousins share a joint estate and are condemned by circumstance to live in close proximity with one another throughout their lives (see chapter 1). Spiritual cousins are more fortunate, perhaps, because they have the advantage of mobility, and it appears that the disciples of important pirs like the Akhund of Swat and Hadda Sahib purposely located themselves at some distance from other disciples so that they would not be competing with one another for support.[45] Nevertheless, it sometimes happened that spheres of influence overlapped and as a result, occasioned spirited rivalries such as that between the Manki and Hadda Mullas.[46]

PIRS AND PRINCES

> Someone reported to Abdur Rahman that Hazrat Sahib [of Butkhak, one of Hadda Sahib's deputies] was giving langar, and Abdur Rahman wanted to know where the expenditures were coming from. "What is the source of his income? Is he an alchemist or something?" Then Abdur Rahman said, "Bring him to me, so I can ask him face-to-face!"
>
> The day that Hazrat Sahib came was a Friday, and Abdur Rahman ordered that [Hazrat Sahib's] prayer carpet be put in the front row [of the mosque]. After the Friday prayers, Abdur Rahman said to him, "I caused trouble for you [in the past]. Now I want to ask you something. Should I ask it here or in private?"
>
> Hazrat Sahib replied, "There is nothing special about my activities, so go ahead and ask."
>
> "I want to know what is the source of your income when you give langar. You have so many expenses. What is the source?"
>
> [Hazrat Sahib] said to him, "Are you a king?"

[Abdur Rahman] replied, "Yes."

"Suppose I come from Butkhak or the mountains and I bring you a gift of a hundred rupees or one hundred rupees worth of gifts. So I, as a poor man, give these things to you. What would you, as a king, do in return?"

He replied, "If you bring a hundred, I must put 1,000 or 2,000 rupees in front of you."

[Hazrat Sahib] said, "This is my alchemy—that I give a piece of bread in the name of God, and He gives me ten in exchange. If I expend one ser [approximately 16 pounds], then immediately God gives me ten ser. If I spend one rupee, God finds ten rupees for me. If you like this kind of alchemy, then you should start giving langar to people and the income will also be coming to you from every direction. This is my alchemy."

* * *

When Hadda Sahib became popular as a saint, his influence grew, and people were coming to him all the time. One of the distinguishing characteristics for which Abdur Rahman was known was his suspicion of those who were becoming influential among the people. When someone was becoming popular among the people, he would feel threatened and worry that he would be challenged. Then he would find pretexts for arresting or expelling that person from the country.

[Abdur Rahman] started opposing Hadda Sahib and tried to destroy his reputation. Finally, he decided to arrest Hadda Sahib, so Hadda Sahib left his home during the night. He left his home in Kabul during the middle of the night, and he reached Miran-i Zarbacha [in the Shinwar territory] before dawn. The people who lived there at that time were his followers. Since they were memorizers [qari] of the Qur'an, they were his sincere devotees. He spent the night there, and when the people of Shinwar were informed [of his arrival], all of them stood determined and expressed their readiness to fight Abdur Rahman.

Hadda Sahib told them, "Jihad against Muslims is forbidden because it will result in the shedding of Muslim blood. I don't want you to start fighting with him. I am going to the border so I will be beyond his authority. I want other Muslims to remain at peace and do not want to have their blood spilled."

Then the father of Feroz Khan—I can't remember his name—

and some people of Mohmand Dara took Hadda Sahib to the ferry crossing. They crossed the river and took him themselves to Mohmand—the free tribal area [*azad qabayel*]. When Hadda Sahib arrived there, his fame increased.

At that time, Hazrat Sahib was in Butkhak, and Abdur Rahman was saying things about Hadda Sahib. At that time, some spies brought a report to Abdur Rahman, "Hazrat Sahib has called you an infidel [*kafir*]. He has given his judgment against you as an infidel."

So Abdur Rahman summoned Hazrat Sahib, and one of my uncles named Azim Jan, who was a young boy at that time, says that he was with him. He says, "I thought if they put him in prison, I'd like to be with him to serve him." He says, "When they took Hazrat Sahib there, they told him to sit and wait."

(Abdur Rahman was a very intimidating king. He was cruel [*zalem*] and merciless [*be rahm*].)

When Abdur Rahman was face-to-face with Hazrat Sahib, he asked him, "Is it true that you called me an infidel?" He told him, "I received reports that you have given a verdict of infidelity against me."

Hazrat Sahib told him, "Our religious law (*shari'at*) doesn't permit a Muslim to call another Muslim an infidel."

(This is in accord with Shari'at law. If any Muslim calls another Muslim an infidel, he himself will be the one who is an infidel.)

Then Hazrat Sahib said to him, "I received some reports that you used bad words against Hadda Sahib who is the leader of the people (*muqtada-i 'alam*). If you have called him these names, then you are an infidel. Do you understand?"

(In other words, "I may have given the judgment against you, but only if you have used these words. Then you are an infidel.")

Then Abdur Rahman used bad words against Hadda Sahib in front of Hazrat Sahib. He even called him a kafir. Hazrat Sahib said, "Now I am sure that you have become an infidel."

Then Abdur Rahman ordered that the beard of Mubarak [Hazrat Sahib] be pulled out. He commanded them to tear it out by the roots, and he issued the order for his execution.

Hazrat Sahib said, "You can't kill me because [the Qur'an] says that God is the only one in the position of life and death. . . . God's is the only power. You are something that can't even cure its own leg." (Abdur Rahman's leg was crippled. He had a problem with his leg that caused him to limp.) "Life and death are in God's hands. If you have the power to kill someone, then you should also have the power to bring them back as well. If you can do that, go to the graveyard and bring someone back to life."

When Abdur Rahman ordered them to tear his beard out by the roots, Hazrat Sahib said, "Thanks be to God. I have been ready to sacrifice my jugular vein, but so far I have suffered very little. I am thankful that this thing has happened in the path of Islam."

The order of execution was not carried out, but seven ser and one *charak* [approximately 4 pounds] of shackles and chain were placed on his feet, and five charak of handcuffs were placed on his wrists: in all, more than eight and a half sers [about 140 pounds]. But when they took Hazrat Sahib to prison with those eight and a half ser of shackles and chains, they broke by themselves.

The jailer told him, "I know that the chains have broken of their own accord, but if Abdur Rahman sees that the chain is not on your neck, he will kill me. If he finds out that you are not wearing your chains, he will accuse me of opening them." Then when Mubarak [Hazrat Sahib] finished his ablution and prayers, he would put the nail [securing the chains] back in place.

He was in prison for two years and some months. Then one day, Tur, the jailer, asked him, "Why don't you put these handcuffs back on?"

Hazrat Sahib told him to come fix them himself. "I won't fix them anymore."

When Tur tried to fix them, they would just break again. Then Hazrat Sahib said to him, "If you can't fix them, why should I?"

Then Tur went to Abdur Rahman and told him that, "We are putting the chains on, but they are breaking by themselves," and Abdur Rahman said, "If they won't remain secure on him, don't put them on."

Every night his bed would turn over, and [Abdur Rahman] would see in his dreams Hazrat Sahib with his *shalgi* [an iron-tipped staff sometimes carried by faqirs]. Hazrat Sahib would say to him, "Shall I stab you, tyrant?," and Abdur Rahman would shout out in his sleep. Then he ordered that the shackles be removed.

During the two years [that Hazrat Sahib was in prison], Abdur Rahman's bed turned over many times, and he saw Hazrat Sahib many times in his dreams.

When Abdur Rahman died, his son, Amir Habibullah Khan, came and kissed the beard of Hazrat Sahib and asked him to excuse his father. Hazrat Sahib said, "I have forgiven all Muslims."[47]

In his autobiography, Abdur Rahman freely admits his antipathy for religious leaders, and from the evidence obtained in my various interviews the feeling appears to have been reciprocated. This is not surprising. A common theme in Sufi narratives is precisely this animosity between the power of the state and the power of religion, and many of the stories told about Hadda Sahib and his deputies, including the ones presented here, reflect this tension.[48] The first of the two stories begins with Abdur Rahman learning through his network of informants of the extraordinary bounty of the langar operated by the Hazrat Sahib of Butkhak. Suspicious, Abdur Rahman goes to see for himself what sort of magic the pir is employing that allows him to supply endless amounts of food to the people.

When Abdur Rahman meets Hazrat Sahib, the Amir expresses his discomfort at speaking in public. We infer that he is used to working in secret—his is the world of manipulation and intrigue. Not so with Hazrat Sahib, who makes it clear that he has nothing to hide from others. His power comes from God alone, and he has no need to cut covert deals—with the king or anyone else. Abdur Rahman then asks the question that has been preying on his mind: how could a humble man like Hazrat Sahib with no apparent source of income manage to feed the streams of people coming day and night to his langar? To Abdur Rahman, this phenomenon is inexplicable and makes him suspicious. Could the pir be a magician of some sort or an agent of the British? And, even if he is neither of these things, the pir is still dangerous, for he attracts people's attention and draws them to him.

To answer the Amir's question, Hazrat Sahib asks one of his own which succinctly illustrates the difference between their two modes of operation. The question concerns what the Amir would do if Hazrat Sahib were to give him a valuable gift. Abdur Rahman's response is to indicate that as ruler, he would be obliged to outdo the pir's gift ten- or twenty-fold. This is the nature of his power: he can allow no one to hold an advantage over him, for to do so would be to admit the other as an equal to himself. To this admission, Hazrat Sahib has his own reply. His authority does not derive from wealth, nor is it subject to contestation. Like the Amir, he can cause vast riches to materialize on demand, but it is God who is ultimately responsible for these riches, not Hazrat Sahib. Unlike the Amir, he feels no need to prove his worth by outdoing potential rivals. He is not required by his position to overwhelm the potential gifts of others and thereby render them socially inferior. Nor does he manifest any particular interest in the quantity of goods moving through his langar. He is merely the agent for this alchemy of riches. The benefactor is God, and it is to God that thanks are due.

Whereas the story does not explicitly challenge the authority of the king, the challenge is nevertheless present, grounded in the contrary notion of benefit and gratitude espoused by the Hazrat. As noted in the last chapter, the king bestows benefits on his subjects and demands gratitude and obedience in return. This story, however, shows the limits of this equation, first, through its implicit depiction of the Amir's use of benefits as a measure of his own dominance, and second, through its demonstration that the king's benefits are not as impressive as they might seem, at least when compared to the greater benefits freely provided by God. The king's attitude is that he is the central conduit through which benefit is bestowed upon the community, but the pir contravenes this notion and demonstrates that all those in a position to provide benefit are merely custodians of God's bounty and that, consequently, gratitude is finally due to God alone. In this sense, the pir's resolute disinterest in the dynamics of material exchange communicates the message that material benefit is not a basis of temporal authority because it is not any person's to give. God alone produces the material resources on which human life depends, and consequently the act of taking credit for that production must be seen as an act of unlawful appropriation.

The second story is more discursive and explicit in its points. The king is afraid of crowds because they are a challenge to his power, and so whenever large groups of people gather, he tries to eliminate the person responsible. In this case, the author of the Abdur Rahman's discontent is Hadda Sahib himself who is forced to flee Kabul in the middle of the night to evade the Amir's plot. However romanticized it might be, this episode does accord with the apparent facts of Hadda Sahib's life. Sometime in the late 1880s, he managed to incur the Amir's distrust and animosity.[49] In an effort to limit Hadda Sahib's power, the Amir tried to convince other mullas to declare Hadda Sahib a "Wahhabi," which is to say, a follower of the militant Arabian leader, Abdul Wahhab, who advocated the demolition of saint shrines and the discontinuation of other beliefs and practices unsanctioned by the Qur'an and the hadith of the Prophet.

Time and again, Afghans have rejected and expelled religious reformers who urged them to abandon their traditional beliefs and practices, and the Amir's accusation was clearly intended to tap this conservative current as a means of discrediting the Mulla with his followers.[50] However, given the Mulla's status as a Sufi pir and the seemingly un-Wahhabi-like quality of his career, the Amir's choice of tactics appears strange, and perhaps desperate. The initiative failed, apparently because Abdur Rahman was unable to convince a large enough number of religious leaders to support his efforts. Subsequently, the Amir reversed directions, asking Hadda Sahib to serve as a mediator when the Ghilzai tribal confederacy rose up against the state. Himself a Ghilzai by birth, Hadda Sahib initially agreed to undertake the assignment on the condition that the Amir agree to limit taxes collected from his subjects. Abdur Rahman refused to accede to this demand and reportedly tried to have the Mulla secretly killed, but Hadda Sahib discovered the plot.

Effecting his escape from Kabul, Hadda Sahib journeyed first to the territory of the Shinwari tribe, which is in fact not far from Hadda itself. Presumably, the Mulla had disciples among the tribe, but he was also familiar with the tribe's leaders from an earlier visit in 1883.[51] On that occasion, Abdur Rahman had sent him to negotiate an end to a long period of antagonism between the tribe and the government, and he had been successful in his mission. Now, four years later, Hadda Sahib openly denounced the Amir as an infidel and was greeted with warm support by the Shinwaris who declared their own willingness to accept the Mulla as their king (*padshah*). In the story, Hadda Sahib refuses this suggestion because of his desire not to "shed Muslim blood." According to Kakar, the Mulla refused because "he did not intend to enter politics."[52] Whatever the reason, the narrative coincides with archival accounts in indicating that the Mulla chose to leave Shinwari territory and continue on to the Mohmand districts, north of the Khyber Pass. Like the Shinwari lands, the Mohmand area was also free of government control, and it had often provided a refuge for political opponents of the British and Afghan states.

Our story is silent about the Mulla's flight and long sojourn among the Mohmand (he was to remain there until after Abdur Rahman's death in 1901). Instead, the narrative shifts to the Mulla's disciple, Hazrat Sahib of Butkhak, who was imprisoned by the Amir about the time of the Mulla's flight. This change in focus occurs partly because the narrator of the story is the grandson of Hazrat Sahib, but it is also because Hazrat Sahib had a more dramatic encounter with the king than did Hadda Sahib, who managed to escape.[53] This episode accords with the known facts, for it is entirely consistent that the Amir would try to force Hazrat Sahib to demonstrate his loyalty to the state by issuing an edict of infidelity against his pir, Hadda Sahib.

It is not simply the reputation of an individual that is at stake in this story, however. Far more significant is the question of which of two different authorities has the right to declare someone an infidel. Through his network of spies, the Amir has discovered that Hazrat Sahib has condemned him. When confronted with this charge, Hazrat Sahib avoids openly stating whether he is guilty as charged, but he does indicate what actions on the part of the Amir would confirm his status as an infidel. Since no Muslim has the right to call any other Muslim an infidel, the Amir has effectively condemned himself in his attacks on Hadda Sahib.[54] For his part, Hazrat Sahib is careful not to fall into the same trap of making unlawful pronouncements. Cleverly, he states the conditions within which a declaration of infidelity would be justified and then allows the Amir to fulfill them, thus making it self-evident to the listener who is in the right and who is in the wrong.

On one level, this dispute seems rather like schoolyard taunting, but the dynamics here are profoundly important. What is at stake in this semantic contest is the right to make pronouncements and categorizations of the most vital sort. The right to decide whether or not someone is a believer carries with it the power of inclusion and exclusion from the community. Abdur Rahman clearly wants this right for himself.[55] As we saw in the last chapter, he preserves to himself the right to appoint each individual to his rightful place and to receive in turn the gratitude that this right carries with it: "Each one stands in his own place and position, and hence you people should be grateful to God and to the King." There is a crucial problem with this equation, however, and that is that the king's authority ultimately derives from God, and while it is understood that God desires one individual to rise above the rest and lead the community of the faithful, there is no specific set of guidelines that can indicate who that individual should be. As we have seen, Abdur Rahman claims that right on the basis of his own qualities of just leadership (dramatically illustrated in the autobiography) and through the mystical vehicle of dreams.

In this story, an alternative framework for determining legitimacy is offered to counter Abdur Rahman's claims. The first element of this framework is control over Islamic legal precedents. Traditionally, Islamic kings have always had to rely on the legal advice and consent of scholars to approve their edicts. Abdur Rahman was no different; he too had to secure the approval of Islamic clerics when he wanted to institute a change in the established way of conducting business or when he wanted to exercise force to secure the obedience of his subjects. In most instances, for example, in the case of a tribal uprising, this approval was not difficult to obtain, but when he sought to attack one of their own number, the clerics bridled and asserted their authority to check his power. That is what is at issue when Hazrat Sahib counters Abdur Rahman's efforts to secure Hadda Sahib's condemnation. The judgment of infidelity is the ultimate sanction that can be leveled against a Muslim: it entails exclusion from the community of the faithful at the least, and execution at the most. Hazrat Sahib not only denies the Amir the right to wield this weapon, he also turns that weapon upon him: illegitimate use of power by the sovereign makes the sovereign himself illegitimate.

This is the first of several reversals that we see in the story. The second comes when the Amir attempts to punish Hazrat Sahib. The Amir pulls out the saint's beard and throws him in prison bound in heavy iron handcuffs, leg irons, and chains. The saint, however, welcomes his punishment and, in so doing, transforms Abdur Rahman's use of symbolic violence (his infliction of a physical punishment that not only harms the body but also communicates a message) into a source of power for himself. That is to say, the saint undermines the absolute nature of the king's sovereignty by conveying his own message of pleasure at having pain inflicted upon himself.

The source of the saint's pleasure is the opportunity that Abdur Rahman's violence affords Hazrat to compare the puny power of temporal violence in relation to the ultimate power of God to bring about life and death, pain and healing. The saint's power, it has been noted, comes from his own actions, particularly his acts of self-abnegation. The king's torment and temptation may be unbearable for most men, but they are a mere shadow of the torment and temptation that Sufi adepts face during their extended retreats in the chilla khana. The king's punishment is therefore welcomed by the saint, for he can do nothing to the saint that the saint has not already done to himself. In communicating pleasure in his predicament, Hazrat Sahib contemptuously derides the limited power of the king while also declaring his own gratitude for the opportunity which the Amir has provided him to demonstrate his faith. The king's prerogative not only to exercise justice but also to inflict a surplus of violence—a prerogative that we saw in the last chapter as central to Abdur Rahman's authority—is thereby taken from him. So, ironically, is his right to expect gratitude and obedience from his subjects, for here gratitude is expressed for the Amir's "benefits" but in a manner that makes a mockery of the Amir's power.

The final reversal in the story comes in the end when the saint uses the means at his disposal to inflict his own pain on the king. Significantly, the principal vehicle for this reversal comes through the medium of dreams which is one of the avenues by which Abdur Rahman himself sought to legitimate his power. Here, however, dreams are used to torment the Amir, not to succor him, and the agent of that torment is the Hazrat himself carrying the iron-tipped staff of the faqir, the Islamic personage who represents more completely than any other the antithetical character of spiritual and temporal power. Ultimately, of course, victory belongs to the saint. The king's chains cannot hold Hazrat Sahib, and the tormentor becomes the tormented until finally the dead father must ask forgiveness through the person of his living son.[56]

The representation in the story of the son asking forgiveness for the father carries an especially strong symbolic value given the charged relationship of fathers and sons in Afghan society. In this instance, the king's lust for power makes him oblivious to the real source of power. Only in death is he brought to his senses, and he must use the medium of dreams to communicate his plight to the living son who alone can alleviate his torment through acts of pious devotion.[57] In this way the saint finally lays hold of the authority that is rightfully his. The king can pursue his triumphs only to the brink of death, but the saint transcends this boundary, thereby demonstrating the primacy of God over human affairs and of religious leadership over the state.

CODA: THE JOURNEY TO KOH-I QAF

To conclude this discussion of the life of Najmuddin Akhundzada, I want to return to the story which began this chapter—the story of the Mulla of Hadda's journey to Koh-i Qaf. The import of this specific story and the more general significance of miracle stories as a narrative genre are clearer in light of the nature and role of Islam in the frontier context. What seemed most striking about this story initially was its admixture of the mundane and the fantastic. The Mulla, after all, is a historical personage of the recent past, yet in this episode he is engaged in acts that seem better suited to a character from the Arabian Nights than a real man.

Similar comments were elicited by Sultan Muhammad Khan's story and by the life history of Abdur Rahman. All of these stories are memorable because they place "real" people in mythical situations. This being the case, what is most important to attend to, in this story as in the others, is precisely the conjunction between myth and history, between the vision of the ideal and the embeddedness of the real. The first point to make in this regard is that the magical elements of the story enshroud what is basically a prosaic tale concerning the religious leader's role in mediating social disputes. Thus, we have a jilted lover (who just happens to be a dragon) prevented from marrying the daughter of a nobleman. Beseeched to intervene on the lover's behalf, the Mulla reluctantly agrees to fly off to the land of the fairies. While attending to this business, Hadda Sahib also arranges and performs sixty-nine other marriage ceremonies.

There are a number of confusing elements in this story; for example, the dragon is revealed to be the prince of fairy land and therefore presumably a suitable marriage partner for any nobleman's daughter. It is also not explained why there is such a backlog of marriages in fairyland. The implication seems to be that the marriages had been held up, perhaps because of disagreements over bride price or some other part of the exchange. We cannot be sure of this interpretation, but one Western reader has suggested that the Mulla's performance of these multiple marriages might represent "an emotional amplification of the perceived 'touchiness' of marital negotiations in general in real life, and the potency of the intervention of a real-life spiritual figure."[58]

Over and above these issues, however, the critical feature of the story is its ordinariness. Within the magical frame lies a quite straightforward narrative about one of the things that religious leaders like the Mulla of Hadda have traditionally done—which is to mediate disputes and offer solutions to the everyday problems that restrict the normal flow of social life. In this context, Koh-i Qaf serves as a kind of mirror world to the world of the everyday. That other world may be more exotic than the world of the frontier, it may contain succulent fruits and metamorphosing dragons, but despite these differences, the fairies must deal with the same sort of problems in their mystical realm that Afghans deal with in their mud-brick villages back home.

At the same time, there are differences between the mirror world of Koh-i Qaf and the real world of the frontier, the most important of which is the relative authority that the fairies give to the Mulla to intervene in their affairs. Comparatively, the Pakhtuns of the frontier accord far less scope to their religious leaders to intervene in social affairs, and—we are to conclude—have a far less harmonious and prosperous society as a result. In this sense then, the story of Koh-i Qaf can be seen as an implicit critique of Pakhtun culture, particularly its failure to treat religious figures with the respect they are due.[59] The world revealed in the miracle story is a world where the divine plan has been worked out by and through those whom God has designated as his instruments. Lost in its temporal concerns, the human world remains unconscious of God's power, just as it is unconscious of the status of God's saints. The miracle story, however, reminds those absorbed in the world of appearances about the existence of a transcendent reality superseding the evanescent order of the material world that holds them in thrall. The majority of men and women cannot experience this realm, of course, but they can at least show a proper respect to those saints who can cross the divide and bring some of the harmony from that other world into this one.

The story highlights the dichotomy between the real and the ideal, and it also reminds the listener that, despite the Mulla's lack of those things that constitute temporal power, he is neither abject nor powerless. To the contrary, the humble faqir has, through his various negations and privations, endowed himself with a pure potency capable of striking terror into the hearts of great men, including kings. The Mulla and his ilk frighten and confound those who align their compasses in relation to more mundane ambitions and desires. With normal men, even the great and powerful, the logic of why and how they act is comprehensible, but the motivation and response of a pir can only be guessed at. His reasons and ways evince a moral calculus that others cannot readily comprehend, and the power that he displays is a power not of human manufacture.

The transmutation of power from powerlessness is an unstable operation, but the story of the Mulla's journey to Koh-i Qaf indicates some of the ways the process can be smoothed and ensured. Thus, for example, it is important to preserve the illusion that the saint's power has not been sought and that the saint does not brandish it for his own sake alone. Just as he shows a distinct disinterest in the transactions of wealth surrounding the langar, so the pir must eschew any display of pride or personal investment if the notion that he is truly God's agent is to be maintained. This attitude is demonstrated in the Koh-i Qaf story by the Mulla's fruitless efforts at hiding his miracles from the sight of those around him and by the fact that it is only Abdul Baqi's meddlesome presence that allows the story to be known at all. The nominal reason for making these efforts to obscure the journey to Koh-i Qaf is that ordinary mortals are not capable of comprehending or withstanding the hidden reality of divine power. For this reason, then, the Mulla must veil himself and his acts. He must dissuade Abdul Baqi from accompanying him, and he must tell him not to tell anyone else what he has seen. Mankind is not ready to absorb the truth of the *batin*, the hidden realm, so for now they can only get hints of that other power on which the Mulla draws.

That is one reason for veiling his miracles. But there is another one, and that is the extreme nature of the miracles that are claimed for the Mulla. In the eyes of many Muslims, the notion that a man—any man—might journey to Koh-i Qaf is too far removed from the realm of the ordinary to be acceptable. It is one thing for the Prophet to fly on the back of his magical horse, Buraq, but it is something else again for an ordinary mortal to consort with dragons and fairies. Those who claim such power mislead the people and commit the gravest of all sins—that of diverting attention from God to themselves. This is infidelity (*kufr*) of the most dangerous sort, for it both imputes divine power to a non-divine source and causes people to stray onto the path of idolatry and polytheism. That is why Abdul Baqi's presence in the story is so crucial. He not only provides a kind of narrative foil for the Mulla—the ordinary mortal whose foolishness complements the Mulla's sagacity—but also serves to insulate him from culpability for the story's extreme claims. Abdul Baqi, the story makes clear, is impulsive. He gets involved in affairs that do not properly concern him, as when he rashly tries to bring a memento back from the magic kingdom of the fairies. These are recognizable sorts of acts, the sort of thing that any one of us might do, and this fact shifts responsibility for the story from the Mulla onto the shoulders of Abdul Baqi, who can be blamed for perpetuating infidelity without any stigma attaching to the Mulla.[60]

Despite Abdul Baqi's presence, however, the story of Hadda Sahib's visit to Koh-i Qaf reveals a fundamental ambiguity that is inherent in the Mulla's social position and that is similar to the ambiguities previously encountered in our examination of other great lives. The actions of Sultan Muhammad obscured the boundary between what is exemplary and what is arrogant; in the end, his position of respect was apparently preserved because his devotion to honor could be seen as mitigating his sometimes unseemingly arrogation of authority. Likewise, Amir Abdur Rahman often stepped over the line of what was just and acceptable for a ruler into the realm of the cruel and despotic, but his reputation remained intact due to the perception that he was bound by higher principles than mere self-interest and that whatever his faults and excesses might have been he did fulfill his responsibility for bringing order and prosperity to his kingdom.

The Mulla of Hadda's story presents a similar ambiguity, for he too trod a narrow path between the acceptable and the unacceptable. This is true of Sufi saints in general, of course, since all those who explore the mystical realm automatically make themselves vulnerable to accusations of infidelity from the narrowly orthodox, who limit appropriate action to that which is explicitly called for in scripture. However, even among Sufi saints, the Mulla of Hadda's case is an extreme one, since relatively few in this category ever did so much as he did or were so involved in the social and political events of their time. Nor do many Sufi saints have the kind and degree of power claimed for them by their disciples that the Mulla did by his. It is one thing, after all, to be associated with making roof beams longer or keeping the langar pot full (particularly since these are actions without clear agents), but it is something else again to converse with dragons and take off on night flights to fairy land.

As with our other heroes, the Mulla's reputation finally overcomes all qualifications and uncertainties. Whatever the orthodox might think of dragons and fairies, no one doubts the Mulla's single-minded devotion to Islam. No one questions his personal piety or the fact that he made great sacrifices to preserve and protect the Muslim community. There are excesses in his stories—instances in which powers are ascribed to the Mulla that surpass what a scripturally minded Muslim can countenance. But what is unseemly and dangerous in Hadda Sahib's stories can be explained away. Others in the past, lesser men like Abdul Baqi, can be held responsible for what transgresses the boundaries of the moral; and having taken the blame away from the Mulla himself, those in the present can then safely revel in the wonder and possibility that the great saint's miracles open up to view.

5 Mad Mullas and Englishmen

LATEST INTELLIGENCE
RISING IN THE SWAT VALLEY
(From our correspondents)
Simla, July 27

Yet another proof has been given of the wave of fanaticism which is sweeping along the North-West frontier of India. Malakand was the scene last night of some sharp fighting, a sudden tribal rising in the Swat Valley taking place during the day. The story is a curious one, as showing how quickly tribesmen can gather and how readily they respond to an appeal to their fanaticism.

The garrison at Malakand consists of one squadron of the 11th Bengal Lancers, No. 8 Bengal mountain battery, one company of Sappers, the 24th and 31st Punjab Infantry, and the 45th Sikhs, or about 3,000 men, of whom 200 infantry and 25 cavalry held the Chakdara post guarding the bridge across the Swat river, on the road to Chitral. Colonel Meiklejohn commands this brigade. Since the Chitral campaign came to an end the Swat Valley has been perfectly peaceful. The trade with Bajaur and the neighbouring countries has developed considerably, and the Swatis generally have been contented. The Chitral road has been kept open by tribal levies, and no signs of disaffection have ever been apparent. The sons of the late Akhund of Swat have, it is true, tried to excite fanaticism, but hitherto unsuccessfully.

Yesterday, without the least warning, the attitude of the population in the Lower Swat Valley underwent a sudden change. The

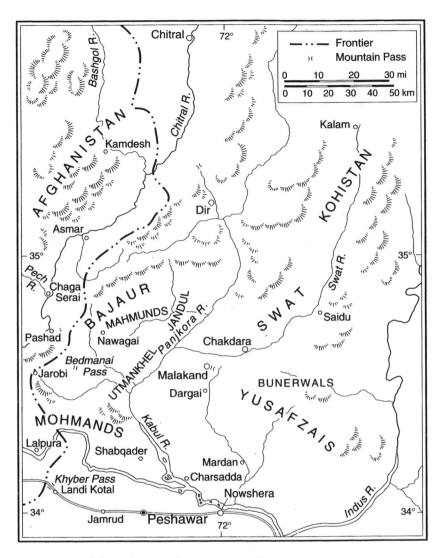

Map 4. North-West Frontier Province, circa 1897

first news which reached Malakand was that a disturbance had taken place at Thana, near Chakdara bridge. A few hours later further news was received that the "mad mullah," a priest who is apparently well known locally, had gathered about him a number of armed men with the view of raising a *jehad*. In the evening it was reported that he was advancing down the valley towards Malakand. Preparations were made to send out a column early the next morning and disperse the gathering. The tribal levies, who fled as the mullah advanced, reported that Malakand itself would be attacked at 3 a.m. The camp was, consequently, on the alert, but the attack was delivered at half-past 10 that night—a very unusual hour for Pathans to attempt a surprise.

In the fight which ensued Honorary Lieutenant Manley, of the Commissariat, was killed; and Lieutenant-Colonel Lamb, of the 24th Punjab Infantry, Major Herbert, staff officer, Major Taylor, 45th Sikhs, and Lieutenant Watling, Royal Engineers, were wounded. The returns of casualties among the rank and file have not yet been received.

Colonel Meiklejohn ordered up the Guides from Mardan to strengthen the garrison, and at daybreak sent out a column consisting of a squadron of cavalry, four guns, and the 31st Punjab Infantry, to reconnoitre towards Chakdara and pursue the enemy. It was then discovered that the whole valley was up in arms, and it was impossible to open communication with the Chakdara post. The tribesmen were plainly not disheartened by the failure of their night attack, but were prepared to renew hostilities. Colonel Meiklejohn accordingly concentrated the garrison in the entrenched position on the Malakand ridge, withdrawing the troops from the north Malakand camp, which was rather exposed. At the same time he telegraphed for reinforcements to be sent immediately.

Orders were at once issued from the Punjab command headquarters directing four regiments of infantry, a mountain battery, and the remaining three squadrons of the 11th Bengal Lancers at Nowshera to move as quickly as possible. This was confirmed by the authorities here.

But little anxiety is felt regarding the Chakdara post, as it is impregnable against any force not armed with artillery. It is well provisioned, and the small body of troops have plenty of ammunition. It is nine miles from Malakand, on the further bank of the Swat river, and commands the suspension bridge, but the latter may be wrecked at night. The Guides should reach Colonel Meiklejohn this evening, as they were to make a double march of 24 miles. Malakand, which is a fortified position, is too strong to be stormed, but the garrison must be reinforced in order that the Swat Valley may be kept clear and that Chakdara may be relieved. Unless this be done, the rising may spread among the neighbouring clans. The news of the attack quickly became known along the frontier, and it may possibly have an effect in Waziristan, stimulating the tribesmen there to action against Major-General Corrie Bird's force in the Tochi Valley. So far, no opposition whatever has been met with there.

The Times, Wednesday, July 28, 1897

A PASSAGE TO INDIA

Winston Churchill was winning money at the Goodwood Races when he heard the news that a tribal uprising had broken out on the northwest frontier of India.[1] Within a matter of hours, the young cavalry officer, who was then on home leave in England from his regiment in Bangalore, booked return passage on the Indian Mail. He also sent off a telegram to an old family friend, General Bindon Blood, who had been appointed to head the column that was being dispatched to relieve the two garrisons at Malakand and Chakdara (map 4) then under siege. General Blood had once made a casual promise to Churchill that he would include him in a future campaign, and with this promise in mind, Churchill set off for the frontier.

To understand Churchill's excitement, one must consider the circumstances. The year was 1897, the British Empire was ascendant around the globe, and that summer Her Royal Majesty Queen Victoria was celebrating the Diamond Jubilee marking her sixtieth year on the throne. The day before the news of the frontier uprising reached London, Churchill had enjoyed a major milestone in his young career when he delivered his first public address to a picnic meeting of the Primrose League of Bath. Churchill's principal theme had been the importance of maintaining the grand empire fashioned during Victoria's reign. Despite the lamentations of "croakers" who believed the British Empire must soon go the way of Babylon, Carthage, and Rome, Churchill urged his listeners to stay the course. The British people, he proclaimed, must continue to pursue "that course marked out for us by an all-wise hand and carry out our mission of bearing peace, civilisation and good government to the uttermost ends of the earth."[2]

Coming on the heels of his first foray into the political arena, the uprising in India offered Churchill an opportunity to dramatically demonstrate the principles he had articulated in his speech. By the time he arrived on the frontier, however, the first wave of the uprising had crested without any major loss being suffered. Most of those who had participated in the siege at Malakand and Chakdara had returned to their homes, but other installations were still under assault, and the job of punishing those responsible for inciting the insurrection remained. General Blood received that assignment—to push into the tribal districts to the north and west of Malakand up to the Afghan border and discipline those who had "dared violate the Pax Britannica." While he was unable to gain assignment to Blood's staff, Churchill did manage to secure a position as a war correspondent attached to his command. With the assistance of his mother in London, Churchill also succeeded in getting a newspaper, *The Daily Telegraph*, to publish his dispatches from the field.[3]

In this fashion, the political career of one of the twentieth century's great statesmen and politicians was launched, but my concern is not so much with the man as with what he witnessed and what he reported. Whereas Churchill's person and life are almost invariably set in the foreground of whatever scene he happened onto (including this one), he will hereafter in this chapter occupy a subordinate role to the other actors who shared the stage with him that summer, actors who have traditionally been cast in supporting roles or as stock heavies in the drama of colonial encounter. Using Churchill's own descriptions of that summer, along with those of other contemporary British journalists and Pakhtu oral accounts collected in the course of my fieldwork, I will try to reconstitute the moral significance of this encounter as it was constructed and understood by those on the Afghan side of the battlefield. Before doing so, however, we must first understand how the British constructed the events of 1897 and the kind of moral value they saw unfolding in these "uttermost" reaches of British authority.

THE EVENTS OF 1897 AND THEIR EXPLANATION

The frontier disturbances that Churchill took such pains to witness began where local political authorities least expected trouble and were initiated by an unlikely antagonist. For some months, British officials had been reporting improved relations with the local people of the Swat valley, and after several years of intermittent hostility, it finally appeared that calm had settled on the region. The postal service now delivered mail to and from the valley, and a medical dispensary located alongside the Chakdara fort was treating patients from the neighboring communities. Most telling of all perhaps, British officers found that they could ride "about freely among the fierce hill men" and were even being "invited to settle many disputes, which would formerly have been left to armed force."[4]

In early July, however, the first hints of disaffection began to appear. The native markets were abuzz with rumors that "great events were impending." At the center of these reports was an obscure faqir and sometime malcontent named Saidullah, whom the British authorities henceforth referred to as the "Mad Fakir of Swat." A native of the region who long before had abandoned his family and home to become a religious mendicant, Saidullah had begun making declarations of an impending holy war in which he would be aided by supernatural forces.[5] A crowd had gathered to hear him, and as it swelled his rhetoric became more inflamed until finally, on the afternoon of July 26, he had set off to attack the British garrisons at Chakdara and Malakand.

Followed at first by only a few of his fellow mendicants and a handful of teenage boys, Saidullah attracted new adherents in each village he passed, gathering some five thousand by the time he reached the fort at Chakdara, located at the confluence of the Panjkora and Swat Rivers, just north of the Malakand Pass that linked the tribal territories with the Peshawar plains to the south. Although their weaponry consisted mostly of primitive flintlocks, swords, and staves, the followers of the Fakir mounted an assault that lasted four days and might have led to the capture of the Chakdara garrison had it not been for the arrival of General Blood's relief column on the first day of August.

The timely relief of the cavalry succeeded in breaking the siege at Chakdara, but no sooner had this uprising subsided than other, equally serious tribal risings broke out in nearby areas along the frontier from the Kohat district in the southwest (where the Orakzais and neighboring tribes attacked a British base on the Samana Ridge) to the Tirah and Khyber districts, directly west of Peshawar (where Afridi and Shinwari tribes attacked British posts protecting the strategically vital Khyber Pass), to the Mohmand territory (where a force of Mohmand, Mahmund, and other cross-border tribes attacked the British fort at Shabqader and the neighboring market at Shankargar, just nineteen miles from Peshawar itself). Although none of these attacks ultimately succeeded in dislodging any of the British garrisons in the region, the simultaneous appearance of so many attacks was worrisome to the British administration.

Since the infamous "Mutiny" of 1857, India had been free of widespread insurrection, but the passing of time and the ensuing peace had failed to assuage the fear inspired by that episode. During the travails of 1857, one of the saving graces for the British had been the failure of the frontier tribes to join the general rebellion, and it had been widely concluded from this experience that, however tough an opponent the tribes were on their home ground, their potential danger to the Raj was mitigated by their inability to make common cause among themselves or to coordinate their actions with others outside their home territory. Such was the received wisdom, but here were these notoriously fractious tribes mounting coordinated assaults on well-fortified garrisons and demonstrating a degree of organization unprecedented in the history of British rule in India. And it also appeared that the decision to initiate the attacks had been influenced by external factors of the sort to which the frontier tribes had previously been oblivious.

In his reports from the frontier, Churchill noted that the tribes were more cognizant of outside events than they had ever been in the past. One reason for this was that the Afghan amir, Abdur Rahman, had been "meddling" in frontier affairs—inviting delegations of tribal elders to meetings in Kabul, keeping large numbers of troops near the border, distributing pamphlets in the tribal areas on the proper conduct of jihad. From the British point of view, the Amir's actions were annoying and provocative, but even without his assistance, the tribes simply knew more about what was going on in the outside world than they had in the past, and they also appeared to have more sense of the possible implication of distant events on political relations at home. A recent victory by the Ottoman Turks over a Greek army had raised hopes in India and the tribal borderlands of an impending Islamic revival, and news of the seizure of Aden and the Suez Canal had likewise encouraged the belief that Great Britain would shortly lose its ability to secure troop reinforcements from Europe.

In explaining the sudden spread of such rumors, Churchill assigned blame to one group in particular—the mullas. It was their vitriolic preaching that had made the tribes aware of distant worlds, their slanders that had magnified British problems in other lands, and their incitement that had produced "a 'boom' in Mohammedanism" in the remote villages up and down the frontier. The motivation of the mullas was not difficult to discern, for in Churchill's view, despite their backward beliefs and practices, they had the "quick intelligence" to recognize that "contact with civilisation assails the superstition, and credulity, on which the wealth and influence of the Mullah depend."[6] So long as British arms produced security in the region and an increase in trade and communication with the outside world, the authority of the mullas was bound to suffer. Therefore, it was critical for them to find a pretext to fight back and reassert their former authority among their tribal followers.

The mullas could not accomplish this task alone. They needed a catalyst capable of "firing the mine." In 1897 that catalyst was discovered in the person of the faqir Saidullah, who, in his apparent derangement, was "convinced alike of his Divine mission and miraculous powers."[7] In Churchill's terms, the frontier uprising was comparable in its intensity and irrationality to the ill-fated Children's Crusade. Playing the role of Peter the Hermit on this occasion was Saidullah. He was the one who marched at the head of his credulous followers into the fiery crucible, but just as Peter had had "regular bishops and cardinals of the Church" standing off to the side, ready to reap the benefits of popular enthusiasm and sacrifice, so Saidullah was surrounded by "crafty politicians," anxious to "seize the opportunity and fan the flame."[8] According to Churchill, these were the masterminds behind the plot of insurrection, and foremost among their number was none other than the Mulla of Hadda.

The Mulla of Hadda casts an ominous shadow in Churchill's writings. Little was known about him, particularly compared to Saidullah, but that lacuna only seemed to increase his stature and significance in British eyes: "In the heart of the wild and dismal mountain region in which these fierce tribesmen dwell, are the temple and village of Jarobi, the one a consecrated hovel, the other a fortified slum. This obscure and undisturbed retreat was the residence of a priest of great age and of peculiar holiness, known to fame as the Hadda Mullah. His name is Najim-ud-din."[9]

Though no one knew much about the Mulla, spies among the tribes had been telling tales about him for years, and it was known that he was a steadfast foe of British influence. The most notable example of his belligerence had come two years earlier when he had taken the lead in organizing a tribal blockade of a column attempting to relieve the British garrison at Chitral, which was then under siege. Since that time, spies had reported other instances of the Mulla preaching to the tribes against British rule in India and of his attempts to coordinate other religious leaders in an effort to destroy British influence in the region.

In the summer of 1897, these efforts finally bore fruit, and Churchill was ready to offer his explanation for the Mulla's success. The first reason he provided was the predilection of the illiterate tribes for taking rumors at face value and passing hearsay on as truth: "The bazaars of India are always full of marvelous tales. A single unimportant fact is exaggerated, and distorted, till it becomes unrecognizable. From it, a thousand wild, illogical, and fantastic conclusions, are drawn. These again are circulated as facts. So the game goes on."[10] In the normal course of events, such stories and rumors do not amount to much, but because of the coordination provided by the Mulla and his allies in the early summer, "a vast, but silent agitation was begun." "Messengers passed to and fro among the tribes. Whispers of war, a holy war, were breathed to a race intensely passionate and fanatical. Vast and mysterious agencies, the force of which are incomprehensible to rational minds, were employed. The tribes were taught to expect prodigious events."[11] In this fashion, rumors had swept through the bazaar and on into the mountain villages, transforming a slightly crazed malcontent into a "mighty man who had arisen to lead them." Likewise, the coincidental occurrence of a number of separate events in different parts of the world were trumped up as a sign that "a great day for Islam was at hand. . . . The English would be swept away. By the time of the new moon, not one would remain."[12]

A second, related factor in creating the synergy between visionary leader and his credible followers was their conviction that he could perform miracles:

> Had the 'Mad Mullah' called on them to follow him to attack Malakand and Chakdara they would have refused. Instead he worked miracles. He sat at his house and all who came to visit him brought him a small offering of food or money, in return for which he gave them a little rice. As his stores were continually replenished he might claim to have fed thousands. He asserted that he was invisible at nights. Looking into his room they saw no one. At these things they marvelled. Finally he declared that he would destroy the infidel. He wanted no help. No one should share the honours. The heavens would open and an army would descend. The more he protested he did not want them the more exceedingly they came.[13]

Related to the belief in the Mad Fakir's miraculous powers was the sense apparently shared by his followers that, so long as they followed their leader, they themselves would be invulnerable to harm. Thus, for most, "bullets would be turned to water," and for the rest, those struck and killed following the Fakir into battle, their succor was the knowledge that a final resting place had been prepared for them "degrees above the Caa[b]a itself"[14] According to Churchill, this belief remained unshaken even after the fighting at Chakdara, where the tribal army had seen a quarter of its number fall upon the field: "Only those who doubted had perished, said the Mullah, and displayed a bruise which was, he informed them, the sole effect of a twelve-pound shrapnel shell on his weird person."[15]

In Churchill's analysis, it is clear that the irrational plays an exceedingly important role in his explanation for the uprising's success. For him, the existence of religious leaders claiming miraculous powers and the readiness of the local people to believe such claims provided irrefutable evidence of the barbaric nature of Britain's adversaries and, concomitantly, the impossibility of sustaining a rational negotiation with them: "Were [the tribes] amenable to logical reasoning, the improvement in their condition and the strength of their adversaries would have convinced them of the folly of an outbreak. But in a land of fanatics common sense does not exist."[16]

For Churchill, this conclusion had important practical consequences for how the colonial authorities should conduct themselves. One could not negotiate with savages. The only language such people could understand was force. "Pax Britannica" had been "violated," and it remained for the authorities to avenge this injury and to teach the tribes the only sort of lesson they were capable of absorbing. Half-measures would not do the trick. The tribes had tasted blood and would undoubtedly mount similar attacks in the future if the government failed to punish those responsible for the trespass and provide an object lesson for those who believed in the miraculous power of their mullas to protect them from harm. To Churchill, this was not simply a political skirmish between the government and a band of malcontent mullas for control of a few outposts; it was more profoundly a battle for the soul of India, a battle that pitted the forward march of civilization against the backward slide of ignorance and superstition.

WAGING JIHAD

In Churchill's writings on the uprising, it is apparent that the author seeks to deny his enemy any claim to moral status by establishing the premise that he is *fanatical*. "Fanaticism" serves as the central trope of Churchill's polemic and fixes the personae of the Mulla of Hadda and Mad Fakir in Churchill's texts much as "cruelty" fixed Abdur Rahman in the writings of Curzon and Martin. And just as I argued in chapter 3 for the value of decoding "cruelty" as a first step toward seeing the Amir clearly, so I would argue here that "fanaticism" must also be taken seriously, explicated, and worked through in order to understand the Mulla in something like a neutral manner. Fanaticism may be a biased term, but it still describes something real that must be deciphered if we are to understand the nature of religious authority and the reasons why the normally insular border tribes chose to follow religious leaders into battle.

In his efforts to deal with the quality of the irrational in the relationship of leaders and followers, Max Weber borrowed the term *charisma* from Christian theology to signify "a certain quality of an individual personality by virtue of which he is set apart from ordinary men and treated as endowed with supernatural, superhuman, or at least specifically exceptional powers or qualities. These are such as are not accessible to the ordinary person, but are regarded as of divine origin or as exemplary, and on the basis of them the individual concerned is treated as a leader." [17] Weber goes on to note that, "in primitive circumstances," a "peculiar kind of deference" is paid to certain kinds of people—leaders in the hunt, great healers, prophets, heroes in warfare—whose capacities and accomplishments seem so far beyond the ordinary that they can only be explained by attributing to them some sort of "magical power." [18]

Weber's definition of charisma retains a quality of vagueness at its core despite his attempts to specify the circumstances within which charisma appears. This vagueness, along with its ubiquity in contemporary social commentary, has led many scholars to reject the term outright, but no one has been able to suggest a better word or to dispel the sense that, however murky it might be, charisma still refers to something real. Whether we choose to define it or not, there is a persistent tendency in human affairs for groups of people to attribute uncanny powers to some individuals and to celebrate and sometimes venerate those who are thus set apart. In the absence of any alternative way of designating that quality of person and relationship, charisma retains its usefulness, a usefulness that is increased in this instance by the fact that the word itself derives from the same root as the term *kiramat* (miracle). [19]

Using Weber's analysis of charisma and its association with the miraculous as a starting point, I want to consider in some depth the role of miracles in the uprising/jihad of 1897. Miracles are clearly at the heart of Churchill's attribution of fanaticism to the tribesmen, but they also seem to have been central to what was actually going on that summer and so are critical to understanding the nature of religious authority. In addition to examining the role of miracles in the jihad, I also want to consider how religious identity and the social formation of religious organization influenced the events of 1897. Here again, Weber's analysis provides an essential starting point, specifically his discussion of the "routinization" of charismatic authority. [20] In contrast to Weber's approach, however, which posits routinization as a later and fundamentally corrupting process, my position is that the appearance of new forms of charismatic authority depends upon prior social and cultural forms.

Just as miracle stories are comprehensible and compelling insofar as they are retellings of older tales, so it is generally the case that each new charismatic leader builds a reputation for himself to the degree that he is familiar with and connected to an ongoing routinized tradition. It could be argued that the tariqat system as a whole stands outside the profane sphere of everyday life and that the example of Najmuddin choosing to build his center in the desert of Hadda proves that to be the case. Likewise, the "anti-economizing" attitude of the Mulla in relation to the wealth circulating through his langar is another example of the way in which the tariqat stands apart from the economic concerns of the society at large. The point I want to make here, however, is that charismatic authority is inherently and necessarily routinized, that its emergence at any particular time is, in fact, a reemergence dependent upon the prior existence of a cultural framework that allows the person and the message of the charismatic leader to appear as something already familiar to the people and therefore a recognizable and legitimate basis for collective political action.

Most of the information that I have been able to collect on the ideological and organizational aspects of the 1897 jihad comes from British archival sources. In the course of my interviews with the offspring of the Mulla's disciples (and a few Mohmand tribesmen from the area where Hadda Sahib resided during his exile from Afghanistan), I found only one set of stories that clearly dealt with the jihad of 1897. However, that set of stories pertains to the denouement of the jihad and is of little help in discovering why the Mad Fakir's first appearance in Swat was greeted with such enthusiasm. (The multiple versions of this story do help with understanding the ultimate meaning of the events of 1897, as will be seen in the last section of this chapter.)

To understand that first stage of the jihad, I will rely on British sources, and consequently will apply the basic principles deduced from the miracle stories in the preceding chapter to the analysis of the British records. Because most of the events during the first stage (and the records pertaining to them) revolve around the Mad Fakir and not Hadda Sahib, I will divide the following analysis into two parts, the first of which has to do with the role of miracles in the actions and pronouncements of the Mad Fakir and the second of which concerns Hadda Sahib himself and his role in organizing and coordinating the tribal armies that both he and the Mad Fakir helped to galvanize into action.

The Scaffolding of Rhetoric

> About the 20th and 21st, the Fakir began giving out that he had
> heavenly hosts with him, that his mission was to turn the British
> off the Malakand and out of Peshawar, as our rule of 60 years there
> was up. He claimed to have been visited by all deceased Fakirs, who
> told him the mouths of our guns and rifles would be closed, and
> that our bullets would be turned to water; that he had only to throw
> stones into the Swat river, and each stone he threw would have on
> us the effect of a gun. He gave out that he had no need of human
> assistance, as the heavenly hosts with him were sufficient.[21]

The first point I would like to make about Saidullah's role in the events
of 1897 concerns the miracles that he promised and the way in which
these miracles occurred. As mentioned earlier, Churchill and other British
commentators were quick to point to miraculous doings as evidence of the
unscrupulousness of religious leaders and the primitiveness of the tribes.
The "fanaticism" so apparent that summer was the result of these two
factors. Setting aside this judgment, I will examine some of the reports of
the Mad Fakir's miracles themselves before attempting to consider what
sense might be made of them. The first such reports that I was able to
discover were dated July 18 and indicated that the Fakir had appeared in
the area, "professing that one small pot of rice, which he had with him,
was sufficient to feed multitudes." He also indicated that he was able to
"multiply to the vision of people a few small flags that he had with him,"
these flags apparently representing the emblems that the people were accustomed to taking into battle with them (thereby implying that their
own number would magically multiply).[22]

The next report was the one above concerning the events of July 20
and 21. From this account, it would appear that the Fakir was claiming
divine assistance in his plan: from an invisible "heavenly host" that accompanied him, as well as from "all deceased Fakirs" who were guiding
his actions and providing magical protection to those who accompanied
him. The reason for their assistance was apparent: the end of one historical
era—that of colonial domination—was upon them, and another was beginning—that of Islamic rule. Perhaps to emphasize the larger historical
design of which they were a part, the Fakir announced to those around
him that one of the several adolescent boys who accompanied him was
"the heir to the throne of Delhi," and he dramatized this assertion by
crowning him on the spot with "a puggrie [turban]."[23]

The response to the Mad Fakir's claims was apparently negligible at first, and he had to be prevented by the people from setting out against the British fort at Chakdara alone. A number of the local chiefs who were on the British payroll spoke out against him, but their exertions seem to have helped rather than hindered his cause. The recent introduction of a policy of providing allowances for local leaders seems to have created resentment and suspicion in the populace, and the efforts of allowance-holders to detain the Fakir appear to have crystallized these resentments and suspicions and drawn the people to a leader who stood ready to oppose all aspects of colonial intrusions into the region.

Whatever it was that finally impelled the people to support the Fakir, we do know that once he had gained a few adherents to his cause, the number of his supporters increased suddenly and exponentially until he had an estimated eight thousand people trailing behind him as he headed down the valley toward the British garrisons at Chakdara and Malakand. The decision of large numbers of people to join the movement appears to have been undertaken without premeditation or planning. That, at least, is the sense one gets from some of the intelligence reports, one of which indicates that the followers of the Mad Fakir were so convinced of his message that they took no measures to prepare for a possible setback: "Cattle and grain, &c., had all been left in the villages, and at Chakdarra the bridge over the Swat river and the cavalry horses in the post, though entirely exposed, were left practically unmolested in the confident feeling that they would be useful when the post was captured."[24]

This and other similar reports indicate that the Mad Fakir's attack was a classic example of a charismatic leader mobilizing people toward millenarian objectives. Thus, one finds here, as in accounts of other millenarian movements, the appearance of a leader promising to reclaim a lost glory by defeating a foreign power that is perceived as responsible for present corruptions. There are also promises of supernatural support, including immunity from the effects of the enemy's weapons for all those who support the leader, and a general lack of concern for the practical needs of the movement (the pervasive feeling being one of unwavering belief in the imminent victory and the consequent irrelevance of logistical concerns). Finally, here as in other accounts, there is apparent the belief that a mythical plan is about to be realized in the domain of real events and that those who participate in the fulfillment of that plan will themselves attain an appropriate reward.

All of these elements are evident in this case, but my interests are less in the practical and political causes of the uprising than in its ideology. In particular, I am concerned with how the Mad Fakir used the medium of miracle stories to embody the principles of sacred authority that were discussed in the previous chapter. In exploring these issues, I will be enlisting the services of an unlikely ally, none other than Winston Churchill himself, and the source of his assistance is an obscure essay entitled "The Scaffolding of Rhetoric."[25] To the best of my knowledge, this essay was never published prior to its appearance in a posthumous collection of Churchill's correspondence and writings, and I have never seen any reference to the work in the recent biographies of Churchill's life; but whatever the reasons for its undeserved obscurity, the essay is of great utility to this project for several reasons.

First, it was written in the summer of 1897, when Churchill made his trip to India. In fact it appears likely that Churchill failed to complete the essay precisely because of his sudden decision to leave England to witness the frontier uprising firsthand. The timing of the essay is of at least marginal interest since its contemporaneity with the events under discussion does afford some insight into Churchill's concerns on the eve of his journey to the frontier. Second, and of more relevance to this work, however, is what the essay says about charismatic authority and the mobilization of popular support in general. Churchill, of course, did not use the term *charisma*. His discourse is rather about *rhetoric* and *oratory*, but the essay nevertheless provides acute insights about the dynamics of popular mobilization from a man who was himself embarking on a career that would make him one of the great charismatic leaders of his time.

The work is essentially a treatise on the sources and requirements of effective political oratory, and Churchill begins it by asserting that the "direct, though not the admitted, object" of political rhetoric is "to allay the commonplace influences and critical faculties" of an audience. One primary attribute which any orator requires for accomplishing this objective is a "striking presence" caused, for example, by a slight speech impediment or even a physical deformity. It matters also that the orator himself believes, if only for the duration of his performance, what he is saying: "The orator is the embodiment of the passions of the multitude. Before he can inspire them with any emotion he must be swayed by it himself."[26]

Besides the personal qualities of the speaker, the quality of the speech itself is significant, and Churchill points to a number of elements in a speech that cause audiences to come under an orator's sway. These elements include the correctness of diction, the rhythm of phrasing, and the overall accumulation of argument that creates a coherent picture and allows the audience to "anticipate the conclusion." More important than these factors, however, is the use of "analogy," through which the orator can "translate an established truth into simple language" or "adventurously aspire to reveal the unknown." While admitting that "argument by analogy leads to conviction rather than to proof, and has often led to glaring error," Churchill discerns that the reason why analogies are so effective in oratory is that they "favor the belief that the unknown is only an extension of the known: that the abstract and the concrete are ruled by similar principles: that the finite and the infinite are homogeneous. An apt analogy connects or appears to connect these distant spheres."[27]

Using Churchill's analysis as a point of departure, we can identify certain similarities between the rhetorical principles governing traditional political oratory and those governing the speech and behavior of Saidullah, the faqir who initiated the upheaval in Swat. The first matter to consider in this regard is the person of Saidullah himself.[28] While I have been unable to ascertain any evidence as to Saidullah's appearance, I have discovered several of the names by which he was known, names which provide indications of his social persona. The first of these names was *sartor faqir* ("black-headed faqir"), which apparently referred to the fact that Saidullah went about in public without any turban, cap, or shawl. Given that men in this region invariably wear some sort of head covering when they venture out into the world, Saidullah's apparent failure to do so might indicate a general lack of concern on his part for the usual markers of social propriety.

So too does a second name by which he was known, a name that is similar to the British sobriquet "the Mad Fakir." This name is *lewanai faqir*, which can also be translated as "mad faqir," but which does not convey the same sense as that intended by the British in their usage of the term. Thus, rather than connoting psychological impairment or mental deficiency, native reference to Saidullah's "madness" implies that he was subject to a kind of "intoxication" that can occur when a spiritual adept comes into close proximity to God. Such a person succeeds in approaching God but cannot absorb the experience in any sustained or coherent fashion. Nearness to God overwhelms him, and he is left permanently, if intermittently, impaired, liable to fits of irrational behavior, and always capable of channeling through himself extraordinary bursts of divine power.

Given his status as a "mad faqir" and the elements of his personal history indicating that he was frequently at odds with local authorities and local custom, it is fair to say that Saidullah was a most "striking presence," even if not of the sort Churchill had in mind.[29] In Swat, as elsewhere in South Asia, the religious mendicant is seen in every town and many villages. Most are ignored, except when they pester passers-by for alms. Many people feel some resentment toward them, secretly suspecting that they have taken up the lifestyle of a faqir to shirk other responsibilities and smoke hashish. At the same time, however, few of those who distrust the motives of faqirs would be willing to openly declare their suspicions. The reason for this hesitancy is simple: people recognize that no matter how many mendacious mendicants might be out there in the world, some are for real, and who can tell the one from the other? Besides, too many stories—stories like the ones recounted in the previous chapter involving Hazrat Sahib of Butkhak and Amir Abdur Rahman—attest to the unhappy fate of those who abuse the faithful of God.

Whether Saidullah consciously intended to draw on the legacy of such stories is impossible to know, but one can say with conviction, if not certainty, that all of those whom Saidullah would have encountered in the summer of 1897 would have been familiar with tales of poor faqirs humbling the mighty. One also suspects that in claiming "to have been visited by all deceased Fakirs," Saidullah was specifically calling attention to this legacy and his presumptive status as standard bearer for all those who have ever battled tyranny while wearing the raiments of religious poverty.

Similarly, in declaring that heavenly hosts would soon descend, that bullets would be turned to water, and that a pot of rice could feed a multitude, the Fakir was not simply "making up" stories, but was rather drawing on deeply rooted narrative traditions with which his audience was abundantly familiar. In this way, the miracles that the Fakir claimed for the future represented events that (as the "twice-told" tales from chapter 3 illustrated) had occurred repeatedly in the past. The fact that his promises could be found in extant narratives did not make them less plausible. On the contrary, the quality of the familiar made them more believable because the possibility of such phenomena occurring had already been attested to in the time-honored arena of legend.

At the same time, it can be argued that miracles function in the discourse of the Fakir like the "apt analogy" of Western political rhetoric in that they too "allay commonplace influences and critical faculties" by making the unknown "an extension of the known." The essential talent of all great political persuaders, whatever their medium of expression or cultural context, is their ability to "appeal to the everyday knowledge of the hearer" in such a way that the hearer will be tempted "to decide the problems that have baffled his powers of reason by the standard of the nursery and the heart." [30]

Like analogies and metaphors, miracle stories make concrete but inchoate experience subordinate to the abstract design of something larger than the experience itself while also making the larger design immediate and perceptible in the concrete instance. When reality is seen through the lens of miracles, transient events are perceived as coherent and directed toward the fulfillment of a larger plan unfolding in time. Miracles thus convey a sense of unity to events that are normally experienced as discontinuous and enable those sensible to the continuity of events to see themselves as part of an ongoing story moving toward its necessary and predetermined conclusion. It matters not that those who believe in the miracles do not understand the nature of the larger design. What matters is that the situation before them, a situation which has no apparent solution, is seen not only to have an outcome but a self-evident and necessary one at that.

Extending our comparison a bit further, we can say that the efficacy of both miracles and metaphors derives not only from their capacity for making people "see" the world in a certain way but also from the fact that they implicate their audiences in their own resolution. That is to say that miracles and metaphors carry with them an implicit sense of moral culpability, so that those who "see" the world anew also "feel" themselves to be responsible for achieving the outcome predicated by the figure. An example of the manipulation of the moral determinacy of metaphor can be seen in the following dispatch written by Churchill and published in *The Daily Telegraph:*

> Starting with the assumption that our Empire in India is worth holding, and admitting the possibility that others besides ourselves might wish to possess it, it obviously becomes our duty to adopt measures for its safety. . . . The most natural way of preventing an enemy from entering a house is to hold the door and windows; and the general consensus of opinion is that to secure India it is necessary to hold the passes of the mountains.[31]

The Londoner reading his newspaper over breakfast may know nothing of India, but he recognizes the imperative of defending what is his and taking reasonable precautions to prevent others from getting the idea that his property could be theirs. What he does not know about India is excluded by the metaphor. The weight of familiar knowledge from the realm of his own experience as a citizen and homeowner thus leads him to ignore what he does not understand—India—and to accept the immediately accessible logic of similarity over the more intractable mystery of difference. In this way, the metaphor serves literally to domesticate what is strange while also pointing to the moral necessity of pursuing a particular line of political action that derives from the sense of inevitability imparted by the figure.

The sense of inevitability is contained in two additional metaphors of imperial control quoted by Churchill in "The Scaffolding of Rhetoric":

> They (Frontier wars) are but the surf that marks the edge and advance of the wave of civilization.

> Our rule in India is, as it were, a sheet of oil spread over and keeping free from storms a vast and profound ocean of humanity.[32]

The first of these quotations was penned by the then prime minister, Lord Salisbury, and uses nature to inculcate a sense of the futility of opposing an inexorable process—the advance of civilization. Never mind that the metaphor also implies that civilization is static rather than progressive; the dominant image is of the wave advancing against sometimes dramatic but ultimately ineffectual resistance. The second example, attributed to Lord Randolph Churchill, Winston's father, implicates the same natural phenomenon but to a different end. Civilization is not nature here but that which tames and subdues nature—in this instance, the uncivilized peoples of India.

As was the case with the miracles of the Mad Fakir, Churchill's analogies present to the imagination of those responsive to them "a series of vivid impressions which are replaced before they can be too closely examined and vanish before they can be assailed."[33] Along with the impressions they create, the figures also engender a sense of providence (called "Allah" by one side, "civilization" by the other) operating in ineluctable and inexorable ways in human affairs. This sense of the providential, in turn, inculcates an attitude both of anticipation for what will happen in the future and of personal responsibility for the proper resolution of the situation framed by the metaphor.

In promising the appearance of heavenly hosts who would protect his supporters from bullets and fill his pot with rice to feed the multitudes, Saidullah was involving himself in a discursive operation that differed from that remarked upon by Churchill more in its cultural content than in its basic constitution. The promises he made were all promises that the people had heard before in the form of stories. In those stories the promises came true, and there was no reason to believe they wouldn't come true in this instance as well, so long as those who listened accepted their role in the resolution of the unfolding narrative. The genius of the Mad Fakir was thus the genius of all great political leaders—Winston Churchill not least among them—of creating through words the vision of a grand historical design and then making those who are susceptible to this vision aware of their own responsibility for its realization.

The Organization of Charisma

> Help from God (awaits us) and victory is at hand.
> Let it, after compliments, be understood by, and known to, the fol-
> lowers of the greatest of the prophets, vis, all the people of Ningra-
> har, the Shinwaris and others, that the people of Swat, Bajaur and
> Boner have all united together and succeeded in annihilating the
> troops of the infidels stationed in Swat, and have plundered their
> property. All the Muslims are therefore hereby informed that the
> Mohmands as a body have joined me in advancing upon (Shankar-
> garh) via Gandab for the purpose of carrying on a jehad. It is
> hoped that you on receipt of this letter will rise up, if sitting, and
> start, if standing, and taking the necessary supplies with you, come
> without fail as soon as possible. God willing, the time has come
> when the 'kafirs' (infidels) should disappear. Be not idle. What
> more should I insist upon. Peace be upon you.
>
> > (sd) *The Fakir of Adda*[34]

I want to turn now from the miracles of the Mad Fakir to the role
played by the Mulla of Hadda in organizing the insurgency. We have seen
that the promise of miraculous events was an important precondition for
gaining the people's confidence, but the Fakir's role, which was to light
the spark, was short-lived. The same was not true of the Mulla of Hadda.
While the Fakir was essentially a solitary figure (his solitariness being in
many respects the key to his charisma) who had neither the resources nor
the capabilities to extend his authority much beyond the range of his own
voice and person, Hadda Sahib was connected to an extensive network of
support and identification through the tariqat system, which provided him
with an organizational structure that was unique in the area. As we have
seen, tribes represent the dominant form of social organization in the region and one that has a particular resiliency in the face of state encroachment, but tribes also tend to be insular in orientation and provide neither
the idioms of relationship that would allow for more far-reaching alliances
nor the resources to support a widespread and sustained mobilization of
manpower.

The Mulla, on the other hand, had symbolic and practical resources
available to him that the tribes did not. Most importantly of course, he
had Islam, which represented the only ideology that was capable of unit-
ing disparate individuals and social polities under a common flag. Whereas
honor was essentially a particularizing code of conduct that specified the

local community as the primary context of moral suasion, Islam was something quite different: a universal system that leveled (if it did not erase) particular marks of identity while delineating a separate and distinct code of moral conduct applicable to all and arbitrated impartially by an implacable deity impressed more by self-effacing piety than self-affirming performances of personal honor. However, while Islam represents a separate moral system from that of honor and tribe, leaders like the Mulla of Hadda were successful to the degree that they could operate within both worlds. Islam could provide an ideological framework for joint action, but it could do so most effectively when those in charge were able to implicate honor and tribe to the cause of Islam rather than drawing attention to the differences between them. This was not an easy task, and the Mulla's organization of the 1897 uprising represents an example of the potentialities and perils inherent in the operation of reconciling Islam and honor for even a limited amount of time and in a circumscribed context.

In the letter that begins this section, we see one dimension of the Mulla's use of honor and Islam within the same ethical frame. Despite being limited in the kind of conclusions we can make because we only have an English translation and not the original document to work from, it is still possible to see in this letter the way in which Hadda Sahib was drawing on his own reputation as a man of God to impose an ethical obligation on those to whom he is writing. In this letter, the Mulla begins by addressing his readers not as Shinwaris and Ningraharis, but rather as "followers of the greatest of the prophets." This is the identity that he wishes to invoke, and it is to their responsibilities as Muhammad's followers that he wishes to draw their attention. At the same time, however, tribal identity does indeed matter and is implicitly manipulated in this message, for the Mulla well knows that to tell one tribe about the heroic actions of another tribe is to goad them to respond in kind. In the culture of honor, all deeds are enmeshed in a dialectic of challenge and response, and consequently when the Mulla tells the Shinwaris that the Mohmands have already accomplished a great deed, he is also implicitly challenging them to match it.

That sense of challenge that is set up throughout the letter is finally solidified in the last lines of the message when he asks rhetorically, "What more should I insist upon." In articulating the point of his letter in this indirect manner he puts the onus of response on those who hear the message. If we assume that a letter such as this would have been read aloud in public assembly, we can see that what the Mulla is doing is setting forth to the group at large the framework of the challenge (the context of an ongoing jihad and the prior action of other tribes in answering the call) and then articulating the challenge itself as a question to which those who hear the message must respond if they do not want to be publicly humiliated by failing to meet the challenge.

A second feature of the message is the way in which the Mulla encodes his own authority. Significantly, he does not order anyone to do anything. To do so would have been to involve his reader/listeners in a hierarchical relationship. Those who were disciples of the Mulla would presumably have been willing to accept an order from their pir, but others probably would not have been and might also have viewed acceptance as a diminution of their own pride of person and autonomy of action. This being the case, it was a far more effective strategy for Hadda Sahib not to command anyone, but rather to put himself in the position of directing the divisive energies of tribal honor to the cause of Islam. The letter effects this end by framing its intent not as an order but rather as a sort of public service announcement: this is who you are (followers of the greatest of the prophets), this is what other groups have done, and this is what you too should do if you want to be judged as their equal.

The "public service" tone of the message is, of course, disingenuous. The Mulla clearly means to prod the tribes to action, but the tone of the letter preserves Hadda Sahib's attitude of indifference to the dynamics of honor and highlights his sole concern for the preservation and betterment of Islam. While we cannot say with any certainty how the message was interpreted by its recipients, a sense of the persuasiveness of his requests for assistance can be at least tentatively gauged from the following letter from representatives of the Khani Khel section of the Chamkani tribe to Sir William Lockhart after the latter had asked the tribe not to join in the uprising: "We cannot deviate from obeying the orders that may be issued (for us) by the Fakir of Swat, the Adda Mullah, the Akka Khel Mullah, and all followers of Islam. It is allowable if our necks are cut off by one single blow from a sword (in obeying their orders). If they make peace with you, we are also at peace, or else we shall sacrifice our lives."[35]

Beyond the ideological advantages which Islam offered, the Mulla also had the practical resources of the tariqat system to draw on in his efforts to organize the jihad. If these resources were not as bountiful as those possessed by the state, they were certainly more potent than those of any individual tribe, and they were also more readily available than the resources of the state, which had to be brought in from outside. The first of these resources which the tariqat system made available was the network of communication that it afforded him and that allowed him to rally support from far-flung and otherwise disconnected tribes and locales on both sides of the border. Throughout the summer and fall of 1897, British reports testify to the extensiveness of Hadda Sahib's network, as British agents continually uncover evidence of agents carrying messages back and forth between him and the different fronts.[36]

The Mohmand territory where the Mulla made his own headquarters was not only relatively protected from British reprisal, it was also probably the most central point from which to maintain communications with the northern front at Swat, the more southerly fronts along the Khyber and in the Afridi Tirah, and Afghan tribes further removed from the border. Those with whom Hadda Sahib was in communication before and during the summer and fall of 1897 included first the Mad Fakir in Swat, who was certainly acting in concert with the Mulla and who may even have been following his orders.[37] In addition, the Mulla also maintained contact with several leaders who, like himself, had some prior connection to the Akhund of Swat, including the sons and grandsons of the Akhund, the so-called Mianguls of Swat, and the Palam Mulla of Dir who, like Hadda Sahib, was one of the deputies of the Akhund. The Mulla also drew heavily upon his own deputies (the name of Sufi Sahib of Batikot is mentioned most often and prominently in British dispatches) for assistance in rallying support from inside Afghanistan, and he also kept in frequent communication with other religious leaders like himself, such as Mulla Said Akbar and the Akka Khel Mulla (the principal religious leaders of the Afridis) and the Karabagh Mulla, the dominant religious figure in Kohat District.[38]

The main conduits in this communications network were the shaykhs and talebs who studied with and accepted orders from Hadda Sahib. Having relinquished ties of family and become his disciples, these individuals were free of other obligations and allegiances that might have divided their loyalties and undermined their obedience to their leader. Furthermore, their lack of other ties and their status as followers of a religious leader enabled the Mulla's men to "move quietly about the country, attract but little notice, and then work more successfully than the known Mullahs with whom they are associated." In the opinion of Harold Deane, the political agent in Malakand at the time of the uprising, it was these students, even more than the leaders like Hadda Sahib himself, who had the larger hand "in creating uneasiness and in trying to rouse the people to a *jehad.*"[39]

Another resource upon which the Mulla could presumably draw was the langar. As previously indicated, Hadda Sahib and his deputies fed large numbers of people in their langars, and one of the sources of their authority was their reputation for always being able to find enough food to feed their guests. This reputation was probably one of the reasons why followers of the Mad Fakir left cattle and crops undisturbed on their way to assault Chakdara. It also seems to have informed the attitude of many of the Mulla's adherents as well, and for a while, at least, it appears that he was able to keep up with demand since there are reports of men carrying loads of food to Mohmand prior to the battle of Shabqader.

It is fair to presume that if the battle had gone more in the favor of the Mulla's forces (particularly if they had succeeded in capturing the Hindu market at Shankargar), then the supplies at their disposal would have sufficed to keep his reputation intact. It did not, and this failure seems to have exposed Hadda Sahib to rebuke and eroded the foundation upon which he had based his authority. Reports indicate that in the days after the assault on Shabqader, as the Mulla waited for reinforcements and additional supplies, the late summer monsoons spoiled both a good deal of the food and much of the ammunition that the tribal force had at its disposal.

The combination of the military defeat that they had suffered, along with the rain and the protracted waiting that ensued following the retreat from Shabqader, also seems to have encouraged a general attitude of belligerence and disrespect in the Mulla's camp that was recounted in British reports with barely suppressed glee:

> The Mullah had a felt ('namad') and a charpoy only and the Ghazis were far and off over the hills lying behind the rocks disaffected with the Mullah. The Ghazis were complaining that good food as promised was not supplied to them from the 'langar.' Some were supplied with food and others were not fed for two days. Bread and atta were pouring into the Mullah from all sides, but nearly half reached him, half being spoiled by the rains and thus rendered unfit for eating.[40]

According to a second report,

> The Mullah said he awaited the outbreak of the Afridis when he would renew the ghaza; this time the arrangements had not been satisfactory, and moreover the Mohmands behaved villainously. The people secretly laughed at what he said, and remarked that after the present experience it was impossible for any one to flock to his standard again.[41]

Other followers of the Mulla were likewise quoted as saying, "We have seen the Mullah's greatness; he was boasting that he could provide food for 10,000 men twice a day, but he could not feed more than 200 even once a day." [42] Perhaps most humiliating of all, and most happily welcomed by the British, was the report in late September of Hadda Sahib's ignominious fall from grace following his final skirmish with British forces:

> There is a good story told that, during the attack on the Badmanai Pass, the Hadda Mullah was seen personally riding among the flying foe, but his pony fell in an awkward place, and they put him into a litter and carried him off. There were women close by, refugees from the villages, who cursed him in their choicest tongue for the trouble he had brought upon them. [43]

THE FAULT LINES OF AUTHORITY

Whether they are true or imagined, stories of the Mulla being laughed at by his followers and cursed by local women force us to consider the question of why the uprising failed. There are a number of obvious factors, among them the apparent superiority of British arms and organization. The British units had at their disposal the best arms and equipment available at the time, and after several generations on the frontier British and Indian soldiers knew how to use them to maximum effectiveness. The frontier tribesmen, on the other hand, had inferior armaments and none of the siege machinery that would have allowed them to breach the well-fortified battlements of British outposts. In addition, the tribesmen also lacked the military organization and discipline that enabled the British to keep men in the field for extended periods of time. In the tribal army, or *lashkar*, each lineage and group fought under its own flag and maintained its autonomy of action. Tribal warriors were loath to accept the authority of any leader, whether it was from within or outside their own group, and this meant that decisions had to be made by consensus.

Tribesmen also resisted the idea of assigning specific roles to different groups, and the notion that an army would work more effectively if some among them accepted a logistical role to ensure the regular shipment of necessary food and supplies was insupportable. Pakhtuns have long looked to battle as an opportunity for besting their personal rivals every bit as much as for gaining larger victories, and this ethos meant that few were willing to accept subordinate or specialized roles. It also meant that many tribesmen, at least in the first stages of confrontation, were willing to go out onto the open field to meet the British enemy face-to-face. This willingness to expose oneself to risk for the sake of honor was well and good when the enemy consisted of other tribesmen, armed like oneself with sword, shield, and flintlock, but it was another matter altogether when the enemy across the way had mounted lancers, maxim guns, artillery pieces, and the latest repeating rifles.[44]

Such problems did not afflict the British army, and as a result of their superior organization, they were able to maintain an extended line of defense around the perimeter of their territory, to sustain logistical support for these perimeter bases over long periods of time, and to respond quickly to threats against these bases. The tribal lashkar was a highly effective military organization in its own way as well, but its limitations were exposed in situations of protracted, stationary combat such as occurred in the summer of 1897. If one could imagine such a thing as a bestiary of military forms, the lashkar would perhaps be compared with the shark in the sense that it is a ruthlessly effective killing organism so long as it sustains its forward momentum. Once it is forced to stop moving, however, the lashkar, like the shark, quickly suffocates and dies. An operation of the size undertaken by the tribes in 1897 required logistical support of the sort that the lashkar could not provide. The number of men attracted by the charismatic promises of the leaders exceeded the ability of those leaders to meet their daily needs, and, as the Mulla discovered to his discomfort, an extended period of inactivity between battles was impossible to sustain, even if one did have the resources of various local langars to fall back upon.

In addition to these logistical problems, Hadda Sahib and his allies were also undermined by political divisions, among them the disloyalty of local potentates who seem to have found the prospect of a successful jihad nearly as threatening as did the British themselves. As Lionel James noted, "In almost every area of revolt the Khans and privileged groups were in secret touch with the British, fearing political anarchy and the uncontrollable and unpredictable religious fanaticism of the 'mullahs'. The predictable dilemma was either to choose the uncertain path to 'national' and religious glory or risk local opprobrium by keeping their options open through contact with the imperial powers."[45]

A second factor in the failure of the uprisings involved the ambiguous role of Amir Abdur Rahman, the old foe of the Mulla, who appears to have mitigated Hadda Sahib's success by first appearing to offer him support for his enterprise and then taking it away. Given the history of animosity between the Amir and the Mulla, one would assume that the Amir would have opposed any adventure in which the Hadda Mulla had a hand. In the same way, it is equally difficult to imagine Hadda Sahib seeking the support of a ruler who had tried to arrest him (and, reportedly, to kill him) and who had imprisoned a number of his principal deputies. More than anything else, however, the Amir was a political realist, and he would have recognized the advantage of having an insurgency mounted against the colonial power on his eastern border without his having to take a leading role. If the insurgency were successful, it would mean that he would have a much freer hand in dealing with the frontier tribes and less to worry about in terms of the British exercising their influence on "his" tribes. If the insurgency failed, then the Mulla himself, along with his allies, would perhaps permanently tarnish their own reputations with their followers. Either way, the Amir came out ahead.

From Hadda Sahib's point of view, alliance with the Afghan state offered several important advantages, regardless of the history of animosity between himself and the Amir. One advantage was obviously that of greater manpower, better armaments, and more reliable supplies. A second advantage was doctrinal. Hadda Sahib does not appear to have imagined himself a king: his rejection of the Shinwari offer of such a title is evidence of this. But, at the same time, he also certainly recognized the importance of such a title, particularly in a time of conflict. Only a properly ordained ruler was entitled to declare a jihad, and without such a declaration any conflict, including even one against an infidel power like Great Britain, was illegitimate. This implied, among other things, that those who died in the course of the conflict would not be considered Islamic martyrs (*shahidan*).

For their part, the British were convinced that the Amir was helping the insurgents, and their correspondence from the summer of the uprising is replete with signs and signals of the Amir's real intentions:

- "Sixty copies of the 'Targhib-ul-Jehad' and the 'Taqwim-ud-din' [two pamphlets on jihad written by the Amir] have reached the Mullah Sahib of Adda from Kunar Haka. . . . The Hakim [governor] of Kunar has sent 200 'kharwars' of wheat and 5 'kharwars' of barley to help Mullah Sahib's supplies";
- Despite the fact that Hadda Sahib had been expelled by Amir Abdur Rahman, they were said to be on good terms and his Commander-in-Chief was reported to have been in communication with the Mulla and to have sent him cash;
- The Amir's officials were secretly encouraging the uprising and are reported to have given the Mulla 25,000 rupees through Sahibzada Jilam of Kama.[46]

Despite the cumulative evidence of such reports, it seems clear that the Amir couched whatever support he offered in such a way that he could never be held accountable for it. Public statements to tribal leaders (which, he was certainly aware, were being reported to British authorities) were noncommittal at best and dismissive at worst.[47] Whatever aid he might have sent to the rebels seems to have been handled through third parties and was of such limited quantity and value that it provided little in the way of practical help or encouragement to the overmatched tribesmen.[48] Likewise, letters sent by Abdur Rahman to the British themselves were supportive of their position and promised assistance in reining in recalcitrant tribes.[49]

Even his incendiary pamphlets on jihad were phrased in such a way that conditioned his support for military action on certain requirements being met, the most important of which was that a jihad be formally declared by the lawful Islamic ruler of the realm. From the British point of view, of course, such rhetorical ambiguity was simply an example of Abdur Rahman's skill in the arts of political manipulation. With "true Oriental subtilty [sic]," one colonial writer noted, he sought to veil the most important passages of his pamphlets with "a double meaning" that allowed him to "argue from either standpoint. If it suited the Amir to set the mechanism working, it evidently has not suited him to openly aid the working of the machine, though he possibly can find means to supply the necessary lubricants, even when expressing righteous indignation at the attitude of the frontier fanatics."[50]

While there is undoubtedly some truth to the judgment that Abdur Rahman recognized the strategic advantages of playing both sides against the middle, it is also true that the matter of who had the right to declare a jihad was tremendously important to him. Religious leaders had great appeal in Afghanistan and, on average, far greater longevity than rulers. During his tenure in office, Abdur Rahman had discovered the weaknesses of most of the leaders who challenged his right to rule. Some could be bought off, some could be lured into compromising positions, and those who didn't have sufficient support he was able to simply eliminate. Hadda Sahib, however, was one of the few, perhaps the only, religious leader who consistently stymied the Amir, staying just beyond his grasp and outside of his control.[51] Consequently, it was important for the Amir to preserve what advantages he had, and one of these advantages was certainly the doctrine that only an Islamic ruler could declare a jihad.

A final factor in the failure of the uprisings had to do with the Mulla's dependence on the tribes themselves. Many of the most important tribal maliks received allowances from the British which they were loath to endanger, and his location in Mohmand also seems to have harmed his ability to function as independently as he had been able to while he was living in Hadda. Thus, while Abdur Rahman was undoubtedly right in being leery of the Mulla's potential for causing him trouble, it was also true that once the Amir had forced Hadda Sahib to take refuge with the Mohmand, his ability to accomplish his political objectives was compromised.

As long as Hadda Sahib was living in Mohmand, his access to his disciples was limited. When he lived in Hadda, close to Jalalabad, anyone who wanted to visit him had only to make the short journey from the city. In the fastness of Mohmand, on the other hand, he was largely cut off from his supporters and dependent on messengers to communicate with his followers in other areas. Thus, despite the relative freedom that the Mulla enjoyed among the tribes and despite the central location of the Mohmand territory along the border, this was still a mountainous area without roads or centers where people from different backgrounds could gather. During the summer of 1897, this isolation not only hampered Hadda Sahib's ability to coordinate strategy between the different fronts, but also limited his ability to personally rally support.

Beyond this, the Mulla's residence with the Mohmands limited his autonomy of person and his status as a religious figure. When he was located in his own center, he was in charge, he was "sahib of Hadda." In Mohmand, his position was restricted. Every move had to be negotiated, often with tribal leaders who, as indicated, were receiving allowances from the British and therefore hesitant to throw their support behind a religious figure who threatened not only to eliminate a reliable source of income but also to introduce new moral demands into the universe of tribal relations.

One concrete indication of how the moral demands of the Mulla came into conflict with the moral demands of tribal honor can be seen in the following report that explained why Hadda Sahib was encountering resistance in his efforts to have his followers support the uprising in Swat: "The tribesmen refused to go towards Swat, because it would be impossible for them to bring back their dead and wounded from so great a distance, but they said that if the Mullah would lead a jehad somewhere closer to their homes they would join him."[52] Time and again in the course of Afghan history, one encounters this reticence over fighting too far from home. On one level, what this phenomenon reveals is a concern for the proper disposition of the dead, but on a deeper level it reflects both the insularity of tribal morality and the ambivalent regard which the tribes have for Islam. If truly committed to the cause, the final resting place of the body would not matter: those who die in jihad are (to reprise the words of Talabuddin Akhundzada) "pure martyrs" and no one need concern themselves with the mortal remains or cultural fallout from their deaths. But, as Sultan Muhammad reminded his father, the dead mind their own business. The living remain behind, and they must keep one eye on those around them even if they choose to focus the other eye on heaven.

TALES OF JAROBI GLEN

Having considered some of the reasons why the jihad of 1897 failed in its efforts to dislodge the British from the frontier, I want to turn to another question that is more puzzling than why the rebellion itself faltered. Given that the Mulla did indeed fail in his efforts to end British rule in the frontier, what were the consequences of this failure for his reputation? Since he is remembered by Afghans today as one of the great saints in their history, we must assume that his reputation remained intact, but if this is the case, how exactly did his reputation survive the defeat of his miraculous claims to divine assistance? Most miraculous promises, we must assume, do not come true. Most claims to supernatural assistance in the prosecution of political objectives ultimately run afoul of practical reality. How then do charismatic leaders like the Mulla of Hadda survive as viable foci of public respect? How is it that their moral authority continues to prosper even when their promises prove hollow?

   This is, of course, a complex problem and one that belies simple answers, but in order to propose at least a partial solution, I want to direct our attention back to the realm of stories in which we began our investigation and to the role of stories in encoding the moral imperatives by which particular societies choose to live. So let us consider the denouement of events in the late summer of 1897, as those events are recounted from the different points of view of those who were involved in the confrontation. The first of these is a journalistic account written by a British reporter named H. Woosnam Mills, who accompanied the expeditionary force into the Mohmand tribal territory in pursuit of the Mulla of Hadda. The second version of the events of that summer is a miracle story that was told to me by a descendant of one of the Mulla of Hadda's deputies. The third and final version of events is contained in a story told by a Mohmand tribesman whose grandfather was also a participant in the uprising and who claimed to be with the Mulla of Hadda during the climactic engagement with the British.

Mills's Tale

After relieving the Chakdara and Malakand garrisons, General Bindon Blood, Churchill's sponsor and family friend, assumed charge of a punitive expedition against the rebellious tribes of Swat and Mohmand. Designated the Malakand Field Force, General Blood's column first secured the submission of the villages of lower Swat directly involved in the siege of the Malakand and Chakdara forts, then turned west to confront the Mohmand and Mahmund tribes that had participated in the attack on the Shabqader fort and Shankargar bazaar. In the course of their westerly traverse into the Mohmand territory, Blood's original force was joined by a second column under General Elles—the Mohmand Field Force—that had been hurriedly assembled in Peshawar in the wake of the uprising. The explicit objectives of the combined operation were, first, to disperse and punish the tribes that had undertaken the assault and, second, to apprehend the author of their discontents, the Mulla of Hadda. From their intelligence reports, the British authorities knew that the Mulla had made his headquarters in the most inaccessible part of the Mohmand territory, astride the border between India and Afghanistan. The location they set their sights upon was the little village of Jarobi, a place that had attained an almost mythical stature in British eyes due to the Mulla's residence there and the fact that no foreigner had ever laid eyes upon it.

As the two columns marched toward the Mulla's stronghold, the British encountered stiff resistance, especially while crossing the Bedmanai Pass (where the Hadda Sahib had reportedly fallen from his horse in his hurry to escape the onrushing British troops). Following this encounter, the only difficulty faced by the invading force was fatigue induced by the stifling heat and "tier upon tier of dusty waste-stretches." The aridity and barrenness of the landscape was sufficiently oppressive, in fact, to cause Mills to wonder if, in fact, the much fabled "Jarobi, the valley of the Mohmands, which overflows with milk and honey" was "but a myth".[53] Such doubts were assuaged, however, when they crossed the pass leading into the undefended valley, and gray hills and dusty plains gave way to a very different scene:

> When the tower was reached at last, the beautiful valley which no European had gazed upon before broke upon the view. . . . The valley opened out and the far side was lost in a lofty range. On the right the hills were lower and gracefully wooded with walnut and pine, while as stepping-stones to the centre of the valley the green fields of Indian corn rose in succeeding tiers, and there on a knoll with a deep grove at its foot stood Jarobi proper,—the

home of the Mad Mullah—nestling against the wooded spurs which rose away from behind it melting away into the bleak barrenness of the separating range.[54]

Before the troops could descend into the valley that they had traveled so far to conquer, however, their progress was suddenly interrupted from an unexpected quarter:

> As the first white men shaded their eyes to the scene, the elements joined, and as if in disapprobation of the sacrilegious advance, dense storm clouds rolled over the peaks and vivid lightning played above the sacred spot, while the artillery of heaven reverberated across the peaceful valley; an ominous forecast of the rude awakening which was about to come.[55]

The odd congruence of natural and human events did not deter the column from continuing on its mission, for even as the monsoon rains were gathering above them, two companies of the 20th Punjab Infantry and a detachment of miners from the Bengal Sappers began their work of destruction, first blowing up the tower that commanded the entrance to the valley and then proceeding on into the village itself, which they intended to burn to the ground. "As they came abreast of the village," however, "the heavy clouds brought rain and hail, and a bitter wind chilled all to the bone as they plodded up the Pass."[56]

To the accompaniment of hail and lightning, the first wave of British troops entered the deserted village to carry out their appointed mission. The only resistance that was encountered came from five swordsmen who had remained behind in the village mosque after the other villagers had fled the scene. No one knows who these swordsmen were or what their mission was, but they "rushed on the 20th Punjab Infantry and died, undoubtedly in their own way, as a sacrifice."[57] While the Sappers "applied the fatal torch" to Jarobi, the infantry pressed on up the narrow defile which was said "to lead to the Mullah's retreat." Here, "a blaze of fire was poured in from either side, and it was evident that the defile was held by the enemy in force."

> The fire was heavy, and four or five men dropped in as many seconds. In the meantime, the firing having declared the position to General Westmacott in the rear, No. 3 Mountain Battery was ordered up, and it made beautiful practice on the hills crowning the left of the 20th, while the remaining half battalion was pushed up to the defile in support. A few minutes after the guns came into action the whole of the valley was in flames, and the main object of the expedition had been attained.[58]

As night was approaching and "a retirement in the dark would not have been desirable, at 3–30 the 'retire' was sounded," and the British troops began their retreat from the defile "under a harassing fire from the most daring of the cragsmen who held on to their rear. . . . By 5 the dangerous part of a most treacherous valley had been cleared and by 5–30 the whole of the troops engaged were in camp." All that remained before "the curtain was finally rung down" was for General Blood's troops to conduct a "Political walk-round."[59] For the most part, this consisted of a demonstration of force and intimidation, one aspect of which was the prying loose of money, arms, grain, and forage from tribes that "owed" what could be extracted as compensation for having acted in a hostile fashion toward the government of India. Hostages were also taken from those tribes failing to turn over the stipulated penalties, new passes and routes were reconnoitered, and all the while an orderly and unhurried retreat was carried out.

Rohani's Tale

Before commenting on the preceding reconstruction of events, I first turn to the account of this confrontation that has been preserved by descendants of the Mulla's deputies. I have collected several versions of this story from various informants, but the one I have chosen to include is the most complete. The narrator is Maulavi Ahmad Gul Rohani, a grandson of Ustad Sahib of Hadda, the deputy who took over the Hadda center after the Mulla's death. Maulavi Ahmad Gul was a judge and religious teacher in Afghanistan prior to the Marxist revolution, and he told me the story during the course of an interview in Peshawar in 1984. This account was introduced with the statement that it was a story "we have heard from our elders:"

> One day the late respected Najmuddin Akhundzada [the Mulla of Hadda], may peace be upon him, gathered [his forces] in Jarobi, and from there they attacked the English and assaulted them and did jihad against them. The English were faced with great trouble because of him. Finally, they brought their troops near the village and gathered there. They called the people of the village and took their elders and brought them to the governor and told them, "If you accept these three demands of ours, fine. Otherwise, I will destroy your village and kill all of your women and children.
>
> They said, "What are these demands?"
>
> [The general] replied, "First, you must sacrifice Najmuddin Akhundzada Sahib (may peace be upon him) so that we will be saved from troublemaking and sit comfortably. And if you can't do

this, send him from your village so you won't be caused trouble and difficulties. Then it will be between him and us. If you don't give him a place to stay, he will go back to Afghanistan."

These were their demands, and the people of the village returned with great worry, grief, and sorrow. They consulted among themselves how it would be possible to disclose these conditions to *sahib-i mubarak* [Blessed Master] and tell him the English words. Finally, they said, "Let us go and consult with Sahib-i Mubarak," and they told him the whole story, that "you must either be martyred or surrendered or sent out from the village."

Sahib-i Mubarak told them, "I will go and sit on the mountain. You go and tell the English, 'We have sent Sahib-i Mubarak from our village. Now it is between you and him.'"

Sahib-i Mubarak went to the mountain and started his worship of God. Then he started his *nawafil* prayers. He was saying his nawafil prayers, and the white beards came to the English and talked to their armies, and they told them, "See! We have sent Sahib-i Mubarak from our village. See! He is sitting on the mountain. Now if you want to capture him or martyr him, do as you wish."

The commander ordered his soldiers—foot and cavalry—to go and surround Sahib-i Mubarak and take him alive and bring him. From there, the English forces moved and were running and finally had almost reached him. Because of his blessed prayers (he was busy with his humble prayers), because he was busy humbly and secretly praying to God (his only creator, the Master of the Universe, and he took refuge in God), by the blessing of God, bees swarmed down on the English, and the bees attacked, and every one of their soldiers was faced with hundreds of bees, and they stung them. Some fell from their horses, and some fell while running, and some died, and some fled.

Thus, they faced defeat, and they came and told their commander, "We were faced with this kind of plague and disaster that all of our bodies were filled with painful poison, and we were unable to reach [the Mulla]. God sent bees against us."

Then [the commander] communicated with his headquarters and told the story to them—that such things had happened up to this minute. "What can we do now?"

Then [the villagers] ordered them, "Take your dead bodies and come, and don't cause him any more trouble." And they confessed, "Even if there is no one with him and he has no weapons or equipment, our power cannot conquer this faqir who has spent his life in the clothing of poverty and piety. This is truly a miraculous and courageous faqir!"

There are no dates attached to this version of events, and none are remembered. The context in which this miraculous occurrence took place had been forgotten by the narrator, if indeed he had ever known much about it. The only reason we know that the narrative concerns the same events as those in the first account is the setting in Jarobi and the involvement of the Mulla of Hadda. Older informants who have been asked to recount additional stories from this time that they might have heard from their elders do not recall any others. This is the story they remember, and while there are significant variations in how the story is told and what elements are emphasized, the miracle of the bees is the central event in all of the versions.

In considering the relationship between the British history and that told by the Mulla's followers, it is appropriate to begin by mentioning the elements that they share in common. This would include the following "facts:" The British came to Jarobi to capture the Mulla, but he was absent from the village. After a confrontation in the mountains outside the village, the British retired from the valley without capturing the Mulla. Finally, both accounts come to closure through an act of submission on the part of the enemy.

Beyond the general similarity of outline, the most intriguing element common to both stories is certainly the "natural" event at the center of each, for it is in this depiction that we recognize that this is the same historical event differently cast in two forms of remembrance. It is also in the representation of this "storm" that we see the most telling difference in the cultural perspectives of the two protagonists. For the British author, the onset of a violent hailstorm at the moment of the expedition's arrival at Jarobi is given an ironic significance. The odd synchronicity of the natural and human events leads the author to introduce the notion of supernatural intelligence conspiring to resist "the sacrilegious advance." The "artillery of heaven," however, is seen to be no match for the "destroying cartridge" of the Sappers, and the supernatural intervention proves to be no more than "an ominous forecast" of the more potent "awakening" about to come in the form of the British expeditionary force as it moves forward to level the village. The effect of this passage is then to appropriate and, through irony, dissolve the sacred world view associated with the Mulla within the rationalizing framework of the British. In the second narrative, however, irony is also implied but in relation to those who believe themselves all powerful when in fact they are powerless before God. This ironic relationship is demonstrated in the initial arrogance of the British and their subsequent humiliation at the hands of the humble faqir.

At the heart of these two stories are very different understandings of the world and of human and divine agency within it. The different metaphysical principles embodied in the narratives can both be exemplified by reference to the same organizing figure: a figure that conveys opposed meanings to the different protagonists and that neatly concretizes the difference that we earlier noted between miracles and metaphors. That figure is often discovered in British colonial accounts and is associated with the act of "lifting the veil" or "lifting *purdah*" and can be seen in the following example taken from Mills's account of the Mohmand expedition: "As far as the Baizais [Mohmands] are concerned, they never can boast that their *purdah* has not been lifted, that a *Sirkar's* [government] force has not swept through their country, and in accordance with the nature of things, it may be fairly presumed that they will keep clear of raids in our territory for many a long day." [60]

On one level, the use of this metaphor expresses the moral duty of civilized society (reprising Churchill's Primrose League speech cited at the beginning of this chapter) to bear "peace, civilisation and good government to the uttermost ends of the earth." Since the tribes lived in what Churchill termed "the unpenetrable gloom of barbarism," it was incumbent upon those blessed by rationality and common sense to push back the curtain of superstition and dispel the darkness. In addition to this abstract reading of the metaphor, a more straightforward sense conveyed by the figure has to do with the political act of asserting dominion.

Thus, the figure connotes the idea of pushing through an impediment to imperial rule, and it does so in terms that are culturally significant to those over whom the colonial power seeks to assert its authority. Specifically, it appropriates the emotionally charged symbol of purdah, the cloth screen or veil used to conceal women and the private space of the home from the public gaze of outsiders. As employed by Mills (and many other colonial writers), the nature of the appropriation is clearly spelled out: invading tribal space is an act of penetrating private space and, as such, an affront to tribal honor that is equivalent to having one's domestic quarters violated by strangers. The British troops are the ones in a position to boast. Their force is the greater one; the tribes must endure the shame of trespass, a shame which British colonial officers well knew had a visceral and highly personal quality to it.

By construing the invasion in these terms, Mills and like-minded writers were in some respects simply putting the best slant on a political reality that had not worked out as well as they would have desired. Despite their superiority in weapons and organization, the British found permanent occupation of the tribal territories to be impractical and, in the final analysis, impossible. Consequently, the effectiveness of campaigns such as the Mohmand expedition depended as much on the exercise of symbolic domination as on actual control. In this instance, symbolic domination was achieved through the act of trespass itself, which was also an act of observation.

As Foucault and others have argued, observation is both a condition and an expression of power; but here the particular salience of observation is in relation to the tribal context—a context in which public and private space are strictly delimited and where trespass is an offense requiring armed retaliation.[61] Although few British officers and even fewer journalists were familiar with the cultural dynamics of honor among the frontier tribes, they were well aware that tribesmen, like their own subject populations in India, placed considerable importance on the sanctity of purdah; they also realized that the act, figurative or literal, of "lifting the veil" was a way of empowering themselves (in their own terms) by unmanning their adversaries (in theirs).

That at least is one way to interpret the metaphor of "lifting the veil," but there is another, and it is this other interpretation which allows us to understand how the Mulla and his followers achieved their own symbolic victory during the battle of Jarobi Glen and how an apparent humiliation could be turned into a signal success. This alternative interpretation derives from the mystical significance of the term "lifting the veil" as it is understood in Sufi cosmology. As indicated earlier in this chapter, the metaphor of "lifting the veil" is a way of talking about the saint's power to perform miracles by drawing upon the resources and potentialities of the hidden realm of the batin, the domain of divine power, to shape events in the world immediately apparent to us.

Although caution must be exercised in making connections between the universe of Sufi cosmology and the domain of social and political relations, it can be argued that the figure of the lifted veil has a paradigmatic significance that informs the moral imperative of the Afghan account equally as well as it does that of Mills. In the story of the bees, divine intervention is brought about when the Mulla moves outside the bounds of human society to devote himself completely to God. Maulavi Ahmad Gul, the narrator of the story, refers several times to the fact that the

Mulla was absorbed in worshipping God, and he specifically mentions that the Mulla was engaged in "nawafil" prayers. This is a potentially significant detail given the fact that the narrator of the story was himself a Sufi and religious scholar and might be presumed to have been familiar with the well-known tradition from the life of the Prophet, according to which God told Muhammad: "When my servant seeks to approach Me through super[er]ogatory works, I entirely love him. And when I love him I become the hearing through which he heareth, the sight through which he seeth, the hand with which he graspeth, the foot with which he walketh." [62]

This tradition is a principal part of the evidence for the belief that men can enter into a state of "nearness" to God through acts of supererogatory worship (*qurban nawafil*) and that God will show His love to those who enter this state through the performance of miracles. Thus, by indicating that Hadda Sahib engaged in nawafil prayers, the narrator appears to be indicating that the Mulla was entering the state of "unveiledness" within which a miracle could be manifested and the Mulla's power as beloved of God revealed to others. [63]

This act of mystical unveiling is the central focus of the second historical narrative, just as the political act of lifting the veil is of the first. Thus juxtaposed, the unveiling in the first becomes an ironic counterpoint of the second, for the British attempt to lift the veil concealing the Mulla provides the condition for the revelation of God's miraculous control over human affairs. That is, of course, quite contrary to what British officials intended to accomplish through their punitive campaign, and it leads to the conclusion that if it is power that allows the British to create their image of the "Mad Mullah," then it is the capacity of this latter individual to use the condition of powerlessness to create himself (or at least to be retrospectively recreated through the transformative medium of miracle stories) that allows charisma to endure.

The British effort to make the Mulla visible and subject to the constraints of their metaphors, their plots, and their terms of narrative closure may effect this end for themselves; however, it failed in relation to the people of the frontier for the simple reason that they have succeeded in remembering the encounter in a way that reflects their own sense of moral determinacy. British reports of the Mulla's defeat gather dust in the archives. No one particularly recalls that in 1897 British troops managed to part the curtain and penetrate to the very heart of tribal territory. What is remembered, at least by some, is that a long-dead saint was saved by the miraculous appearance of bees. Through this story, a divine act of intervention that reaffirmed the Mulla's status as one of God's beloved has eclipsed evidence of his human vulnerability and his defeat at the hands of the British. Defeat may indeed have been his fate, but the events of that day were soon consigned to the domain of narrative, and it is within that domain that the possibility of future miracles and future leaders like the Mulla of Hadda remained alive.

Shahmund's Tale

And so it would appear to conclude—the British and the Mulla, each claiming (or having claimed for them) a kind of victory for their labors, each framing their victories in an unassailable language of moral necessity. But, the situation becomes more complicated when we add a third version of events from an altogether different source: the Mohmand tribesmen who were the other principal party in the battle of Jarobi.[64] The narrator of this third account is the Mohmand elder, Shahmund (who was quoted in the first chapter on the subject of what a man inherits from his parents). Shahmund comes from a branch of the Mohmand tribe, the group with whom the Mulla had been living for most of the decade prior to the uprisings of 1897. Shahmund's account goes like this.

> My grandfather told me that Hadda Sahib was staying temporarily at the Taib mosque in Dara Adam Khel when the *ferangi* [English] attacked the Khawezai tribe who lived there. Many other tribes such as the Musa Khel marched toward Dara to help and take part in the battle. My grandfather told me that Hadda Sahib lived in Dara at that time, but he did not have a horse to take part in the battle.
>
> My grandfather said, "Since he was a very old man, I offered to carry him on my back to the battlefield. He was very eager to take part in the battle, so he accepted my offer and I had the opportunity of serving him for a good cause."
>
> My grandfather said that he was pretty sure that he could carry Hadda Sahib for a long distance because he was very skinny. I must mention that my grandfather was one of Hadda Sahib's sincere and loyal followers. My grandfather said, "When we got close to the battlefield, Hadda Sahib said, '*Pahlawan Shaykh* [mighty shaykh], let me down!'"
>
> Then Hadda Sahib prayed for the help of God. My grandfather said that he was impatiently waiting for the results of the praying

when suddenly dark clouds covered the sky and a heavy rain started to fall. Meanwhile an army of bees, hornets, and wasps appeared over the English army and from the other side the tribesmen attacked them. In a matter of a few hours the army was almost completely defeated. The hailstones were pouring down like bullets from the sky.

Amazingly, the army was defeated more easily than anyone could have ever expected. The skulls of their horses' heads are still over there in that place where the battle was fought. The Mohmands followed them all the way to Shabqader, shouting, "Allah Akbar, Allah Akbar! [God is Great! God is Great!]" This was a very clear miracle of his.

When I reencountered this story after it had been transcribed from tape, I noticed elements in Maulavi Ahmad Gul's version of events that I had failed to appreciate when I first heard it. One such element is the way in which the Maulavi's story depicts the Mohmand tribesmen as passive and even somewhat craven in their relations with the British. Thus, when the people return to the village after being informed of the British demands, they are represented as being full of "worry, grief, and sorrow." We can almost imagine them bemoaning their fate and wringing their hands before finally concluding that the Mulla alone can decide what to do. When Hadda Sahib goes off by himself to confront the British on the mountaintop, no Mohmands are depicted as being present, and no mention is made of the Mohmands being involved in any way in the ensuing battle. When the Mulla leaves the village, they essentially wash their hands of the struggle by saying, "Now it is between you [the British] and him."

In the Afghan scheme of things, the people presented in this account are more like peasants than tribesmen and more like women than men, as seen in a variety of ways, one of the most telling of which is the depiction of the tribal elders as intermediaries with the British side. In tribal custom, when one party to a dispute wants to sue for peace, they will send a delegation of mullas (or other religious functionaries), carrying with them a Qur'an and often accompanied by a group of women, to negotiate with the other side. Mullas and women can perform this role because they are considered noncombatants. While the mullas discuss the terms of a truce, the women will sit in the domestic quarters of the other side until arrangements have been made, and then they return to their own people. In this story, however, the usual roles are switched as the Mulla remains behind while the elders go off to hear the British general announce his conditions for withdrawing from the area.

In keeping with the place assigned to them in the story, the Mohmands play no role in the ensuing combat. Hadda Sahib bravely goes forth to meet his destiny, but the villagers fearfully stand apart from the fray. No one steps forward to protect the Mulla from the British. No man among them is willing to rise up to defend the old man who has been resident among them for so many years. What is not stated here is that such passivity would open the Mohmand to the vilest criticism, for in their unwillingness to protect the Mulla, the Mohmand villagers would be violating a fundamental obligation in tribal culture: that of defending those who have taken refuge among them. The Mulla may have been among them a very long time. He may even have overstayed his welcome, but he was still a guest of the tribe, and the men of the tribe were obligated to defend his life with their own.

Although such behavior would be considered contemptible in the tribal world, its depiction here is intended not to sully the reputation of the Mohmand but rather to advance that of the Mulla. The Mohmands (who are never referred to in the Maulavi's story by name) serve simply as stock characters. Their point of view is unimportant to the story, which is more concerned with finding evidence of victory in the incident of defeat. What might have been a doubly humiliating reversal for the Mulla (his rejection by the tribe and his defeat by the British) is thus turned into a moment of mastery over both the local tribesmen and the encroaching forces of state rule.

Not surprisingly, the Mohmand narrative doesn't view the tribe's relation to the Mulla or their involvement in the battle in exactly the same terms as that of the Mulla's disciple. In Shahmund's rendition, Hadda Sahib plays a major role in the battle, but so also do the Mohmands. The first mention of the Mulla in this alternative account is of his being in one of the local mosques when the war broke out between the "ferangi" and the local people (not, significantly, between the British and the Mulla). Following this introduction, the narrator notes that the Mulla didn't have a horse at the time, that he was (apparently) old and frail, and that the narrator's grandfather, who was one of the Mulla's disciples, offered to carry him on his back.

In none of this is there any sense of subservience. Rather, one gets the impression of a younger man with strength to spare shouldering the burden of an elderly and infirm man who might have some trouble taking care of himself. Hadda Sahib himself is in no way abased in this depiction, for after telling us how his grandfather carried him on his back, the narrator goes on to describe how the Mulla ordered the younger man to set him down when they reached the battlefield. Just as the younger man has provided a service for the old man and, in the process, demonstrated his strength, it is now time for the Mulla to come to the aid of his followers by demonstrating the power that is at his command.

The next section of the story contains elements similar to ones found in both the British version and Maulavi Ahmad Gul's, for here rain and hailstones, as well as a variety of swarming insects, suddenly appear to greet the British troops. It is perhaps significant that Shahmund's account mentions the appearance of more natural elements than any of the others: rain, hail, and, in the insect category, hornets and wasps, along with the bees of which we have already heard. The contrast between Shahmund's version of events and Maulavi Ahmad Gul's makes one suspect that, for the Maulavi, bees were sufficient. The confrontation he depicts, after all, was not a clash of arms and men, but "a kind of plague and disaster" in which the bodies of the dead filled up with poison, and all who did not die a presumably excruciating death were forced to escape panic-stricken from the battlefield.

Shahmund's version of the engagement with the British troops has a mythic cast to it as well, but of an entirely different sort than in the other account. His template is not a biblical plague but a heroic battle in which ancestors join in common cause to counter an invading army and send them fleeing in headlong retreat. In keeping with this orientation, Shahmund's story has a firmer sense of the tribal setting within which the action transpires. The narrator, after all, has lived near Jarobi most of his life and knows the terrain on which the battle took place. To my knowledge, Maulavi Ahmad Gul never went anywhere near the locations he describes (having lived most of his life in and around Jalalabad) and would not know, for example, that in a particular spot near Jarobi one can find the bleached skulls of horses that, according to local lore, date back to this very battle. He would also be unaware that in Mohmand territory travelers are as likely to encounter hornets and wasps as they are bees, which tells us, of course, that these insects are not from some other world (like the fruits Abdul Baqi brought back from Koh-i Qaf) but rather local creatures enlisted (like the tribesmen themselves) to assist in the cause of vanquishing an invading army.

Beyond the mythic or ordinary identity of the creatures, another point of difference between the two accounts has to do with how much credit the bees should receive for the outcome of the battle. As Shahmund tells the tale, the insects are present when the battle is joined, but they are not given credit for carrying the day. Rather, it would appear to be a joint victory in which the Mulla plays his role and the Mohmands theirs. Neither role is clearly more important than the other, and both are represented as contributing to the general good.[65] In this way, the Mulla's role is certainly not dismissed in Shahmund's account (as the Mohmand role is negated in Maulavi Ahmad Gul's rendition), but it is also not represented as decisive. Shahmund judiciously divides responsibility by indicating that both the Mulla and the Mohmands deserve credit for expelling the British from the valley. Both participated, and both share in the glory of the moment.

The Trouble with Heroes

In the earlier chapters on Sultan Muhammad Khan and Amir Abdur Rahman, the existence of alternative endings to the stories raised the possibility that the stories had more ambiguous meanings encoded within them than first might be supposed. The same can be said of these alternative versions of the battle of Jarobi Glen, for in reading them one is forced to reevaluate whose victory this is and how it is to be decided. In the British narrative, victory belongs to the best armed and organized, but it is a victory that belongs as well to the most advanced. The act of penetrating the territory of the Mohmands plays out on a small scale the grander project of civilization overcoming barbarism, of reason vanquishing superstition.

The Mohmand version shares one element with the British account: it valorizes great deeds and the image of men contesting with one another on the field of battle. Tribesman and statesman alike glorified this ideal, but beyond this one shared aspect, there is only difference. Shahmund's story centers on his grandfather's actions, and the story itself figures as part of his own patrimony. History is an inheritance—it is the flesh and sinew that animates and quickens the genealogical skeleton around which social life is organized. Shahmund's story illustrates this idea and also the way in which tribal histories, like tribal genealogies themselves, turn inward, for ultimately it is not what objectively happened on a particular day that matters but what one's ancestors accomplished before the eyes of their peers.

Maulavi Ahmad Gul's story is like the British version as well in one regard, for it also encodes a more universal interpretation of history than does the more narrowly focused Mohmand account. For the British, the events in Jarobi could be seen as a simulacrum of larger historical processes, and the same is true for the Mulla's disciples who envision in Hadda Sahib's miraculous escape the intervention of God on behalf of one whom He has chosen as His *wali*, His friend. Beyond this, the story also reveals in crystallized form the transmutation of power from powerlessness that is at the center of the Sufi's world view and practice. Thus, even though the Mulla faces the onrushing might of the British Raj without aid of weapon or ally, we see that he is precisely where he wants to be. He has chosen his fate, and as he ascends the mountaintop, we realize that he is not approaching the end of his power but rather the source of its renewal. On the mountaintop, he is exposed for all to see, but he is also alone, a solitary figure, turned inward in prayer. The image that returns to me when I imagine the scene is of the Sufi adept alone in the dark recesses of the meditation chamber, bent and rocking as he rhythmically and repeatedly recites the formulas of zikr. In this instance, however, the Mulla is not alone in a room; he sits atop a mountain peak and harnesses the power that is his life's work, the power of the ascetic, the power of the marginal man to defy comprehension or capture.

The discrepancies between the three accounts are revealing but so too is the element that all of the stories share—namely, the sense of the Mulla's difference and of the strange combination of power and powerlessness that he seems to have embodied. To some extent, these attributes are unique to the pir, but on another level, they are ones that the Mulla shares with the other two heroes we have been examining in this book. In this regard, I would note the similarities that exist among three striking scenes from each of these lives. These are, first, the moment recorded by a British observer of the Mulla falling from his horse at the Bedmanai Pass and being spat on by tribal women for the harm he had brought them; second, the recollection by Samiullah Safi of his father dismounting from his horse each time he passed the house of one of the women whose relatives he had killed; and, third, Frank Martin's description of how Abdur Rahman's body could not be carried through the streets of his own capital for fear that it would be torn apart by furious mobs.

At these moments, we see that the authority wielded by these figures was less secure than we might have originally supposed. In each case, we see the hero of the story standing apart from his society—the man of determination and action suddenly reduced in stature, unable to pass safely among his own people for fear of the retribution that might befall him, retribution that his own actions, his own relentlessness have engendered. Veneration is thus shown to be transmutable into belligerence and disdain, and, to the extent that their authority rested on some form of controlled violence, we see that violence to be of a mimetic nature and capable of changing signs, so that the energies that had been originally projected outward onto other objects can as easily reverse themselves and implode upon their progenitors.

In considering the significance and similarity of these three scenes of heroes scorned, it is worth remembering the etymology of the word *qahraman* (hero) that was discussed in the introduction of this book. The hero is the one who harnesses fury, who molds passionate anger into exemplary violence. By its very nature, this operation must be full of hidden perils, and, by his very nature, the hero as the alchemist of this transformation must be a dangerous figure, to himself and to society at large. Images such as these—of heroes vilified and violence redirected—remind us that the qualities embodied in the hero are at their root deeply antagonistic to the common pursuit, that they threaten the security and happiness of the many, even as they provide them with an avenue of meaning and transcendence. They also remind us that the moral imagination is more complex than it is sometimes thought to be and capable of redirections and reversals even within the protected realm of the story.

CONCLUSION

In the introduction, I indicated that my objective was to shed light on the sources of the contemporary civil strife laying waste to Afghanistan. I was interested in uncovering the "deep structure" of the Afghan conflict beneath the level of competing parties, sects, ethnic groups, and tribes. The most significant fault lines of Afghan society were not those one reads about so often in the news reports, nor could the blame be laid entirely at the feet of the various outsiders who have interfered in Afghanistan's internal affairs over the years. Rather, I contended that Afghanistan's central problem was Afghanistan itself, specifically certain profound moral contradictions that have inhibited the country from forging a coherent civil society. These contradictions are deeply rooted in Afghan culture, but they have come to the fore in the last one hundred years, since the advent of the nation-state, the laying down of permanent borders, and the attempt to establish an extensive state bureaucracy and to invest that bureaucracy with novel forms of authority and control.

I have not attempted to explain these latter developments but rather to lay a conceptual foundation for understanding why these efforts have failed to bear fruit by revealing, in as pure a form as possible, the central moral schemas that Afghans bring to bear in the conduct of their political affairs. The form that this analysis has taken has been that of an exegesis of key texts that I have encountered over many years of living in and near Afghanistan and researching its history and culture. In giving priority to stories, my intention has not been to argue that politics can be reduced to texts (of any sort) or that Afghanistan has floundered because of the inadequacy of its narratives or of its exemplary figures. Instead, my objective has been to provide a foundation for the analysis of the moral codes undergirding Afghan political life and to lay bare certain contradictions within and between these moral codes—contradictions that helped to bring about the conflict in Afghanistan and that have subsequently impeded efforts to create a civil society.

In recounting and analyzing the story of Sultan Muhammad, I wanted to succinctly illustrate both the compulsion of honor as a basis for individual action and its potential destructiveness for social and political relations. The autobiography of Abdur Rahman provided a case study of the moral imperative of kingship and the way rulers can use Islam and honor to supplement their own claims to authority; however, Abdur Rahman also proved a complex figure whose claims to virtue and right—and the means he employed to instantiate those claims—ultimately outstripped the moral basis on which those claims were premised. As with Sultan Muhammad, the extremity to which Abdur Rahman went in his treatment of those around him appears not to have been simply the result of ambition or greed. In both cases there is evidence that extremity of action was the result of the protagonist advancing the moral logic of his position to its ultimate conclusion. Seen through the lens of miracle stories, the Mulla of Hadda appeared as an extreme figure of a somewhat different stripe. Both Abdur Rahman and Sultan Muhammad justified their actions on religious grounds and assumed their success to be evidence of divine support. Abdur Rahman went a step further in his use of dreams as a vehicle for legitimating his right to authority and in his assertion of divine intervention at critical junctures of his life story; however, neither the Amir nor the khan ever professed (or had professed for them) that they were capable of flying off to mythic realms, multiplying pots of food, or otherwise evading the laws of nature.

The Mulla's miraculous capabilities were an important source of his authority, but it is clear that these capabilities (and the heightened expectations that resulted from them) were the source of his greatest vulnerability as well. Indeed, in all three cases, the greatness of the man and of his claims to authority served to magnify his potential weakness, a weakness that in all three cases was represented in terms of *exposure*—of the great man being unveiled for all to see as counterfeit and insubstantial. This is a quality that all three sets of stories impart to the lives they depict, and in doing so they provide telling evidence of the contradictions lying at the heart of each of these moral codes. I would also contend, however, that something else is revealed as well—namely, the instability that all three moral codes share (individually and collectively), an instability that prevents their coalescing in any coherent fashion for any length of time.

The events of 1897 provide a case study of one attempt to overcome the inherent contradictions dividing Islam, honor, and rule as bases of political action and relationship. The ultimate failure of the jihad initiated by the Mulla of Hadda in the summer of that year can be attributed to a number of circumstantial factors, of course: the superior organization and firepower of the British, the difficulty of mobilizing and coordinating scattered groups of fighters over long distances for protracted periods of time. Factors such these were significant to the outcome of the jihad, but to me they are also insufficient by themselves, or at least tell only part of the story. The evidence assembled in this chapter is hardly conclusive; however, it does provide evidence that the Mulla and his religious allies had problems other than the British army; for example, there are suggestions that various tribes were working at cross-purposes to the Mulla, even while nominally supporting him, just as there are also indications that the Afghan amir was undermining the Mulla's efforts even as he was offering nominal assistance and support.

It is, of course, the case that such evidence need not be taken as proof of deep-seated structural differences between honor, Islam, and rule. A more obvious explanation would center on the personal rivalry and apprehension felt by both tribesmen and Amir that any power gained by the Mulla would be power lost to them. I don't negate the importance of this explanation, but I also don't believe it to be sufficient or satisfactory— first, because it ultimately lays the impetus and direction of historical events entirely at the feet of a few ambitious men and, second, because it discounts the role of the masses who choose either to follow the great or to ignore their call. In the final analysis, I cannot say why large numbers of tribesmen chose to follow the Mad Fakir in his precipitous siege of the Chakdara fort in July 1897. Nor can I say why, a few days later, his throng of ardent supporters began to dissipate and decrease. I am equally hesitant, however, to parrot Churchill by arguing that it all had to do with the enthusiasm of the moment, with some sense of irrational euphoria that caused the tribesmen to briefly pitch forward into a utopian dreamscape. An element of utopianism certainly pervaded the Mad Fakir's message, but underwriting this utopianism was a strongly anchored belief in the potentiality of God to intercede in the affairs of humans and of the role of certain sorts of culturally familiar humans to act as mediators for such intercession. Likewise, whereas the frustration of the Mad Fakir's plans may have led his erstwhile followers to question his charismatic claims and to return to a more realistic cast of mind, it is also the case that there was strong impetus to regain the moral sphere centered on family and tribe and to leave behind the more unfamiliar sphere of intense religious devotion and the submissive cast of mind that it entailed.

The point I want to emphasize is that, while it is impossible to ascertain exactly what is going on in people's minds when they make choices, we must nevertheless avoid the tendency to reduce those choices to mere expediency, psychology, or ambition. My goal here has been to outline an alternative reading of history in which actions are premised on moral grounds. Such grounds and consequences are never straightforward or deterministic. Pakhtuns, no less so than other groups, have available alternative moral maps to guide them in their life decisions. In retelling and analyzing the stories collected in this book, I have attempted to provide some sense of what those maps might look like and how they might be read. But I have also tried to indicate the inconsistencies that exist between these maps and the paradoxes and complexities that an individual faces in trying to reconcile the routes that each map offers with the decisions he faces in his life. Reading a chart is not the same thing as taking a journey, of course, and the particular texts and tracings brought together here likewise leave us far short of an adequate understanding of contemporary Afghan politics and society. Nevertheless, the narratives provided in this book—worn and faded as they might appear—can still tell us a great deal about the enduring values of Afghan culture. And, in similar fashion, the compasses that we begin to calibrate as we read and ponder these oft-told tales can also provide a vital sense of orientation and bearing as we set out to cross the treacherous terrain of the present.

6   Epilogue

From: [Ghairat@aaa.edu][1]
Newsgroups: soc.culture.pakistan, soc.culture.afghanistan
Subject: The ignorant and Murderer Mullaahs are again on
            the street
Date: 4 Nov 1994 04:14:34 -0800

I just found out from back home that the Jamatis[2] and locals have
taken to the streets again. They have taken over Police Stations,
Court houses, Air ports, and other govt. offices. They want Islamic
Law in Malakand division (Swat, Dir, Buner, Chitral districts). Several [parliamentary representatives] have been taken as hostages
along with the Judges. One [member of the provincial assembly]
Badi-u-Zaman from Besham has been shot dead by the culprits, idiots with beards. His car was stopped when he was on the way to receive the Chief Minister Sherpao. He was to be made hostage when
his driver opened fire and shot two of the armed men. They killed
Badi-u-Zaman during his captivity, in retaliation. The govt. responded with some paramilitary deployment but they have been
blocked by some new idiots in Dargai and Sekhakot, down the hills
from Malakand. I don't know what is the govt. going to do next. I
hope they send troops and kill the culprit Jamati leaders who are
taking the law in their hands and stop killing representatives in
cold blood. They are carrying AK-47s and Machine guns, and stopping every bus for check up. The local people have also joined
them. They are out in every village, town, city along the roads. It
is said to resemble 1976–77. On top, they are provided with food,
tea, water, etc. I think they should be poisoned rather. These idiots,

cold blooded murderers. I will see their braveness if they stand up
to the regular troops.

—[Ghairat Khan] (Very angry and am posting
    at 4:00 o'clock in the morning)

RE: POSTING ON THE INTERNET

As I began to write the concluding section of this book, I discovered via
the Internet that Swat, Malakand, and the neighboring tribal districts of
northwest Pakistan were again in turmoil. The text reproduced above is
the first message that appeared concerning this fighting. It was posted on
two Internet newsgroups—*soc.culture.pakistan* and *soc.culture.afghani-
stan*—early in the morning of November 4, 1994. The author of this initial posting, whom I have called "Ghairat," identified himself as a native
of the region, and from what he wrote, it is likely that he had just received
news of the fighting via telephone from Pakistan. A half-hour later, the
same Ghairat posted a second account taken from a Voice of America
(VOA) report originating from Pakistan. According to this report, a group
of religious leaders had been mobilizing local people to resist the government's attempts to implement civil law in the region and demanded the
institution of Islamic law.

The conflict is the most recent in a series of confrontations between
residents of the northern districts and the government that began in Feb-
ruary 1994, when a Pakistan supreme court ruling replaced local legal
codes with uniform civil statutes. In addition to the new law, the court
also decided that local councils had to relinquish their right of deciding
legal matters to the government courts. According to the VOA correspondent in Islamabad, the antigovernment action was led by the Organization
for the Enforcement of Islamic Law, a spokesman for which was quoted as
saying the group would lay down its arms only when "it is satisfied that
the Pakistani government is sincere about bringing Islamic law to the remote area."[3]

On November 5, additional messages that provided new information
appeared on the Internet. One report noted that thirty-five soldiers and
fifteen local people had died in this recent round of fighting, and various
posters related the news that a government helicopter had also been shot
down over Dir—apparently it was the target of sophisticated weaponry
imported from Afghanistan. A later VOA report also identified the leader
of the uprising as Maulana Sufi Muhammad, who is said to be associated

with a movement known as the Black Turban Group, a name that conjures up (in my mind at least) memories of Saidullah, the Mad Fakir, a.k.a. *sartor faqir*—the Blackheaded Faqir.

The following day, November 6, Ghairat logged on the Internet with another early morning update, apparently supplied by eyewitnesses in Pakistan, that told of the military's operation to retake the area and what appeared to be the resolution of the affair.

Update news along the road to Mingora:

The Para-Military forces were blocked at Malakand Pass, thirty five miles from Mingora toward Peshawar. They took an alternative route from Topi-Swabi and via Buner district, where they met little resistance and entered Swat, Dir etc. Remember, last May eleven people were killed in Buner by the PM forces. As the Military pushed forward toward the city of Mingora, the capital, Saidu Sharif, and the Saidu Airport at Kanju, they engaged in three major encounters on the main highway toward Mingora at Odigram, Balogram and Qamber. Hillicopter, tanks and closed armed vehicles were used. At odigram, three tribemen and five troops are dead. One of the tribemen was a retired army man who almost shot the hellicopter down. He was killed by a bomb or grenade dropped from the hellicopter. As the Military cleared the road there, they advanced to Balogram. Two tribesmen and three military men are dead there.. . . One of the guy was killed cold blooded.. . . the military raided his home, got him out of his home and killed him.. . . The next town was Qamber, where people had fortified themselves in advance as they heard of the fighting in the next two towns. As the army reached there and came face to face with the people in the fortified mountains, some of the women from the town came out and put Quran in the middle and asked both sides for a truce. Which eventually both sides accepted and no shots were fired.. . .

The Military might be facing a bigger threat in the areas across the river, due to the reasons that Jamiat is more stronger at that side and those people have routes to Dir and Afghanistan, where they get some of these advanced weapons. It is all so sad. [This area] has never witnessed grenades, bombs and tanks' shots for as long as I remember. The only thing I know is the Historic grave yard and the old ruins between the hills (between odigram and Balogram). [This is] Where Mahmud Ghaznawi[4] fought with the

Hindu Raja Gira and defeated him after a bitter struggle. His Commander Pir Khushal and two sons who got killed are still burried there. The olive trees can be seen all over the grave yard.

Anyway, the curfew is lifted and everything is suppose to be getting back to Normal over there.. . . . The Chief Minister has announced that the Islamic Sharia Law would be implemented as soon as possible. The leader of the movement who happens to be from Dir district has been arrested. Maulana Fazle-Rahman condemns this movement.
—Ghairat Khan

In July 1897, when Saidullah led the people of Swat and surrounding valleys against the British fort at Malakand, civil unrest was inspired by government attempts to expand its influence and authority into the tribal areas. Nearly one hundred years later, it would appear that the same issues are being contested, even though roads, schools, post offices, an electrical grid, and other extensions of the nation-state have long been in place in the region. Despite these innovations and intrusions, however, the people of Swat and neighboring districts have been able to preserve a sense of themselves as separate from the rest of Pakistan, in part because of the continuation of customary law. The government's attempt to replace that law with its own civil code (an amalgam of Islamic law and colonial era statutes) is viewed by the people as an assault on one of the last bastions of traditional society, and faced with this threat, they have turned once again to Islam. The call to implement Islamic law makes a good rallying cry against a national government that, despite its long-declared intention to "Islamicize" the country, has been unable to implement that law of its own accord. Faced with the challenge from the north, the government must explain why it has not done so fifty years after the departure of the British and the establishment of the Islamic state of Pakistan.

At the same time, while the strategy of attacking the government on religious grounds is a time-honored one, I can assume only that this alliance of religious and tribal forces, like the one that arose in 1897, is temporary. Are the people of Swat and neighboring districts really prepared to accept the leadership of mullas and maulavis and help them in bringing about the replacement of traditional legal codes with *shari'a* law? Or will the people of these areas eventually withdraw their support from Sufi Muhammad and his confederates and quietly return to the old ways of doing business, solving disputes, and rendering judgment once the threat of government intrusion has been pushed back, which is, of course, what happened in 1897. Once the Mulla of Hadda had withdrawn into Afghanistan and the Mad Fakir had disappeared into the upper reaches of the Swat Valley, the colonial authorities and local residents reverted to established practice, which apportioned to the government a percentage of tax revenues and ceded control in areas such as transportation and commerce, but which also retained some autonomy for the local people in many of their affairs. Given the present context, will tradition win out as it has in the past, or will the price for mounting a unified resistance to the state be acceptance of a shari'a code far stricter than any that has held sway before?

At present, there is not enough information to answer these questions, but what is known about the ongoing situation in Swat is sufficient to demonstrate that the fault lines delineated and analyzed in this book still exist on the frontier, albeit in novel forms. The events themselves say as much, and so too do the messages that I have been monitoring over the Internet—messages that have not only relayed information about the events on the frontier to a far-flung network of expatriate Afghans and Pakistanis but that have also transmogrified those events into new forms of moral exchange. Thus, while the fighting on the frontier was beginning to decline in intensity, spirited combat on the Internet was only just beginning. This became evident later in the day on November 6 when a second Internet user whom I have named "Ejaz Ahmed" posted a message indicating his view that the events in Pakistan had nothing to do with Afghanistan and should be kept off the Afghan news group, because the "issue of tribesmen taking The NWF Province is entirely a domestic issue to Pakistan and Pakistanis and does not concern Afghans at this point." This opinion notwithstanding, Ejaz Ahmed went on to assert his belief as to the central significance of the Qur'an and the hadith in Pakhtun society. Contrary to Ghairat, who condemned the movement and "the ignorant and murderer mullaahs" who were behind it, Ejaz Ahmed's position was supportive of the leadership and the goals of the frontier uprising:

> pakistanis should not forget that Islam and Islamic law is in the fabrics of life in the Pashtoon land both in Afghanistan and Pakistan and people have already realized that the only solution to our problems as a human society comes from Qura'an and Hadis. We as muslims should be aware that today, the western media and government along with a bunch of self-sold elements of our society are tring to discredit Islam in anyway possible from shooting rockets on cities to associating Islam with terrorism. We should bare in

mind tha Islam is not a product of a few fanatics such as Gulbud-
din/Rabbani or Qazi Hussian Ahmad,[5] but Islam is the Message of
Allah (SWT) through his Rasoul [Prophet] Mohammad Mustafia
(PBUH) for betterment of human society. There is nothing wrong
with impowering Islamic law as long as those who are impowered
by this law have an honest will for implementing Shari‘a.

Despite the cessation of hostilities along the frontier, animosities inten-
sified on the Internet as different posters began to pursue one another on
a variety of pretexts. Following the usual pattern of Internet exchanges,
messages would be added on to, with later posters interjecting their responses at appropriate places within the preceding message. The effect of
this style of exchange is very much like a heated face-to-face confrontation in which each party interrupts the other to debate an issue or score a
point. One of the most acrimonious exchanges occurred between Ghairat
and Ejaz Ahmed. This exchange evolved from the original series of messages that were posted during the uprising. As the exchange continued
over several days, new messages were superimposed on top of the ones
already there. In the final version that is transcribed here, Ghairat's most
recent comments appear flush to the left margin while an earlier response
is indicated by two angle-brackets. Ejaz Ahmed's latest messages are
preceded by a single angle-bracket next to the left margin, and his first
postings are preceded by three angle-brackets. The text begins with
Ghairat:

> I apologize to the net people in advance. Actually I don't like to
> insult his family but this guy is asking for it. If you are using a
> fake name and aliases, that doesn't mean you shouldn't look in
> the mirror and think if you are realy a man, after I get through
> with you. I don't doubt you can be even a low life dirt from Paki-
> stan/India/Afghanistan. No matter how much you want people
> to be believe.
> »The issue of tribesmen taking over The NWF Province is en-
> »tirely a domestic issue to Pakistan and Pakistanis and does not
> »concern Afghans at this point. I am requesting all Pakis to take
> »this discussion to SCP [soc.culture.pakistan] and spare SCAians
> »time. There are other issues that has to be discussed on SCA
> »[soc.culture.afghanistan].
> »I don't think you are in any position to make a statement like
> »that. As I have previously stated, your dady or moma doesn't
> »own the net or SCA.

›No, but this is not Herria Mundi either.[6] So, you cannot show
›your naked butt
I feel sorry for people who are born in Hera Mundi. It ain't my
fault that you get so angry, better ask your mom.
›On SCA, we have seen enough of it. You are a self-sold Paki-
›stani who not only has forgotten his ethnic roots and "Nang"
›but also has no clue what so ever of his people's desire for imple-
›mentation of a noble law.
All I condemned was violence of any sort. I welcome Islamic
Law if the Sharia Bench is educated enough to distinguish
wrong and right.
»Go hide your face under a blanket. How many times do I have
»to humiliate you? I guess you have no shame MR. alias user.
›No I don't. Do you? How many people on SCA and how many
›time have [they] asked
Don't shout like a dog with out any facts to back up your
claims.
›you to get lost? You claim to be a "nangaily" Pashtoon. Well, I
›don't see any "nang" in you. There must be something wrong
›in your genes. Just a guess, could it be possible that you might
›be British or Panjabi from Father side? Just a question.
Don't compare your paternal traits with others, specially if you
are born in Hera Mundi. You may consult your mother about
your genes. She can probably tell you who it was, unless she instructed you to do research. In that case I may help where to
look up :-)
»Having said that, these events are related to Afghanistan. It is
»due to the inflow of weapons and theology from there which
»has inspired these kind of events across the border.
›First of all, if these people are Muslim, they need not be inspired
›by anyone but Prophet Mohammad (PBUH) and the teachings
›of Islam, not from
Humans get more effected from the surroundings. That shows
your lack of any intelligence. I may be wrong, but using your
theory of genes, it ain't your fault but your genes. Get your
facts straight.
›Afghans. Secondly, the weapons? I think we just borrowed
›them, the unused portion of Rockets, mortors etc must be re-
›turned and used. Since it seems we have enough of everything,

›we are going to send them back to Pakistan so Pakistanis see
›how a rocket launcher works.
Shame on you and your coward Paternal traits.
›I am sure nothing will happen to you or your relatives as it
›seems they have the protection of their fathers i.e. Punjabi army
›of Pakistan.
Don't compare your piece of shit family with others, dude. . . .
Wasn't it your family living in Hera Mundi, which is located in
Punjab? I hope you are not from Karachi or Lahore, which I
doubt. If some Pashtoon soldiers had your family up in the corner, what fault is that of others??? Then don't come crying who
your dady was, better ask your family. After all thats what the
doctors order. . . . :-)

—Ghairat
›Afterall, it is time for the army to pay the price. . . . :-)

›Ejaz Ahmed

EMBEDDED CODES

The sheer vehemence of the exchange between Ghairat and Ejaz Ahmed
is what stands out most as one reads through these communications, but
there is more going on here than mere nastiness. The debates one encounters on the Internet reflect perplexing issues that confront Afghans and
Pakistanis in general. This confusion can be seen, for example, in the controversy about whether Afghans and Pakistanis have the right to comment on events in the others' country. The question of who has the right
to post messages and where is a longstanding source of contention in the
two news groups, and after having followed the various arguments for
some time I wonder if the debate and the fervor of opinion that it gener-
ates is not itself a legacy of the Durand Line, which I have discussed at
various points in this book. The line that is being drawn here has no
physical status, of course. It is rather a discursive divide that has been
constructed by and between Pakistani and Afghan computer users on cam-
puses, in homes, and in corporate offices across the United States, Canada,
and Europe; but the heated nature of the rhetorical exchanges that develop
between members of the two groups and the frequent revisiting of the

subject of boundaries make one realize that the antagonisms and uncertainties set in motion by the British boundary commissioners one hundred years ago have in no way diminished with the passage of time.

On the Internet, just as on the frontier itself, aspects of identity that had once seemed inseparable (or at least negotiable) have been rendered as distinct layers in the centrifuge of civil strife, and it is understood that every individual must make his loyalties known: Are you a Pakhtun first or a citizen of your country? Is your primary loyalty to your tribe or your ethnic group, or is it to Islam? The view that "Pakhtunness" is the core of identity is encouraged, of course, by the centrality of the Pakhtu language, which is not only the mother tongue of most frontier residents, but also a source of great pride because of its rich poetic tradition. Then there is the Pakhtun claim to an exalted ancestry and history: the role of Pakhtuns as conquerors of Delhi, the heroic stature of local chieftains like Khushhal Khan Khattak, and the lore of memorable engagements with various imperial invaders, from the Moghuls to the Sikhs to the British. Finally, reinforcing Pakhtunness is honor itself, the sense of personal nobility inherited from exalted ancestors and confirmed by personal action. While honor is a concept central to many peoples of south and southwest Asia, the Pakhtuns have long held the conceit that it is their own special prerogative and that the honor of others is not quite like their own. This attitude is apparent in the language of Ghairat, who conveys in his messages the enduring significance of honor, even for expatriate Pakhtuns far from their homeland. But, just as his postings indicate honor's hold, so too do they reveal the insecurity of honor and the way it can degenerate into a narrow-minded chauvinism when removed from its proper social context.

In terms of their identification with their respective states, it is clear that Pakhtuns on both sides of the Durand Line take pride in being associated with one or another national community, albeit that pride is frequently tinged with disgruntlement and occasional chagrin. To a great extent, the sense of national identification is a product of segmentary dynamics, as is tribal identity, which is to say that the experience of identifying with one's own group comes as a result of disparaging another. For Pakistanis in general national fellow-feeling is principally a product of the long rivalry with India. Separatist sentiments in each of the provinces that make up Pakistan are held in check, first, by the relative strength of the military and, secondly, by the recognition that a divided Pakistan would stand little chance against the forces of a united India. With regard to its western neighbor—Afghanistan—feelings are very different, especially among residents of the North-West Frontier Province. On the one hand, N.W.F.P. Pakhtuns look upon their westerly neighbors with barely disguised condescension—as rough-hewn country cousins who are a bit short on education and a little bumptious in their adherence to out-of-date customs.[7] On the other hand, Pakistani Pakhtuns also recognize that, in their simpler and more direct ways, their Afghan cousins are more authentically "Pakhtun," more like the tribal heroes of old, the image of whom all Pakhtuns venerate.[8]

Islamic identity—what it demands, what its limits are, what it allows one to do—is the source of greatest controversy and uncertainty today for Afghans and Pakistanis, whether at home or abroad. One representative source of tension related to Islamic identity seen repeatedly on the Internet has to do with the familiar question of who has the right to post their messages in which news groups. Here, the problem is not just between Pakistanis and Afghans but also with other Muslims, particularly those who are referred to by some on the Internet as "fundamentalists" or simply "fundis."[9] For many of the so-called fundis, national boundaries are artificial distinctions, and they reflect this belief in their practice of dispatching their computer messages to multiple news groups. For their part, many of the regulars who post to *soc.culture.afghanistan* and *soc.-culture.pakistan* resent these cross-postings. In their view, the arrogance displayed by the fundamentalists who post their messages indiscriminately in different national news groups replicates the problem that Afghans and Pakistanis face in real life: that of having politically motivated ideologues—sometimes from their own countries and sometimes outsiders from other lands—interfering in their nations' internal affairs.

Beyond this problem of who has the right to participate in the discourse of different news groups, there are many other issues that arise on the Internet that also reflect the concerns of Afghans and Pakistanis regarding the maintenance of Muslim identity in the modern world. Questions of this sort include whether or not it is permissible to get married over the phone, what Islamic law says about oral sex, and if there are any stipulations in shari'a against investing in mutual funds and other novel financial instruments. Although most of these issues are particular to the better-off immigrants coping with the modern diaspora, there are nevertheless similarities between these questions and those that arose in the mud-walled refugee camps where I conducted research in the mid-1980s. The refugee camp, like the Internet, is an unprecedented place to be working out issues of identity and community, and in both settings there are many matters that had previously been unproblematic but that have now ac-

quired major significance. Thus, in the refugee camp, Afghans pondered
whether it was better to adhere to custom and continue arranging marriages with kinsmen who might be far away or to accept the reality of
their status and make matches with neighbors in the camp or even with
local Pakistanis. Before the war, such unions would have been scorned, but
their utility is self-evident in present circumstances.

Another source of uncertainty centers around the general question of
how one should comport oneself. During my time working in the camps,
mullas and especially the young party ideologues associated with the more
radical political parties like Hizb-i Islami Afghanistan insisted that people
should be serious and maintain a gravity appropriate to a time of jihad.
Since *mujahidin* warriors were sacrificing their lives across the border, it
was only appropriate the people in the relative safety of the camps would
respect their sacrifice by abjuring all frivolity and celebration. To enforce
this position, mullas and party loyalists would berate anyone who permitted dancing at their weddings or who played music on their tape recorders.
Even the act of telling a story, if it were frivolous enough, could bring
censure down on an individual, and the people with whom I associated
were always careful to monitor their company and surroundings before
they would tell a joke or express an opinion that was scornful of the new
moralism that held sway in the camps.

The tensions and sources of uncertainty that were evident in the refugee camp are not the same as those that generate anxiety on the Internet,
but there are still certain shared features. In both contexts, strangers have
come together out of common need and have been forced by circumstance
to share an unaccustomed *space.* Although these strangers share much in
common, the exigencies of living in this new space and negotiating common protocols have helped to make established beliefs and procedures of
everyday life subjects of debate and discord, especially under the influence
of a vocal minority demanding the adherence of all to a rigid set of religious beliefs and postures. Under this pressure to conform, individuals
must announce their choices—for or against. Compromise becomes impossible. One is a Muslim or one is an infidel, and with the erosion of any
middle ground the discourse of identity becomes surly, self-righteous, and
enraged.

In the case of the Internet, the most innocent discussion inevitably
becomes ensnarled in bitter polemics. An example is the exchange between Ghairat and Ejaz Ahmed, and it is almost always evident in the
postings of either the Afghan or Pakistani news group. One particularly
telling example involves an American high-school student who posted a

message on *soc.culture.afghanistan* asking for assistance with a homework assignment he was working on. The student seemed to want a thumbnail sketch of Afghan culture and history—presumably one he could copy directly into whatever social studies paper he was writing. However, what he actually got, whether he realized it or not, was much more revealing than his question warranted, for the posters who responded soon forgot about the student's inquiry and launched into a set of diatribes for and against the various Afghan political parties. In that exchange, like the one that introduces this epilogue, each poster interjected his message interlinearly within that of the preceding poster, and consequently what one saw in following the debate over several days was the gradual erasure of sensible discourse as each new response was laid down on top of the previous one and the text as a whole became progressively more shrill, garbled, and ultimately unintelligible.

The deterioration of discourse encountered on the Internet rather accurately approximates the general fracturing of Afghan society—inside and outside the country's borders—after more than fifteen years of war. At the same time, however, there are differences between the kinds of deterioration one finds inside Afghanistan or in the camps and in the farther-flung diaspora of the Internet. The rockets and artillery shells launched each day in Afghanistan are aimed at real people, and they do not discriminate as to whether those they strike are from the enemy side or innocent children. Likewise, when refugees crammed side by side in their squalid compounds are unable to resolve their disputes and the few avenues of mediation available prove unworkable, they usually end up seeking redress in the old-fashioned way. Only now, the instruments and protocols of vengeance have changed. Automatic weapons are plentiful, and so too are stealthy paybacks: bombs tossed into compounds, the use of hired gunmen to conceal responsibility, and the proliferation of street-corner kidnappings.

Debates on the Internet sometimes aspire, in their rhetorical way, to the level of violence that exists "on the ground," but the fact that these debates have been adapted to the electronic space of the computer distinguishes them both in their practice and in their outcome. In a camp, a dispute, whether engendered by a personal feud or an ideological disagreement, will often lead to bitterness and killing, but in cyberspace, words that elsewhere provoke violence are articulated through glyphs and cursors, and no one gets harmed—at least physically. Violence remains in the minds of the beholders, and the escalation that occurs in a physical feud never develops because of the faceless quality of communication on the

Internet. The image that comes to mind when I think about this new technology is the old technology of the panopticon. The new is a reversal of the old, however, for the new technology does not have a single observer viewing each of the cells located on the outer ring of the circle. Rather, the panopticon has been inverted so that all of the observers on the periphery now look inward to the central space of the Internet. In this space, posters dream their dreams, vent their rage, and assume their identities and poses. The antagonisms can be vicious here, but no one really knows who it is they are striking. No one suffers the consequences of their anger, and it is all ultimately rather futile.

Despite this apparent harmlessness, however, there still seems something particularly troubling about exchanges such as that between Ghairat and Ejaz Ahmed, particularly the knowledge that those tossing invectives back and forth so carelessly are the best educated and most fortunate sons of the Afghan-Pakistani frontier. Beyond this, however, are the idioms of denunciation themselves: the jokes about rape, the proud flaunting of race and nationality, the self-righteous intolerance. Is this what it comes down to? Are the moral codes of honor, Islam, and rule—codes which begin with idealized notions of commitment and community and purpose—finally reduced to base slander? The evidence of these electronic exchanges, not to mention the ongoing events in Afghanistan and the Frontier, indicate rather definitively that, while the Afghan (and maybe even the Pakistani) state is fast disintegrating, the moral codes that I have been examining in this book are very much alive and still inspire great fervor among both resident and expatriate Pakhtuns.

But what is it that survives? With the fragmentation and scattering of tribes, is honor reduced to petty chauvinism—the exaltation of mythic ancestors and racial purity? Is rulership finally stripped of its pretensions of rightmindedness and responsibility, and accepted as nothing more than untempered self-interest? And, what role is left for Islam in such a universe? It was once the binding cement of frontier society. When all other bases of identity turned in upon themselves or proved hollow in their pretensions to unity, Islam remained as a refuge for the homeless and a succor for the bereaved. So it is today for many, but for others it is something more as well. Islam migrates better than honor or nationality. As a transportable system of belief and practice whose locus is personal faith and worship, it can be adapted to a variety of contexts and situations, but estranged from the familiar settings in which it arose, is it not also more resistant to the mundane negotiations and compromises that everyday life requires?

Given the pertinence and persistence of such questions, the concerns of this book—with heroes, with stories, with the past—might seem rather disconnected. I don't believe them to be so, however, for the simple reason that it is with such stories and the moral truths embedded within them that one must look for the sources of the current crisis, just as it is also here that one must hope to find a solution. The multiple fissures that one sees now in Afghanistan are between leaders and parties—ethnic groups and different religious sects—but they begin somewhere else. The imposition of the nation-state is one source, I have argued, but more than this, it is what the nation-state was imposed upon: the moral fault lines of honor, Islam, and rule. These fault lines are not unique to Afghanistan. To the contrary, their impact can be seen in the earliest histories of the Islamic era in the battles that the Prophet Muhammad and his party of believers fought against the independent Bedouin tribes of the Arabian desert and the entrenched mercantile oligarchy of Mecca. Following the Prophet's death and up to the present, the same divisions have persisted and found various expression in different regions of the Muslim world. Afghanistan's version of this configuration is a product of its own particular history and its unique combination of tribes, ethnic groups, and sects; but in its general outlines the divisions are the same as those one encounters throughout the Middle East.

What is the origin of these divisions? From what roots do such fault lines arise and what factors cause them to perpetuate themselves through history and across cultural divides? I have no idea and am loath even to suggest that an answer can be found. I am also frankly discomfited to be portraying history in the way that I have here because of its insinuation that Afghans—unlike ourselves—are held irrevocably by "the dead hand of tradition," that their fate is somehow obscurely determined by a "deep structure" beyond their control. The danger in comparing geological and moral structures is, of course, that it becomes all too easy to draw the concomitant conclusion that in such a situation nothing can ever change, that Afghans—in their violence, their zeal, their resistance to compromise—are finally irredeemable. Such a judgment, reminiscent as it is of Churchill's analysis of frontier fanaticism, is one we must avoid, but at the same time we must also seek to account for the periodic surfacing of certain structural forces and for the often determinate impact of these structural forces on historical events.

The crisis engulfing Afghanistan was certainly precipitated by the Marxist coup d'etat and subsequent invasion of the Soviet Union, but it cannot be reduced to this any more than it can be construed simply as a legacy of Great Game skullduggery or as the sole doing of the political leaders now shelling each other's forces in and around Kabul. There are momentous occasions in a nation's life that, while triggered by particular people and circumstances, quickly outstrip and outweigh the characters and events that initiated them. What confluence of factors sets such a process in motion is mysterious, but the result is that the moral core from which communal loyalties and passions derive is exposed to view—with all of its contradictions and inconsistencies intact. For Americans, the Civil War was such a moment, when something dark and cancerous at the nation's heart—something more troubling even than the carnage itself—appeared, as though from the bloody ground itself. And while that conflict has long been ended, the rancor and discord (one wants to say *evil*) that those events unleashed have never been entirely quieted. The same can be said of Afghanistan, which has yet even to find the proximate end to its strife. That being the case, this much at least can be hoped for and prayed—that even if the fault lines dividing the Afghan nation cannot finally be mended, the people themselves will some day soon gain respite from the rage they now endure.

Notes

1. INTRODUCTION

1. Sahlins 1981, 1985.
2. White 1981, 14.
3. Ibid., 20.
4. The center of concern in this study is the frontier between British India and Afghanistan (see map 2). This frontier runs south to Baluchistan, but the area that I am primarily interested in is that bordered by Chitral in the north and the tribal territories surrounding the Khyber Pass in the south. The two dominant commercial and political centers in this region are the Afghan city of Jalalabad in the west and the Indian (later Pakistani) city of Peshawar. At the heart of this area, residing in the bare hills and mountains that straddle the border in this area are a number of politically independent Pakhtun tribes, including the Mahmund, Mohmand, Safi, Shinwari, Khogiani, and Afridi. As one moves further from the frontier and the mountains into the broader plains that ring Peshawar in the east and Jalalabad in the west, one encounters more peasant populations that have been traditionally under the control of the state and linked directly to the national economy.
5. British control over Afghanistan's foreign policy remained a sticking point for years and provided one of the explicit rationales for the third and final Anglo-Afghan war in 1919, a war that was provoked by Abdur Rahman's grandson, Amir Amanullah Khan (see Adamec 1967).
6. On the invention and spread of the nation-state, see especially Seton-Watson 1977; Anderson 1983; Gellner 1983; and Hobsbawm 1990.
7. One of the leaders of the abortive Panjshir uprising was Ahmad Shah Massoud, who would later gain fame during the jihad as the commander of the Panjshir Valley resistance. Other equally fruitless attacks occurred that same day in Laghman, Surkh Rud, and Paktia. All were organized by the Muslim Youth Organization, which was severely damaged by the failure of these attacks and the capture of most of its leaders.
8. The best example of this sort of analysis applied to Afghanistan is the intro-

duction written by Richard Tapper to his edited volume on tribe-state relations in Iran and Afghanistan (1983).

9. I encountered one notable exception to this rule while conducting research in an Afghan refugee camp in 1984. That exception was the Ahmadzai tribe, most branches of which come from the region south and east of Kabul. The Ahmadzais are a numerous and successful branch of the Ghilzai confederacy, which essentially ceased to exist as anything more than a name following Amir Abdur Rahman's suppression of a Ghilzai tribal revolt in 1888. Due in part to their proximity to Kabul and an effective leadership, the Ahmadzais continued to wield considerable influence in national politics at a time when other tribes were fragmenting and losing ground. Following the Marxist coup, the tribe was split as some members (the most prominent of whom was Dr. Najibullah, the leader of the Parcham party, who succeeded Babrak Karmal as president of the Democratic Republic of Afghanistan) sided with the government and others took up arms against it. Again, because of their proximity to Kabul, many of those who resisted were forced to flee the country early in the war, and those who did were scattered in refugee camps throughout the North-West Frontier Province of Pakistan.

Despite these ruptures, the Ahmadzais have continued to maintain a degree of coordination that few other tribes evince. Within the camp I studied, the Ahmadzai groups were unique in having maintained their coherence as segmentary tribal sections—that is, all of the male heads of house in a given residential group were related by descent from common (paternal) ancestors. Likewise, the Ahmadzai khans in the camp where I worked met periodically in assembly with the khans of other tribal sections in other camps, and the tribe kept an office in Peshawar, as they once had done in Kabul. These and other acts of group solidarity indicated that the tribal idea was alive and well, at least for this one group. (For background on the economic and social situation of the Ahmadzais and other Ghilzai tribes prior to the war, see Jon Anderson's excellent ethnographic articles on the Ghilzai of Logar and Ghazni, especially "Tribe and Community among Ghilzai Pashtun" (1975) and "Khan and Khel: Dialectics of Pakhtun Tribalism" (1983).

10. See Azmat Hayat Khan, "Afghan Resistance and National Leadership" (1981).

11. In noting the greater attention paid to organizational than to symbolic dimensions of political relationships, Steven Caton has argued that more research is needed that would "focus on the significant individual and not just segmentary groups—using culturally laden signs in concrete acts of communication" (Caton 1990b, 99). In Caton's view, concern for the nature of political groupings has obscured the role of individuals and clouded as well the nature of Ibn Khaldun's own model, which "hinges crucially on a Weberian notion of charismatic personality, in the guise of either the desert chieftain or the prophet" (Caton 1990b, 89–90).

12. Two of the first articles that I wrote on my research dealt with the maintenance of cultural forms by refugees (Edwards 1986d, 1990). While I still hold to the conclusions I presented there, I also recognize now that the situation was more complicated than I realized and that the urge for order in my own mind led me to focus on small triumphs of cultural survival that individual families and groups

were achieving while underrepresenting the larger picture of chaos and dissolution.

13. For examples of Rafiq Jan's poetry and an analysis of its significance, see Edwards 1993a. My enthusiastic response to Rafiq Jan's poems was undoubtedly conditioned by my earlier reading of Michael Meeker's book, *Literature and Violence in North Arabia*. Meeker's poetic analysis offered an answer to a problem faced by Middle Eastern specialists interested in symbolic analysis, and that problem had to do with the relative paucity and stereotypical nature of ritual expression in most Middle Eastern societies. In the late 1970s and early 1980s, many of the influential symbolic studies that were then shaping the discipline centered around ritual, but in the Middle East, ritual did not seem to be at the center of cultural identity and practice, at least not in the distinctive way that it was in other cultural areas. Meeker's focus on poetry and narrative circumvented this difficulty by offering an alternative arena within which to think through symbolic issues. Meeker, it should be admitted, was not the first or only Middle Eastern scholar to call attention to poetry. Both Alois Musil (1928) and Ignaz Goldziher (1967; originally 1889–1890) had written on Arabic tribal discourse generations earlier, while a number of other scholars published significant works having to do with poetry and poetic production shortly after Meeker's book came out. These scholars include Samatar (1982), Abu-Lughod (1986), and Caton (1990a).

14. Such a notion was probably never realistic given that Massoud is an ethnic Tajik (and therefore never one who would have seriously contended for power in the past), while most of those with whom I interacted (and the vast majority of the refugees in general) were Pakhtuns. Pakhtuns constitute a slim majority of the Afghan population, always controlled things in the past, and were unlikely to cede control now to a non-Pakhtun. But the very fact that Pakhtuns of my acquaintance were willing to discuss the possibility of having a Tajik in a position of political power illustrates how little faith they had in their own immediate Pakhtun political leaders.

15. In the mid-seventies, there were not that many people interested in the oral history of early uprisings and fewer still who were focusing on Islam as a dynamic social force in Afghan society. With his idiosyncratic and omnivorous appetite for all things Afghan, Louis Dupree had dealt with both oral history and Islam in a number of articles, and so too had a few other scholars (e.g., Poullada 1973; and Canfield 1973). But the majority of scholars (and I probably would have been among them if I had been conducting research then) seemed to view Islam as part of a quickly receding and largely irrelevant past that had little to offer outside antiquarian interest. Afghanistan scholars were not alone in holding to this view, of course. The same sense pervaded scholarship of the sixties and early seventies throughout the Middle East, and a classic expression of this tendency can be seen in the introduction of Richard Mitchell's classic work on the Muslim Brothers, in which he obliquely apologizes for choosing a subject that "has had its moment in history, and that for very few of [whose] leaders will historians reserve a place larger than a footnote" (Mitchell 1969, xv).

16. There were several reasons why rural elites chose to settle in Peshawar. First, Peshawar was centrally located and contained most of the relevant offices

(e.g., the offices of the Commissioner of Afghan Refugees and of the resistance parties) that they would need if they were to secure assistance and employment. Secondly, Peshawar has long enjoyed the status of being the hub of Pakhtun culture. This status goes back centuries, and while it was partially diminished by the imposition of a national border at the end of the last century, that border has always been porous, and Pakhtuns, whether nominally of Afghan or Pakistani citizenship, have never relinquished their affection for the place. A third factor is that whereas the rural elites with whom I dealt were not wealthy on any objective scale, they had greater resources to draw on than most refugees and could consequently afford Peshawar rents. Thus, in addition to whatever resources elites received from either the political parties or the Pakistan government, many also continued to receive income from land that tenants farmed throughout the war. The owner's share was far smaller than it had been before the war, but the continued payment of the share provided some income while also preserving the owner's claim to the land into the future.

17. While I have taken the tack of focusing on just a few individuals in this book, I have availed myself of some of these interviews in other published articles (1986b, 1986c, 1987, 1989, 1993b, 1993c, and 1995).

18. Geertz was not the first or only person to recognize the value of life histories for the study of cultures (Paul Radin and Edward Sapir both come to mind as early pioneers in this field), but he was the one with whom I was most familiar and who has probably had the greatest influence in developing this line of research among anthropologists of the Middle East. Whether the debt is explicitly acknowledged or not by individual authors, *Islam Observed* clearly anticipates a number of influential works that center on Middle Eastern lives, including Crapanzano 1980; Dwyer 1982; Munson 1984; Eickelman 1985a, 1985b, 1991; Mottahedeh 1985; Loeffler 1988; Friedl 1989; Lavie 1990; Beck 1991; Abu-Lughod 1993; and Burke 1993. For a general review of life histories in anthropological research, see Peacock and Holland 1993; and see Schwartz 1987, for an excellent example of a "Durkheimian" life history focusing on the social uses to which great lives are put.

19. See especially Nagy 1979.

20. While the ethnographic literature on Islam in Afghanistan was relatively limited prior to the war, relevant ethnographic work had been done in the neighboring North-West Frontier Province of Pakistan by Fredrik Barth (1959a). Barth's initial work has also been supplemented by Ahmed (esp. 1976, 1980, 1983), Lindholm (1982, 1986, 1992), Grima (1992), and Jahanzeb (1985), all of whom provide interesting insights into Islam's role in Pakhtun tribal society. Recent work pertaining to Islam in Afghanistan includes Shahrani and Canfield 1984; J. Anderson 1984; Ashraf Ghani 1978, 1983, 1987; M. Mills 1991; Roy 1986; and Edwards 1986b, 1986c, 1986d, 1993b, 1993c, and 1995.

21. The cultural nature of perception and of narrativity is a principle deeply rooted in anthropology, going back most significantly to the work of Edward Sapir and Benjamin Whorf. Others who have foregrounded texts and textual questions in ways that I have found fruitful include Basso (1986), Rosaldo (1986), and Bowen (1993); and—among scholars working in the Middle East—Goldziher

(1967), Mottahedeh (1980), Abu-Lughod (1986), Dresch (1989), Caton (1990a), and Messick (1993).

22. As in the case of my decision to focus on "axial figures," I cannot claim originality for my view of the importance of particular kinds of historical texts for the understanding of other, historically situated minds since I had been aware of Le Roy Ladurie's *Montaillou* (1978) before embarking on my fieldwork and read works by Darnton (1984) and Ginzburg (1985), among others, on my return.

23. See B. Anderson 1983 for a perceptive analysis of the symbolic and social implications of this division. Also, see Lindholm 1992 for a similarly insightful comparison between Afghan and Moroccan conceptions of the division between tribe and state.

24. It can be argued, of course, that documents like these are incommensurable with oral histories such as the ones I use to discuss honor and Islam. Histories of any sort reflect the times in which they are recorded. Abdur Rahman's autobiography and proclamation are solely of the past and represent its concerns, whereas the oral histories I collected represent the present of the teller along with the past of the told. This objection would have merit if I were concerned either with the performative context in which the oral histories were told or with the way in which they were being strategically deployed in the present. But what I am interested in here are the traditional moral orders that held sway during a significant moment in Afghanistan's recent past, and the oral sources on which I rely are not only the best sources available for considering these moral orders, but they also give every appearance of being relatively fixed.

I will discuss the fixity of these stories at appropriate points in the relevant chapters, but it is worth noting here the general grounds on which I base this judgment. As indicated previously, almost all of the stories told about the Mulla of Hadda are miracle stories, and they are virtually identical to those associated with other Muslim saints from India and Afghanistan. Having read several hundred of these stories from different times and places, I have become convinced not only that the stories are relatively stable, but that stability is one of their key features. With regard to the story of Sultan Muhammad Khan that is the centerpiece of chapter 2, I have less proof that it has not been transformed over time by different tellers in different contexts, but it is clear from certain aspects of the story itself that the story is not Safi's own, that it has been told to him by others in a relatively set format, and that its style and structure offer limited scope for revision. Safi does make occasional remarks in the course of telling the story that are intended to clarify points that might be obscure to me, but the rhetorical bracketing of these remarks makes it clear that they are meant to stand outside the narrative itself.

25. James 1898, 5.

2. THE MAKING OF SULTAN MUHAMMAD KHAN

1. *Gulistan* (The Rose Garden) and *Bustan* (The Scented Garden) were both composed by the thirteenth-century Persian poet, Sa'di. *Bustan* is a collection of didactic poetry on a variety of mystical and moral subjects, including "Justice,

Equity, and Governmental Administration," "Benevolence," "Love (Physical and Mystical)," and "Modesty." *Gulistan* combines a mixture of poetry and prose and is likewise concerned with ethical matters. Long staple texts for instruction, both collections have also served as source books for scribes seeking proverbs, pithy sayings, rhetorical formulations, and other sorts of bon mots. See Levy 1969, 116–26.

2. The concept of namus will be discussed in depth in the text, but briefly it signifies those people (especially his wife, mother, sisters, and daughters), objects (e.g., his rifle), and properties (especially his home, lands, and tribal homeland) that a man must defend in order to preserve his honor.

3. The informant cited above made the following observations about the potential danger of marriage to the dilution of one's honor: "See, the fingers of the hand are different from one another. The same kind of difference exists between people. The asil man is the one whose father and mother are from his own *nasab* [stock, parentage, kind]. He is all right. If the mother is one thing, and the father is another, the foal of that donkey will be *kacha* [unbaked]. Surely he would do some mistake. Look at my brothers-in-law. The mother and father are both asil. Were they lions or not? . . . I don't have much information about the distant past, but for at least the last 600 years our family runs well. It is the glory of almighty God that he makes each century better than the others. If the potter's vein had joined with ours, or the ferryman's vein or the weaver's vein, truly nasab would be destroyed by the mother's side. If you were to say 'Boo!' to the children, they would lose heart." For an informative discussion of the concept of nasab in an earlier era, see Mottahedeh 1980, 98–104.

4. It is not surprising that the government should look to religious leaders to play this role. Prior to Abdur Rahman, the dominant political force in Kunar had been another religious family (the Padshahs of Kunar) that traced its descent ultimately to the Prophet Muhammad and more proximately to a famous Sufi saint known as Pir Baba whose popular shrine is located across the Pakistani border in Buner. Many (if not most) of the important local dynasties in the region claim a religious pedigree, the most famous examples being the Nawabs of Dir and the Walis of Swat. In both of these instances, the religious authority of the family's ancestor combined with other more material advantages: control of one of the principal Central Asian trade routes (in the case of the Nawabs of Dir) and alliance with the dominant Afghan and British States.

5. For an extended discussion of patrilateral cousin rivalry within the Mohmand tribe, see Akbar Ahmed 1980, especially pages 181–202.

6. One of the most eloquent ways in which the son's relationship with his father is expressed is in the phrase *qibla ga sahib,* by which a man will refer to his father to someone else when he is not present. In its most common use, *qibla* or *qibla ga* (place of qibla) refers to the direction of Mecca, which is often marked in a mosque by a hollow space known by the term *qibla.* Used in relation to the father, it indicates the almost reverential respect which a father expects from and is usually accorded by his son.

7. Additional research also uncovered the fact that the daughter who had been originally promised to Sultan Muhammad never left her father's house and later committed suicide after the deaths of her brothers rather than allowing herself to be taken by Sultan Muhammad.

8. Jon Anderson has noted that "Namuws comprehensively refers to integrity (completeness) and identifies what is subject to trespass and how. It links adultery, house-breaking, and land-theft—all uninvited entry—in a trilogy of capital crimes equivalent to the murders to which these and other torts of trespass often lead in the feud" (1979, 77). The use of the term *trespass* here is appropriate, for what is involved in each instance is the integrity of objects possessed by men and, consequently, the integrity of the individual and the group of which he is a part. Honor and integrity are inexorably intertwined, and the concept of namus is where that correlation is most completely realized.

9. In Pakhtun culture, an act of vengeance is thought to be particularly noteworthy if it comes after the passage of time. As a familiar proverb expresses it, "People say of the Pakhtun who took revenge after a hundred years, 'He took it quickly.' " In this light, Sultan Muhammad was not unjustified in feeling that his mother had acted in an overly hasty manner. At the same time, because of his youth, his lack of allies, and his absence from the area, it is also not surprising that the mother might question her son's ability to fulfill his obligations to his father. Whatever the truth of the matter might be, it is a curious, though by no means illogical, feature of the Pakhtun ethos of revenge that the longer an individual can endure the existential limbo that an unavenged act of violence brings about, the greater will be the interest that accrues once he has repaid the debt of honor.

10. Pitt-Rivers 1977, 1.

11. Recall that it was as part of such an agreement that Paindo's daughter was also supposed to go to Sultan Muhammad and also that much the same thing happens at the end of the story when Sultan Muhammad married off the female relatives of his slain enemies.

12. Martin 1907, 166–67.

13. Usually those who join together in mutual defense of one another are those who "share the same blood," therefore, those who are most closely related. Since agnates share most immediately in the honor of the deceased, it is expected that they will act most vigorously in gaining his revenge. But there are no fixed rules as to who must gain revenge for whom, and it is not unusual to see affinal and maternal relatives involved in enmities. When such participation takes place, individuals try to explain alliances in agnatic terms. Because of the frequency of patrilateral cross-cousin marriage and of cousin marriages in general, Pakhtuns can generally calculate almost any set of kinship relationships at least two or three ways. This allows considerable flexibility in how people conceptualize kinship connections and permits them as well to preserve the ideological integrity of the patrilineal system even when it is being contradicted in action.

14. E. Peters 1990, 59.

15. An ancient feud among the Mohmands that I investigated had been restarted on two occasions by an ambitious and belligerent young man (referred to by informants as a *badmash:* a ne'er-do-well or a troublemaker) after tribal jirgas had twice reached mutually agreed-upon solutions to terminate hostilities. However much the community at large wanted the conflict over with, this one man's actions disallowed resolution and caused the feud to continue for decades.

16. One fallout of the endemic feuding that exists in the tribal areas is that

there are many individuals who (like, the young Sultan Muhammad) are forced to take refuge outside of their home area. Those who follow this path do not demean themselves by doing so, but if they fail to make any moves toward taking revenge and remain "in the shade" of a khan for an extended period of time, they gradually lose their status as equals (sials) and come to be seen as servants, subject to the khan's directives.

17. An interesting case for comparison is offered by Mottahedeh in his analysis of oaths of political association undertaken during the Buyid dynasty (1980). In his study, Mottahedeh includes the following letter written by the caliph al-Muqtadir to his troops which asks for support on grounds that resemble those invoked in our story: "Most of your benefits (singular: *ni'mah*) are from me, but it would not be my way to reproach you with any favor that I have conferred, and that I regarded at the time—and still regard—as small compared with your merits; rather, it suits me to fertilize and increase them . . . [and] I long to bring you to the utmost limit of your aspirations. . . . I claim from you that oath of allegiance (*bai'ah*) which you have affirmed time after time" (p. 40). Mottahedeh also quotes Ibn Khaldun to the effect that "when people of group feeling (*'asabiyah*) take as followers people of another descent; or when they take slaves and clients into servitude and enter into close contact with them . . . the clients and followers share the group feeling of their masters and take it on as if it were their own group feeling" (pp. 89–90).

18. Bourdieu's comments on honor and domination in Kabyle society are pertinent to this case: "In a society in which overt violence, the violence of the usurer or the merciless master, meets with collective reprobation and is liable either to provoke a violent riposte from the victim or to force him to flee . . . symbolic violence, the gentle, invisible form of violence, which is never recognized as such, and is not so much undergone as chosen, the violence of credit, confidence, obligation, personal loyalty, hospitality, gifts, gratitude, piety—in short, all the virtues honoured by the code of honour—cannot fail to be seen as the most economical mode of domination, i.e., the mode which best corresponds to the economy of the system" (Bourdieu 1977, 192). Relevant here, as well, are Abu-Lughod's comments on the importance of voluntarism in societies bound together by honor but also characterized by an unequal distribution of wealth and power: "One way those at the bottom resolve the contradiction between their positions and the system's ideals is by appearing to defer to those in authority voluntarily. . . . What is voluntary is by nature free and is thus also a sign of independence. Voluntary deference is therefore the honorable mode of dependency" (Abu-Lughod 1986, 104).

19. According to Caroe, "The denial of sanctuary is impossible for one who would observe Pakhtu; it cannot be refused even to an enemy who makes an approach according to *Nanawatai*—a verbal noun carrying the meaning of 'coming in'. This is an extension of the idea of *Melmastia*, hospitality, in an extreme form, stepped up to the highest degree" (Caroe 1965, 351).

20. It is interesting to compare this Pakhtun paragon with the two great Greek heroes—Achilles and Odysseus—particularly with regard to their use of cunning. Achilles is a man who is single-minded in his concern for honor but less given to cunning. Odysseus, on the other hand, is less single-minded in his purposes and

sometimes directs his cleverness to less than honorable ends. Sultan Muhammad has features of both, being clever like Odysseus but also single-minded like Achilles. Thus, in putting a spy into the house of his enemies, cobbling together a band of retainers to do his bidding, and finally luring his enemies into his trap, Sultan Muhammad demonstrates a strategic capability similar to that displayed by Odysseus when he managed to overcome the suitors. And like Odysseus he ultimately executed his plan in the confines of his own guest house—though, in the case of Sultan Muhammad, the enemies were tricked into entering the guest house while in Odysseus's, the slaughter was undertaken in response to a prior invasion of his domestic space.

Likewise, Sultan Muhammad shows the kind of unwavering devotion to the ideals of honor that Achilles demonstrates, but he is like Achilles as well in his narcissistic self-absorption. All three heroes, in fact, show this flaw. For Odysseus, it is most succinctly revealed in his taunting of Cyclops, which condemns him to prolonged wandering and separation from his native society. For Achilles, self-absorption leads to his sulking retreat from battle and later to his defilement of the body of his fallen enemy, which in turn helps to bring about his own death. For Sultan Muhammad, the final outcome of self-absorption fuses elements of both of these stories: like Odysseus, his single-minded concern for honor leads to his estrangement from the normal affections of society; and while he never makes Achilles' mistake of investing too much of himself either in the honor of a woman or the love of a friend, his actions (like those of Achilles) cause a great destruction.

21. A proverb of the Dangam tribe of Kunar expresses the symbolic significance of land trespass this way: "When a man becomes sick he must wear the skin of an animal. When the land becomes sick, it must wear the skin of a man" (M. Rasul Amin and Hakim Taniwal, personal communication). This proverb equates an earlier custom of wrapping the sick in the skin of a sacrificed goat or sheep as a cure for their illness and the need to sacrifice a man to solve property disputes. It also nicely illustrates one of the moral justifications for Sultan Muhammad's killing of his enemies.

22. Lindholm 1982, 240–41.

23. Romantic relations with women can never aspire to this level of trust in Pakhtun society for the simple reason that women make men vulnerable. The story makes that fact clear from the first scene when it is a woman who is used as bait to snare Sultan Muhammad's father. Later, this act of deceit is reciprocated when still another woman is placed in the enemies' home as a spy, and finally we see Sultan Muhammad's attitude toward the threat of female involvement in his gesture of dismounting from his horse whenever he rode past a home where one of the female relatives of his enemies resided.

24. White 1981, 14.

25. The relentlessness that is associated with honor is perhaps relevant in relation to Sultan Muhammad's father and the motivation that led him to assume the role of the pious Muslim. The system wears men down, and religion provides not only solace regarding the next world, but also a refuge from the ceaseless demands of honor.

26. The archetypal form of female paighur is the *landai*, a form of poetry that women make up and recite among themselves. According to Inger Boesen, who

has studied landai composition among women in Kunar, landais are often bawdy, display a contemptuous attitude toward husbands, and extol the virtues of the daring lover who is willing to defy social custom to pursue his desire:

> Come and sit beside me, my beloved!
> If shyness prevents you from taking me in your arms,
> I shall take you in mine.

> Oh my God! Again you send me your dark night
> And again I tremble from head to feet, because much
> against my will, I have to lie down in the bed I hate.

> My beloved! Jump into my bed, don't be afraid!
> If it breaks, the Little Awful One [i.e., the husband] will repair it!

> (Boesen 1983, 120–21)

In Boesen's opinion, such verses "challenge and transgress the norms of Pakhtun society by demonstrating active sexuality; and by negating the honour of their husbands through escaping their control" (Boesen 1983, 121). But she also recognizes that the nature of this transgression is a contradictory one that reinforces the morality of honor at least as much as it undermines it. Thus, while the act of taking an illicit lover breaches customary norms of behavior, it also reinforces the ideal of individual self-determination (*ghairat*) since anyone who would undertake the path of illicit love must demonstrate traits highly esteemed among Pakhtuns, including a courageous disregard for danger and the cunning to overcome obstacles placed in one's path. The fact that landais could elicit such contrary responses leads to the conclusion that this verse form exemplifies the same tension between individual self-assertion and communal acquiescence revealed in the story of Sultan Muhammad. Landais articulate this tension in a somewhat different manner, however, in that they more directly address the problematic status of sexuality and gender relations. These areas of social engagement are implicated in Sultan Muhammad's narrative as well, but they are muted by their being presented in a male voice.

Given the manner in which landais elevate female sexuality, belittle domineering husbands, and celebrate the violation of social norms, one might suppose that they represent a female "culture of resistance" among Pakhtun women, but I believe Boesen is essentially correct in discounting this notion. As she indicates, the composition of landais do constitute an "outlet" for women's creativity and anger, but they do not represent "a basic challenge to the existing male-dominated society." To the contrary, landais reveal more than anything else that women are as ensnarled in the ethical crosscurrents of honor as men. This fact is illustrated by several landais which I collected in the course of my research from Pakhtun women via male relatives of my acquaintance:

> Oh, my love! Sacrifice your head for the homeland.
> Don't leave me to the taunts of my girlfriends.

> He who doesn't have arms must not be called man.
> It is better for him to put henna on his hands
> and make-up on his eyes for the young men.

It might be argued, of course, that the transmission of these verses through male hands ensured that they would reflect ideals consonant with those of honor, but the existence of similar landais in Boesen's work (e.g., "My lover fled from the battle. Now I regret the kiss I gave him yesterday.") and my own sense of the essential integrity of honor as an encompassing moral system convince me that men and women are equally in honor's thrall and equally vulnerable to the contradictions of its demands. For an elaboration of this point, see Boesen 1980, 1983. On Pakhtun women's lives and poetry more generally, see Grima 1992.

27. MacIntyre 1984, 126.

3. THE REIGN OF THE IRON AMIR

1. Curzon 1923, 69. While Lord Curzon translated most of the document, he did not analyze it or provide transliterations of key terms. As a result, I have included here a revised translation of the document that I prepared with the help of Nasim Stanazai. The same document, it should be noted, is also reproduced by Vartan Gregorian (1969, 131), but neither he nor Curzon examined the document in any depth. Note that the date of the proclamation—1898—is four years after Curzon's visit to Kabul, which would indicate that Curzon collected the document at a later point in his career, presumably during his tenure as Viceroy of India between 1899 and 1905.

2. Curzon notes, "Great as was his contempt for his people, he did not mean to run any risks or to give them any opportunity of getting rid of him before his time. On one occasion he was suffering severely from toothache and decided to have the offending tooth taken out. The surgeon prepared chloroform, whereupon the Amir asked how long he would have to remain insensible. 'About twenty minutes,' said the doctor. 'Twenty minutes!' replied the Amir. 'I cannot afford to be out of the world for twenty seconds. Take it out without chloroform!' " (Curzon 1923, 94).

3. The best studies of Abdur Rahman's reign are two works by Hasan Kakar (1971, 1979). In addition, Gregorian's book (1969) has useful sections, both on Abdur Rahman's reforms and on the place of the Amir in the larger history of Afghan state-building.

4. In contradistinction to the Durkheimian vision of nation-state as a form of "organic solidarity" (different parts making a complexly unified whole) and the tribe as a form of "mechanical solidarity" (similar parts linked by their sameness), Abdur Rahman's vision is of the nation-state as a mechanical solidarity in which each separate unit subordinates (or, better yet, dispenses with) its uniqueness while accepting a common identity in relation to the center. There is hierarchy here, of course, but what is more telling perhaps is the assumption that identity is more or less uniform and undifferentiated. The social vision articulated to me by a number of tribal Pakhtuns was arguably more complex than Abdur Rahman's, for it recognized differences between individuals and groups as fundamental. It also supposed a functional interdependence of subgroups within the social whole since it assumed that different groups have their own proper and indispensable

place in the social order (e.g., certain groups are by nature potters, ferrymen, or peasant laborers).

5. On the question of why the two sides came to accept the idea of demarcating fixed boundaries with Great Britain, Fraser-Tytler has made the following observations: "Abdur Rahman, though anxious to settle his south-eastern boundaries, was also anxious to include under his temporal as well as his spiritual authority as much as possible of the territory occupied by his Islamic followers. And so throughout the eighties he watched with displeasure any tendency on the part of the British to advance their boundaries. He was much disturbed when they, 'having cut a tunnel through the Khojak hill, were pushing the railway line into my country, just like pushing a knife into my vitals.' In reply he pushed forward his outposts into Waziristan, threatened the Turis of the Kurram, assumed virtual sovereignty over the Afridis and strengthened his connexion with the Mohmands. If unchecked, his dominion would in a few years have extended to the administered border of India, and threatened Peshawar. In the north-east he disregarded the Government of India's injunction not to meddle with Bajaur and Dir by seizing the district of Asmar. By 1893 relations were becoming increasingly strained, and the settlement of some form of boundary to check these encroachments was becoming urgent" (Fraser-Tytler 1950, 188).

6. S. M. Khan 1980, 2:175–77. (*The Life of Abdur Rahman: Amir of Afghanistan* was originally published by John Murray, London, in 1900.)

7. Hasan Kakar, the preeminent scholar of this period of Afghan history, has provided the following information on the Amir's autobiography: "only the first part [of *The Life of Abdur Rahman*] covering the events of 'Abd al-Rahman's early life up to his arrival in Afghanistan, was written by the Amir himself. The manuscript is undated and preserved in the Mss Department of the Kabul Public Library. It is not definite when the Amir wrote it, but in 1303/1886 it was published under the title of *Pandnamah-i dunya wa din (A Book of Advice on the World and Religion)*. Sultan Mahomed has simply incorporated its English translation in the so-called Autobiography of the Amir" (Kakar 1971, 217–20). The provenance of the second volume of *The Life* is a good deal more uncertain, for although Sultan Mahomed claims that he wrote it directly from the Amir's dictation, it appears more likely that the account has been cobbled together from a number of original documents and Sultan Mahomed's own eyewitness testimony. According to Kakar, Abdur Rahman commissioned Sultan Mahomed Khan to compose an account of his administration and his views on various issues—such as indeed appears in the second volume of the autobiography. However, since Sultan Mahomed Khan fled Afghanistan prior to completing the manuscript (reportedly because of his embezzlement of government funds) the finished work was never officially approved by the Amir himself.

While the authenticity of the first volume appears certain, the quality of the English translation is another matter, and it is one that has never been closely considered as far as I can ascertain. Sultan Mahomed Khan claimed to have "translated every word of the Amir's own narrative of his early years," including the "Eastern stories" that the Amir loved to recount and that are "an object of special interest to the European mind" (S. M. Khan 1980, xxx). The only alteration that the Amir's former secretary acknowledges is to "have given different titles to the chapters from those given by the Amir. The change, however, does not affect the book itself, or its real '*Matlab*' [meaning]" (S. M. Khan 1980, xxxi). For further details on the autobiography and Sultan Mahomed's role in its production, see Kakar 1971, 217–20.

8. S. M. Khan 1980, xxxi–xxxii.

9. Ibid., 46.

10. Ibid., 48.

11. Ibid., 55.

12. Ibid., 67.

13. Ibid., 77.

14. In emphasizing the supremacy of God and the responsibility of the Muslim ruler for ensuring that his subjects are able to lead a good Muslim life, Abdur Rahman is drawing on time-honored principles of Islamic political authority. As Bernard Lewis has noted, "The worth of the state, and the good and evil deeds of statesmen, are measured by the extent to which this purpose is accomplished. The basic rule for Muslim social and political life, commonly formulated as 'to enjoin good and forbid evil,' is thus a shared responsibility of the ruler and the subject, or in modern terms, of the state and the individual" (Lewis 1988, 29).

15. S. M. Khan 1980, 138–39. It should be noted that Abdur Rahman himself was renowned for cruelty, and the same condemnations that he leveled against the king of Bokhara have frequently been made against him. Indeed, if even half of the stories told of him have any basis in reality, then the forms and extent of his violence matched—if they did not exceed—what he attributes to the king of Bokhara. The implications of this violence will be discussed in depth in the final section of this chapter.

16. Ibid., 37–39. Margaret Mills has pointed out the similarity between this story and the account of the Prophet's first Qur'anic revelation. According to this account, Muhammad was either asleep or in a trance when the angel Gabriel appeared to him and three times commanded that he "read." The first two times, Muhammad replied that he could not read, but after the third command he found that he could. Upon awaking, the words remained "as if inscribed upon his heart" (Margaret Mills, personal communication). See N. J. Dawood's introduction to The Koran (1990, x) for a description of this scene.

17. On the subject of dreams in Muslim culture, see the collections edited by G. E. von Grunbaum and Roger Caillois (1966) and Ewing (1980).

18. S. M. Khan 1980, 231–33.

19. Ibid., 171.

20. Ibid., 172–73.

21. The general cultural pattern in Afghan society is for fathers to maintain an air of reserve in front of their sons, whereas sons are expected to be deferential and circumspect in the presence of their fathers (and all other senior agnates). Thus, while "kindness and mercy" may have been the natural feelings that fathers experienced for their sons, the expression of this feeling was generally muted, as can be seen in the following report concerning Abdur Rahman's own family relations: "The Amir, although always treating his sons in a kindly manner, was never familiar with them, and his attitude toward them was that of king to subject, rather than father to son. If they committed a blunder or offended in the discharge

of their duties, he punished by ordering them not to show themselves in durbar, and so kept them under the ban of his displeasure for a longer or shorter time, which he ended by sending them an order to come to him, and then the one in disgrace would come and kneel before his father, and be allowed to kiss his hand in recognition of forgiveness" (Martin 1907, 120–21).

22. Lewis 1988, 17.

23. S. M. Khan 1980, 46.

24. Ibid., 88. British political observers of the day had long been speculating on the rivalry between Abdur Rahman and his uncle and fully expected the death of Muhammad Afzal to be followed by a full-scale dynastic war. It must have come as a surprise to them, therefore, when the following communication (dated 9 October 1867) was received from their native reporter and not only confirms the accuracy of Abdur Rahman's description but also employs the same metaphoric language to describe the reconciliation between uncle and nephew: "Sardar Abdul Rahman Khan at first entertained the belief that on the demise of his father, the Wali (Sardar Muhammad Afzal Khan), he would succeed to the throne, his uncle, Sardar Muhammad Azam Khan, taking the second place in the conduct of affairs as Naib; but Sardar Muhammad Azam Khan, sending for his nephew . . . explained in a private audience that, in event of his (Sardar Abdool Rahman Khan's) being able to undertake the responsibilities of the Government, he (Azam) was willing to bow to his will, and reside at Candahar or Khooram, or any other place he might indicate . . . and that he would always look on him (Abdool Rahman Khan) as his son, and would do nothing to injure his own family. The Sardar, owing to his isolation (tunhaee) and to diversity of opinions at Cabul, replied that he would give way to his uncle, and consider him in the light of a parent; accordingly, to day, after the conclusion of third day's mourning for the Wali, the Sardar Abdool Rahman Khan in public Durbar made over the sword of his deceased father to Sardar Muhammad Azam Khan and tendered his allegiance to him" (Enclosure 6 in No. 11, "Correspondence Respecting the Relations between the British Government and That of Afghanistan since the Accession of the Ameer Shere Ali Khan" [Great Britain. Parliament, 1882]).

25. S. M. Khan 1980, 134–35.

26. Ibid., 54–56.

27. Ibid., 26–27.

28. Mottahedeh 1980, 72–73.

29. On Abdur Rahman's efforts to reform the army, see Kakar 1979, 93–115.

30. S. M. Khan 1980, 216 n. Sultan Mahomed, the editor of the autobiography, notes in this footnote that Parwana Khan was "the most trusted" of the Amir's courtiers and that his sons continued to enjoy a position of importance in the court of Abdur Rahman's son, Amir Habibullah Khan.

31. Ibid., 110.

32. Ibid., 94.

33. Ibid., 101.

34. Ibid., 127.

35. Ibid., 57. Similar offense is also expressed concerning an incident that occurred during his exile in Russian Turkistan when he was taken from his house and arrested by Russian authorities. At the time of his arrest, it appeared that he

faced an uncertain future and might be imprisoned for a considerable period of time. Unexpectedly, however, he was released that same day and returned to his home that night to find the garden door locked: "On ordering my servants to open it I found my cousins, with their friends, already asleep, and quite regardless of what might happen to me. . . . I was disappointed and heart-broken at seeing my cousins and all my servants asleep. I had brought these men up like my children, and this was my reward" (Ibid., 157). This ingratitude on the part of his servants is clearly meant to contrast with the compassion and concern which he, their master, feels for those who enter his service. This benevolence is seen in several places in the autobiography, including a scene in which Abdur Rahman and his followers have just succeeded in crossing a Turkistani desert during which endeavor they had found no water for days and had lost a number of men to the heat. At this moment of distress, Abdur Rahman indicates that his thoughts turned not to himself, but to "my lost servants, and [I] could not help weeping at their fate" (Ibid., 133. See also, 105).

36. Ibid., 83.

37. Ibid., 89. One of the ways Abdur Rahman signals the self-interested nature of courtiers is by depicting their manners, particularly at table, where they are shown "eating the food before them, like so many cattle, who also require no plates" (Ibid., 57; see also, 225–26). The Amir is likewise disparaging of the intelligence of his officials as seen in the following anecdote: "Once, when bread and flour were very dear in the market, there was fear of famine; and my ministers, whom I consulted at that time, strongly advised me to nail the ears of the corn and flour sellers to the doors of their shops, in order to force them to make the corn and flour cheaper. I could not help laughing at this valuable advice, and since that day till the present time, I have never asked advice from my counsellors!" (Ibid., 226).

38. According to the British engineer Frank Martin, who worked for Abdur Rahman for a number of years in Kabul, Abdur Rahman had a view of women that was remarkably similar to that of Sultan Muhammad: "The Amir seldom spent much time in the harem serai amongst his women, it being his custom to devote an occasional evening to them only, and his opinion of women in general was not a high one. On some occasions he spoke rather plainly of the length, and lying propensities, of a woman's tongue, and her general inaptitude for anything of worth, and love of intrigue" (Martin 1907, 106).

39. S. M. Khan 1980, 261.

40. Ibid., 261. It is worth noting here the resemblance between Abdur Rahman's association of actions and heredity and that of Shahmund, the Mohmand tribal elder quoted in chapter 1, who noted that "the foal of the donkey" will inevitably prove itself "unbaked."

41. Ibid., 262.

42. Ibid., 262.

43. Ibid., 263.

44. Ibid., 264.

45. Ibid., 267. The declaration of faith (shahadat) which is the sine qua non of Muslim belief is as follows: "There is no god but Allah, and Muhammad is His messenger."

46. Ibid., 270.

47. Ibid., 34.

48. See page 218 of *The Life* for mention of this practice by the Amir. Other references are contained in Bell 1948, 13; Martin 1907, 163; and Curzon 1923, 65. I have also seen photographs of such cages, including one taken by the American journalist Lowell Thomas during a trip through the Khyber Pass in the mid-1920s.

49. S. M. Khan 1980, 35.

50. Ibid., 21.

51. Curzon 1923, 66.

52. Frank Martin devotes two chapters of his Afghan memoirs to the subject of "Prisons and Prisoners" and "Tortures and Methods of Execution," the latter of which has the following lively subheadings,

Amir's Iron rule—Hanging by hair and skinning alive—Beating to death with sticks—Cutting men in pieces—Throwing down mountain-side—Starving to death in cages—Boiling woman to soup and man drinking it before execution—Punishment by exposure and starvation—Scaffold scenes—Burying alive—Throwing into soap boilers—Cutting off hands—Blinding—Tying to bent trees and disrupting—Blowing from guns—Hanging, etc. (Martin 1907, 157).

53. Curzon 1923, 59.

54. S. M. Khan 1980, 219.

55. Martin 1907, 151.

56. S. M. Khan 1980, 172. In *The Life*, we see examples of a thief disguising himself as a *sayyid* (descendant of the Prophet) (p. 113); traitors masking their evil intentions by intoning Qur'anic oaths (p. 154); and the aforementioned instance of Isaq Khan, Abdur Rahman's great rival, assuming a quasi-messianic identity in his attempt to subvert Abdur Rahman's authority (p. 263).

57. Ibid., 218.

58. Ibid., 252.

59. In discussing the instability of the government at the time of his ascension, Abdur Rahman notes that his predecessor, Sher 'Ali, "being unable to fight against the chiefs of his subjects himself, introduced another system, which he thought was a very wise one. This was to set his own chiefs and officials against each other, and to encourage them to cause bloodshed, and a law was made, that if any one wanted to kill his enemy, he had only to place 300 rupees per head in the Government Treasury and to kill as many as he liked" (Ibid., 227). However much of an exaggeration this might be, it is nevertheless the case that Afghan rulers have long relied on their ability to divide their subjects in order to rule the country. On a number of occasions when local rebellions threatened to get out of hand, Abdur Rahman himself was forced to use one tribe or group in order to defeat another, but he was also aware of the long-term dangers of this practice and was determined to develop a sufficiently loyal military that his successors would not have to resort to this tactic.

60. Foucault 1979, 47–48.

61. Samiullah Safi noted in one of our interviews that his father had once summarily shot a man and a woman who had been flirting with one another near his house. He also recounted another incident in which his father had captured a

man who had committed adultery and turned him over to the husband of the woman with whom he had been involved.

62. As we will see in the next chapter, religious leaders have traditionally interposed themselves in the space afforded by these different interpretations of rule. In some cases, their role was to support the king by branding recalcitrant tribesmen as infidel for resisting the king's legitimate authority. In others, religious leaders have sided with tribes against authoritarian rulers, branding them despotic and unfit to govern. Such leaders forfeited their moral entitlement to rule under Islamic law, and the people who believed themselves yoked to such a tyrant could look to a number of legendary examples in early Islamic history of tyrants whose acts of injustice caused them to lose their thrones.

63. Martin 1907, 128.

64. Ibid., 129.

65. Ibid., 129.

66. Ibid., 130.

4. THE LIVES OF AN AFGHAN SAINT

1. One of the other two informants with whom I discussed the career of the Mulla of Hadda was Shahmund, who is quoted in chapter 2 on honor and descent. An elder of the subsection of the Mohmand tribe with which the Mulla took refuge in his later years, Shahmund had heard a number of stories from his grandfather about the Mulla, one of which is recounted at the end of chapter 5. The second informant without a direct ancestral connection to the Mulla's Sufi order was Khalilullah Khalili, a poet, politician, and former government official, who was in his eighties when I met him in Pakistan. The son of the *mustufi* (chief of finance) under Amir Habibullah, Khalili had been close to the center of Afghan political life from boyhood; he is, in fact, mentioned (and photographed) in the memoir of an American engineer who was in Kabul during Habibullah's reign (Bell, 1948). Khalili enjoyed the unique position of having served both Bacha-i Saqao, the "bandit-king" responsible for overthrowing Amir Abdur Rahman's grandson, Amir Amanullah (1919–1929), and Zahir Shah, the Afghan king who ruled from 1933 to 1973. In addition to being intimately apprised of the workings of the royal court, Khalili was also a personal acquaintance of several of the Mulla's principal deputies, including the Mulla of Tagao.

2. "Karama," in Gibb and Kramer 1974, 216.

3. Gilsenan 1982, 75. See also, Gilsenan 1973, especially 20–35.

4. Ibid., 83–84.

5. Temple 1882, 325–26.

6. The term *pasanai* (upper) is a form of reference that those from the Indian subcontinent have traditionally used in relation to Afghans who were known as "people of the upper land." Here, Najmuddin is referred to as "upper mulla," which means essentially "mulla from the high country," therefore, from Afghanistan.

7. This story was told to me by Sayyid Abdullah Pacha, a grandson of Sayyid Ismail Pacha of Islampur, one of the Mulla of Hadda's principal deputies. Fazil Aziz, who told me the story of the journey to Koh-i Qaf, also provided a story

that is remarkably similar to this one, though more complicated. This story, which involves the Mulla of Hadda and his deputy, Turangzai Sahib, goes as follows:

One day before I became a disciple of Hadda Sahib, I went to *Baitulla-i Sharif* [Mecca]. At that time, traveling to Baitulla-i Sharif was full of trouble because you had to go by foot. When I arrived there, I sought to establish good relations with the head *imam* [prayer leader] of the Ka'ba. I presented him with the things which I had brought, and I made a practice of helping him with his sandals in order that one day he would assist me by assigning a man to take me to the shrine of *pir-i piran* ["the Pir of Pirs," Abdul Qadir Jilani, the founder of the Qaderiya Order] in Baghdad. One day he said to me, "Oh, you sir, you have tried to get close to me. What business do you have with me?"

I said, "I hope that God will help and that you will pay attention to my problem. My intention is to go to the shrine of *ghaus ul-'azam dastagir* [an honorific title for Abdul Qadir Jilani] if you will only help me."

Then he said to me, "I can't do that, but on Fridays a person comes and sits between these two columns at such-and-such a time. When he comes, go and sit behind him. When he leaves, you go along behind him. Ask him, and maybe he can take you."

I waited at the proper time and found that person and sat behind him. After prayers, I went out behind him when he left. He walked very fast, and I also followed him at a fast pace so I wouldn't lose him in the alleyways of Mecca. Finally he stopped and asked me, "What business do you have with me that you are following behind like this?"

I said, "Dear sir, I am hoping that you will take me to the shrine of Pir-i Piran."

He said, "You are here, and Pir-i Piran Sahib is in Baghdad. I don't have any money to give you, and it is very expensive."

While we were talking, the man suddenly vanished, and I found myself in the desert. I couldn't find my way to glorious Mecca. Finally, I saw a person who asked me where I was going. I said that I was going to Baitulla-i Sharif, but that I had lost my way.

He said to me, "May God be kind to you, for this is Baghdad, and that is the shrine of Pir-i Piran Sahib."

After the pilgrimage, I returned to Turangzai. Some of the scholars, spiritual people, and elders gathered and said, "Hadda Sahib has come to Mohmand. Let us go and see him."

After that event [of finding myself in Baghdad], I was always trying to visit the mullas who were known as good people in order to try to find that person who took me there, so I also went with them and arrived in Jarobi [Hadda Sahib's home base in Mohmand]. There were many people standing, and some were serving, and Sahib-i Hadda was sitting. When I saw him I said, "This is the one who took me to Baghdad when I was praying at *haram-i sharif* [the Ka'ba]."

When I went up to him, he put his hand to his mouth, so that I wouldn't tell anyone. When I took his hands, I couldn't say anything no matter how hard I tried. My mouth was sealed. Sahib-i Hadda got up and took me to a separate room. He told me to be careful. "As long as I am alive, don't tell anyone this story. After my death, you can if you want. But, if you tell the story while I am alive, you will be responsible for any harm that comes to you."

When I saw him I said that, "Without doubt, he is a *wali* [friend of God] and a *kamil pir* [perfected saint]."

8. While many religious titles are found throughout the Islamic world, the meanings attached to these titles frequently vary from country to country. In the eastern part of Afghanistan, one finds a number of different terms used in reference to religious figures. By and large, there is uniformity in usage throughout the region, but even within this relatively restricted domain, there are local variations. Thus, the definitions I use in this book and that are summarized here may not conform to idioms in other parts of the country.

The most basic terms are *mulla, akhund,* and *imam,* all of which are applied to men who have received a basic religious education and whose status in the group is related to their association with Islam. While the terms are often used interchangeably, there are differences. For example, an imam specifically refers to someone who is employed as a prayer leader of a mosque, and the use of the term *imam* therefore relates to the individual's assumption of that role in his community. A mulla usually is also an imam, but not necessarily. In addition to their responsibility for leading prayers, imams and mullas have several additional jobs as well. These include teaching basic religious beliefs and practices, along with appropriate Qur'anic phrases, to local children; performance of marriage ceremonies and funerals; recitation of the call to prayer (*azan*) into the ears of newborn children; the recitation of Qur'anic phrases for healing (*dam*) and the writing of amulets (*tawiz*); participation in local assemblies; and mediation between warring factions. The term *akhund* is also used to refer to someone with a basic religious education, but in my experience it is most often employed for individuals in the past and its primary significance is as a family designation: for example, in the names Talabuddin Akhundzada and Najmuddin Akhundzada. In addition to these terms, others related to the scholarly class include *maulavi,* which is used for those with advanced religious training, especially those who have trained in India and/or Pakistan; *maulana,* which is more or less synonymous with *maulavi,* but appears to be used particularly for those who received their advanced training at the Deoband madrasa in India; *qazi,* which is used for those who served as (or received the training to serve as) a judge; and *talab ul-'elm* and *charai,* both of which refer to religious students.

A second category of religious terms is applied to those whose authority is primarily spiritual and mystical in nature rather than scholarly. This category includes *pir,* which is used to refer to Sufis who have completed the sequence of zikrs in one or more orders and who have been authorized by their teacher(s) to take students of their own; *mauzun* and *khalifa,* synonyms which refer to those students of a pir who have been authorized to take on students and establish centers of their own (mauzuns/khalifas would thus also be pirs); *murid,* which means disciple and refers to all those who visit and take lessons from a pir; *shaykh,* which is used to refer to those disciples who attend to the needs of a pir and take care of the business of the pir's center. In addition to these titles, there are also a number of terms for religious mendicants, including *faqir*, which is the most common expression one hears in eastern Afghanistan, *malang* and *qalandar*, which are both more common in Pakistan, and *darvish*, which seems more often found in poetic discourse than in daily usage.

A final set of titles is associated with spiritual families whose status is based on descent from a revered ancestor. The most common of these titles include the following: *sayyid*, reserved for descendants of the Prophet Muhammad; *mia* (in the plural, *miagan*, and in reference to a lineage, *miakhel*) and *pacha* (*pachagan* in the plural), which are both sometimes used as synonyms for *sayyid* but which additionally refer to the descendants of revered saints of the past; and *hazrat* (*hazratan* in the plural), used for those who claim descent from Umar, the second Islamic caliph, and best known in relation to the Kabul-based spiritual family known as the Hazrats of Shor Bazaar. Many titles, such as *akhund* and *pir*, can also be turned into a family name through the addition of the suffix -*zada*.

9. Whatever salary an imam or mulla receives is usually not sufficient for his family's needs, and most village clerics also keep a flock of animals and till a small amount of land, which is often lent, rented, or given over to them by the local people. According to one of my informants whose father was one of the Mulla of Hadda's deputies and who assumed control of the center at Hadda after the Mulla's death, "villagers give wheat, maize, and rice to their local mulla. In some places, the amount of the salary is fixed, and in some other places, it is variable. For example, when the residents of a particular village decide to hire a good mulla to teach their children and lead prayers at the mosque, they sit among themselves and decide on the quantity of food or amount of money to pay him, whether it is ten *sir* of wheat per family or a thousand Afghanis [the unit of currency in Afghanistan] in cash. Whatever [the arrangement], it is decided on beforehand by the villagers. This arrangement is different from *zakat*. . . . Because zakat is for poor people, it should be given first to indigent relatives. The amount of zakat is fixed, and it is given by each individual."

10. The best known articulation of the scriptural/mystical division in Islam is probably to be found in the work of Ernest Gellner on Moroccan Islam (e.g., 1981). I base my own contention as to the relative absence of a scholarly/mystical split in Afghan Islam primarily on the evidence of my own interviews and observations of the present situation. Whether I was speaking with the descendant of a great Sufi pir, a scholar, or a judge, biographical accounts tended to weave together the scholarly, the legal, and the spiritual. Thus, most of the great scholars ('ulama) of the past about whom I was able to gather information seem to have engaged in mystical practices, while stories told of Sufi pirs usually emphasize their scholastic learning. On a practical level, though, the absence of a split also seems to be a result of the institutional matrix of Islamic practice characterized by the absence of a centralized or hierarchical structure of authority and by the prevalence (at least in eastern Afghanistan) of a pattern whereby religious seekers traveled indiscriminately from madrasa to khanaqa in their search for knowledge and communities of interest. In addition, the Sufi beliefs and practices one encounters in Afghanistan tend to be relatively tame in comparison with some other Muslim

countries where Sufis are known to go into ecstatic trances, attribute almost god-like powers to their pirs, and otherwise to indulge in extreme activities. Afghan Sufis generally steer clear of such practices, and even when they attribute miraculous powers to their saints, they are careful to indicate that the saint is only a vehicle through whom God has chosen to manifest himself and not an independent actor. This attitude is summed up in the oft-heard expression that the Muslim must attend first to *shariʿat* (Islamic law), then to *tariqat* (the Sufi path).

11. The approximate date of 1850 would place Najmuddin's tenure in Kabul sometime near the tumultuous First Anglo-Afghan War. Whether or not Najmuddin participated or witnessed events associated with this war, it appears that he spent a formative period of his life in Kabul during a time of great upheaval in which dynastic strife within the ruling elite was endemic and the specter of European influence first appeared as a major force in Afghan society.

12. Himself the son of a shepherd (some say from the Gujar tribe), the Akhund (born Abdul Ghafur) became a disciple of a local pir of the Qadiriya Sufi order named Sahibzada Muhammad Shwaib, who taught him the ritual formulae that are recited in the practice known as zikr. Thereafter, the young Abdul Ghafur isolated himself for twelve years in a cowshed by the banks of the Indus River. During this time, he devoted himself to prayer, meditation, and zikr, and, according to local legend, subsisted on nothing more than grass, millet, and water: a diet which, with the addition of buffalo's milk, he was to maintain for the rest of his life. While he sometimes served as a unifying leader of the tribes in operations against the British, the Akhund was primarily renowned as a Sufi pir who attracted devotees from throughout northern India and Afghanistan to his center in the town of Saidu Sharif in the lower Swat Valley.

13. Every Sufi order has its own set of zikrs which must be learned sequentially and under the guidance of a recognized master. Those who are interested in learning these spiritual exercises will go to a pir who has himself completed training under a pir and received formal permission (*ejaza*) from him to teach these exercises. The pir will permit the student to learn each new exercise at the speed the pir deems appropriate, and most disciples never receive the complete set. If the pir decides that a disciple has the ineffable qualities of true spiritual insight and devotion, however, he will teach him all of the exercises associated with a particular order and give him permission to teach disciples of his own. As is often the case in Afghanistan and the frontier, the Akhund had received training in four different Sufi tariqats, or orders: those of the Qaderiya, Naqshibandiya, Chishtiya, and Suhrawardiya. Most disciples of the Akhund learned the zikrs of the Qaderiya Order. Some went on to learn those of the Naqshibandiya, and a smaller number received those of the Chishtiya and Suhrawardiya Orders as well. For concise overviews of Sufi history and philosophy, see Baldick (1989) and Schimmel (1975). For general information on Sufi orders, see Trimingham (1971). Among the best studies dealing with individual orders are Abun-Nasr (1965), Eaton (1978), Eickelman (1976), Evans-Pritchard (1949), Gilsenan (1973), and O'Brien (1971).

14. It should be pointed out that the Akhund of Swat had two sets of progeny. On the one side were his disciples and deputies who collectively assumed the mantle of Sufi leadership. On the other were his own sons and grandsons, known by the title of *miangul* (flower of the saints), who took over the Akhund's position

of political leadership in Swat and also inherited a degree of spiritual authority from him as well. Although the younger of the Akhund's two sons (Miangul Abdul Khaliq) followed his father on the ascetic path, most of the Akhund's biological descendants devoted their time to politics rather than religion, in the process squandering the better part of the spiritual respect earned by their forebear. For a fascinating description and analysis of the political universe of Swat and the role of the Akhund's family therein, see *The Last Wali of Swat*, written by one of the Akhund's great-grandsons, Miangul Jahanzeb, with the help and additional analysis of Fredrik Barth (Jahanzeb, 1983).

15. Spiritual genealogies are not as exclusive as tribal ones because individuals can and often do belong to more than one. Most of the important pirs about whom I have heard stories mastered the zikrs of several orders and received permission from their masters to provide training in each. While there is some flexibility in tribal affiliation (refugees from other areas sometimes being gradually incorporated into local genealogies), I have never heard of a situation in which an individual claimed membership in more than one tribe.

16. This story was told to me by Maulavi Abdul Hakim Zhobul, grandson of Sufi Sahib of Faqirabad.

17. The tendency for saints to locate themselves (or to have their shrines located) on the border between tribes or tribal sections was first noted by Evans-Pritchard (1949) and further developed by Ernest Gellner (1969). The interstitial location of Hadda is somewhat different, being essentially between tribe and state rather than tribe and tribe, but the principle seems essentially the same.

18. Both Clifford Geertz and Lawrence Rosen have noted the important social role played by markers of identity in negotiating social interactions in Morocco. See Clifford Geertz, "From the Native's Point of View," in Geertz, 1983; Geertz, et al. 1979; and Rosen 1984.

19. Rabinow 1975, 28.

20. This story was told to me by Maulavi Muhammad Gul Rohani, grandson of Ustad Sahib of Hadda, one of Hadda Sahib's principal deputies.

21. This story was told to me by Maulavi Abdul Hakim Zhobul, grandson of Sufi Sahib of Faqirabad.

22. According to one informant, there are two kinds of chilla. The first, called *chilla aurad*, lasts only a few days and so is sometimes undertaken by less experienced disciples with the approval of their pir. A second chilla, known as *chilla-i tariqat*, lasts forty days and is undertaken only by those who have just completed all of the lessons of the order. The restrictions on who can perform this chilla exist because of the danger which it presents. During the confinement, Satan himself can appear to the adept, and if he is unprepared for this challenge he can lose his sanity or even his life. For those who have the wherewithal to handle this challenge (and it is the saint's responsibility to make the determination who is and who is not ready), the forty-day retreat is generally initiated ten days prior to the beginning of the month of Ramazan.

23. As one Afghan refugee—a religious judge before the war and a descendant of Ustad Sahib of Hadda—expressed it, "Jihad is a struggle against the enemy, whether the enemy is in the person's body or another human being. Both are

enemies of Islam. The foundation of Sufism [*tasawuf*] is the Qur'an and the hadith, and it says in the Qur'an and hadith that we should do jihad against our *nafs* and Satan. We should also do jihad against those who oppose our shari'a [Islamic law], but when the Prophet Muhammad came back from the Battle of the Trench, he said to his companions that, 'We have returned from the smaller jihad to the greater one.' "

24. One such zikr, referred to as "negation and affirmation" (*nafi wa isbat*), centers on the phrase *la illah il lallah:* There is no God but Allah. When performed correctly, the first, negative part of the phrase (there is no God) must be uttered so that the breath starts from the left breast and moves up and out of the body through the right shoulder. The second section of the utterance, which affirms the oneness of God, is then directed inward, "to purify the heart."

25. Amir Habibullah, the son of Abdur Rahman, was known to be much more pious and respectful of religious figures than his father, and one mark of this attitude was that he set aside a special *sarai*, or enclosure, where faqirs could eat and sleep. Arthur Jewett, who worked as an engineer in Habibullah's court for a number of years, noted in a letter that the Amir was not alone in caring for poor faqirs: "Some of the wealthier Afghans support and keep these holy beggars in their homes, with the idea that they will thereby acquire merit and that it will bring them good luck. The mustofi [chief of finances] kept one of these lunatics in his home in Kabul. The old idiot used to wear a skullcap all studded with Bokharan coins. He was given the best of food and everything he asked for and was treated with ceremonious respect. If he were tired, some of the household would massage his legs, while he reclined on cushions and babbled rubbish. Even the great mustofi himself would defer to him and make him presents" (as quoted in Bell 1948, 304). In explaining the position of faqirs, Jewett records two Persian proverbs that express opposing points of view as to the status of faqirs. The first of these proverbs, which he does not supply the original for, is "God has taken their minds, and God speaks through them." The second, more cynical point of view is expressed in the proverb that the faqir is "Crazy, but in his own interest wise" (*diwana, laken ba kar-i khud ushyar*) (as quoted in Bell 1948, 304).

26. This analysis is taken from the famous eleventh-century treatise, *Kashf-al-Mahjub* (1980) by 'Ali bin Uthman al-Hujwiri (better known in the subcontinent by the name Data Ganj Bakhsh). The title of the treatise can be translated as "The Unveiling of the Veiled," and refers specifically to the process by which mankind is made aware of "the subtlety of spiritual truth" (al-Hujwiri 1980, 4). The work is probably the best known work of Sufi philosophy in Afghanistan and the subcontinent and provides the most complete summary of the mystical principles that inform the Sufi tradition in the Afghan context.

27. Ibid., 226.

28. This story was told to me by Maulavi Ahmad Gul, grandson of Ustad Sahib of Hadda.

29. This story was told to me by Maulawi Abdul Hakim Zhobul, grandson of Sufi Sahib of Faqirabad.

30. On the Pakistan side of the border, the largest active langar is at the tomb of Pir Baba in Buner. Smaller langars also continue to operate at other tombs as well,

although most of the active tombs that I am familiar with serve food only during the annual festival that commemorates the anniversary of the saint's death.

31. Son of Kajuri Mulla, personal communication.

32. Most of the deputies who chose to return to their native villages appear to have been from established religious families. At least four of Hadda Sahib's most important deputies were from such families, and, in at least one case—that of Pacha Sahib of Islampur—the family was also very wealthy.

33. Maulavi Abdul Hakim Zhobul, the grandson of Sufi Sahib, recalled the vivid impression made upon him when, as a young child, he first beheld the great copper pots that had been used in his grandfather's langars, pots large enough that "a whole cow could be cooked in them." The grandson recalled that he once met his grandfather's servant who kept the storeroom where all the supplies such as grain and flour were kept. There was another man who looked after the meat and other foodstuffs needed for cooking, and a third who supervised all of the pots and pans. In addition, there were three people whose principal job was to pour water over the guests' hands before and after meals.

34. In Afghanistan, there are a number of different kinds of charitable donations. Qalang, referred to above, is a voluntary contribution generally made on an annual basis to spiritual figures. The best known form of charity is zakat, which is supposed to represent 2.5 percent of a person's wealth and is usually given to poor people or mullas. Another general category of religiously stipulated charity is known as 'ushr and involves the relinquishment of 10 percent of a person's annual produce, again to the poor or to local religious functionaries. In the frontier, 'ushr is also sometimes conflated or superseded by another form of charitable donation known as ara. This is a donation given to religious functionaries at harvest time. In earlier times, ara was taken to the home of whichever religious figure was to be the beneficiary. In more recent times, the religious figure or his descendants will go themselves to collect the donation which usually amounts to around 7 "wet" kilograms (or 5 "dry" ones) donated for every kharwar (560 kilograms) produced. Alms that are voluntarily given, for example, in the collection box at a shrine, to poor people during annual Eid celebrations, or at the time of funeral or marriage ceremonies are referred to as khirat. Sadaqat is the donation which an individual pledges for the fulfillment of some vow or prayer. Sarsaya is a donation made during the month of Ramazan prior to the Eid prayers that conclude the fast. It is a one-time donation of food given to poor people (generally to mullas), usually amounting to approximately 5 pounds of wheat or an equivalent amount or value of some other grain or meat.

35. The only group that seems to have been exempted from this pattern of social leveling were Islamic scholars who received especially good treatment, at least at some of the langars. Thus, the grandson of Sufi Sahib indicated that scholars were served meals in a different room than other visitors. In addition, "every scholar ['alem] who left the langar was given a present such as a turban or overcoat. Even tea would be given. At that time, tea was very scarce. [Sufi Sahib] would also give money, and everyone who asked permission to leave was told not to go away empty-handed and had to take something with them. Some didn't like to take anything away from the langar, so they would just take home one or two

small pieces of cornbread as a memento [*tobaruk*]" (Moulawi Abdul Hakim Zhobul, personal interview, August 31, 1983).

36. A number of informants discussed the role which their saintly forebears played in resolving individual and group disputes. Following a pattern discussed by Barth (1959a), some of the deputies of Hadda Sahib also appear to have established centers in particular areas at the behest of local headmen who sought outside mediation in solving long-standing tribal conflicts.

37. Amin, n.d.

38. The sense of being "bound" to the pir leads many disciples to perform acts of extreme veneration including such practices as acquiring mementos from the saint such as pieces of his clothing or his leftover food. When a piece of bread is taken home from the langar, it will frequently be mixed in with fresh bread dough and eaten by family members so that all can enjoy the baraka of the pir. It also sometimes occurs that people will eat dirt taken from the precincts of a saint's tomb, and ashes from the fireplace in the langar will sometimes be removed and placed in the mouths of young children to protect them. While these forms of veneration are quite commonly encountered, many view them critically. Thus, for example, those who subscribe to what might be called a more orthodox view of Islamic ritual practice believe that such acts divert the attention of the believer away from God toward the pir himself and as such constitute a form of polytheism (*shirk*). Many "orthodox" Pakhtuns base their objection less on religious grounds than on the fact that such practices are demeaning to the individual and contrary to the independent spirit of Pakhtun culture.

39. Despite the fact that there is no shame attached to following a pir, it is the practice in some areas for disciples to keep secret their involvement with pirs. The reason for keeping this attachment a secret is difficult to ascertain, but it seems at least in part to keep the moral worlds of honor and Islam separate and thereby avoid the kinds of contradictions that ensue when the two overlap. An alternative explanation is offered by an informant from Paktia Province who explained the practice as follows: "Most disciples do not want to reveal that they are followers of a pir. They think that [revealing this fact] would be a way of projecting yourself as a good person, which is [an attitude] that Allah wouldn't like. Basically, one becomes a disciple to seek guidance on the right path to Allah. One doesn't do it for any other reason, and it should be kept secret as much as possible. In the case of our family, it happened so many times that one of our family members became a disciple without our even knowing about it. Because of this attitude on the part of the disciples, it is difficult to know how many have accepted the tariqat."

40. This story was told to me by Fazil Aziz, a nephew of Hazrat Sahib of Butkhak.

41. Political Abstract of Intelligence, Punjab Police, August 18, 1896 (Peshawar Archives).

42. Majrooh n.d., 5.

43. As will be noted in the next section, there is some evidence that the Manki Mulla was supported by Amir Abdur Rahman, but that support appears to have been distant. It does not appear that the Manki Mulla was acting as an agent of

the Amir or that he was put up to the confrontation by him. To the contrary, all of the (admittedly limited) evidence that I have been able to assemble leads to the conclusion that the two religious leaders were operating independently.

44. The most dramatic example of this kind of rivalry was in Swat, and has been well analyzed by Barth (1959a; and in Jahanzeb 1985). I have not found many instances of dual factions developing on the Afghan side of the border, but I have heard of at least one case in the village of Kot, in Ningrahar Province, where two khans who were most active in the 1920s squared off in a long-standing rivalry that is continued into the present by their descendants.

45. No informant would actually admit to an economizing logic in the decision of where to situate Sufi centers, but it is the case that all of the principal deputies of the Akhund of Swat and Hadda Sahib were located at some remove from one another. This was especially true of the Akhund whose deputies came from as far away as the Punjab in the east and Ghazni in the west. Significantly, however, it appears that none of the Akhund's deputies came from Swat itself, an observation that might be explained by the fact that the Akhund's own biological descendants remained in the area. The Mulla of Hadda, of course, had no descendants, but in keeping with the pattern I have noted, it appears that he made sure that his deputies all went to areas where there were no other "spiritual agnates" present with whom they might compete for disciples.

46. Since British intelligence records indicate that disciples of the two leaders were still contesting the issue three years later, it seems that no unanimous winner emerged from this debate. We know that Hadda Sahib himself was soon to be embroiled in other matters—the anti-British jihad that will be taken up in the next chapter—so his interest in the subject might have waned of its own accord. A subsequent, well-publicized debate over the issue of raising the finger in prayer involved Mulla Muhammad Azam of Bannu, purportedly a disciple of the Manki Mulla, and one Mulla Muhammad Sharif, who is referred to in British records as a disciple of Hadda Sahib. The two appeared in Kohat in the summer of 1899 and debated the matter, but again no final winner appears to have emerged from this exercise. (Most of my information on these debates comes from a letter from the District Commissioner, Peshawar, to the Secretary, Government of the Punjab, July 6, 1899 [Peshawar Archives]).

47. Both of these stories were recounted by Fazil Aziz, a nephew of Hazrat Sahib of Butkhak.

48. A typical example of this sort of story is found in the seventeenth-century chronicle *Makhzen Afghani.* In one of the sections of this history, a ruler named Islam Shah decides to punish a darvish accused of opening a shop in the market-place solely for the purpose of spending "his whole time in conversation with the women of the town" (p. 169). The darvish is brought before the king, who denounces him and has him bastinadoed. The darvish is silent throughout the ordeal until the end when the king threatens to have him burned for any future violation of the law. To this threat, the darvish replies, "Burn me, if thou dost not burn thyself." The next morning, a boil appears on the king which quickly becomes a burning inflammation that spreads throughout his body. When the king attempts to find the darvish to beg forgiveness, the man is nowhere to be found, and the king soon dies of his affliction. (*Makhzen Afghani* was compiled by Niamatullah

[Neamet Ullah], a scholar in the employ of the Mughal emperor Jehangir, and published in English under the title *History of the Afghans* [1965]).

49. The specific reasons for their disagreement are unclear, but the historian, Hasan Kakar, has noted the Amir's fear that "a man like [the Mulla] can raise disturbances whenever he likes" (Kakar 1979, 156).

50. See Ashraf Ghani 1978, 282–83 and Kakar 1979, 156.

51. Kakar 1979, 156.

52. Ibid., 156. One incident mentioned by Kakar that is not touched upon in the story concerns contacts made between the Mulla and the Safi tribe. This event occurred in 1888 when the Safis took up arms against the Amir in protest over the construction of a road into the valley of Chawkai. Incited by "agents" of the Mulla, the Safis decided to rise up against the "infidel" Amir, but the effort fizzled when the two sides reached an agreement halting road construction but requiring the Safis to pay tax revenues in kind, something they had hitherto refused to do (Kakar 1971, 101–102).

53. Some stories I have heard indicate that Hadda Sahib was also imprisoned by Abdur Rahman but that the pir magically removed himself from his prison cell. Following his escape, Hadda Sahib traveled the entire distance from Kabul to the Shinwari territory—a journey that would normally take several days—in the hours between midnight and dawn. According to various descendants of the Mulla's deputies, Amir Abdur Rahman at one time or another imprisoned the majority of Hadda Sahib's deputies, including Shaykh Sahib of Sangar, Mia Sahib of Baro, Pacha Sahib of Islampur, and the Mulla Sahib of Tagao.

54. Use of the term *muqtada-i 'alam* in reference to Hadda Sahib is significant in this context, for what seems to be implied is that, while Abdur Rahman occupied the official position of Amir of Afghanistan, Hadda Sahib was the true leader of the people. The term *muqtada* carries the meaning not only of "leader," but also of "the one who is imitated." This implies that Hadda Sahib's authority arises out of the qualities of person that lead people to emulate him, not from the position that he occupies or the powers of coercion and control that he can wield against those below him.

55. Martin provides an interesting example of another exchange with a religious leader over the categorization of "kafir." In this case, however, the story is told from the Amir's point of view: "The late Amir once told me a story of a moullah in Kandahar who had dubbed him a 'Kafir' (infidel) when inciting the people to rise against him. They had to make him out a 'Kafir,' as otherwise it is against the religious law for the people to rise against the King, who is also their spiritual head. When the ensuing rebellion had been put down the Amir was told that this man had taken refuge in the sanctuary [presumably the local mosque-shrine in which a garment reputed to be the mantle of the Prophet is kept]. Then the Amir, turning the tables on the man, said that the sanctuary was for Mussulmans only, not for such infidels as men who rose against their king; and, taking his sword, he went to the musjid [mosque] and killed the man in the very place" (Martin 1907, 15).

56. Martin writes that after Abdur Rahman's death, three or four of "the oldest and holiest of the moullahs were appointed to stop at the late Amir's tomb and pray there, and it was afterwards said by some of the people that the tomb, to

which all had access to pray for his soul, had blue flames coming out of it, and this was a sure proof that this spirit was in Hades" (Ibid., 135). Not surprisingly, Martin doubts the authenticity of these reports, noting instead that "the tomb was three times set on fire" by unknown persons who wished to "disgrace" the Amir's final resting place. This explanation was rejected by Martin's informants, however, who insisted on assigning a supernatural source to the tomb's propensity to burst into flame, it being "commonly said that the heat of the Amir's soul was the cause of the fires" (Ibid., 135).

57. In one version of this story I have heard, Habibullah is induced to seek forgiveness from Hadda Sahib after he himself has been visited in dreams—in this case, by his dead father who tells him of the sufferings which he has had to endure on account of his injustices and informs his son that the only way he can be freed from his torments is to receive the forgiveness of Hadda Sahib.

58. Margaret Mills, personal communication. After reading this story in a draft version of this chapter, Mills called my attention to a case in Erika Friedl's *Women of Deh Koh* (1989), in which the women of the bride's family, commenting on an unhappy marriage, indicate that they didn't want to agree to the match but were persuaded when his people sent an elderly religious woman to ask.

59. Traditionally, Pakhtun tribes have relied on the jirga assembly and tribal law (*nerkh*) to solve their problems. Concomitantly, there has long been a tendency to treat mullas more as ratifiers than as arbiters of tribal accords, and one rarely hears accounts of religious figures intervening to settle disputes, except occasionally when matters have reached a total impasse. Thus, I have heard of several incidents involving nationally renowned pirs, such as the Hazrat of Shor Bazaar and Pir Gailani (Naqib Sahib), who were called in at the last minute to settle major tribal disputes that were on the verge of open war.

60. The tendency for disciples to attribute excessive power to their pir is indicated in an oft-quoted proverb: "Though the pir himself does not fly, his disciples would have him fly." Interestingly, many of those who told me such stories, including Islamic judges and others well-versed in Islamic tradition, would never say explicitly whether or not they believed them, even though it was clear that they enjoyed telling them. What seemed most important was that they might be true, that such power potentially existed. The closest I came to an outright rejection occurred when I repeated this story to the deputy amir of the "fundamentalist" Hizb-i Islami political party, who stated unequivocally that such stories were the product of illiterate people who used them to bolster their own importance. At the same time, however, his attitude was mitigated by his willingness to accept the believability of some sorts of miracles. Pirs flying to Koh-i Qaf, he refused to accept, but other miraculous acts he had no problem with, for example, that the descendants of a saint who was famous for curing snakebites could be endowed with this same talent, or that the practice known as *dam* (in which a person recites a passage from the Qur'an while breathing on an injured part of the body) might be efficacious. These acts were ones he could find precedents for in the Qur'an or hadith, and so they were acceptable. Those that had no justification were not.

5. MAD MULLAS AND ENGLISHMEN

1. Churchill's account of the 1897 uprising was originally published as *The Story of the Malakand Field Force: An Episode of Frontier War*. This work is most readily available in a collection of Churchill's war reports published under the title of *Frontiers and Wars* (1962). In addition, see Frederick Woods, ed. (1972) and Churchill's published correspondence, collected by Randolph S. Churchill, ed. (1967).

2. Quoted in R. S. Churchill 1967, 1(2):774.

3. Churchill's correspondence from this period shows his initial disappointment at not being given a formal staff position with General Blood. It is clear in retrospect, however, that Churchill's career was better off for this misfortune, for contrary to usual procedures, General Blood allowed Churchill to wear his uniform on the field of battle while also serving as a reporter. In the former capacity, Churchill was able not only to experience war firsthand, but also to add a battle-field commendation to his resume of accomplishments. In his capacity as a journalist, Churchill was able to gain a wide and influential audience (including such luminaries as the Prince of Wales and the prime minister, Lord Salisbury) that thrilled to the achievements of General Blood's field force and much appreciated Churchill's polemics in praise of imperial power and vigilance.

4. W. S. Churchill 1962, 28.

5. This and other information on Saidullah, "the Mad Fakir," is taken from a telegraph from the Deputy Commissioner in Peshawar to the Foreign Department of the Government of India, dated August 8, 1897 (Punjab Civil Secretariat, Foreign/Frontier Files, Proceedings, August 1897). Note that the archival references given in this chapter refer to the filing system in place at the archives of the Peshawar Library. The filing system I encountered at the library was dilapidated, and items were frequently out of place or in unmarked files. It should also be noted that the system employed at this facility may differ from those employed at the India Office Library or at the archives in New Delhi.

6. W. S. Churchill 1962, 28–29. For the original dispatches from which the book-length account was drafted, see Woods 1972, 9–10.

7. W. S. Churchill 1962, 29.

8. Woods 1972, 29.

9. W. S. Churchill 1962, 66.

10. Ibid., 29–30.

11. Ibid., 28.

12. Ibid., 30.

13. Woods 1972, 29–30.

14. Ibid., 30.

15. Ibid., 30.

16. Ibid., 10.

17. Weber 1968, 48.

18. Ibid., 48.

19. See "Karama," in Gibb and Kramer 1974.

20. Weber 1968, 54–61.

21. Letter from Harold Deane, the political agent at Malakand to the secretary of the Foreign Department, Government of India, August 8, 1897, Punjab Civil Secretariat, Foreign/Frontier Files, Proceedings, August 1897.

22. Ibid.

23. Ibid.

24. Ibid.

25. R. S. Churchill 1967, 816–21.

26. Ibid., 818.

27. Ibid., 818–19.

28. Most of the biographical information I have uncovered on Saidullah comes from a telegraph sent from the deputy commissioner, Peshawar, to the secretary of the Foreign Department, Government of India, August 8, 1897, and from the diary of the political agent, Khyber Agency. Both in Punjab Civil Secretariat 1897, Foreign/Frontier Files, Proceedings, August 1897.

29. I discovered very little about Saidullah in the interviews I conducted in the area and in the Peshawar archives. Despite this paucity of material, however, the few bits of evidence collected by British intelligence agents at the time do provide some significant clues as to what sort of person Saidullah might have been. Among these bits of evidence is the information that about twelve years prior to the uprising, Saidullah had abandoned his home and family to live in the shrine of Pir Baba in neighboring Buner.

A few years after this event, he had begun preaching on the need to reform local Islamic customs, but mullas in the area had opposed his efforts and he had been forced to leave the frontier for an extended tour of Central Asia and the Middle East. Rumors picked up and reported by local spies indicated that Saidullah lived in Mecca and Medina for some years before returning home a few months prior to the onset of hostilities in 1897. On his journey back to the frontier, it is claimed that he visited Kabul and was there granted an audience with Amir Abdur Rahman. Following this visit, he is also supposed to have paid his respects to the Mulla of Hadda at his residence in Mohmand, immediately prior to his return home to Swat.

An additional story told of Saidullah has it that during his first absence from home, when he was staying at the shrine of Pir Baba, patrilineal cousins killed his son in a quarrel. According to the British agent who reported this information, "Saidulla called up his son's murderers and told them that he had given up Afghan ways, as well as worldly affairs, and that therefore, instead of avenging his son's death, he forgave them" (Punjab Civil Secretariat 1897, Foreign/Frontier Files, Proceedings, August 1897). Saidullah's decision—so different from that of Sultan Muhammad Khan in a comparable situation—apparently led to his disgrace and further estrangement from his native society, but it does not seem to have affected his standing as a faqir. To the contrary, people expect the unexpected from a faqir, and they also expect the faqir to devote himself fully to God, even if it means the loss of everything else that matters in life. The fact then that Saidullah refused to be drawn back into an affair of honor meant that his dedication to God was so single-minded that he was even willing to sacrifice his honor to serve Him.

30. R. S. Churchill 1967, 819.

31. Woods 1972, 9–10.

32. R. S. Churchill 1967, 820.

33. Ibid., 818.

34. This letter was captured by the British in 1897 (Punjab Civil Secretariat, Foreign/Frontier Files, Proceedings, September 1897).

35. Contained in a letter from W. R. H. Merk to the chief secretary, Punjab Civil Secretariat, November 13, 1897 (Punjab Civil Secretariat, Foreign/Frontier Files, Proceedings, August 1897).

36. To some extent, the repeated appearance of reports indicating a regional conspiracy of anti-British elements represents a tendency on the part of the British to overestimate the cohesiveness of their enemies. Having only a rudimentary understanding of what was going on in the tribal areas, the colonial authorities tended to assume a far more intricate organization than actually existed. Nevertheless, the Mulla had succeeded in cobbling together a widespread regional unity that had a greater degree of coherence than any previous mobilization, with the possible exception of the earlier Ambeyla uprising in 1867 that was led by, among others, the Akhund of Swat.

37. Communications with the Fakir, it was believed, had begun long before the commencement of the uprising when the Fakir had traveled to Mohmand to meet Hadda Sahib on his return from making the pilgrimage to Mecca. Subsequently, a "Kunari sayyid," who secretly acted as a British agent, reported that the Mulla had been in touch with the Fakir between 18 and 20 July, immediately preceding the attack on Chakdara. Later reports indicate contact between the two on the twelfth of August and again toward the end of that month (Punjab Civil Secretariat, Foreign/Frontier Files, Proceedings, August 1897).

38. The army, or *lashkar*, of Hadda Sahib was reported to include Mohmands (of the Musa Khel, Isa Khel, Miro Khel, Bara Khel, Lashkar Khel, Atamar Khel, and Koda Khel branches from the British side of the border; and of the Khwazai and Khuga Khel branches from the Afghan side of the border). In addition, there were smaller numbers of Safis and Shinwaris, along with otherwise unidentified Kunaris, Ningraharis, and ex-soldiers from the Afghan army. The total number of the Mulla's force at the battle of Shabqader was estimated between 3,700 and 14,000. One report indicates that the Mulla's force suffered at least 22 killed and 47 wounded, but it then goes on to note that both of these numbers were probably too low insofar as some of the dead and wounded were carried off by their own family members before they could be counted. Following the Shabqader battle, the Mulla's force was supposed to have been supported by an additional 2,500 men from more distant locations, including Tagao and Laghman. It is quite probable that some of these late arrivals were recruited by deputies of the Mulla, who were based in these areas (Punjab Civil Secretariat, Foreign/Frontier Files, Proceedings, August 1897).

39. Communication from Major Harold Deane, Political agent (Malakand), August 15, 1897, Punjab Civil Secretariat, Foreign/Frontier Files, Proceedings, August 1897. In large part because they were so difficult to monitor or control, talebs inspired the fury of British administrators probably more than any other class of religious functionary. This anger can be seen in the following statement in a political report published in 1901: "The preaching classes absolutely swarm in this country. Among them, especially among the village Mullahs and Kazis, are men

of real religion and good lives, but the majority are mere religious adventurers, who play on the superstition of the people and batten on their alms.

"Worse even than the bigger men are the *Talib-ul-ilm* (seekers after knowledge). These are men, chiefly young men, who contemplate following the religious profession. They flock to the shrines of this country and attach themselves to some religious leader, ostensibly for religious education. Their number far exceeds those required to fill up vacancies in village mullahships and other ecclesiastic appointments, and they are reduced to seek other means of livelihood. They are at the bottom of all the mischief in the country, the instigators and often the perpetrators of the bulk of the crime. They use their religious status to live free on the people, who are too superstitious to turn them out, even when they destroy the peace of the family circle" (McMahon and Ramsay 1981, 22–23).

40. Punjab Civil Secretariat 1897, Foreign/Frontier Files, Proceedings, August 1897.

41. Punjab Civil Secretariat 1897, Foreign/Frontier Files, Proceedings, September 1897.

42. Ibid.

43. H. W. Mills 1979, 165.

44. The frontier tribes are storied fighters, but their least effective engagements have tended to be those when they have been on the offensive, particularly when their objective has lain across open terrain. Their greatest moments, on the other hand, have generally been when they have been defending territory from outside invasion. This posture allowed them to choose their own moments of counterattack and, most important of all, to resort to guerrilla tactics: spreading out, attacking from cover, picking off stragglers, harassing lines of retreat, and wearing down the enemy both physically and psychologically.

45. James 1898, 109. An additional problem for the Mulla was the backbiting and intrigues that he had to endure from a number of his fellow religious leaders, who also worried about their own prospects and revenues should the British cease to operate as a major power in the frontier. This was the case, for example, with the Mianguls of Swat, who were the sons and grandsons of the Akhund of Swat. Despite the religious basis of their authority, the Mianguls were well on their way to shedding the mantle of sanctity in order to participate more whole-heartedly in the internecine power struggles that defined politics as usual in the area.

While the Mianguls do not seem to have supported the Mulla very strenuously, they also do not appear to have opposed his movement. The same cannot be said of Hadda Sahib's old rival, the Manki Mulla, who had engaged with him in the debate the year before over the propriety of raising a finger during prayer. Beyond their history of animosity, the Manki Mulla also had another reason to be leery of Hadda Sahib's challenge to British control since he himself had chosen to live within the British dominion rather than outside it, as Hadda Sahib had done. Whatever his reasons, however, at least one British dispatch indicates that he was disdainful of his rival's enterprise: "The Ranizais and Thana people who first joined are followers of the Manki Mullah, not of the Mian Guls, and the Manki Mullah's reply on his own account to the Fakir was 'the Malakand is a hill of hornets; I advise you not to touch it,' whereby he has gained much credit amongst the people as a man of foresight" (letter from H. Deane to the secretary, Foreign

Department, Government of India. Punjab Civil Secretariat, Foreign/Frontier Files, Proceedings, August 1897).

46. Punjab Civil Secretariat, Foreign/Frontier Files, Proceedings, August 1897.

47. According to Frank Martin, the Amir was greatly distressed by letters he received from the Indian Government, accusing him of secretly aiding the tribal insurgents and threatening to remove him from his throne if he did not openly renounce the uprising. On receipt of one such letter, the Amir read the message "in a public durbar held for the occasion, and to which all leading men were summoned, and after reading it, he accused his people of doing that which brought upon him disgrace at the hands of his ally" (Martin 1907, 110). About the same time, Abdur Rahman granted Martin a private interview, during which he "spoke for several hours on the Afridi rising, and the trouble the border tribes had caused him." During this meeting, he "seemed particularly bitter against the Haddah moullah, Maulavi Najmudeen Aghondzada, who was the principal instigator of the rising. He said that since he came to the throne, rebellions had been frequent, and though each revolt had been put down with a strong hand (those who know the Amir's methods will understand what his 'strong hand' meant), it had not been sufficient to prevent further risings, for his people were not only the most unruly, but the most fanatical of people." In response to the suggestion that he might openly support a religious leader like the Mulla of Hadda, the Amir explained to Martin that such a course of action would be destructive of his own interests, since "the people once risen and flushed with any little success, would become beyond the control of any man, and there were old scores to be wiped off between the border tribes and the Afghans, so that any rising was a menace to himself. And in addition to this, a rising in one part of the country would undoubtedly lead to similar risings and revolt in other parts, and it was only by his firm ruling and the stringent methods adopted towards those who sought to agitate the people, that the country was kept quiet" (Ibid., 110–11). Such testimony is by no means conclusive, of course. Abdur Rahman probably assumed that the substance of any conversation he might have with Martin would eventually make its way to the British authorities. At the same time, the logic of what he had to say to Martin is also apparent and coincides with other information we have concerning Abdur Rahman, especially his bitter distrust of religious functionaries.

An additional piece of evidence indicating that the Amir went out of his way to discourage participation in the uprising is contained in a letter captured by British agents. Dated October 25, 1897, the letter is from one Qazi Mira Khan of the Adam Khel Afridi to Mulla Sayyid Akbar, an ally of Hadda Sahib and the leader of the Afridi front. In this letter, the Qazi noted that the Amir "advised us not to fight with the British Government, and this was and has been his advice ever since" (India, Army Intelligence Branch, [1908]: 118).

48. According to one British intelligence report dated September 4, 1897, the Amir's commander-in-chief sent Hadda Sahib three mule-loads of cartridges and seven Martini rifles. Not only would such limited supplies have been of negligible importance—especially at that late date—but the fact that they were accompanied by a letter from the Amir ordering the Mulla to halt the assembly of his army until he received further orders from Kabul indicates the Amir's ambivalence about the operation and his desire to be in charge of whatever transpired along

the frontier (Punjab Civil Secretariat, Foreign/Frontier Files, Proceedings, August 1897).

49. In a letter from Abdur Rahman to the Viceroy of India dated November 25, 1897, the Amir states that he has ordered Hadda Sahib either to remove himself from Afghanistan or to proceed at once to Kabul. Upon his appearance in Kabul, the Amir promised to dispatch him at once to Mecca or Medina via Persia. If he failed to follow one of these two paths, the Amir promised to order his troops to arrest the Mulla (Punjab Civil Secretariat, Foreign/Frontier Files, Proceedings, August 1897).

50. James 1898, 94.

51. On the occasion of his meeting with Martin during the middle of the 1897 uprisings, Amir Abdur Rahman alluded to the curious elusiveness of the Hadda Mulla: "The Amir said that no one knew to what country the Haddah moullah belonged, for he had no known relations, and during Shere Ali's reign the moullah had been allowed to do much as he liked with the people, and raise revolt at his pleasure. He himself, however, had made inquiries, and found out the moullah's mode of procedure, and had arranged to capture him, but the moullah received timely information of his intention, and escaped across the frontier, where he shortly afterwards raised the Shinwari and other tribes against him, and for some months gave considerable trouble, and it was not until four thousand or so had been killed that the tribes were quieted. And this was the man whose actions he was held responsible for [by the British authorities who accused him of aiding the uprising]." The Amir claimed to Martin that the Mulla had sent his agents through eastern Afghanistan to induce his subjects to join the uprising under the pretext that "the Amir had given permission." Abdur Rahman, Martin reports, "said that of their leaders he had four sheikhs and two maliks, who carried the green jihad flag, in prison in Kabul, and he knew what to do with them, but the other leaders had escaped" (Martin 1907, 111–12).

52. Undated and unsigned letter to the chief secretary, Government of the Punjab, Punjab Civil Secretariat, Foreign/Frontier Files, Proceedings, August 1897.

53. Mills 1979, 161.

54. Ibid., 162.

55. Ibid., 163.

56. Ibid., 163.

57. Ibid., 163.

58. Ibid., 163–64.

59. Ibid., 164.

60. Ibid., 165.

61. Foucault 1979. In the prison environment studied by Foucault, the rationalization of power demanded that all marks of the individual's personal identity be transformed into signs of institutional dominance. In a similar way, dominance on the frontier is exercised by having that which is most intimately linked to tribal culture (in this case the institution and accouterments of female seclusion) appropriated and made part of the political language of the invading power.

62. Al-Bukhari, quoted in Gibb and Kramer 1974, 432 ("Nafila").

63. See Schimmel 1975, 133; and al-Hujwiri 1980, 226–27. It should also be noted that while I never specifically asked the narrator of this story about the

significance of the Mulla's performing nawafil prayers and whether it related to his entering the state of unveiledness, the metaphoric description of miracles as a form of unveiling is a common one among Afghan Sufis and came up a number of times in my interviews, including with the narrator of this story who referred to the capacity of a pir to know what is in someone's heart or mind as the quality of "unveiling the heart" (*kashf ul-qolub*).

64. The first version of this chapter appeared in 1989 as "Mad Mullahs and Englishmen: Discourse in the Colonial Encounter," *Comparative Studies in Society and History* 31 (4):647–68. After completing that manuscript in 1988, this third version of the Jarobi story came to light in the course of transcribing a number of interviews conducted during a second stint of fieldwork.

65. It should be noted that I elicited this story in my interview with Shahmund by asking him if he had ever heard any stories about the Mulla of Hadda. This very well might account for the emphasis in the story on the Mulla's miracle, and it might also be the case that if I had elicited the story in a different way—for example, in relation to his grandfather's deeds in battle—that the Mulla's role might have been more diminished than it was in the version recorded.

6. EPILOGUE

1. The following text and others that appear in the epilogue were taken from the *soc.culture.pakistan* and *soc.culture.afghanistan* newsgroups between November 4 and November 8, 1994. Misspellings and awkward syntax abound on computer newsgroups, and consequently I have had to edit these postings in places to ensure comprehension. Where comprehension was not at stake, I have left errors intact to preserve the sense and syntax of the original. I have also removed identifying information regarding the posters and have employed pseudonyms throughout rather than actual names. Since newsgroup posters themselves frequently use pseudonyms, however, it is quite possible that my pseudonyms are pseudonyms of pseudonyms, but that somehow is in keeping with the strange amalgam of secrecy and openness that one encounters on the Internet.

2. Member of the Jama'at-i Islami Pakistan political party, which was founded by Maulana Ala Maududi. The Jama'at has been the principal voice for radical Islamic reform in Pakistan.

3. Douglas Bakshian, VOA correspondent report, No. 2–168709, 3 November 1994, Islamabad.

4. Sultan Mahmud of Ghazni (988–1030), the ruler of the Ghaznavid empire.

5. The references are to Gulbuddin Hekmatyar, amir of Hizb-i Islami Afghanistan, Burhanuddin Rabbani, amir of Jami'at-i Islami Afghanistan, and Qazi Hussain Ahmad, amir of Jama'at-i Islami Pakistan. The first two groups are the principal political parties fighting for control of Afghanistan. The third is the dominant Islamic party in Pakistan, which has repeatedly aided and abetted the two Afghan parties since the late 1960s.

6. References to Hera Mundi occur repeatedly in this exchange. The implication of being born in Hera Mundi is that the individual is a Punjabi rather than a Pakhtun. For many Pakhtuns born in Afghanistan or the North-West Frontier, this is considered especially insulting.

7. The more cultivated and refined image that Pakistani Pakhtuns have of themselves is seen by Afghan Pakhtuns as quite the opposite. To them, Pakistanis are citified and slightly effeminate, and they might advise you to look at the clothes favored by each side in order to understand the essence of the difference: Pakistani Pakhtuns favor *shalwar-kamez* made from light-weight, light-colored fabric that is carefully tailored and that shows dirt at the slightest soiling; Afghans wear darker-colored clothing made from rougher, thicker cloth that can be worn for long periods of time and that holds up to the vagaries of hard living. For a similar distinction that held between city and country Pakhtuns in Afghanistan prior to the war, see Jon Anderson (1983).

8. Expatriate posters to the Internet may be insulated from such distinctions in their own lives, but their arguments and debates nevertheless reflect the same sentiments of identity and difference encountered on the frontier. Thus, Pakistani Pakhtuns on the Internet often manage to convey the same smugness vis-à-vis their Afghan interlocutors as I repeatedly saw in the behavior of Pakistani refugee-camp administrators dealing with Afghan tribal elders. In the same fashion, Afghans on the Internet will condescend to Pakistanis, often on the presumption that their paternity is impure compared to Afghans' and that their honor is so much the less secure as a result.

9. However problematic the term *fundamentalist* might appear to academics, particularly in relation to Muslim radicals, it has nevertheless become a standard term in the discourse of the news groups. Among refugees in Pakistan, fundamentalists are usually referred to—sometimes interchangeably—as *hizbis* and as *maktabis*. The former refers especially (but not exclusively) to members of the Hizb-i Islami Afghanistan political party led by Engineer Gulbuddin Hekmatyar. The latter, which can be translated as something like "schoolies," refers to young, secularly educated adherents of Islamist ideologies. The relevant distinction that is implied by the name, *maktabi*, is to mullas and maulawis who have been trained in religious madrasas. A large number of maktabis (especially Pakhtuns) belong to the Hizb-i Islami party, and they can usually be identified by their short-trimmed beards and general air of trained efficiency and righteous condescension. On the development of the Islamist parties in Afghanistan, see Roy (1986) and Edwards (1993b and 1995). On the role of the parties in the refugee camps, see Edwards (1986d and 1990).

Glossary

Note: This work includes stories, texts and commentaries in both Pakhtu and Afghan Persian (Dari). The majority of the words that are included in this glossary are found in both languages. In those cases where a word is unique to one or the other language, I have added the designation (P) if it is found primarily only in Pakhtu. Following each word (as it appears in the text), I have provided in parentheses a transliteration with appropriate diacritical marks. The system of transliteration used here is that employed for Persian by the *International Journal of Middle East Studies*. Pakhtu has several letters and sounds that are not found in Persian. These include four retroflex phonemes (indicated by *ḍ, ṇ, ṛ,* and *ṭ*) and three additional consonants (indicated by *zh, kh* and *tz*.) Pakhtu also has a complex system of endings which I have not tried to reproduce here.

adab (adaḅ)	politeness
afghaniyat (afghānīyat)	the customs of Afghans
akherat (ākherat)	the next world
akhund (akhūnd)	religious scholar
akhundzada (akhūndzādah)	son of a religious scholar
ʿalaqadari (ʿalāqadārī)	rural administrative district
amir (amīr)	commander, ruler, king
andiwal (anḍīwāl) (P)	friend, companion
asil (asīl)	genuine, pure, uncorrupted
awliya (awalīya)	saints, friends of God
azad qabayel (āzād qabāyel)	independent tribal area
azan (azān)	call to prayer

badal (badal) (P)	exchange; an exchange marriage involving sisters; feud
badmash (badmāsh)	reprobate or outlaw
barakat (barakat)	blessing
batin (bātin)	domain of extrasensory understanding apprehended only by prophets and saints
be abru (bī ābrū)	dishonor, disgrace, indignity
be ghairat (bī ghaīrat)	cowardice, dishonor
be ghairati (bī ghaīratī)	cowardly, dishonorable
be rahm (bī rahm)	merciless
buzurg (buzurg)	large, great, religious saint
chilla (chillah)	period of ascetic retreat (usually 40 days long)
chilla khana (chillah khānah)	cave, room or building where retreats are undertaken
dala (dalah) (P)	cuckold, someone who is insipid or of impoverished self-esteem
dam (dam)	breath, the curative act of reciting verses of the Qur'an while blowing on a sick or injured individual
daraja (darajah)	rank, degree, class
daus (dawūs) (P)	cuckold
darvish (darvīsh)	religious mendicant (*see also* faqir, qalandar, *and* malang)
dehqan (dehqān)	peasant, tenant farmer
din (dīn)	religion
dost (dūst)	friend
drund (drūnd) (P)	heavy, great, consequential
dunya (dūnyā)	world
dushman (dushman)	enemy
'elm-i batini ('elm-i bātinī)	esoteric knowledge of the hidden, supernatural realm
faqir (faqīr)	religious mendicant (*see also* qalandar, dervish, *and* malang)
ferangi (ferengī)	Englishman, European, foreigner
firman (firmān)	proclamation, command, order

ghairat (ghaīrat)	courage, zeal, bravery
gharur (gharūr)	pride, vanity
ghulam bacha (ghulām bachah)	slave boy, court servant
hadith (hadīth)	traditions and sayings associated with the life of the Prophet Muhammad
hakim (hakem)	rural government administrator
hamsaya (hamsāyah)	neighbor, tenant farmer, someone dependent on another for his livelihood
harim (harim)	domestic area, off-limits
hujra (hūjrah)	guest house
hukm (hukm)	order, verdict
imam (imām)	prayer leader
jihad (jehad)	effort, struggle on behalf of Islam; holy war
jirga (jirgah)	tribal council or assembly
jumat (jūmat) (P)	mosque
kafir (kāfir)	unbeliever
kaka (kākā) (P)	paternal uncle
kashf (kashf)	discovery, detection, unveiling
khadem (khādem)	servant
khalifa (khalīfah)	someone granted the right by a recognized pir to teach mystical lessons; someone appointed by a pir as his successor (*see also* mauzun)
khanaqa (khānaqāh)	center of activity associated with a sufi pir
kha tzwan (khah tzwan) (P)	"good youth"; a man who adheres to Pakhtun norms
khedmat (khedmat)	service
khilat (khel'at)	robe of honor
kibr (kibr)	pride, arrogance, insolence
kiramat (kirāmat)	miracle
kotwal (kūtwāl) (P)	chief police officer, home minister
kufr (kufr)	infidelity
landai (landai) (P)	short verse form generally composed by women

langar (langar)	eating area for disciples and visitors to a sufi pir or associated with a saint's tomb
lashkar (lashkar *or* lakhkar)	army
liaqat (līyaqat)	ability, competence, merit
luchak (lūchak) (P)	shameless
madrasa (madrasah)	religious school
malang (malang)	religious mendicant (*see also* darvish, faqir, *and* qalandar)
malatar (malāṭar) (P)	supporters, usually kinsmen "who bind their waists together"
malgarai (malgarai) (P)	companion, attendant of a khan
mama (māmā)	maternal uncle
masjid (masjid)	mosque
maulana (mūlānā)	an advanced religious scholar, similar to maulavi (although more often associated with those whose training has been in India/Pakistan)
maulavi (maulavī)	an advanced religious scholar, similar to maulana
mauzun (mauzun) (P)	someone granted the right by a recognized pir to teach mystical lessons; someone appointed by a pir as his successor (*see* khalifa)
melmastia (mīlmastīa) (P)	Pakhtun obligation to offer hospitality
mia (mīya)	honorific used for descendants of certain venerated saints; sometimes used in the Afghan frontier for descendants of the Prophet Muhammad
miangul (mīangul)	"flower of the saints"; title bestowed on descendants of the Akhund of Swat; the family line of the ruler (wali) of Swat.
mubarak (mubārak)	blessed
mulla (mullā)	a man who earns all or part of his income supervising a mosque, teaching religious lessons, or otherwise engaged in religious activities
munshi (munshī)	secretary, writer, clerk

murid (murīd)	disciple of a Sufi pir
nafs (nafs)	self, soul, passions, senses, carnal desire
namaz (namāz)	prayer
namus (nāmūs)	honor, that which a man possesses that cannot be violated
nanawatai (nanawatai) (P)	Pakhtun custom of offering protection
nang (nang)	honor; reputation, esteem
naqsha (naqshah)	map, design
nasab (nasab)	lineage, parentage, identity
nasib (nasīb)	share, portion
nerkh (nerkh) (P)	custom, law, rate
nikagan (nīkahgān) (P)	grandfathers; patrilineal ancestors
ni'mat (ni'mat)	blessing, riches, favor
nokaran (nūkarān)	servants
padshah (pādshāh)	king, sayyid
paighur (paīghūr) (P)	taunt, reproach
pakhtun (pakhtūn) (P)	those who speak the Pakhtu (Pashto) language and who claim descent in one of the commonly recognized lines of Pakhtun tribal descent
pakhtunwali (pakhtūnwalī) (P)	Pakhtun code of honorable behavior
pandnama (pandnāmah)	book of advice
pir (pīr)	master of a sufi order
por (pūr) (P)	debt; an act—often of violence—that must be reciprocated in kind
Qaderiya (qāderīya)	prominent sufi order in Afghanistan and Pakistan
qahraman (qahramān)	hero, champion
qalandar (qalandar)	religious mendicant (generally used in the Indian subcontinent)
qalang (qalang) (P)	donation
qari (qārī)	memorizer of the Qur'an
qaum (qaūm)	tribe
qazi (qāzi)	judge
qur'an (qur'ān)	word of God revealed to the Prophet Muhammad

ra'iyat (ra'iyat)	subject (of a king)
Ramazan (Ramazān)	ninth month in the lunar calendar, the Islamic month of fasting
roza (rūzhah) (P)	fast
ruhaniyat (rūhāniyat)	spirituality
sahib (sāheb)	honorific meaning "master" or "sir"
sarhad (sarhad)	border, frontier
sayyid (sayid)	descendant of the Prophet Muhammad
shahid (shahīd)	martyr
shari'a (shari'a)	religious law
shaykh (shaykh)	attendant of a pir; custodian of a shrine, a Hindu converted to Islam
shirk (shirk)	polytheism
sial (sīal) (P)	a rival; someone of equal status
silsila (silsilah)	chain, series, order, hierarchical organization
sud (sūd)	fixed interest
Sufi (sūfī)	a person who devotes him to the mystical path (tasawuf)
sunnat (sunat)	tradition, customary or expected, circumcision
talab ul-'elm (tālab ul 'elm)	religious student, seeker of sacred knowledge
tana (ta'nah) (P)	taunt, reproach
tarbur (tarbūr)	patrilateral parallel cousin; one's father's brother's son.
tarburwali (tarbūrwalī)	the code of cousin rivalry; the expectation that a Pakhtun male will seek to outdo his paternal cousins, an expectation that often leads to feuds
tariqat (tarīqat)	Sufi order
tasawuf (tasawuf)	Sufism
ta'wiz (ta'wīz)	amulet
tura (tūrah) (P)	sword
'ulama ('ulama')	religious authorities
'urs ('urs)	annual ceremony commemorating the death day of a religious saint

wali (walī)	saint, friend of God, master, governor
watan (watan)	homeland, residence, home territory
wazir (wazīr)	minister
zahir (zāhir)	the domain of outward 'sensory appearances (opposed to batin)
zakat (zakāt)	religious tax incumbent on all Muslims (for other forms of religious contribution, see chapter 4 n.33)
zalem (zalem)	cruel, tyrannical, tyrant
ziarat (zīārat)	shrine
zikr (zikr)	mystical act associated with sufism involving the repeated recitation of sacred phrases
zulm (zulm)	tyranny

Bibliography

Abu-Lughod, Lila.
   1986   *Veiled Sentiments: Honor and Poetry in a Bedouin Society.* Berkeley: University of California Press.
   1993   *Writing Women's Worlds.* Berkeley: University of California Press.

Abun-Nasr, Jamil M.
   1965   *The Tijaniyya: A Sufi Order in the Modern World.* London: Oxford University Press.

Adamec, Ludwig.
   1967   *Afghanistan, 1900–1923.* Berkeley: University of California Press.
   1975   *Historical and Political Who's Who of Afghanistan.* Graz, Austria: Akademische Druck-u. Verlagsanstalt.

Afridi, Omar Khan.
   1980   *Mahsud Monograph.* Peshawar: Home and Tribal Affairs Department, Government of the North-West Frontier Province.

Ahmad, Aziz.
   1970 [1964]   *Studies in Islamic Culture in the Indian Environment.* Karachi: Oxford University Press.

Ahmed, Akbar S.
   1975   *Mataloona: Pukhto Proverbs.* Karachi: Oxford University Press.
   1976   *Millennium and Charisma among Pathans: A Critical Essay in Social Anthropology.* London: Routledge & Kegan Paul.
   1977   *Social and Economic Change in the Tribal Areas.* Karachi: Oxford University Press.
   1979   *A Bibliography of the North-West Frontier Province.* Peshawar: Home and Tribal Affairs Department.
   1980   *Pukhtun Economy and Society: Traditional Structure and Economic Development in a Tribal Society.* London: Routledge & Kegan Paul.
   1983   *Religion and Politics in Muslim Society: Order and Conflict in Pakistan.* Cambridge: Cambridge University Press.
   1983   Tribes and States in Waziristan. In *The Conflict of Tribe and State*

in Iran and Afghanistan, edited by Richard Tapper. New York: St. Martin's Press.

1984   Religious Presence and Symbolism in Pukhtun Society. In *Islam in Tribal Societies: From the Atlas to the Indus,* edited by Akbar S. Ahmed and David M. Hart. London: Routledge & Kegan Paul.

Ajmal, Mohammad.

1984   A Note on *Adab* in the *Murshid-Murid* Relationship. In *Moral Conduct and Authority: The Place of Adab in South Asian Islam,* edited by Barbara D. Metcalf. Berkeley: University of California Press.

Amin, Haji Muhammad.

n.d.   *Silsilah Qaderiya.* Peshawar.

Anderson, Benedict.

1983   *Imagined Communities: Reflections on the Origin and Spread of Nationalism.* London: Verso.

Anderson, Jon.

1975   Tribe and Community among Ghilzai Pashtun. *Anthropos* 70: 576–600.

1979   Doing Pakhtu: Social Organization of the Ghilzai Pakhtun. Ph. D. diss., Department of Anthropology, University of North Carolina.

1983   Khan and Khel: Dialectics of Pakhtun Tribalism. In *The Conflict of Tribe and State in Iran and Afghanistan,* edited by Richard Tapper. New York: St. Martin's Press.

1984   How Afghans Define Themselves in Relation to Islam. In *Revolutions and Rebellions in Afghanistan,* edited by M. Nazif Shahrani and Robert L. Canfield. Berkeley: Institute for International Studies.

1985   Sentimental Ambivalence and the Exegesis of 'Self' in Afghanistan. *Anthropological Quarterly* 58 (4):203–11.

1992   Poetics and Politics in Ethnographic Texts: A View from the Colonial Ethnography of Afghanistan. In *Writing the Social Text: Poetics and Politics in Social Science Discourse,* edited by Richard Harvey Brown. New York: Aldine de Gruyter.

Antoun, Richard T.

1989   *Muslim Preacher in the Modern World: A Jordanian Case Study in Comparative Perspective.* Princeton: Princeton University Press.

Asad, Talal.

1972   Market Model, Class Structure, and Consent: A Reconsideration of Swat Political Organization. *Man* (n.s.) 7 (1):74–94.

Ataye, M. Ibrahim.

1979   *A Dictionary of the Terminology of Pashtun's Tribal Customary Law and Usages.* Kabul: Academy of Sciences of Afghanistan, International Centre for Pashto Studies.

Attar, Farid al-Din.

1966   *Muslim Saints and Mystics (Episodes from the Tadhkirat al-*

Auliya'). translated by A. J. Arberry. London: Routledge & Kegan Paul.

Azoy, G. Whitney.

1982   *Buzkashi: Game and Power in Afghanistan.* Philadelphia: University of Pennsylvania Press.

Baldick, Julian.

1989   *Mystical Islam: An Introduction to Sufism.* New York: New York University Press.

Barfield, Thomas J.

1981   *The Central Asian Arabs of Afghanistan: Pastoral Nomadism in Transition.* Austin: University of Texas Press.

Barth, Fredrik.

1959a   *Political Leadership among Swat Pathans.* London: Athlone Press.

1959b   Segmentary Opposition and the Theory of Games: A Study of Pathan Organization. *Journal of the Royal Anthropological Institute* 89 (5):5–21.

1969   Pathan Identity and Its Maintenance. In *Ethnic Groups and Boundaries,* edited by Fredrik Barth. Boston: Little, Brown.

1981   *Features of Person and Society in Swat: Collected Essays on Pathans.* London: Routledge & Kegan Paul.

Basso, Keith.

1986   'Stalking with Stories': Names, Places, and Moral Narratives among the Western Apache. *Antaeus* 57 (Autumn):95–116.

Beck, Lois.

1986   *The Qashqa'i of Iran.* New Haven: Yale University Press.

1991   *Nomad: A Year in the Life of a Qashqa'i Tribesman in Iran.* Berkeley: University of California Press.

Bell, Marjorie Jewett, ed.

1948   *An American Engineer in Afghanistan.* Minneapolis: University of Minnesota Press.

Bellew, H. W.

1977 [1864]   *A General Report on the Yusufzais.* Lahore: Sang-e-Meel Publications.

1977 [1891]   *An Inquiry into the Ethnography of Afghanistan.* Karachi: Indus Publications.

Boesen, Inger W.

1980   Women, Honour, and Love: Some Aspects of the Pashtun Woman's Life in Eastern Afghanistan. *Afghanistan Journal* 7 (2):50–59.

1983   Conflicts of Solidarity in Pakhtun Women's Lives. In *Women in Islamic Societies: Social Attitudes and Historical Perspectives,* edited by Bo Utas. London: Curzon Press.

Bourdieu, Pierre.

1966   The Sentiment of Honour in Kabyle Society. In *Honour and Shame: The Values of Mediterranean Society,* edited by J. G. Peristiany. Chicago: University of Chicago Press.

1977   *Outline of a Theory of Practice.* Cambridge: Cambridge University Press.

Bowen, John R.
1993   *Muslims through Discourse: Religion and Ritual in Gayo Society.* Princeton: Princeton University Press.

Brinner, William M.
1987   Prophet and Saint: The Two Exemplars of Islam. In *Saints and Virtues,* edited by John S. Hawley. Berkeley: University of California Press.

Brown, Peter.
1981   *The Cult of the Saints: Its Rise and Function in Latin Christianity.* Chicago: University of Chicago Press.
1987   The Saint as Exemplar in Late Antiquity. In *Saints and Virtues,* edited by John S. Hawley. Berkeley: University of California Press.

Burke, Edmund, III.
1993   Middle Eastern Societies and Ordinary People's Lives. In *Struggle and Survival in the Modern Middle East,* edited by Edmund Burke, III. Berkeley: University of California Press.

Campbell, J. K.
1992   The Greek Hero. In *Honor and Grace in Anthropology,* edited by J. G. Peristiany and Julian Pitt-Rivers. Cambridge: Cambridge University.

Canfield, Robert L.
1973   *Faction and Conversion in a Plural Society: Religious Alignments in the Hindu Kush.* Anthropological Paper No. 50. Ann Arbor: University of Michigan Museum of Anthropology.

Caroe, Olaf.
1965   *The Pathans.* London: Macmillan.

Caton, Steven C.
1985   The Poetic Construction of Self. *Anthropological Quarterly* 58 (4):141–51.
1987   Power, Persuasion, and Language: A Critique of the Segmentary Model in the Middle East. *International Journal of Middle East Studies* 19 (1):77–101.
1990a   *Peaks of Yemen I Summon: Poetry as Cultural Practice in a North Yemeni Tribe.* Berkeley: University of California Press.
1990b   Anthropological Theories of Tribe and State Formation in the Middle East: Ideology and the Semiotics of Power. In *Tribes and State Formation in the Middle East,* edited by Philip S. Khoury and Joseph Kostiner. Berkeley: University of California Press.

Christensen, Asgar.
1980   The Pashtuns of Kunar: Tribe, Class and Community Organization. *Afghanistan Journal* 7 (3):79–92.
1982   Agnates, Affines, and Allies: Patterns of Marriage among Pakhtun in Kunar, North-East Afghanistan. *Folk* (24):29–64.
1988   When Muslim Identity Has Different Meanings: Religion and

Politics in Contemporary Afghanistan. In *Islam: State and Society*, edited by Klaus Ferdinand and Mehdi Mozaffari. London: Curzon Press.

Churchill, Randolph S., ed.
1967   *Winston S. Churchill Companion*, Vol. 1, Pt. 2, *1896–1900*. Boston: Houghton Mifflin.

Churchill, Winston.
1898   *The Story of the Malakand Field Force: An Episode of Frontier War*. London: Longmans, Green.

1962   *Frontiers and Wars*. London: Eyre & Spottiswoode.

Colonna, Fanny.
1984   Cultural Resistance and Religious Legitimacy in Colonial Algeria. In *Islam in Tribal Societies: From the Atlas to the Indus*, edited by Akbar S. Ahmed and David M. Hart. London: Routledge & Kegan Paul.

Crapanzano, Vincent.
1980.   *Tuhami: Portrait of a Moroccan*. Chicago: University of Chicago Press.

Crocker, J. Christopher.
1977   The Social Functions of Rhetorical Forms. In *The Social Use of Metaphor: Essays on the Anthropology of Rhetoric*, edited by J. David Sapir and Crocker. Philadelphia: University of Pennsylvania Press.

Curzon, George.
1923   *Tales of Travel*. New York, George H. Doran Co.

Dani, Ahmad Hasan.
1969   *Peshawar: Historic City of the Frontier*. Peshawar: Khyber Press Mail.

Darnton, Robert.
1984   *The Great Cat Massacre and Other Episodes in French Cultural History*. New York: Basic Books.

Dawood, N. J.
1990   Introduction to *The Koran*, translated by N. J. Dawood. London: Penguin.

Dekmejian, Richard H., and Margaret J. Wyszomirski.
1972   Charismatic Leadership in Islam: The Mahdi of Sudan. *Comparative Studies in Society and History* 14 (2):193–214.

Di Bella, Maria Pia.
1992   Name, Blood, and Miracles: The Claims to Renown in Traditional Sicily. In *Honor and Grace in Anthropology*, edited by J. G. Peristiany and Julian Pitt-Rivers. Cambridge: Cambridge University Press.

Dresch, Paul.
1986   The Significance of the Course Events Take in Segmentary Systems. *American Ethnologist* 13 (2):309–24.

1989   *Tribes, Government, and History in Yemen*. Oxford: Oxford University Press.

1990   Imams and Tribes: The Writing and Acting of History in Upper
                Yemen. In *Tribes and State Formation in the Middle East,* edited
                by Philip S. Khoury and Joseph Kostiner. Berkeley: University of
                California Press.

Dupree, Louis.
1974   The First Anglo-Afghan War: Folklore and History. *Afghanistan*
                26 (4):1–28.
1980   *Afghanistan.* 3d ed. Princeton: Princeton University Press.
1984   Tribal Warfare in Afghanistan and Pakistan: A Reflection of the
                Segmentary Lineage System. In *Islam in Tribal Societies: From
                the Atlas to the Indus,* edited by Akbar S. Ahmed and David M.
                Hart. London: Routledge & Kegan Paul.

Durand, Col. Algernon.
1977   *The Making of a Frontier.* Karachi: Indus Publications.

Dwyer, Kevin.
1982   *Moroccan Dialogues: Anthropology in Question.* Prospect
                Heights, Ill.: Waveland Press.

Eaton, Richard M.
1978   *Sufis of Bijapur, 1300–1700. Social Roles of Sufis in Medieval In-
                dia.* Princeton: Princeton University Press.
1984   The Political and Religious Authority of the Shrine of Baba Farid.
                In *Moral Conduct and Authority: The Place of Adab in South
                Asian Islam,* edited by Barbara D. Metcalf. Berkeley: University
                of California Press.

Edwards, David B.
1986a   Pretexts of Rebellion: The Cultural Origins of Pakhtun Resistance
                to the Afghan State. Ph. D. diss., Department of Anthropology,
                University of Michigan.
1986b   The Evolution of Shi'i Political Dissent in Afghanistan. In *Shi'ism
                and Social Protest,* edited by Juan R. I. Cole and Nikki R. Keddie.
                New Haven: Yale University Press.
1986c   Charismatic Leadership and Political Process in Afghanistan. *Cen-
                tral Asian Survey* 5 (3/4):273–99.
1986d   Marginality and Migration: Cultural Dimensions of the Afghan
                Refugee Problem. *International Migration Review* 20 (Sum-
                mer):313–28.
1987   Origins of the Anti-Soviet Jihad. In *Afghan Resistance: The Poli-
                tics of Survival,* edited by Grant M. Farr and John G. Merriam.
                Boulder: Westview Press.
1989   Mad Mullahs and Englishmen: Discourse in the Colonial En-
                counter. *Comparative Studies in Society and History* 31 (4):647–
                68.
1990   Frontiers, Boundaries and Frames: The Marginal Identity of Af-
                ghan Refugees. In *Pakistan: The Social Science Perspective,* edited
                by Akbar S. Ahmed. Karachi: Oxford University Press.
1993a   Words in the Balance: The Poetics of Political Dissent in Afghani-
                stan. In *Russia's Muslim Frontiers: New Directions in Cross-*

Cultural Analysis, edited by Dale Eickelman. Bloomington: Indiana University Press.

1993b   Summoning Muslims: Print, Politics, and Religious Ideology in Afghanistan. *Journal of Asian Studies* 52 (3):609–28.

1993c   The Political Lives of Afghan Saints: The Case of the Hazrats of Shor Bazaar. In *Manifestations of Sainthood in Islam,* edited by Carl W. Ernst. Istanbul: Éditions Isis.

1995   Print Islam: Religion, Revolution, and the Media in Afghanistan. *Anthropological Quarterly* 68 (3):171–84.

Eickelman, Dale F.

1976   *Moroccan Islam: Tradition and Society in a Pilgrimage Center.* Austin: University of Texas Press.

1982   The Study of Islam in Local Contexts. *Contributions to Asian Studies* 17:1–16.

1985a   *Knowledge and Power in Morocco: The Education of a Twentieth Century Notable.* Princeton: Princeton University Press.

1985b   Introduction: Self and Community in Middle Eastern Society. *Anthropological Quarterly* 58 (4):135–40.

1989   *The Middle East: An Anthropological Approach.* 2d ed. Englewood Cliffs, New Jersey: Prentice-Hall.

1991   Traditional Islamic Learning and Ideas of the Person in the Twentieth Century. In *Middle Eastern Lives: The Practice of Biography and Self-Narrative,* edited by Martin Kramer. Syracuse: Syracuse University Press.

Einzmann, H.

1975   Religious Folk Tradition in Afghanistan, Pilgrimage, and Veneration of Saints. In *Islam in Southern Asia: A Survey of Current Research,* edited by D. Rothemund. Weisbaden: South Asian Institute.

Elphinstone, Mountstuart.

1972 [1815] *An Account of the Kingdom of Caubul.* 2 vols. Karachi: Oxford University Press.

Evans-Pritchard, E. E.

1949   *The Sanusi of Cyrenaica.* Oxford: Clarendon Press.

Ewing, Katherine Pratt.

1980   The Pir or Sufi Saint in Pakistani Islam. Ph. D. diss. Department of Anthropology, University of Chicago.

1984   *Malangs* of the Punjab: Intoxication or *Adab* as the Path to God? In *Moral Conduct and Authority: The Place of Adab in South Asian Islam,* edited by Barbara D. Metcalf. Berkeley: University of California Press.

Fahim, Muhammad.

1978   British Relations with the Akhund of Swat. *Islamic Studies* 17 (1):57–66.

Fernandez, James W.

1986   *Persuasions and Performances: The Play of Tropes in Culture.* Bloomington: Indiana University Press.

Foucault, Michel.
1979   *Discipline and Punish: The Birth of the Prison.* New York: Vintage Books.
Fox, Richard G.
1985   *Lions of the Punjab: Culture in the Making.* Berkeley: University of California Press.
Fraser-Tytler, W. K.
1950   *Afghanistan: A Study of Political Developments in Central Asia.* London: Oxford University Press.
Friedl, Erika.
1989   *Women of Deh Koh: Lives in an Iranian Village.* Washington, D. C.: Smithsonian Institution Press.
Garthwaite, Gene R.
1983   *Khans and Shahs: A Documentary Analysis of the Bakhtiyari in Iran.* Cambridge: Cambridge University Press.
Geertz, Clifford.
1968   *Islam Observed: Religious Development in Morocco and Indonesia.* Chicago: University of Chicago Press.
1983   From the Native's Point of View. In *Local Knowledge: Further Essays in Interpretive Anthropology,* edited by Clifford Geertz. New York: Basic Books.
Geertz, Clifford, Hildred Geertz, and Lawrence Rosen, eds.,
1979   *Meaning and Order in Moroccan Society: Three Essays in Cultural Analysis.* Cambridge: Cambridge University Press.
Gellner, Ernest.
1969   *Saints of the Atlas.* Chicago: University of Chicago Press.
1981   *Muslim Society.* Cambridge: Cambridge University Press.
1983   *Nations and Nationalism.* Ithaca: Cornell University Press.
1990   Tribalism and the State in the Middle East. In *Tribes and State Formation in the Middle East,* edited by Philip S. Khoury and Joseph Kostiner. Berkeley: University of California Press.
Ghani, Abdul.
1980 [1921] *A Review of the Political Situation in Central Asia.* Lahore: Aziz Publishers.
Ghani, Ashraf.
1978   Islam and State-Building in a Tribal Society, Afghanistan: 1880–1901. *Modern Asian Studies* 12 (2):269–84.
1983   Disputes in a Court of Sharia, Kunar Valley, Afghanistan, 1885–1890. *International Journal of Middle East Studies* 15:353–67.
1987   Islam and Counter-revolutionary Movements. In *Islam in Asia,* edited by John L. Esposito. Oxford: Oxford University Press.
Ghobar, Mir Ghulam Muhammad.
1967   *Afghanistan dar Masir-i Tarikh.* Kabul: Government Printing House.
Gibb, H. A. R., and J. H. Kramers, eds.
1974   *The Shorter Encyclopedia of Islam.* Leiden: E. J. Brill, p. 216.

Gilmartin, David.

1984   Shrines, Succession, and Sources of Moral Authority. In *Moral Conduct and Authority: The Place of Adab in South Asian Islam,* edited by Barbara D. Metcalf. Berkeley: University of California Press.

Gilmore, David D.

1987   Introduction: The Shame of Dishonor. In *Honor and Shame and the Unity of the Mediterranean,* edited by David D. Gilmore. Washington, D.C.: American Anthropological Association.

Gilsenan, Michael.

1973   *Saint and Sufi in Modern Egypt: An Essay in the Sociology of Religion.* Oxford: Clarendon Press.

1982   *Recognizing Islam: Religion and Society in the Modern Arab World.* New York: Pantheon.

Ginzburg, Carlo.

1985   *Night Battles: Witchcraft and Agrarian Cults in the Sixteenth and Seventeenth Centuries.* New York: Penguin.

Goldziher, Ignaz.

1967 [1889–1890]
         Muslim Studies, edited by S. M. Stern. Chicago: Aldine.

Great Britain. Parliament.

1882   Afghanistan and Central Asia: Papers presented to Her Majesty, 1870–1882. London: Harrison and Sons.

Gregorian, Vartan.

1969   · *The Emergence of Modern Afghanistan: Politics of Reform and Modernization 1880–1946.* Stanford: Stanford University Press.

Grima, Benedicte.

1992   *The Performance of Emotion among Paxtun Women.* Austin: The University of Texas Press.

Harding, Susan.

1987   Convicted by the Holy Spirit: The Rhetoric of Fundamental Baptist Conversion. *American Ethnologist* 14 (1):167–81.

Hart, David M.

1985   *Guardians of the Khaibar Pass: The Social Organisation of the Afridis of Pakistan.* Lahore: Vanguard Press.

Hensman, Howard.

1978 [1881] *The Afghan War of 1879–80.* Lahore: Sang-e-Meel Publications [London: H. Allen].

Herzfeld, Michael.

1985   *The Poetics of Manhood: Contest and Identity in a Cretan Mountain Village.* Princeton: Princeton University Press.

Hobsbawm, Eric.

1990   *Nations and Nationalism since 1780: Programme, Myth, Reality.* Cambridge: Cambridge University Press.

Hobsbawm, Eric, and Terence Ranger, eds.

1983   *The Invention of Tradition.* Cambridge: Cambridge University Press.

Howell, Evelyn.
    1979 [1931] *Mizh: A Monograph on Government's Relations with the Mah-sud Tribe.* Karachi: Oxford University Press [Simla: Government of India Press].
Howell, Evelyn, and Olaf Caroe.
    1963   *The Poems of Khushhal Khan Khatak.* Peshawar: Peshawar University Press.
al-Hujwiri, 'Ali bin Uthman.
    1980   *Kashf-al-Mahjub,* translated by R. A. Nicholson. Lahore: Islamic Book Foundation.
Ibn Khaldun.
    1969   *The Muqaddimah. An Introduction to History,* translated by F. Rosenthal. Princeton: Princeton University Press.
India, Army Intelligence Branch.
    1908   *Frontier and Overseas Expeditions from India.* Vol. 2.
Jahanzeb, Miangul.
    1985   *The Last Wali of Swat: An Autobiography as Told to Fredrik Barth.* New York: Columbia University Press.
James, Lionel.
    1898   *The Indian Frontier War: Being an Account of the Mohmand and Tirah Expeditions 1897.* London: William Heinemann.
Jamous, Raymond.
    1992   From the Death of Men to the Peace of God: Violence and Peace-making in the Rif. In *Honor and Grace in Anthropology,* edited by J. G. Peristiany and Julian Pitt-Rivers. Cambridge: Cambridge University Press.
Jones, Schuyler.
    1974   *Men of Influence in Nuristan: A Study of Social Control and Dispute Settlement in Waigal Valley, Afghanistan.* London: Seminar Press.
Kakar, Hasan.
    1971   *Afghanistan: A Study of Internal Political Development, 1880–1901.* Lahore: Punjab University Press.
    1979   *Government and Society in Afghanistan: The Reign of Amir 'Abd al-Rahman Khan.* Austin: University of Texas Press.
Keddie, Nikki R.
    1972   *Scholars, Saints, and Sufis: Muslim Religious Institutions since 1500.* Berkeley: University of California Press.
Keiser, Lincoln.
    1991   *Friend by Day, Enemy by Night.* Fort Worth: Holt, Rinehart and Winston.
Keppel, Arnold.
    1977 [1911] *Gun-Running and the Indian North West Frontier.* Quetta: Gosha-e-Adab.
Khan, Azmat Hayat.
    1981   Afghan Resistance and National Leadership. *Central Asia* 9 (Winter):163–76.

Khan, Muhammad Fahim.
    1977   The Life and Times of Hajji Sahib of Turangzai. *Islamic Studies* 16 (1):329–41.

Khan, Muhammad Hayat.
    1981 [1874] *Afghanistan and its Inhabitants.* Henry Priestley, trans. Lahore: Sang-e-Meel Publications.

Khan, Sultan Mahomed.
    1980 [1900] *The Life of Abdur Rahman, Amir of Afghanistan.* Karachi: Oxford University Press [London: John Murray].

Khoury, Philip S., and Joseph Kostiner.
    1990   Introduction: Tribes and the Complexities of State Formation in the Middle East. In *Tribes and State Formation in the Middle East,* edited by Philip S. Khoury and Joseph Kostiner. Berkeley: University of California Press.

King, L. White.
    1984 [1900] *The Orakzai Country and Clans.* Lahore: Vanguard Books.

Kurin, Richard.
    1984   Morality, Personhood, and the Exemplary Life: Popular Conceptions of Muslims in Paradise. In *Moral Conduct and Authority: The Place of Adab in South Asian Islam,* edited by Barbara D. Metcalf. Berkeley: University of California Press.

Lavie, Smadar.
    1990   *The Poetics of Military Occupation: Mzeina Allegories of Bedouin Identity under Israeli and Egyptian Rule.* Berkeley: University of California Press.

Le Roy Ladurie, Emmanuel.
    1978   *Montaillou: The Promised Land of Error.* New York: George Braziller.

Levy, Reuben.
    1969   *An Introduction to Persian Literature.* New York: Columbia University Press.

Lewis, Bernard.
    1988   *The Political Language of Islam.* Chicago: University of Chicago Press.

Lindholm, Charles.
    1981   The Structure of Violence among the Swat Pukhtun of Northern Pakistan. *Ethnology* 20:147–56.
    1982   *Generosity and Jealousy: The Swat Pukhtun of Northern Pakistan.* Columbia University Press.
    1986   Leadership Categories and Social Processes in Islam: The Cases of Dir and Swat. *Journal of Anthropological Research* 42 (1):1–13.
    1992   Quandaries of Command in Egalitarian Societies: Examples from Swat and Morocco. In *Comparing Muslim Societies,* edited by Juan R. I. Cole. Ann Arbor: University of Michigan Press.

Loeffler, Reinhold.
    1988   *Islam in Practice: Religious Beliefs in a Persian Village.* Albany: State University of New York Press.

MacIntyre, Alasdair.
   1984   *After Virtue: A Study in Moral Theory.* Notre Dame: University
                 of Notre Dame Press.
Majrooh, Sayyid Bahouddin Majrooh.
   n.d.   Education in Afghanistan: Past and Present (unpublished manu-
                 script). Peshawar: Afghan Information Center.
Malyon, F. H.
   1980   *Pushtu Folk Stories.* Islamabad: National Institute of Folk Heri-
                 tage.
Marcus, Michael.
   1985   History on the Moroccan Periphery: Moral Imagination, Poetry,
                 and Islam. *Anthropological Quarterly* 58 (4):152–60.
   1987   'Horsemen are the Fence of the Land': Honor and History among
                 the Ghiyata of Eastern Morocco. In *Honor and Shame and the
                 Unity of the Mediterranean,* edited by David D. Gilmore. Wash-
                 ington, D. C.: American Anthropological Association.
Martin, Frank.
   1907   *Under the Absolute Amir.* London: Harper and Brothers.
McMahon, Capt. A. H., and Lieut. A. D. G. Ramsay.
   1981 [1901]   *Report on the Tribes of Dir, Swat, and Bajour Together with the
                 Utman-Khel and Sam Ranizai.* Lahore: Saeed Book Bank.
Meeker, Michael E.
   1976   Meaning and Society in the Near East: Examples from the Black
                 Sea Turks and the Levantine Arabs. *Journal of Middle East Stud-
                 ies* 7:243–70; 383–422.
   1979   *Literature and Violence in North Arabia.* Cambridge: Cambridge
                 University Press.
   1980   The Twilight of a South Asian Heroic Age: A Rereading of Barth's
                 Study of Swat. *Man* (ns) 15:682–701.
   1989   *The Pastoral Son and the Spirit of Patriarchy: Religion, Society,
                 and Person among East African Stock Keepers.* Madison: Univer-
                 sity of Wisconsin Press.
Merk, W. R. H.
   1984 [1898]   *The Mohmands.* Lahore: Vanguard Books.
Messick, Brinkley.
   1993   *The Calligraphic State: Textual Domination and History in a
                 Muslim Society.* Berkeley: University of California Press.
Metcalf, Barbara D.
   1978   The Madrasa at Deoband: A Model for Religious Education in
                 Modern India. *Modern Asian Studies* 12 (1):111–34.
Mills, H. Woosnam.
   1979 [1897]   *The Pathan Revolts in North-West India.* Lahore: Sang-e-Meel
                 Publications.
Mills, Margaret.
   1988   Structure, Texture, and the Personal Voice in Afghan Folktales.
                 Edebiy'at 2 (1–2):77–115.

1991   *Rhetoric and Politics in Afghan Traditional Storytelling.* Philadelphia: University of Pennsylvania Press.

Mitchell, Richard.
1969   *The Society of the Muslim Brothers.* London: Oxford University Press.

Mottahedeh, Roy P.
1980   *Loyalty and Leadership in an Early Islamic Society.* Princeton: Princeton University Press.
1985   *The Mantle of the Prophet: Religion and Politics in Iran.* New York: Pantheon Books.

Munson, Henry.
1984   *The House of Si Abd Allah: The Oral History of a Moroccan Family.* New Haven: Yale University Press.
1993   *Religion and Power in Morocco.* New Haven: Yale University Press.

Musil, Alois.
1928   *The Manners and Customs of the Rwala Bedouins.* American Geographical Society: Oriental Explorations and Studies, No. 6. New York: Crane.

Nagy, Gregory.
1979   *The Best of the Achaeans: Concepts of the Hero in Archaic Greek Poetry.* Baltimore: Johns Hopkins University Press.

Neamet Ullah.
1965 [1829–36]
            History of the Afghans, translated by Bernhard Dorn. London: Susil Gupta.

Nevell, Capt. H. L.
1977   *Campaigns on the North-West Frontier.* Lahore: Sang-e-Meel Publishers.

Nicholson, Reynold A.
1914   *The Mystics of Islam.* London: Routledge & Kegan Paul.

O'Brien, D. B. Cruise.
1971   *The Mourides of Senegal: The Political and Economic Organization of an Islamic Brotherhood.* Oxford: Oxford University Press.

Ohnuki-Tierney, Emiko.
1990   Introduction: The Historicization of Anthropology. In *Culture Through Time: Anthropological Approaches,* edited by E. Ohnuki-Tierney. Stanford: Stanford University Press.

Olesen, Asta.
1988   Afghanistan: The Development of the Modern State. In *Islam: State and Society,* edited by Klaus Ferdinand and Mehdi Mozaffari. London: Curzon Press.

Paine, Robert.
1981   When Saying Is Doing. In *Politically Speaking: Cross-Cultural Studies of Rhetoric,* edited by Robert Paine. Philadelphia: Institute for the Study of Human Issues.

Peacock, James L., and Dorothy C. Holland.
1993   The Narrated Self: Life Stories in Process. *Ethos* 21 (4):367–83.

Pennell, T. L.
1909   *Among the Wild Tribes of the Afghan Frontier.* London: Seeley & Co.

Peters, Emrys.
1990   Aspects of the Feud. In *The Bedouin of Cyrenaica: Studies in Personal and Corporate Power,* edited by Jack Goody and Emanuel Marx. Cambridge: Cambridge University Press.

Peters, Rudolph.
1979   *Islam and Colonialism: The Doctrine of Jihad in Modern History.* The Hague: Mouton.

Pitt-Rivers, Julian.
1966   Honour and Social Status. In *Honour and Shame: The Values of Mediterranean Society,* edited by J. G. Peristiany. Chicago: University of Chicago Press.
1977   *The Fate of Shechem or the Politics of Sex: Essays in the Anthropology of the Mediterranean.* Cambridge: Cambridge University Press.

Poullada, Leon.
1973   *Reform and Rebellion in Afghanistan, 1919–1929.* Ithaca: Cornell University Press.

Rabinow, Paul.
1975   *Symbolic Domination: Cultural Form and Historical Change in Morocco.* Chicago: University of Chicago Press.

Raverty, Capt. H. G.
1980 [1860] *A Dictionary of the Pukhto, Pushto or Language of the Afghans.* Karachi: Indus Publications.

Renard, John.
1993   *Islam and the Heroic Image: Themes in Literature and the Visual Arts.* Columbia: University of South Carolina Press.

Robinson, Capt. J. A.
1978 [1934] *Notes on Nomad Tribes of Eastern Afghanistan.* Quetta: Nisa Traders.

Rosaldo, Renato.
1980   *Ilongot Headhunting, 1883–1974: A Study in Society and History.* Stanford: Stanford University Press.

Rosen, Lawrence.
1984   *Bargaining for Reality: The Construction of Social Relations in a Muslim Community.* Chicago: University of Chicago Press.

Roy, Olivier.
1986   *Islam and Resistance in Afghanistan.* Cambridge: Cambridge University Press.

Sabir, Mohammad Shafi.
1964   *Story of Khyber.* Peshawar: University Book Agency.

Sahlins, Marshall.
1981   *Historical Metaphors and Mythical Realities: Structure in the Early History of the Sandwich Islands Kingdom.* Ann Arbor: University of Michigan Press.

1985   *Islands of History.* Chicago: University of Chicago Press.

Salik, S. A.
1953   *The Saint of Jilan (Ghaus-ul-Azam).* Lahore: Ashraf Publications.

Samatar, Said S.
1982   *Oral Poetry and Somali Nationalism: The Case of Sayyid Mahammad 'Abdille Hasan.* Cambridge: Cambridge University Press.

Schimmel, Annemarie.
1975   *Mystical Dimensions of Islam.* Chapel Hill: University of North Carolina Press.

Schwartz, Barry.
1987   *George Washington: The Making of an American Symbol.* New York: Free Press.

Seton-Watson, Hugh.
1977   *Nations and States: An Enquiry into the Origins of Nations and the Politics of Nationalism.* Boulder: Westview Press.

Shah, Sirdar Iqbal Ali.
1978 [1928] *Afghanistan of the Afghans.* Quetta: Gosh-e-Adab.

Shahrani, M. Nazif.
1986   State Building and Social Fragmentation in Afghanistan: A Historical Perspective. In *The State, Religion, and Ethnic Politics: Afghanistan, Iran, and Pakistan,* edited by Ali Banuazizi and Myron Weiner. Syracuse: Syracuse University Press.

Shahrani, M. Nazif, and Robert L. Canfield.
1984   *Revolutions and Rebellions in Afghanistan: Anthropological Perspectives.* Berkeley: University of California Press.

Shah Wali Allah.
1973   *A Mystical Interpretation of Prophetic Tales by an Indian Muslim* [translation of Ta'wil al-ahadith]. Leiden: E. J. Brill.

Sharif, Ja'far.
1972 [1921] *Islam in India, or the Qanun-i-Islam,* translated by G. A. Herklots. London: Curzon Press.

Smith, Harvey H., et al.
1980   *Afghanistan: A Country Study.* 4th ed. Washington, D. C.: American University.

Spain, James W.
1972   *The Way of the Pathan.* 2d ed. Karachi: Oxford University Press.
1985 [1963] *The Pathan Borderland.* Karachi: Indus Publication.

Subhan, John A.
1970   *Sufism: Its Saints and Shrines.* New York: Samuel Wieser.

Sykes, Sir Percy.
1940   *A History of Afghanistan.* 2 vols. London: Macmillan.

Tapper, Nancy.
1983   Abd al-Rahman's North-West Frontier: The Pashtun Colonisation of Afghan Turkistan. In *The Conflict of Tribe and State in Iran and Afghanistan,* edited by Richard Tapper. New York: St. Martin's Press.

Tapper, Richard.
    1983   Introduction to *The Conflict of Tribe and State in Iran and Afghanistan*, edited by Richard Tapper. New York: St. Martin's Press.
    1984   Holier Than Thou: Islam in Three Tribal Societies. In *Islam in Tribal Societies: From the Atlas to the Indus*, edited by Akbar S. Ahmed and David M. Hart. London: Routledge & Kegan Paul.

Tate, G. P.
    1973 [1911] *The Kingdom of Afghanistan. A Historical Sketch.* Karachi: Indus Publications [Bombay: Times Press].

Temple, R. C.
    1882   Twice-Told Tales Regarding the Akhund of Swat. *The Indian Antiquary* 11 (November):325–26.

Thorburn, S. S.
    1978 [1879] *Bannu; or Our Afghan Frontier.* Lahore: Sang-e-Meel Publications [London: Trubner and Co.].

Thornton, Ernest, and Annie Thornton.
    1910   *Leaves from an Afghan Scrapbook: The Experiences of an English Official and His Wife in Kabul.* London: John Murray.

Trimingham, J. Spencer.
    1971   *The Sufi Orders of Islam.* Oxford: Clarendon Press.

Turner, Bryan.
    1974   *Weber and Islam: A Critical Study.* London: Routledge & Kegan Paul.

Utas, Bo.
    1980   Notes on Afghan Sufi Orders and Khanaqahs. *Afghanistan Journal* 7 (2):60–67.

van Bruinessen, Martin.
    1992   *Agha, Shaikh, and State: The Social and Political Structures of Kurdistan.* London: Zed Books.

von Grunebaum, G. E., and Roger Caillois, eds.
    1966   *The Dream and Human Societies.* Berkeley: University of California Press.

Wadud (Badshah), Miangul Abdul.
    1962   *The Story of Swat (as Told by the Founder Miangul Abdul Wadud Badshah to Muhammad Asif Khan).* Peshawar: Feroz Sons.

Warburton, Sir Robert.
    1970 [1900] *Eighteen Years in the Khyber, 1879–1898.* Karachi: Oxford University Press [London: John Murray].

Weber, Max.
    1968   *On Charisma and Institution Building,* edited by S. N. Eisenstadt. Chicago: University of Chicago Press.

White, Hayden.
    1981   The Value of Narrativity in the Representation of Reality. In *On Narrative,* edited by W. J. T. Mitchell. Chicago: University of Chicago Press.

Woods, Frederick, ed.

1972   *Young Winston's Wars: The Original Despatches of Winston S. Churchill War Correspondent 1897–1900.* London: Leo Cooper Ltd.

Wyatt-Brown, Bertram.

1986   *Honor and Violence in the Old South.* London: Oxford University Press.

Yapp, Malcolm.

1983   Tribes and States in the Khyber, 1838–42. In *The Conflict of Tribe and State in Iran and Afghanistan,* edited by Richard Tapper. New York: St. Martin's Press.

Index